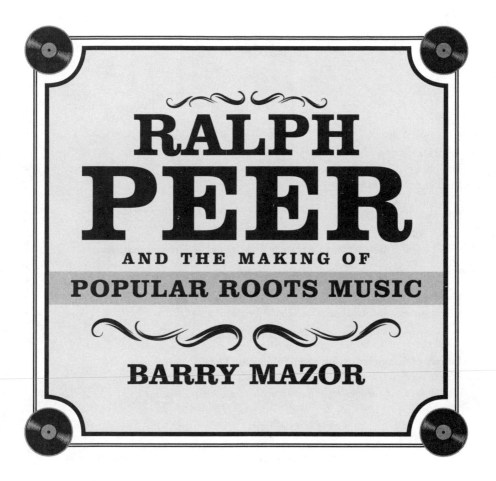

RALPH PEER

AND THE MAKING OF
POPULAR ROOTS MUSIC

BARRY MAZOR

CHICAGO
REVIEW
PRESS

An A Cappella Book

Published by Chicago Review Press, Incorporated
814 North Franklin Street
Chicago, Illinois 60610
ISBN 978-1-61374-021-7

All photos are courtesy of the Peer Family Archives unless otherwise indicated.

Library of Congress Cataloging-in-Publication Data
Mazor, Barry.
  Ralph Peer and the making of popular roots music / Barry Mazor.
    pages cm
  Includes bibliographical references and index.
  ISBN 978-1-61374-021-7
 1. Peer, Ralph Sylvester, 1892–1960. 2. Sound recording executives and producers—
United States—Biography. 3. Sound recording industry—United States—Biography.
I. Title.

  ML429.P37M39 2014
  781.64092—dc23
  [B]
                              2014029263

Interior design: Jonathan Hahn

Printed in the United States of America
5 4 3 2 1

Contents

Introduction

"Something New—
Built Along the Same Lines"

Iɴ 1955 ꜰᴏʟᴋʟᴏʀɪꜱᴛ Jᴏʜɴ Gʀᴇᴇɴᴡᴀʏ sent a letter to the celebrated A&R man and music publisher Ralph S. Peer, pressing him to assess his own impact on American music over the previous thirty-five years or so—specifically, on "folk music." Peer answered Professor Greenway directly and succinctly, in an unpublished letter that, in its thrust, must have taken the protest song chronicler by surprise:

"As a pioneer in this field, I perhaps set the pattern which has resulted in a really tremendous new section of the Amusement Industry. I quickly discovered that people buying records were *not* especially interested in hearing standard or folkloric music. What they wanted was something new—built along the same lines."

It was perfectly characteristic of Peer that his response concerned what appealed to "people buying records"—consumers of commercial, popular music. He had never been driven by any particular desire to contribute something to traditional music, by any musical theory or ideology, by any sense that it was "good" to make or sell some flavor of music rather than some other, or even by his personal taste, but by decades of mounting practical experience about what evoked a positive audience response, provoked it again and again. Finding an untapped opportunity that worked—an audience unaddressed, a style of music underexplored, a new way to freshen what was already available—was

1

precisely what excited Ralph Peer, spurred him to musical and music business experimentation, as the discovery of some new reaction or interaction might galvanize an applied scientist. His music-changing experiments proceeded for some fifty years, with enormous consequences.

Ralph Peer developed and executed a business strategy that bordered on an aesthetic. At its core was a simple idea: untapped roots music—music that evidences rich history, that has moved a specific people of some distinctive place and culture and reflects their lives and rhythms—could appeal to much broader audiences by far, if handled properly as a commercial musical proposition. He never, of course, referred to the arena he was commercializing and popularizing as "roots music," as we commonly do now; he died at the dawn of the 1960s, and nobody used the term in his day. But he talked about "local" music, "regional" music, and occasionally "traditional" or "standard" or even "legendary" music. He knew what he was after.

Before very long, so did the industry he worked in. Step-by-step, he was entrusted with exploring and developing more and more popular music derived from the range commonly included under the "roots music" umbrella today. In the twenty-first century, we can take it for granted that there's a "rooted" side to pop, at times more in favor, at times less so, but it remains an available direction for popular music to take. That wasn't always so, and it wasn't inevitable that it would be.

When the business of creating, promoting, and selling music on a mass scale first took hold, published sheet music was the medium, and its use by professionals in performances was the key to getting the music widely known, so their musically literate audiences might want to buy and play it, too—at home, in a school band, or perhaps semiprofessionally, at a wedding or some community band shell or restaurant. Focused that way, the music business hardly concerned itself with artists or songwriters with little or no formal training, or who specialized in some regionally favored music less known and less appreciated outside of its limited home base, music most typically favored by those who didn't read music at all, music apparently without "universal" commercial pop prospects as they understood them. The early music publishers and professional concert and show producers of the Tin Pan Alley era saw music outside of the Broadway, concert hall, and broadest parlor sheet-music mainstream as marginal propositions, and as a consequence, the structure of the industry they built across the Western world marginalized it still further, without giving the matter much thought.

Surprisingly, perhaps, that didn't change even when recording arrived at the end of the nineteenth century, when making something out of music that hadn't been composed or appeared as sheet music became so very much easier. If anyone, even then, saw broader potential or musical power in the down-home roots music being skipped over so cavalierly, they certainly weren't doing anything about it.

In the United States, the excluded, underestimated, marginalized music included all but the most schooled music made by African Americans, virtually all music of rural and small-town white Southerners other than hymnal lyric sheets, and while there had already been, in Jelly Roll Morton's famous description, a "Spanish tinge" detectable in American popular music for many years, Latino music, and Latin American songs, weren't going to cross the border into American parlors or stages, either.

And then Ralph Peer came along. He saw as much potential in passed-over, underexplored, professionally neglected music, and did as much to make something of it, as any one person ever has. He knew that no working idea in the music business could stay unexplored by others for long, and didn't put much stock in "great-man theories," as was amply evident when, late in life, he was asked directly whether the popularizing of roots music's various flavors would have happened without him.

"I do think that if I hadn't, somebody else would have," he answered. "There was a bigger demand for [those] records, and they'd eventually give them the artists they wanted."

And maybe so—but "eventually" can take a long time. Ralph Peer made it happen the way it happened. He virtually always, as he put it himself, looked first for music "that was local in nature," precisely because it would be novel everywhere else. He was not a musicologist, or a performer, or a composer, but a modernizing businessman, a "record man" and a music publisher, and it was as a businessman that he pulled the lever that budged the musical world. It took—and, even in this interconnected age, still takes—a music industry structure equipped to convey and promote untapped music for us even to be aware of it. Because Peer opened the music business's door to unheard regional music and implemented some serious ideas about what to do with it, the very structure of the industry evolved, and so did the sounds audiences could hear. Durable genres with musical power and lasting, growing enterprises developed, and pop music broadened in the United States and around the world.

A record company A&R ("artist and repertoire") executive's job, in Ralph Peer's day, much as in our own, was to find artists and songs that could work, to record them in the right setting, and to release and promote the result with an awaiting audience in mind. Repeat the process for an identified audience and you may have a continuing genre. It's a commercial job, and making hit records is the central goal. A music publisher's day-to-day work is closely related, which is why publishers would eventually have A&R professionals working for them, as well. It's about placing songs—for recording or any other sort of performance—where they will have the greatest, potentially lasting impact; songs just might come around again. Both lines of work, mastered and to a degree defined by Ralph Peer, are about identifying talents, enabling them, bringing them forward in the most appealing settings, and broadening their reach. Sometimes the results are disposable. Sometimes they are art.

In the course of his career, Peer singled out a historic list of musical jewels and placed them in settings that got our attention. In no small measure because of the work that he did, we share the musical legacies of Jimmie Rodgers and of the Carter Family and have had the pleasure of the solo stardom of Louis Armstrong and Fats Waller, of the recorded gospel of both the Southern white and African American flavors, of the raucous folk-jazz of the Memphis Jug Band, and of Blind Willie McTell's everlasting blues.

We've likely heard Agustín Lara's "Granada" and Consuelo Velázquez's "Bésame Mucho" as well, and even those of us for whom Latin music was *not* originally part of our own culture, or the songs in our language, have seen our mothers or grandmothers taking mambo lessons. If rhythms of the Americas from Mexico or Cuba flourished just close enough to parts of the United States to function much like more ethnic regional music that Peer could help bring further to the fore throughout the States, Latin music in general had been quite cut off from the broader world stage by the limitations of the music industry of Central and South America. Once Peer's musical ideas reached global execution, they were singing "Bésame Mucho" in Moscow and Tokyo, and the ever-increasing amount of Latin music made within US borders found a larger domestic and global audience.

His efforts were important in preparing broad audiences across the United States and ultimately in most parts of the globe to accept new, rooted popular music styles as they came along, from blues to swing and western swing to pop Latin (dance by dance), country, western, bluegrass, rhythm & blues, rock 'n' roll, soul, and well after Peer himself was gone, the likes of Dirty South hip-hop, with its strong regional connections.

Peer served the underserved and ignored because it made good business sense to venture where others hadn't committed to go—but serve them he did. He seldom romanticized "the old tunes" of any flavor, familiar or otherwise, or of older, fading lifestyles, though he did have some specific music-changing ideas about how people related to their own culture's past. He stayed focused on what was happening right now, what might be possible *next*. What, after all, did providing "something new along the same lines" really mean, anyway, and how did you provide it?

Popular music demands novelty; "roots" music, by definition, maintains ties to the traditional. What, then, would the best workable hybrid sound like at any given time—and how could you make it appealing and keep that new genre working, record by record and song by song, if you happened to figure it out?

Ralph Peer didn't stick with, or get stuck on, any one answer; there weren't locked musical rules for him, just new things to try. That temperamental flexibility sheds some light on the intentions behind one of his best-known contributions to popular music, a contribution that has had its critics—his central role in establishing specialized lines of recordings separate from the "mainstream" pop of the day, for the music of African American artists aimed at black audiences, and then for what came to be referred to conversationally as "hillbilly" and later "country" music by and for rural and small-town, working-class Southern whites. Those, too, were marketing ideas designed to speak to previously ignored people Peer recognized as potential new music consumers. Establishing the genres was intended to be about recognition, about serving a market, not about limiting performers, songwriters, or audiences—or locking music makers into segregated netherworlds.

When artists working in those fields demonstrated the ability to expand on their own vistas, repertoires, and styles, and an interest in doing it—a soloing (and, eventually, pop-singing) Louis Armstrong or Fats Waller, a Jimmie Rodgers—Peer took steps to facilitate that, enabling them to move further into general popular acceptance. As he worked to expand what sounds, themes, and even types of musical outfits might be included in the genre categories he'd designed, often pulling a tradition-formed genre further into pop music in the process, he played a key role in breaking down the walls those genres tended to erect, including even, to a degree, society's racial walls.

Critics and more than a few music fans have long argued whether one flavor of popular roots music was more "true" to its roots than another, more "authentic," or whether the music was better off in some allegedly pristine condition prior to its popularization. These arguments would never have arisen if we'd never gotten to hear or recognize the music and its variations in the first place, if it really had just stayed back home where it was born. The broad range of flavors to compare and argue over within roots genres is in part a legacy of Ralph Peer's experiments.

Of Peer, an often quiet, reserved man, enigmatic to some who knew him only briefly or superficially, his son Ralph Peer II observes, "He was not a person to *display* a wide range of emotion, in my experience, but I've found that there was considerable affection for him." The senior Peer, for all of his reticence, was motivated not just by business ambition and a taste for experimenting, but also by his personal fondness for making connections with music makers and sellers across the globe. He developed friendships and found prescient, reliable colleagues of every ethnic stripe to help in his work—some celebrated in their own right, some who worked for him for decades, others who learned what they could from him and moved on.

There were also predictable misunderstandings along the way, stemming from the meeting—or collision—of out-of-the-way local cultures and the rough national and global music business world in which Ralph Peer worked. Peer guided regionally based, often spottily educated roots music performers and songwriters toward far-reaching levels of recognition and professional careers (and very few ever complained about *that*), but he also introduced them to a music industry culture that they may or may not have understood well or been fully prepared for, with its inevitable highs and lows, and the forever freshly shocking truth that the pop-music business could, and often would, be finished with anyone who didn't keep on producing hits.

With Ralph Peer their sole conduit into pop music, when their heydays and their flow of income from records, performances, and songs ebbed, some no-longer-prominent down-home performers and songwriters suggested to music chroniclers of the 1960s and '70s that their career limits must have been about what he, for some unexplainable reason, no longer did for them. It was rare, at the time, for such musicians' and songwriters' complaints ever to be checked against documentation to see if they were justified—or, for that matter, to find music chroniclers who were familiar with the basic practices of the music business and song publishing in particular, let alone the intricacies of rights and royalties. The worst horror stories in the history of the pop-music business were often assumed to be universal. Peer himself was rarely asked to comment while he was around to do so, so there's been an imbalance in the limited picture of his work and life available ever since.

And that's not surprising. Roots music has deep cultural associations, and its makers and many of its chroniclers have tended to be proprietary; it's by definition music that feels like and in real ways *is* "ours," whoever the "we" in question might be. Ralph Peer was obviously not African American, or a rural Southern white, or any nationality of Latino, or (and for some, this would be at least as significant) a *musician*—though few were likely to know much about what his own roots actually were, since he didn't go out of his way to advertise them. To some commentators over the years Peer seemed not quite "one of us," but an outsider or even an interloper, and since he didn't commit his life and career solely to whichever genre they happened to hold dear, that was more reason for some to make light of his key contributions to the story of "their" blues, their jazz, their country music, their samba.

Research for this book—which for the first time looks into what Ralph Sylvester Peer thought he was doing in those far-flung rooms himself, what he was after, what he did, and how and why he did it, in context—revealed a different, less predictable, less vague and cartoonish story than has sometimes been suggested or simply supposed.

His life and career take us from the age of parlor piano and cylinder recordings to the age of stereo systems, color TVs, and rock 'n' roll. At about the time of Professor Greenway's question, when Peer had been in the music business in some capacity, changing its ways, for over fifty years, a high school–educated truck driver from Tupelo, Mississippi, was beginning to attain an astonishing level of pop stardom on records, broadcasts, and in the movies. People responded to Elvis Presley's mix of blues, country, gospel, and Tin Pan Alley pop across continents and classes. One side of his very first released recording, for Sun Records in 1954, was a blues Arthur "Big Boy" Crudup had recorded for RCA Victor; Ralph Peer had had a hand in popularizing blues in the first place, and first introduced the genre to that record label. The B side of Elvis's breakthrough single was a new, more pop-sounding, rhythmically altered version of Bill Monroe's "Blue Moon of Kentucky," a song, as the Sun label attests, that was published by Peer Music. When Presley returned to Sun's Memphis studio a star, and was captured singing with the down-home Southern gang now recalled as "the Million Dollar Quartet," he toyed with Agustín Lara's "Solamente Una Vez," both in a little Spanish and in its American English translation, "You Belong to My Heart." It was a song that the young Tupelo trucker never would have known at all if Peer hadn't brought it across cultures and borders from Mexico. There is no record of Elvis Presley having met Ralph Peer, but he lived, took in musical ideas, and became a global phenomenon in a world Ralph Peer played a key role in making.

In the summer of 1951, long since finished with the work for which he's most famous—his A&R work in the recording side of the business—and focusing on music publishing exclusively, Peer was featured on the *Luncheon at Sardi's* interview program broadcast from that famed New York theater district restaurant, then heard daily across the United States on the Mutual Broadcasting System radio network. He was asked a pair of simple questions by the host, sportscaster and game show emcee Bill Slater: "This music publishing business—how did you ever start in it? Did you used to write songs yourself?"

And Peer, who rarely agreed to interviews at all, responded, "No, you couldn't possibly be a success—at least, it would be unusual to be a success—if you knew *too much* about music. You have to be a businessman and a prophet, and you also have to be somewhat of a gambler." He qualified that thought on a later occasion. "The real secret," he admitted, "is continuous activity. You can't rest."

This is the story of a businessman and a popular-music prophet. The temperament of Ralph Peer the man, and the nature of his restless "continuous activities," his gambles, his explorations, his experiences and hunches, the very style of his work with the talents he found and the tunes he chose to bring to the world, have shaped our ideas of what popular music is—who we include in it, and what and how it reaches us—to this day, over a century after he first walked into an early record player manufacturer's warehouse to pick up some spare parts and platters for his father's shop.

We can still hear the difference he made.

1

Starting Out: Independence, 1892–1919

IN THE LATE 1920S, WHEN RALPH PEER was finding, recording, and helping make global stars out of makers of country, blues, and jazz music, more than one down-home Southern performer or local music shop owner he encountered took him for a New York–raised, upper-crust, Ivy League–style sophisticate slumming in their homespun music, swooping down from somewhere far north and far above. They were wrong about the vital particulars, but the misperceptions were understandable. When they met Peer he was in his midthirties. He had already been in the music business for decades, and he was dapper, urbane, energetic, and, by his own admission, often downright cocky.

The truth was, this executive who would eventually head the world's largest independent global music publishing company had never been to college, let alone the Ivy League, and had begun life the son of a displaced farmer turned shopkeeper and a coal miner's daughter. He was not from the North at all, but from that particular place where America's Midwest, South, and West meet, Kansas City, and more specifically, from just east of that storied city, a most appropriately named town: Independence, Missouri.

Ralph Sylvester Peer was born in Independence on May 22, 1892, the first and only child of Abram Bell Peer, 28, and Ann Sylvester Peer, 20, who'd married in Detroit, Michigan, the year before, then relocated.

Their goal in moving to that nexus of American regions was opportunity, as heading west was for so many from their notably working-class, rural Great Lakes area backgrounds—a chance to build a stable, more comfortable middle-class life. One sign that the newlyweds envisioned a life more modern and "up-to-date" (as Rodgers & Hammerstein described the rural view of the place in the song "Kansas City" in their show *Oklahoma*) was that until this move Abram had been known by his legal given name, Abraham, and Ann as Anna. The freshly tweaked names registered as more urban and more modern, and they stuck with them.

Abraham Peer was born and raised in the rural East Bloomfield–Canandaigua area of upstate New York, not far south of Rochester and Lake Ontario, a farmer's son, and a working farmhand himself into his twenties. His father, Benjamin Peer, Ralph's grandfather, was an Irish immigrant, originally from the far-southwestern shipping village of Crookhaven in County Cork, and Roman Catholic—although Peer men seemed to make a habit of marrying Episcopalian/Anglican women. (Peers had not been in Ireland very long; Benjamin's father Andrew, Ralph's great-grandfather, had moved to Crookhaven from southern England.) Young Abraham was one of eight siblings, just two of them boys. His older brother was the one destined to maintain the farm in the future, so Abraham had to explore other possibilities. The life of the new generation of "drummers," traveling salesmen, was his not-untypical choice.

There are neither lingering family legends nor concrete evidence describing how Peer's parents first met. It may well have been in Detroit; the Great Lakes area figures in both of their early stories. His mother was born Ann Sylvester, in Oil City, Pennsylvania (about two hundred miles from Canandaigua), north of Pittsburgh, east of Cleveland, Ohio, and not far from Lake Erie. The American oil boom had begun in that area just a generation before her birth. Her parents, William and Mary Sylvester, were recent British immigrants who soon settled in tiny Clinton, Pennsylvania (near today's Pittsburgh International Airport), where William worked in the bituminous coal mines. In the 1880 census, Ann's brother John, born in England, at age ten, and just two years older than she, was already listed as a working coal miner as well. That's certainly suggestive of the Sylvester family of eight's life conditions at the time.

One prerequisite for the explosion of pop culture that took place in the United States in the late 1890s—the coming of nickelodeons, dance halls, and machinery-heavy amusement parks, of records, and player pianos, and of the ragtime, jazz, blues, and country music that followed—was the ongoing migration of millions of rural Americans to towns and cities. The young Peers were examples of that mass movement themselves. In Kansas City the farmer's son and miner's daughter rented a series of apartments and modest bungalow-style houses, some in the central city, some out in the nearby town of Independence or on the Kansas City outskirts close to it. There were multiple reasons for the regular moves. It was common practice for landlords to offer a month's free rent to new tenants at the time, and for families to move every year to enjoy an annual rent-free month. Moreover, which neighborhoods in the formerly untamed, sometimes still-wide-open cowboy cattle town were actually compatible with a quiet, middle-class life was not yet fully determined. (Repeated outbreaks of Jesse James–style train robberies were still being reported in 1898.)

When baby Ralph Sylvester was born, Abram (or "A. B.," as he was often referred to in business) was listed in the area directories as a "confectioner" in "travelling sales." That was a substantial industry in the city at the time; the American Biscuit Company, maker of crackers and candies, for example, employed hundreds (they'd soon be known as Loose-Wiles, the manufacturer of Sunshine Biscuits and Hydrox cookies). By 1896, however, when Ralph was four, Abram was in a different sales field, one that would prove crucial in his son's life and future career, and for music history. He became a salesman of sewing machines, first as a traveling salesman for Singer, then as manager of a sewing machine dealership on downtown Kansas City's West Tenth Street, near the later site of the Central Library. The senior Peer had a penchant for things mechanical, as his son would; his farmhand background seems to have played a role in that. The 1900 US census describes his occupation as "machinist."

By 1902 Abram was working for Singer's key competitor, White Sewing Machines, at first from home at Fifteenth and Winchester near Kansas City's eastern limits, and then in his own retail storefronts, under the name the Peer Supply Company. In his store, which would soon be located on Lexington Avenue on the main square and shopping district of Independence, A. B. Peer added to the sewing machine line a second sort of mechanical device built on revolving wheels, cranks, and replaceable needles—talking machines, as record players were still called; specifically, those manufactured by the Columbia Phonograph Company and known as Graphophones. He also sold records for those machines, some still old-style cylinders, others the new flat 78 rpm platters, produced by the same firm.

Ralph proved to be a quiet, conscientious, studious sort of child, with stamp collecting one chosen hobby, likely suggesting, as it often does, an early fascination with the faraway places those stamps came from. His childhood preoccupations were markedly solitary. If he developed any significant childhood friendships, they've left no trace; school aside, he appears to have lived, through the multiple family relocations, in a world of adults. There is no evidence that he showed any interest in team sports typical of the time, but on Peer family visits back to the family farm in upstate New York, he showed conspicuous pleasure in the outdoor life, as photos showing him at play with the farm equipment and around the spread bear witness. Ralph Peer's first dose of personal notoriety came in 1901, as he recalled in a brief memoir he wrote near the end of his life, and it was a result of another solitary pursuit:

> In Kansas City, Missouri when I was nine years old, a local newspaper offered prizes for "backyard" gardens belonging to amateurs. At that time my mother and father lived in an apartment house not far from what is now the business center of Kansas City. In back of this house was a high bluff. I laboriously carved out a spot for a small garden. . . . The fact that I was only nine years old, and the unique character of the garden, earned for me a prize of $10 and created an ardent interest in gardening for the rest of my life.

This prefigured a lasting, somewhat unexpected secondary interest for the businessman of the future.

Ralph Peer would always have an introverted side that favored undisturbed, quiet, solo situations—a level of apparent shyness he was going to have to overcome in the profession he'd eventually choose. At about

that same time, though, Ralph began helping out in the stockroom at
Peer Supply, and by 1903 he began taking the new light electric rail line
that ran right past the store into downtown Kansas City, where Columbia Phonograph's regional office and warehouse were located. There, he
met still more adults—adults who would affect his future.

"I was going in and out of Kansas City, back and forth, forty-five
minutes travel," he recalled. "I would go in to pick up the packages of
records, for example, or some repair parts, and then this led to acquaintance with the Columbia organization in Kansas City."

Just that simply his work in the music industry had begun, at age
eleven. It continued, nearly uninterrupted, for the rest of his life.

That ride on the new streetcar line was a mark of a changing town;
as late as 1910 the streets of Independence still saw more horses and
carriages than autos. It was in many ways an archetypal midwestern
American small town of the time, for all of its proximity to Kansas City.
The population reached twelve thousand in 1900. Saloons operated—
apparently raucously—seven days a week, until the mayor ordered them
closed on Sundays in 1898, followed by the suspension of all forms of
gambling, including the previously popular slot machines.

The center of entertainment was the Music Hall, where touring minstrel shows as well as African American vocal ensembles, Tin Pan Alley
song-and-dance men, and touring theater companies appeared, along
with homegrown productions of operettas. The local press heralded the
"good taste in theatrical matters" of the town, both in local productions
and attendance of the theater in downtown Kansas City, while reporting,
nonetheless, on the popular traveling circuses, repertory companies, Buffalo Bill's Wild West Show, and even a send-up "burlesque farmers' street
parade" that all came through Independence to excited response. The
annual fair, the occasion for young Ralph to win that gardening prize,
was a major town event. Big-screen movie clips, in the form of Thomas
Edison's Projectoscope (or Projecting Kinetoscope), reached Independence in the summer of 1898, when Ralph Peer was six. Storytelling
motion pictures such as *The Dog and the Sausage*, *The House of Terror*, and
even *Les Miserables* first reached town in 1907. New telephone services
were competing for customers; one firm took pride in having "120
instruments" in place.

Among prominent, publicized visitors to Independence in Peer's childhood years were five-time presidential candidate William Jennings Bryan (who in 1900 was nominated at the Democratic convention in Kansas City), Carrie Nation, of saloon-hatcheting fame, and the aging outlaws Frank James and Cole Younger, who made public appearances at Confederate army and Quantrill's Raiders reunions (Younger was also an investor in the new streetcar lines). Independence's most famous resident-to-be, Harry S. Truman, born in 1884, entered elementary school the year Ralph Peer was born and in 1898 was working, first sweeping floors, then as a clerk, at Clinton's Drug Store, on the same town square where the Peer Supply Company would soon be located; he graduated from high school there in 1901. There is no certainty as to whether the music-loving Truman purchased phonographs or records from Peer Supply—but he could have.

By 1907 Ralph Peer was commuting into the city daily to attend Kansas City's Central High School. His developing fascination with the evolution and production of consumer technology was apparent when his lengthy prize-winning essay describing the latest production processes used in the making of incandescent electric lights appeared in the school's *Centralian* yearbook, though he was still only a sophomore that year. The writing is clear, very precise, and suggests that a nascent professional technical writer was at hand; it also shows no sign of actively cultivating popular favor. A sampling of the 1907 Peer prose: "Most modern manufacturers use what is known as the 'squirting' process in making filaments. Cotton or fiber paper is dissolved in chloride of zinc solution made acid with muriatic (hydrochloric) acid. . . . This solution is filtered hot and placed in a vacuum . . . then forced through small holes, forming threads, and run into large jars of wood alcohol. Whenever a jar is full, the thread, which is now white cellulose (paper) is taken out and washed for several hours, and then dried on drums."

It should be no surprise that the same man later showed so much relish for describing the process of recording sound at lock-steady speeds out on location, or wrote scientific papers on horticulture on the side.

That same year the local Independence weekly, the Jackson County *Examiner*, reported on an episode in which his father, Abram Peer, arranged a phonograph concert at the poor farm on the edge of town.

There seems to have been considerable local pride in the historically racially integrated, recently modernized institution, for its centralized steam heating, clean new buildings, and reportedly abundant food—though this was still, of course, a government institution in which even the elderly indigent worked long days farming to pay for their own keep. The elder Peer no doubt understood the goodwill to be generated, since he took along the unnamed author of the article, but he nevertheless had no specific sales targets apparent in the effort, which was about introducing the power of recorded music to poor folks who had no access to it—people who had no immediate likelihood of purchasing any of the lavish, cabinet-size Graphophones he sold, or even the more compact Grafonolas. His fifteen-year-old son had to have been aware of this family precedent for interest in extending music's reach down home:

> A.B. Peer of the Peer Supply Company, accompanied by a reporter for The *Examiner*, took a large concert gramophone to the county poor farm Friday afternoon and treated the inmates to a concert. The inmates seemed to thoroughly enjoy every minute of the music. . . . Arriving at the farm, the gramophone was placed on an improvised platform between the men's building and women's building, and the concert began. Before the first piece was half finished, the old men and women began bobbing towards the "music stand" from every direction; those who were unable to leave their rooms could be seen peering curiously out of the windows. From the actions and the faces of many, it could be seen that they had never heard music "made" in this way before. Several requests were made that some of the old familiar songs be played, and when it was possible to comply it was pitiful to see the deep impression that was made.

(That "made" in quotes is a reminder that many were still astonished that music came from anything but instruments, even at that date. Young Ralph Peer would later witness the emotional responses evoked by "old familiar songs" on a much broader scale.)

The senior Peer's community outreach included Peer Supply furnishing a lavish "$50 phonograph" as a prize at the annual Independence fair, won by a Miss Ava Seckles for undetailed accomplishments. The Columbia talking machines also came up in a controversy of a variety long forgotten, in which some local motion picture exhibitors were playing records before running their silent films as free added attractions, to the displeasure of other exhibitors who weren't. The Independence city council actually passed a law adding additional annual taxes for theaters that played records before shows, then limited the time the records could be played to ten minutes—recorded music quotas. (Live organ or piano would have accompanied the silent pictures themselves in either case.)

It is natural to wonder if teenaged Ralph Peer was developing any marked musical interests at that age when individual musical tastes so often develop, but little indication of them remains, besides his ongoing early involvement in the retail side of the record business. His relation with Columbia Phonograph had only intensified. As he later recalled, "During the summertimes, they would ask me to take over [jobs]; I'd be the shipping clerk while the shipping clerk was on a summer holiday, or I'd be a stock clerk or what-not."

Still, it's important to understand that the music he heard, the music regularly featured at the Independence Music Hall, at the town fairs and parades—the operettas, marching bands, barbershop quartet–style pop harmonizing, and sentimental or novelty Tin Pan Alley songs—was the popular musical fodder of the Kansas City area, and of most of the United States. Ralph was not directly involved in the making of any Columbia records of the time—they were, as he noted wryly later, "very mysteriously made in some super secret studio in New York"—but among the hits the label was pushing as he worked overtime there in those summers were such "roots" items as the comic sketch "Backyard Conversation Between Two Irish Washerwomen," semi-anonymous city-studio-musician versions of "The Arkansas Traveler" and the ragtime "Creole Belles," and a few recordings by African American Broadway headliners Bert Williams and George Walker, including Williams's famed "Nobody." (The recording of famed Broadway stars was just beginning to develop; recording African Americans remained uncommon before Peer's own A&R years.)

However aware he was of such records—and, given what he and his father were doing, he had every reason to be—young Peer was certainly *not* spending time at hoedowns or in raucous jazz or blues clubs. The adventurous, seminal African American–led Kansas City jazz and blues shouter scene in the Eighteenth and Vine neighborhood had not yet flowered; that was a phenomenon of the 1920s and '30s, made possible, in part, by the rise of the Pendergast Democratic political machine, circa 1920, which permitted, even encouraged, the rise of that wide-open but geographically contained entertainment district.

Just over a decade later, Ralph Peer would oversee a historically important record label line featuring African American blues, jazz, and gospel artists, treating the talents involved with respect and encouragement, and giving the go-ahead to a number of then-daring racially integrated recording sessions. Yet he was quite capable of talking about some of the same people involved in demeaning ways utterly unacceptable today, notoriously describing Lil Hardin Armstrong, for example—with whom he actually had had a trusting two-way working relationship, and whom he recorded along with her husband Louis and Jimmie Rodgers— as "an awfully nice old nigger girl."

At least contributing to that perplexing dichotomy and to the inexcusable vocabulary were the complex racial attitudes, mores, and relations of Kansas City and Independence of that era. In many ways, race relations and black opportunities in the area were considerably better in those years before World War I than after. African Americans accounted for about 10 percent of the Kansas City, Missouri, population between 1890 and 1920, but the population increased right along with the burgeoning population of the area, and there were substantial numbers of blacks in surrounding locations such as Independence and Kansas City, Kansas, as well.

While, in practice, Kansas City did perpetrate some Jim Crow–era racial segregation regarding schools, theater seating, and hotel occupancy, for instance, the ambiguous "South but West" regional geography also made for anomalous, casually accepted sorts of integration unseen in the Deep South or other areas of the United States at the time. There were essentially no local segregation statutes operating in Kansas City before 1913, as Peer was growing up, other than a ban on interracial marriage; housing restrictions didn't begin to appear until after World War I. The racial mix of neighborhoods was no more set in stone than which neighborhoods were considered tony and middle class. There were at least seventeen black policemen on the Kansas City force; there were black firemen and streetcar operators. Your postman in Independence might be black, whatever your own race, and there were numerous examples of successful middle-class African Americans, as regularly appealed to and advocated for in the black owned and operated *Kansas City Sun* newspaper. It would not have been particularly unusual for black people interested in music to shop in a local phonograph store such as the Peer Supply Company.

A news story in the *Sun* of December 15, 1917, both underscores that integrated history in music retail and indicates how the situation was beginning to deteriorate. The largest, most successful music dealer in Kansas City, the six-story-high J. W. Jenkins' Sons store downtown, featuring prestigious Steinway pianos and Victor Talking Machines (number one to Columbia's number two), shocked African American customers by suddenly "drawing the color line," as the paper put it, in the player piano department: "One lady who is paying for a six hundred dollar player . . . had been told by the store people that the practice of playing 'rolls' for Colored people has been discontinued. . . . It was learned that the question . . . has become a very embarrassing matter for the store on account of the crowded conditions . . . and also . . . the prejudice of some white purchasers. . . . The Jenkins people say that Colored people have not been explicitly barred from their former accommodations at the store. A little room has been set apart for the hearing of 'rolls.'"

While by 1917 Ralph Peer was residing elsewhere, he grew up in an Independence and Kansas City in which casual white-black integration was in many respects the workaday norm, in which there were, incidentally, a substantial set of middle-class African Americans who *were* purchasing $600 player pianos, but where use of the word *nigger* was common currency among those taken to be respectable in white society, the business elite and local politicians included. And there is no doubt that by this time the ways the respectable and successful comported themselves were being observed closely by this first-generation middle-class teenager who was increasingly intent on rising in the world.

In 1908, in his junior year in high school, Peer was again recognized in the yearbook, as a member of the Kelvin Club, which consisted of "boys who display a special aptitude in science." Serious study remained the closed-mouthed, ambitious young man's style, as tending his own garden had been, and a career in applied science seemed to be in his future. In his 1909 senior class group photo the following year, clad in a tightly buttoned celluloid collar and suit jacket, Peer stares directly, intensely into the camera as the other young gents in the photo look off to the side, perhaps distracted by something that did not divert the focus of Ralph Sylvester Peer.

The young man staring at us was in a hurry to grow up, as were so many of his generation—in the Midwest, it seems, especially so. He'd already donned a suit, and however guarded and reserved he was in private life, he quickly adopted for public consumption the commanding, confident ways in which successful men presented themselves. For the shy young Peer, one of the attractions of so quickly becoming a commanding adult may well have been that having the recognized upper hand in a room provided social armor. It may not have come entirely naturally to him, may not even have come easily, but he was determined to become a take-charge guy.

This was a generation raised to admire go-getters, executives, the big shots who got things done, who made things happen, young men (and they pretty much had to be men) who, with the ambition to join those ranks, willingly buckled down and applied themselves. Harry Truman, who'd soon try his hand at running a haberdashery downtown, was one such figure in town. Another, who moved back to his native Kansas City from Chicago just after Ralph Peer graduated from high school and founded an animation company there right after World War I, was Walt Disney—whom Peer eventually encountered and knew well, far from home. These were young men who came out of Kansas City with large ambitions, determination, and strong ideas about whom they meant to be, professionally and socially.

At graduation time, the *Centralian* editors described the technically focused and hardworking Ralph Peer, satirically though apparently affectionately, in terms very much like those a later generation would reserve for "nerds": "A hard student, veritably a regular grind. He is a regular attendant at school, not having missed one day in five years. Judging by his past record we can safely say that he will be on hand promptly when the roll is called up yonder."

On graduating high school, his practical scientific ambitions still held sway; Ralph S. Peer was described in the 1910 census as a "chemist for a packing company," living with his parents on Euclid Avenue, in Kansas City's Parkview neighborhood, not far from downtown. He may well have been working toward tuition to further a career in that direction; he suggested later that he'd been thinking about attending the University of Kansas, which was not far from home and had a well-known electrical engineering and physics department. He never went there; within months, before he was nineteen, he was back at the Columbia Phonograph Company, clerking full-time.

Costs may well have been an unspoken factor in Peer's change of direction, but so was some rethinking about what he wanted to do in life, and what he could most likely build on. His best practical option seemed a reasonable approximation of destiny: "The nut of it was," he later explained, "it was just very *natural* for me to do. . . . I worked very hard for them [Columbia] for a number of years; I was enthusiastic about the business."

It happened to be a moment of immense growth and excitement in the mass music industry. The wholesale value of sheet music in the United States—sales of which were still a central interest and income source for most of the industry, along with placement of the published songs in performance—had tripled since 1890. Piano sales were booming, player piano sales were booming, and some twenty-seven million records—platters and cylinders—were sold in 1909 alone. Not untypically for boom times in music, fights over pieces of the enlarged pie broke out, battles that set the basic rules and laws for the music business Ralph Peer worked in throughout his career.

There were, at that point, limited ways for songs and music publishers to make money—first and foremost through copyrights, which, much as with books, gave the copyright holder the exclusive right to distribute the work, to allow its use in performance (to "license" its use), and to permit some derivative work to be made from it. That mainly meant selling copyrighted, printed sheet music, perhaps licensing the song's use in other countries, and sometimes cutting deals for licensed use of the songs in live performances. In practice, the publishers often wined, dined, cajoled, or outright bribed Broadway show, concert, or vaudeville producers in order to place their songs in a show, which was known as a "plug," as placed by song "pluggers," and they did that primarily because the public exposure sold more sheet music.

Just as Ralph Peer was entering the record business full-time in 1909, publishers and composers were asking industry-shaking questions about the makers of those millions of hot-selling records and player piano rolls, who were typically not paying for use of published songs at all—on the grounds that recorded music wasn't written down, so copyright didn't apply. The dated laws being leaned on were ripe for change, and the music publishing and younger recording industries, which had been quite distinct in their interests and activities, were forced to come to terms with each other. A major reworking of United States copyright law was put into effect that year to reflect those changes.

The trust-busting Theodore Roosevelt administration had been alarmed to find that the eighty-seven members of the Music Publishers Association had signed an agreement that granted exclusive rights for piano roll recordings of their songs to just one manufacturer, Aeolian. Player piano rolls, strange as it may seem in retrospect, were still selling so strongly that it wasn't clear that they might not outpace records in sales forever. After considerable lobbying, and hearing testimony by different segments of the music industry, the US Congress enacted the Copyright Act of 1909, which, among other things, in an effort to punish those eighty-seven publishers, introduced a new, fixed royalty rate (two cents) for use of copyrighted songs on "mechanical" reproductions. By mechanicals, they mostly meant those piano rolls, but the fixed mechanical royalty rate paid to the copyright holder for use of the song also extended to music on records. (If the publisher was going to pass along any percentage of that two cents per side sold to the songwriter, that was for the publisher and writer to negotiate.)

The law, clearly aimed at preventing future monopolies of the Aeolian piano roll sort, also introduced a "compulsory licensing" provision that in time would have vast business and even musical implications not at all well understood when it was enacted. The provision said that once the first license to record a copyrighted song was granted—for a player piano roll or phonograph recording—the publisher (or any copyright holder) of the song recorded then *had to* let anyone else who wanted to record the song do so, and at the same, set two-cent-per-recording-sold rate. These fundamental rules of payment for copyrighted songs on records, of how mechanicals were to be paid, would be in effect for the rest of Peer's life, shaping some of the key ideas and innovations he would come up with in the course of his career.

Before long, he had an additional reason to want to be a dependable breadwinner in an industry with so much momentum and potential. For the first time, the romantic side of the teased high school "grind" was showing itself in earnest. This serious romantic interest was Sadie Hildebrand, whom Ralph might easily have met on any given day, since she and her family lived just a few blocks away in the same Parkview neighborhood. Born in August 1890, she was nearly two years older than Ralph. That was not, of course, the standard-issue male-female age relationship of the time, but for Peer, who was repeatedly attracted to rather than intimidated by relatively self-defined and assertive women, the age difference was not an obstacle.

Most likely the young couple met because the two families had some preoccupations in common. Sadie's father, Emil, who'd been born in Russia but was ethnically German and, like many from just that background, had immigrated to that Midwest region in his youth, had been a longtime Western Union telegraph operator. He had just recently switched trades to retail music sales at that grand downtown Jenkins' Sons. Music retail circles in Kansas City not being large, he might easily have encountered either Ralph, from Columbia Records, or retailer A. B. Peer in the course of work.

But then so might have Sadie, who had strong visual sensibilities that later served her well in fashion and interior design, and athletic capabilities as well, but she was working at the time as a piano teacher, a burgeoning profession given the boom in piano sales. Perhaps she had one of those Steinways they sold at Jenkins' Sons. All of these were talents—if an impressive parcel of them—generally considered acceptable for the highly defined women's roles of the time; Sadie, like Peer's mother, Ann, exhibited considerable curiosity about the wider world but remained essentially domestically focused. It is unrecorded whether his employer's hit 1910 Columbia Quartette record "I Want a Girl Just Like the Girl That Married Dear Old Dad" appealed to Ralph Peer or not.

Thinking about marriage seems to have come quickly, and early, but the couple would not actually marry for several more years, until January 1913. Peer, in the meantime, was on a steady upward path toward more responsibility and higher pay at Columbia Phonograph. "I was promoted to their credit department; I became their credit manager," he recalled. "We never heard about recordings in Kansas City; that all came later, but I did learn the record business, because I went right through the thing. I was the credit manager, and then I was the retail manager, and I was a traveling salesman."

The Peer family continued their regular moves around town; by 1912 they had an upstairs apartment above and to the left of the Peer Supply storefront in Independence. Father and son both made the papers that year, for nearly opposite reasons—centrifugal versus centripetal force. In March Abram Peer made local news when he conceived and fostered a "buy in Independence" (as opposed to downtown Kansas City) campaign that had local businesses signing on for "At Home Day" with varied promotions advertised together to make it work. (A. B. Peer's idea—promoting the "our own small town" local angle for the store because that tack was available—prefigured a later interest in emphasizing "always local" music on his son's part.)

On the other hand, in December, just a month before his marriage to Sadie, Ralph Peer saw his first mention in the national music press for his work in getting *out* of town. The *Music Trade Review* ran a feature on "Men Identified with Progress of Columbia Co." that included a full page of photos illustrating, in top-down order, "some of the wholesale hustlers who are building Columbia business." Of the eighty-nine staffers portrayed, two of those "hustlers" are of particular interest. Ranked number six was the district manager for the middle-west states, W. C. Fuhri, based in Chicago, who'd been with the firm since 1898, was close to dealers throughout the heart of the country, and was effectively Ralph Peer's boss. Coming in at number twenty-six, and sporting a new, dapper haircut, was "Ralph Peer, traveling out of Kansas City."

Young Mr. and Mrs. Ralph Peer soon resided at 3923 Walnut Street, near the city's Hyde Park, home even then to public tennis courts. Sadie emerged as a nationally ranked player in the fast-growing sport within four years. With Ralph on the road as much as he was then—checking in with dealers, getting records and phonographs placed, and seeing how the dealers were moving them—she must have had a lot of time to practice.

The pop records Ralph Peer was peddling to those dealers were getting more rhythmic—and plain hotter. In 1910 the ubiquitous, wildly successful, if nearly anonymous, studio recording vocalists Arthur Collins and Byron Harlan scored a hit with young Irving Berlin's "Alexander's Ragtime Band." By 1913 Columbia would add Al Jolson to the short list of Broadway stars recording for them, as previous fame began to be more of a factor in choosing recording artists, and came up with a series of dance band recordings, some by the popular Prince's Orchestra, to respond to the demands of the syncopated dance craze set off by Vernon and Irene Castle—fox-trots and turkey trots. The label was also right on top of the Hawaiian music craze set off by the appearance of steel guitar players and hula dancers at the 1915 Panama-Pacific International Exposition in San Francisco; Toots Paka's recording of "Aloha Oe" alone sold over three hundred thousand copies.

Peer was learning the ropes, getting a handle on what made a record stand out, hearing dealer reports on record buyers' reactions, and he was doing well. When Peer was twenty-three, in 1915, Fuhri promoted him to assistant manager of the whole Midwest region. "I wasn't old enough to be assistant manager," Peer mused later, "but that's what I was." Practically, he'd have to spend most of his time in the Midwest's business heart, Chicago. In an ill portent for their marriage, two years on, Sadie did not relocate with him. "Chicago, of course," Peer continued, "was a very much bigger business, and I began to meet the top executives, and to really learn about the record business, how it was really done."

In Kansas City and Chicago and on the road through the Midwest as a sales rep, Ralph Peer learned much about the record business's back end—sales, marketing, and promotion. For example, as number two to Victor's number one, Columbia had no single answer to the commanding, bigger label's signing and massive personal promotion of Enrico Caruso, but they could "hit them where they're not," signing four top Metropolitan Opera tenors and running trade magazine ads that could claim, truthfully if not entirely revealingly, "four out of five top tenors are on Columbia."

Peer was learning what a Columbia dealer in a Minnesota town said customers preferred, in contrast to, for instance, those in Texas cities. He was there as Columbia tried some rudimentary marketing of ethnic language records to immigrant populations in his territory—Norwegian songs, Polish polkas, Yiddish records—and he also saw how well some English-language ethnically defined releases could do, records on the order of "Mother Machree" and "When Irish Eyes Are Smiling," which the now rarely recalled Broadway star Chauncey Olcott recorded for Columbia in 1913.

Peer saw, too, how the firm was reaching out to establish subsidiaries and relationships overseas. He learned how decisions about what music was recorded were so often determined by the technical capabilities of the "shout in the horn" technology available. The systems weren't very good at picking up some of the female vocal range, so there were not many female vocalist recording artists; they couldn't record bass tones very well, either, so the industry avoided classical pieces heavy on that end. And the Kansas City lad surely noticed that virtually everything Columbia recorded, whether with their studio recording artists or the new Broadway star roster, reflected New York preferences, sensibilities, and perceptions.

In the summer of 1914 some key promulgators of those New York sensibilities, from Tin Pan Alley ragtime songwriters to leading operetta composer Victor Herbert, banded together to form the American Society of Composers, Authors, and Publishers, ASCAP, with the express purpose of increasing the industry leverage of their members. Instead of having to press or pay to get songs heard, they set up, collected, and enforced fees for use of their songs in performances from concert halls, cabarets, and shows, and divvied up the proceeds, according to allocation rules they set for themselves among the songwriters and the publishing houses. If you didn't pay for performance rights (they'd be known as a "performance rights agency"), you weren't going to have the music that was in demand available to you. It took some years and a few court victories to put in place the mechanisms to make that work, but ASCAP and the established publishers and writers who founded it became a formidable industry factor—capable for the next thirty years of fostering exclusively, and at the expense of others, both the established styles of music they favored and the founding, "grandfathered" publishing firms that built the organization.

While working in Chicago, Peer sometimes began to get tantalizingly close to groundbreaking music makers who had those New York connections. The African American Memphis-based "Father of the Blues" W. C. Handy had already seen success with numbers he'd composed, especially with "St. Louis Blues," which Ethel Waters and Sophie Tucker both sang on Broadway. Unable, however, to find a single publisher to publish his songs on a mass level, in 1912 Handy had started a small publishing company with his occasional songwriting collaborator Harry Pace—the Pace and Handy Music Company, which ASCAP only admitted as a signatory in 1924, a decade after the performance rights organization was founded. Meanwhile, Columbia's Prince's Orchestra got out the first recording of "St. Louis Blues" in 1916, and then the label took the next step of signing Handy himself to record.

"W.C. Handy and his band from Memphis passed through Chicago on the way to New York to record," Peer recalled, "and I was given the job of looking out for [him] . . . to see that he transferred from one train to another. He wasn't accustomed to traveling in Northern cities, and somebody had to make sure he got [around]. . . . I think we put them all on a bus and took them from one place to the other." This fleeting connection proved significant a few years later, and Peer always remembered the heady encounter.

Columbia transferred Peer back to Kansas City in 1917, assigning him more responsibility there, but the return home and to Sadie was short-lived. The United States declared war on Germany on April 6, coming in close to the end of the Great War that had been raging for over three years—heading, as the George M. Cohan song had it, "Over There." In the summer of 1918 Peer returned to Chicago for what he would jokingly refer to (though some would report it seriously) as his time "at college"—two months of US Navy officer's training.

"In 1918," he recalled, "I enlisted in the United States Naval Reserve Officers Training School at the University of Chicago, and in due course made a 'training trip' on a merchant vessel which landed me in Liverpool, England." The man for whom world travel and international business would become a way of life was for the first time in his life, at age twenty-six, in another country. He learned that the Great War had actually ended by the time he arrived in Great Britain, and rather than "lie around in a camp for six months," though he was still in the navy, he signed on as second mate on a freighter owned by the Imperial Munitions Board, drawing two salaries at once. It was more than a little cheeky, but he got away with it. He found a longtime Kansas City friend, George T. Bye, working in England as a foreign correspondent for both the *Kansas City Star* and the military's *Stars & Stripes*. (Later, Bye would be a famed literary agent who represented authors Eleanor Roosevelt, Laura Ingalls Wilder, Deems Taylor, and Alexander Woollcott.) His old buddy somehow helped him wrangle hard-to-obtain papers to go to France, where Peer either would or wouldn't wear a navy uniform as the occasion seemed to call for.

He would always relate these shenanigans, and the sheer joy of discovering these places for himself, with particular relish. He made train trips all over France, until he finally "got tired of the whole thing" and headed back to London to return home on a Red Cross ship—but not before he was interviewed as an interesting American boy abroad by the Associated Press, probably by George Bye. In a lengthy article that ran in papers all over the United States in late July 1919, preceding his arrival back home, Ralph Peer detailed his adventures at sea, mentioned his father back in Independence, suggested that "running a ship was much easier than running a motor car," and stated that he might just have to consider a career change.

"I love to stand on the bridge in a gale," he told them. "It makes me laugh, somehow. . . . They say that if you stay at sea for five years you will be with it for life, so I must drop it before it gets a hold on me. I expect to stay in the shipping business [though]."

That was not, of course, the direction his life was going to take.

2

Getting the Music:
Okeh, Records, and Roots,
1919–1926

RALPH PEER SAILED HOME FROM EUROPE on the steamer *Harrisburg* out of Liverpool, arriving in New York on June 26, 1919. He was quickly discharged from the navy in the place that he requested—back at the US Navy training station at Great Lakes, Illinois.

He was returning to a peacetime economy in which the music business was already on the decided upswing. Back in his native Kansas City, for example, music dealers were reporting that sales had doubled on a year-to-year basis, with upscale, middle-class homes sporting new pianos and lavish high-end record player cabinets, including some wicker-covered models for the porch, and others ready to be brightly painted in a fad-modern cubist-like style. The increasingly sophisticated recording industry, already about thirty years old, was witnessing and working to sustain an extraordinary boom, with sales surpassing $100 million in 1921—a threshold not crossed again until after World War II.

While there were some immediate postwar dislocations, these were the beginnings of an economic upsurge for much of the Western world, the one recalled as "the Roaring Twenties." These were also years of sometimes violent left-right political clashes in Europe and of racial upheaval in the United States, as increased expectations of African American war veterans met the backlash of a resurging, unnerved Ku Klux Klan. That casual racial interplay of the Kansas City of Ralph Peer's youth was coming to an end, as witnessed by the development of a spate of new whites-only suburban housing developments in the area, and, in 1923, a series of bombings of the homes of blacks who attempted to move into increasingly segregated white neighborhoods. Nevertheless, a growing middle class, black and white—including many people who'd previously been poor—displayed both a thirst for mass entertainment and the "disposable" pocket cash to pay for it. This boom brought dramatic changes to the definition of "popular music" and the understanding of its audience, changes that Ralph Peer often found himself spearheading.

Young Peer's fleeting if quite in-character ambition to stay in the maritime shipping business as "a manager of a line, rather than a captain," described with such enthusiasm to that reporter in London just days before his return stateside, had passed quickly, if not his intention to be an in-charge higher executive of *something*. The US Navy's physical and psychological report at the time of his discharge describes him as "4.0 for sobriety and obedience" (their highest rating), five foot ten inches tall, 157 pounds with brown eyes and hair and a "ruddy" sailor-like complexion.

Still sober-sided but toughened, he was heading back *not* to Kansas City and Sadie, but to Chicago, as he explained in a formal demobilization letter and request to the training station commandant on July 8, 1919: "Immediately upon my release from active duty I shall accept a position which I have secured in Chicago, Illinois, and I desire to make that city my home in the immediate future. I hereby waive all claim to transportation to my home . . . Kansas City, Missouri."

Peer was ready to resume the Chicago position they'd held open for him at the Columbia Graphophone Company. All of the evidence suggests that his nearly five years away, first at that Columbia Chicago office and then off on his European adventures, drained whatever enthusiasm he'd had left for his hometown and his wife. Since Sadie Hildebrand Peer had never had any interest in relocating anywhere, Ralph Peer's waiver of transportation to Kansas City amounted to an acknowledgment that his youthful first marriage was over.

By the following April, lawyers would be involved; Sadie's suggested, "Mrs. Peer can doubtless get this divorce very speedily." It was indeed a relatively acrimony-free proceeding between two young parties who had both come to understand that they had been too young and too different in their goals for the marriage to work. The divorce would became final on March 14, 1921, with Ralph paying alimony of fifty dollars per month—though, tellingly, keeping up with that not-insignificant amount proved to be a challenge to him for the next few years of his career. A final cash settlement resolved that issue in late 1927, by which time he was remarried, and his financial situation was dramatically improved. Sadie never remarried, but she was soon thriving in Kansas City on her own—parlaying her early clothing design business experience and her time as an art instructor at the city's Art Institute into long-standing work as a decorating consultant at Kansas City's Robert Keith Furniture and Carpet Company. She also emerged, through the early 1920s, as a headline-making regional tennis star, particularly successful in mixed doubles matches, appearing in national press reports as "Mrs. Sadie Peer" or "Mrs. Ralph Peer."

As it turned out, only a few days after Peer's return to Chicago in 1919, W. C. Fuhri, his old boss and mentor at Columbia, jumped ship to become general sales manager of the ambitious new record division of the Otto Heineman Phonograph Supply Company, just established in midtown Manhattan on Forty-Fifth Street, near Fifth Avenue. Fuhri recruited Peer to join him as his assistant manager there, and the "married but single" Ralph Peer, as he described himself at the time, relocated to East Orange, New Jersey, where many Heineman employees resided. The town was both close to the firm's New Jersey manufacturing facility and just a short train ride from the city.

Heineman's four-year-old company had rapidly become a leading supplier of motors, tone arms, and needles to US manufacturers of record players. A Jewish German, Otto Heineman (the name had been spelled Heinemann back in Germany) had been a director of Carl Lindström A.G., a leading supplier of the same phonographic parts in Europe. He'd found himself stranded, unable to return home when World War I broke out, and saw founding his own US firm as a way to remain in competition with leading phonograph and record makers Victor and Columbia, both of which he'd apparently even attempted, but failed, to acquire outright. Clearly, he was well capitalized.

In 1918, intent on making a mark in the record business, Heineman had bought the facilities of the defunct Rex Talking Machine label and thereby inherited its music director, prolific songwriter Frederick Hager, who'd once led Edison Records' concert band. A greater coup was Heineman's buyout of the recording studio of Charles L. Hibbard, which had been used to record sessions for Rex and its short-lived successor Imperial Talking Machine. An already legendary recording engineering talent with a history that went back to the earliest Edison cylinder recording days, Hibbard became Heineman's technical director. The new company, soon known for the high sonic quality of its records, was dubbed General Phonograph, and the record label Okeh. (The "Okeh" name, sometimes rendered as "OKeh" or "OkeH," was based on Heineman's initials and an older, once-common spelling of "OK," which is how the brand is pronounced. The word was allegedly derived from Native American sources, so a young brave was depicted on early labels.)

Ralph Peer had to have wondered, as the modern reader would, what exactly an "assistant general sales manager" of this new firm was going to be doing. Fuhri had been recruited for his experience in dealing with the users of the firm's phonograph part products—phonograph manufacturers, and the phono dealer/distributor chain—not with record-buying consumers. Heineman Phonograph Supply was what would later be called an "OEM," an original equipment manufacturer catering to finished product makers, and not much attuned to attending to the needs of end-users, until Heineman entered the recording business.

As assistant to Fuhri, Peer was going to be spending considerable time traveling, tending to and keeping tabs on regional distributors of General Phonograph products and record dealers—the latter being the industry people closest and most sensitive to consumer interests and demands. This time out, Fuhri intended for Ralph Peer to handle much more than clerical work or driving W. C. Handy around town. And since this was a fledgling record company that, like many start-ups, needed to have staff wear multiple hats, Fred Hager, the musical director, was going to make some use of young Ralph Peer's as-yet-untested ear as well.

Hager needed the help; Okeh's roster of recording artists hardly compared to that of Victor, for example, for quality. As Peer recalled, "They were way down; I think they sold about three or four million records a year, which was nothing. . . . When I went to New York, they were just starting; they didn't have anybody. . . . We used what I should call 'house orchestras;' we'd name them just anything." And, indeed, the early Okeh catalogs are dependent on such ersatz studio-born outfits as the Okeh Concert Band, Hager's Dance Orchestra, and Hager's Novelty Orchestra, and also some of the most overemployed and prolific recording vocalists of the era—Henry Burr, Billy Murray, Arthur Collins, Ada Jones, Irving Kaufman—all aging, near-anonymous singers who'd sold an enormous number of records since the turn of the century while rarely performing outside of recording studios. There was no Al Jolson, Enrico Caruso, or John McCormack recording there, and no name orchestra, either, on a level potentially competitive with Paul Whiteman's dance band, which had been signed by Victor in 1920 and was soon one of the few recording acts of the 1920s to sell in the millions. Popular music sales, not for the first or last time, were generally dance-driven; Vernon and Irene Castle's popularizing of the fox-trot had been shaping record sales of hot dance bands since 1914; the Charleston was just up the road. But in those generally exciting times for recording companies, Okeh had a meager pop roster.

Otto Heineman's European connections helped in the classical music arena, as he licensed recordings from European labels for their first American release on American Odeon, set up as a sister label to Okeh. For a name hot dance band to call Okeh's own, Fuhri and Peer, in his first major artist involvement, found and signed a new Portuguese-American dance band leader from Brooklyn, Vincent Lopez, a specialist in rhythmic, ragtime-tinged pop that veered ever so slightly toward jazz. They didn't have to venture far to find him; Lopez was appearing regularly just blocks away, at the Hotel Pennsylvania across the street from New York's Penn Station. He would be around for decades.

Where, then, would you have found engaging American roots music on record as Ralph Peer's work at Okeh began—music recorded in the performance style of its originators, reflecting the flavor of the region and people it came from? The short answer is, you wouldn't.

That's not to say that there weren't some obvious precursors of what lay ahead—in Okeh's case, such releases as the successful, white, all-male Peerless Quartet's 1918 "Way Down Yonder in the Cornfield," in a minstrelsy-meets-concert-hall style, and raggy twelve-bar instrumental blues recorded by other white acts, such as "Yellow Dog Blues" by Paul Biese & His Novelty Orchestra (1920).

Heineman, with a combination of ambition and idealism, envisioned greatly expanding the audience for records, as he made clear in an interview in the lavish *Talking Machine World* trade magazine in May 1919: "Today, there is a machine within the reach of every laboring man. Now it's simply a question of a systematic and thorough canvass of this vast country . . . and my slogan of 'A Phonograph in Every Home' will be no mere slogan, but a wonderful fact." He wanted, and regularly demanded, more detailed market information about where they were trying to head—better data about what "every laboring man" actually wanted to hear and might buy—but he firmly believed that there were emerging opportunities "downscale."

Those polite Okeh blues and hillbilly precursor records were not, however, the significant first step by the firm in the direction of popularizing specialized American roots music, or approaching the less affluent, down-home audiences Heineman surmised were out there. That was an expansive and expanding series of recordings aimed at foreign language–speaking American ethnic audiences, released by General Phonograph on Odeon. At first, these were simply imports that had not been issued in the United States, which came cheap and were included in Heineman's European licensing agreements. Nobody had shown interest in releasing those records in the United States, despite America's increasingly large ethnic immigrant population. That's precisely what made them an attraction for an upstart firm trying to make some money in places that Victor and Columbia hadn't much cared to go. General Phonograph released recordings in Russian, Turkish, and Chinese, then additional releases in Yiddish, Italian, Polish, German, Hungarian, Greek, Slovak, and the Scandinavian tongues. They were all languages widely spoken within the United States in the 1920s, and the records were quite marketable in stores in the specific neighborhoods where the languages were prominent—music of local American interest if you knew where to go.

Okeh's strategy was to develop its own essentially undeveloped, less contested arena rather than competing head-on in mainstream pop, where it was weak. This "hit it where they're not" approach would leave a lasting, significant impression on Ralph Peer. It was the context in which one of the milestone recordings and subsequent marketing break-throughs in the history of American popular music came about: the recording and aftermath of "Crazy Blues" by African American vaudevil-lian Mamie Smith, at Okeh in New York City on August 10, 1920, with Ralph Peer on hand.

Writing in *Collier's* magazine, the more politically liberal general-interest competitor of the *Saturday Evening Post*, in April 1938 (by which time the event was understood to have been a recording milestone), Kyle Crichton paraphrased Peer's memory of what had ensued: White vaude-ville star and sometime blues belter Sophie Tucker had been slated to record "You Can't Keep a Good Man Down" for Okeh, but was pre-vented from showing up by her previous recording contract with Vocalion. Perry Bradford, a song plugger for W. C. Handy's publishing firm and a fledgling publisher and artist manager himself, suggested to Peer that he could quickly provide another good singer for the recording date—Ms. Mamie Smith, a black woman with a "loud raucous voice" who, the article suggests, had been working as a cleaning woman in some theater. (That fanciful and demeaning Cinderella story was far from accurate; in truth, Smith had been singing in a Broadway show that fea-tured songs composed and copyrighted by Bradford, who was himself African American.) When this first Mamie Smith recording sold a sur-prising seventy-five hundred copies in a month, the Okeh crew had her return to the New York studio, and she brought along a band known as Mamie Smith and Her Jazz Hounds to record "Crazy Blues," a record that sold ten times as much in its first month alone. In the article, "Thar's GOLD in them Hillbillies," Peer described that one as "the most awful record ever made, and it sold over a million copies."

While calling attention to the spectacular rise of American roots-derived records, with its caustic tone Crichton's article displayed all of the classic mainstream media condescension of the day toward hillbilly, blues, early gospel, and even Cajun, beginning with conflating all of them under that "Hillbillies" headline even with a big photo of Bessie Smith on its opening page—a reminder, at least, that broad "down-home roots music" connections were well understood long before the term came along.

Peer himself nowhere else dismissed "Crazy Blues" as he did in that one later account, and he may well have been dissembling, finding it both useful to provide Crichton and his comfortable, if progressive, readership precisely the musical evaluation of the record that they were assumed to want to hear—as confoundingly lucrative, compared to their favorites. (The article pegged those favorites as swing records that didn't swing too hard, and the Metropolitan Opera, as popularized by Lily Pons—acceptable tastes among the aspiring middle class of the era.) Whatever his personal reaction to these early blues recordings was, for public consumption at that point in his life Peer was certainly careful to portray himself as outside and above the records he'd produced. He knew very well that, in fact, despite the dismissive, cavalier presentation, he'd actually worked closely with Mamie Smith for over eighteen years by then, shared her success, treated her with respect, and given every indication in his life and manner of having enjoyed blues, vaudeville-style and beyond.

Crichton, with Ralph Peer clearly his source, goes on to tell us, quite accurately, that from the moment of the release of the first Mamie Smith record, dealers soon "began to report a curious trend. . . . Negro Pullman porters on trains going South invariably left New York with as many as twenty-five records a piece" for resale down South. "Mr. Peer went south to investigate," Crichton continues. "He found a) that the Negroes *were* buying records of their own people in great quantities and b) that the Negroes of Richmond, Virginia invariably referred to themselves as 'The Race.'"

Years later, Peer said of those provocative weeks, "I discovered and developed the idea of making recordings by Negro artists exclusively for sale to Negroes. I saw that this was really a business like our foreign record business, so I decided that, like the German [records] were all on [their own series], we had to give them a different series."

The popular blues craze, its promotion, and the regular recording of black artists with the intention of appealing to the black audience did, in fact, take off from there. "Crazy Blues" was neither the first blues ever to be recorded, since there had been plenty of renditions of twelve-bar blues songs recorded by white men and women, including many recordings of

Handy's "Memphis Blues" and "St. Louis Blues," nor the first recording by an African American—two often repeated but erroneous claims. Bert Williams and George W. Johnson, for instance, had recorded years earlier, but this was indeed the first blues record to be recorded with a black vocalist, and the record that changed thinking and directions in the recording industry—not to mention definitions of popular music. Ralph Peer was so highly involved in the nailing down of information about the market and outlook in the field for Okeh that Fuhri promoted him to recording director of the new "race" records line he'd identified as an ongoing commercial possibility. He became what would later be called an A&R man, in charge of artists and their repertoire, putting together the right combination of the two in search of broader popular success.

There was, to be clear, nothing demeaning about the use of the term "race" in that context at the time, though the term "race records" would often be found objectionable years later and would be dropped throughout the recording industry. What Peer heard in Richmond, and would also have seen in editorials of the country's leading black newspaper, the *Chicago Defender*, was a positive use and promotion of the term by sophisticated African Americans; being "a race man," for example, was a compliment, suggesting rightful interest, pride, and activist advocacy.

Details of how "Crazy Blues" was produced have long been a subject of controversy. The least-heard phrase in all of popular music history is no doubt "I'm sorry, but I'm given too *much* credit for that," so memories and placement of credit for the historic session and its musical consequences vary. In Perry Bradford's 1965 memoir, which is relied on heavily in later accounts that understandably—but unhelpfully for getting at the complex facts—very much wanted the breakthrough to have been exclusively African American conceived and executed, Bradford claims, "I was wholly responsible for the first recording of a Negro girl singer with a Negro combination jazz band accompanying her." (The record was, in fact, also an early example of true improvisational jazz band backing.) He quickly amends that claim to include the man he recalls as having given him the go-ahead on the session: "I must right here, however, start giving credit where credit is due. The number one man in the successful operation was Mr. Hager, the recording manager of the Okeh Recording Company."

In the course of Bradford's broad account-settling, often contentious narrative (which makes bebop era jazz critics special targets for retaliation), he relates how he'd first attempted to sell the idea of Mamie singing "You Can't Keep a Good Man Down" to Victor to no avail, but got in to see Fred Hager at Okeh on the recommendation of Bill Tracy, a white songwriter they both knew, and sold Hager on the idea that "There's fourteen million Negroes in our great country [mainly in the South] and they will buy records if recorded by one of their own." Hager told him that they feared boycotts and retaliation by segregationists for any move to record "a colored girl," but nevertheless said yes. When the first record did well, despite backing by an undistinguished white band, Hager then OK'd the "Crazy Blues" session for Mamie and the all-black jazz band behind her, a session led by Bradford himself, as he would lead her sessions to follow, with Charles Hibbard as the recording engineer.

In that account, Ralph Peer is never mentioned as being part of the two historic recording sessions at all, let alone having been sent to investigate the dependability of claims like Bradford's that a Southern African American record audience was waiting, and what might be done about it. That's not entirely surprising; as an outside song plugger not part of the Okeh staff, Bradford wasn't necessarily informed about the research— or about Otto Heineman's known interest in looking before he leaped. (This was not, as a matter of fact, the last time Ralph S. Peer was sent on a fact-finding mission about potential musical markets only to emerge as a chief developer of the field he'd scoped out.)

Piano great Willie "the Lion" Smith, prominent in Mamie Smith's Jazz Hounds band, painted quite a different picture of the "Crazy Blues" session in his own memoir, with Bradford constantly pestering Ms. Smith to become her manager. He related how "Mamie and I went down to an old-fashioned studio and performed some selections for Ralph Peer, the guy in charge at Okeh, and he told us to get a band together. The day in August 1920 we went to make the sides, there was only Mamie, Ralph Peer, myself, and the band in the studio. I can't recall that Bradford was anywhere in sight." He added, pointedly, "There have been a lot of inaccurate stories printed about that 'Crazy Blues' record."

In a moment-by-moment account of the day offered by bandleader and later Fats Waller manager Ed Kirkeby, who spoke with a number of the participants, Fred Hager called Peer with Bradford's initial proposition to record Smith on "You Can't Keep a Good Man Down," and Peer gave the go-ahead even for that first record (already being in the position to do so), then Bradford and Peer were both on hand for the actual recording, which required several takes because of wince-inducing sound problems. Peer and Hager both OK'd the follow-up "Crazy Blues" session with the superior African American band.

The disputed history essentially comes down to the question of exactly when Peer was first put in charge of recording sessions. Years later Peer referred to musical director Hager as "this man I had [at the time]," as a recording director might of his orchestra leader; it is quite plausible that Fuhri and Heineman could have been trying Peer out as the recording director for a session or two, as Willie Smith and Ed Kirkeby suggest, before the promotion that instantly followed. Indeed, the opportunity may have happened precisely because the sessions had been considered marginal "experiments" that, what the hell, you might as well hand over to an in-house novice.

What's unquestionable is that the "Crazy Blues" record was a sensation, selling somewhere between eight hundred thousand and a million copies. Many of those sales were in more economically developed black neighborhoods such as Harlem; some were in the barbershops, pool halls, and such that those Pullman porters necessarily worked with in the commercially underdeveloped black South, where there simply were no black-owned record shops to approach. On the side, some sales were to a white audience through the existing retail chain, where segregated stores said yes to carrying it. However questionable his version of the story, Perry Bradford certainly was paid substantial royalties as the songwriter (or, at least, the copyright holder of the songs), and he certainly was responsible for coaxing Fred Hager to consider recording the songs and Okeh to consider Mamie Smith as a barrier-busting singer.

What were listeners responding to? This was not the blues of the rural Delta or, of course, of postwar Chicago, but horn-backed vaudeville blues, what was once called "classic" blues. In retrospect, Mamie Smith is rarely rated the most nuanced blues singer who has ever come along, but her theatrical background and polish were well displayed and she delivered a level of exuberance and assertiveness unheard on records until then. The band was improvising, swinging, on a level also unheard on records till that point, taking a real step away from the pop ragtime era. There's rhythm and drama and also, in what had to have been a shock and thrill for many in the black audience in particular, a no-holds-barred lyric that climaxes with Ms. Smith's announced, song-ending gangsta rap–anticipating intention to "Do like a Chinaman, go and get some hop; get myself a gun and shoot myself a cop."

Brand-new A&R man Ralph Peer was definitely involved with putting out something different there, all right. It was instantly distinguishable from anything in Okeh's pallid catalog of the time, and briefly at least, from anybody else's—music from a place not heard before on record, built on experiences and tastes not reflected before on record, startlingly speaking to you if you were in the targeted black minority audience, Southern or Northern, who knew the place and the life. The material was nervy and novel and, if you were from the white American majority and happened to hear it, exotic.

The response by African Americans to records explicitly intended for them, performed by one of them with a hot and credible jazz band, was not much different from what other ethnics felt when hearing records speaking to them about their lives in their own languages. As Peer was able to certify, Perry Bradford had not been wrong at all about the potential size of this particular ethnic audience, whose contributions and interests had never been marginal to American culture, but had been ruthlessly marginalized by the music industry, and the recording industry in particular. The musical and cultural impact on the popular music of the United States and the world beyond of the mass distribution of the music of American black people would, of course, be enormous, and Ralph Peer would play a key role in beginning the process of making it so. At age twenty-seven, as the newly appointed recording chief of Okeh's 8000 series race recordings, his own lasting musical impact began right there as well.

Other record companies soon jumped on the blues craze bandwagon—Vocalion, Columbia (which signed the era-defining Bessie Smith in 1923), Paramount, and, if only briefly, the black owned and operated Black Swan, founded by W. C. Handy's publishing partner Harry Pace. The competitive pressures, the ongoing business interest in identifying opportunities where competitors were not, and his own experimenting adventurousness led Peer toward an expanding and expansive view of what sounds, styles, and levels of sophistication might be included and sold under the "music by and for Negroes" banner.

What sorts of records the race series and field might include was an open question; this was a very new recording market. Peer was, as all of his actions demonstrated, well aware of what he *didn't* know, though it would be difficult to nominate anyone who knew all that much more. Anybody who'd worked in popular music back to the Tin Pan Alley sheet music days would have understood that a balance needed to be found between familiarity and novelty to keep sales rolling. It was the natural inclination to apply similar rules to commercialized African American blues, jazz, and gospel music, yet there was a learning curve as to where and how to find new talent, sounds, and songs, and how far you could veer from the early Mamie Smith model without getting off track.

At first, Peer and company didn't look much further away, literally, than they had for Vincent Lopez in pop—just around Manhattan, especially in Harlem nightclubs—for music much like the "Crazy Blues" sensation. But temperament mattered here again; Peer proved to be self-confident enough to be comfortable with the understanding that he really didn't have to know everything. He just had to be wise about identifying people who knew more about the needed specifics—to find people worthy of his trust and to trust them.

The first of his notable line of musical trustees to be hired on full-time, rather than serving as an outside musical scout, was his contemporary Clarence Williams, an African American songwriter, vaudeville singer, pianist, and shrewd businessman who, with some smart timing, moved from New Orleans to Chicago in 1920 to operate music stores there. He'd married blues singer Eva Taylor and, having seen how the Mamie Smith records were selling in his own stores, quickly relocated to New York. He set up a new publishing company at 1547 Broadway, the same building that housed W. C. Handy's publishing firm, Bert Williams's, and Perry Bradford's. All of these small, fledgling black-owned firms were naturally pitching songs to Okeh, and that meant pitching them to Ralph Peer. Peer's close working relationships with Clarence Williams and soon with Handy and his firm as well were still at work a decade later when he was a publisher himself, extending the marketing for their smaller houses' songs.

Peer began to employ Clarence Williams as a producer at Okeh, as an in-house A&R assistant, one with connections and songs who was a good session organizer to boot. One of Williams's early signings for Peer was Sara Martin, a highly successful, deep-voiced if not particularly expressive singer originally from Louisville, a smart veteran of the African American vaudeville circuit, sometimes referred to as "the black Sophie Tucker," who later served as an Okeh talent scout herself. They began to record Sara with varying keyboard-led backings—Williams's own piano, Handy's orchestra—and, on a song that would last, "T'ain't Nobody's Biz-ness If I Do," piano by a very young Thomas "Fats" Waller.

It is hardly a wonder, working out of Manhattan, that keyboards were so prominent in these early blues records—since players as exciting as Waller and Willie "the Lion" Smith were close at hand. Peer soon recorded Waller's mentor as well, the great James P. Johnson, inventive master of the syncopated, blues-related stride piano style that bridged ragtime and jazz. Many musicologists cite "Carolina Shout," which Johnson recorded with Ralph Peer in October 1921, as the very first jazz piano recording, and it was unquestionably the record that established Johnson as the "father of stride piano." Just two years later, he composed a little number called "The Charleston" for the Broadway show *Runnin' Wild*, changing the way America and then much of the Western world moved.

Tracking the musical settings Peer and Williams put behind Ms. Martin over the following four years, including a yodeling duet with Williams's wife, Eva Taylor; backing by the great jazz clarinetist Sidney Bechet; and the more lowdown, Louisville-based jug band leaders Clifford Hayes and Earl McDonald (Peer later had them back Jimmie Rodgers), shows the close relation that swiftly developed between maintaining novel sounds and expanding popular roots music's possibilities.

A truly portentous experiment occurred on October 24, 1923, when Peer recorded Sara Martin at the New York studio backed simply by the fluid fingerpicked guitar of Sylvester Weaver on "Longing for Daddy Blues." This was the very first blues vocal ever backed on record by a guitar. Then, just nine days later, Peer recorded Weaver playing solo for a two-sided release, "Guitar Blues" and "Guitar Rag." The latter is none other than the infinitely catchy bottleneck slide guitar tune later generations came to know when Bob Wills's band adapted it for western swing as "Steel Guitar Rag." Peer's job included direct involvement in deciding how acts would be marketed and presented, and he quickly had Okeh promoting the deft Sylvester Weaver as "the Man with the Talking Guitar." Okeh's ads would note that he "plays his guitar in a highly original manner, which consists chiefly of sliding a knife up and down the strings while he picks with his other hand." On records, that popular blues guitar commonplace began right there.

A note Peer sent to Sara Martin a few months later, a little over three years after the "Crazy Blues" session, one of the few from him from that time that survives, at once bears witness to the level of comfort he'd come to feel in his executive position as A&R chief of the race records line; his growing decision-making confidence, cunning, and musical authority; and his competitive nature—all necessary ingredients for his emergence as an experimenting "gambler." He'd tell Ms. Martin:

> "Roamin' Blues" with guitar accompaniment is the biggest seller you have had since "Sugar Blues." It might be well for you to rearrange your act so that this is your feature number using guitar accompaniment. It seems to me that this would make a wonderful encore number to be used very near the end of your act. . . . I want to advertise Weaver as an exclusive artist. . . . It is my intention to keep him satisfied so that he will not want to work for any one else if offered the opportunity. . . . Please extend my regards to Weaver, and tell him to bear down hard when he is picking the strings.

Ralph Peer's growing direct involvement as a career and even performance advisor to contracted recording artists, and his attention to audience responses to Okeh offerings, are suggested in these sentences as well. (For the record, within a year of that note, vaudeville blues women were recording with guitar backing on multiple labels, and the step-by-step march toward the guitar's lasting ascendancy in recorded blues had begun.)

The still-young executive was held responsible for signing off on every act recorded for the race series, which recordings were released, and when; this was the central aspect of the job. As Peer later explained, "I recorded all of them. . . . I *don't* mean I was always actually present at the recordings [and he didn't need to be, with someone he trusted as much as Clarence Williams, for example, working with him] . . . but *I* decided to use them."

His secondary responsibilities continued to include some tending of the dealer chain: he worked with Fuhri to see how well records were being stocked, displayed, and promoted in retail stores, and how the label could help make all of those work better. Given his unmarried status and developing taste for travel, he certainly did not see the jam-packed schedule that resulted from those work obligations as a problem. What leisure time he managed to set aside and personal relationships he had in this period appear to have been offshoots of his work, or were indistinguishable from it. If in the immediate wake of his move east and 1921 divorce he was dating anyone with any consistently, no trail or on-the-record references have been left. In any case, he was attending industry conventions and the firm's marketing events, and enjoyed evenings at musical performances in New York and on the road.

Peer's leisure time, limited as it was, tended to involve the close-knit "family" of General Phonograph and Okeh employees around East Orange, New Jersey. Heineman would stage regular executive dinners and company picnics, and while it's difficult to picture Ralph S. Peer engaged in three-legged races, a favorite at the picnics, he did take up golf at that time, and personal developments would tighten his ties to the local community. Apparently having given up hope of making a sufficient living in the retail phonograph business in Independence, in 1922 A. B. Peer signed on as a traveling salesman again, and Peer's parents relocated to Roanoke, Virginia, which was a home base closer for visits in either direction. When A. B. died suddenly the following year and was buried back home in upstate New York, the widowed Ann Peer moved up to East Orange to be nearer to her son, and was soon getting to know Okeh-connected neighbors herself.

But Ralph Peer was increasingly on the road and, naturally, ideas for potential recording acts came up, whether he spotted them or, as happened, the record dealers that he checked in with suggested them. Given the increasing competition in the field and thirst for novelty, such talent spotting was slowly becoming a deliberate, more organized process. As *Talking Machine World* reported of talent scouting trips he led for Okeh that autumn, "For months the company's representatives had been touring the South in search of artists who were capable of interpreting realistically the old-fashioned Negro spirituals, and they recently discovered this quartet [the Virginia Female Jubilee Singers] in the country regions of Virginia and engaged them for the Okeh library." The range of Peer's race line was broadening further, and his own continuing explorations had helped make that possible.

Newspaper advertising for Okeh race artists, many in trade journals such as *Talking Machine World*, reflected Peer's marketing ideas as director of the record line; they were a way to stretch the reach of the records and they functioned as sales pitches to dealers. Others, placed in papers such as the *Chicago Defender*, were intended to reach black record buyers. The ads were evidence of the firm's early uncertainty about the tone to take in this new realm of marketing, and, at times, even exactly what audience was being chased.

One industry ad, reminding dealers how smart it was to have plenty of Mamie Smith records in stock, would be all business and highly respectful; the next might feature an astonishingly off-key (if not unfamiliar) illustration of the race line's customer as "Mr. Public Opinion," a top-hatted minstrel in blackface telling General Phonograph dealers, "I's heard Blues, but I's telling you Mamie's beats 'em all. O man, her voice is as sweet as honey! It Jus flows and flows and ev'ry note gets richer and richer until I can just sit back and expire with joy."

When Peer signed another Virginia outfit in 1921, the all-male a cappella vocal harmony group the Norfolk Jazz Quartet, recording numbers with them such as "Preacher Man Blues," and "Cornfield Blues," their repertoire was described in industry advertisements as traditional music made less "monotonous" with the addition of "more harmony and weird jazz chant . . . an appeal to the white people to revive negro minstrelsy . . . the old-fashioned folk music of this country. . . . We see in this group a means to boost sales."

That the supposedly "monotonous" old folk chants had been *modernized*—"jazzed up" with new rhythms and harmonies—can be readily heard on the records. Peer and his recording line's deliberate modernization of older styles for modern listeners, his merging of an already somewhat pop-ularized type of roots music with new, up-to-date sounds and rhythms, perhaps attracting a white audience in the process, was another key step in the process of creating fresh pop styles.

New ideas for hits were especially in demand just then. There was rising pressure on the whole recording industry to come up with some: 1921's $105 million–plus in sales had proved to be a high point; by 1923 that was down to $79 million, off some 25 percent. Technology was changing things. Radio was in operation at the local and regional levels and was initially greeted with mixed feelings in the record business; it was suspected that the novelty of free broadcasts was cutting into record sales wherever people had radios, but—as with the advent of digital downloading later—it was not clear how much the new medium was contributing to the sales downturn, or whether it might potentially rep-resent an untapped *promotional* opportunity.

In May 1922 Okeh began experimenting with staging live shows featuring its recording artists on radio broadcasts. One was at a station run by the Army Signal Corps on New York's Bedloe's Island. Another was at Newark, New Jersey, and featured classical selections but also a Miss Virginia Burt, soprano, "introducing her own compositions and original Hawaiian steel guitar imitations"; Harry Reiser, the vaudeville banjo star; and Byron Harlan with "rural interpretations and songs." None of this was a casual accident; Otto Heineman announced the establishment of his firm's radio manufacturing spinoff, the General Wireless Corporation, at the same time.

Puzzle pieces adding up to a new recording era were coming together. Okeh now had in place location appearances by their acts, and regional scouting for Peer's race recordings, especially in the South, where talent for the line was considered most likely to be found. There was that grow-ing demand to identify new acts and material to rekindle sales, and bur-geoning local radio outlets to contend with, especially in the cities. Con-sidering the cost of bringing act after act to New York to record when you found them—and that you couldn't, then or any time after, be sure just how many of the newcomers you recorded would see successful record sales—it was a perfectly logical and simple step for the Okeh management team to ask a potent question more economic than artistic:

wouldn't it make sense just to go record where the talent is, especially talent already being promoted in the area by regional radio?

At just that time, apparently coincidentally, Peer was promoted at Okeh to the position of general recording manager, still overseeing the race music line but increasingly responsible for the label's broader output as well. In a series of era-marking if little-known spring 1923 articles in the *Atlanta Constitution*, we can follow the movement of the Okeh management team toward the beginning of on-location recording and, with it, as an almost accidental by-product, the historic beginnings of a whole new enterprise that would eventually be called "country music."

On April 22 of that year, the paper reported that Warner's Seven Aces, a popular Atlanta outfit that was appearing on the city's WGM radio and sponsored by the *Constitution* itself, owner of the station, had been "selected" to record for Okeh. The Aces were a white, horn-driven society dance band that played some relatively jazzy blues but specialized in popular numbers in the "flaming youth" mode—snappy songs about sheiks and frat houses. The paper reported feeling "a bit of pride in the New York engagement secured by the Aces, because the orchestra has been an outstanding feature of broadcasts from this station for many months."

The Warner's Seven Aces society band had been brought to Peer's attention by Polk C. Brockman, one of Okeh's more successful regional jobbers—agents who negotiated shelf space in stores for the label's records and displays and targeted the records best to push at individual retail outlets. He'd been appointed an Okeh regional rep for his successful work promoting Peer's race line within the phonograph and music-centered downtown store of Atlanta furniture dealer James K. Polk (Polk was Brockman's maternal grandfather). Brockman had an eye out for potential recording talent in the area, if not many connections to the African American talent pool, and he knew the Aces, whom he lined up with Peer.

A week later, on April 29, the *Constitution* noted that Atlanta Aces fans wouldn't be seeing them perform the week beginning May 16, since they'd be in New York to record, and continued to confirm that in articles right through May 3. There was then a sudden change.

In a May 6 feature accompanied by a large photo of the Aces orchestra, the *Constitution* reported that "another angle of interest in the contract for the Aces to make records is that the phonograph company, one of the largest producing companies of its kind in the world, will soon open a recording studio in Atlanta and the Aces' records will be made here. The exact date has not been announced, but it will be about May 20." This was not, in fact, an announcement of the opening of a new permanent "recording studio," of course, but of a temporary location recording stand—for which there wasn't even a vocabulary. It occurred later than first projected, during the week of June 12, 1923, when, as the paper duly noted, "This week, the General Phonograph company, of New York, makers of Okeh records, will make records of a number of orchestrations which Warner's Aces have made famous wherever radio broadcasting is received."

The label's concept of recording locally promoted broadcast artists couldn't have been more straightforwardly expressed. The radio-publicized Aces fit the bill, so their Atlanta home base would be the place where location recording would begin—not just of the Aces, but of other promising acts found there as well. The challenge had been to produce—to invent, really—transportable recording equipment capable and dependable enough to do the job and do it repeatedly. Heineman's General Phonograph, with a reputation for sonic quality within the acoustic play-into-the-horn scale of the time (one version of their printed label read "The Record of Quality"), was not going to compromise on the sound of their released products simply for the economies of going on location.

Heineman, Fuhri, and Peer had put Charlie Hibbard, their technological ace in the grooves, to work on precise, reliable acoustic recording equipment that could be shipped out in a few trunks. He didn't quite achieve that much compactness, and no one elsewhere had either, but he came up with a setup that, fitted into more than a few trunks, could be taken on location to produce professional recordings. Finally, the Okeh team believed they had transportable recording equipment advanced enough to enable making the on-location recordings they'd wanted.

This relatively transportable professional technology, it should be understood, was entirely different in precision and function from the "fits in a car trunk" recording machines folklorists such as Robert W. Gordon and John and Alan Lomax took on the road a few years later to document music makers in the field for the US Library of Congress. The folklorists were looking simply to keep an aural record, quite literally, of what they found—for sound documentation. Commercial release was not a goal, and the small units they used could capture what they needed for that.

Ralph Peer described what his Okeh team had at the ready that May: "The machines themselves were practically handmade. . . . They ran with weights, so you had to have a thing, say, six feet off the ground, like a tower made of wood, that would fold up and be put in a trunk. [A] spring motor isn't accurate enough; the weight thing is *entirely* accurate. It was just like a cuckoo clock."

While several European companies, including Lindstrom, Heineman's old employer, had sent some recording crews to remote locations around the globe to record, and there had been a few examples of American outfits as large as the Mormon Tabernacle Choir being recorded at home because of the sheer expense of bringing them to New York, Okeh's Atlanta expedition would be the first by a US record label planned with the goal of searching the area, identifying acts, and recording them. This was the first sustained effort to record remotely, repeatedly, as a matter of course, and the first to head into the rich Southern region to accomplish that.

Inconveniently, though, other plans had already been made for late May: Peer, Fuhri, Heineman, and Brockman were all scheduled to attend the annual National Association of Music Merchants convention (NAMM) at Chicago's Drake Hotel, so they chose to send Hager and the equipment on to Atlanta to get set up while they were out in Chicago. Brockman stopped up at Peer's office in New York before they headed west to the convention.

In the version of the Atlanta location recording genesis story most often repeated and reprinted since 1965, when it was first reported by chronicler Archie Green in his seminal article "Hillbilly Music: Source and Symbol," Brockman happened to stop in at the Times Square all-day newsreel film house just before that pretravel meeting. They were running some news film about an old-time fiddlers' convention in Virginia, and that struck a chord; there were fiddling conventions and contests like that around Atlanta, too, and an older Georgia man Brockman had heard on the radio there came to mind. At that point, the familiar story goes, Brockman himself thought of and hurriedly arranged the Okeh recording session in Atlanta, focusing on that hillbilly fiddler.

The Atlanta recording session had, in fact, been scheduled a month earlier, with the Aces the prime focus, and Polk Brockman had never actually met the radio fiddler or knew much about him. He had to look into the matter further, and no doubt didn't want to promise the availability of an act he wasn't sure he could deliver, which would account for his not mentioning it at that point. Peer had him consider whether there were other unrecorded but radio-promoted acts around Atlanta besides the Aces that they might record while they were there; perhaps they might even "uncover some new idea," Peer later recalled suggesting.

Ralph Peer's central job focus remained getting new music for the race line he was overseeing, so finding appealing new black artists for that series was the main goal. Brockman thought he had a "church singer" lined up for that; though, as it turned out, she didn't show up. Peer, however, was also a more general "recording manager" by this time, as witness his involvement with the Aces session, and he was certainly not ruling out turning up presold white radio acts for his vague category of "some new idea" that might yield hits.

After the Chicago convention, where Peer and Brockman manned the company's sales booth, they proceeded directly to Atlanta, meeting the engineering crew in a small vacant warehouse on Nassau Street that Hibbard had decked in blankets, hoping to make the acoustics work. There was some urgency about the scheduling since, somewhat ironically, their very *next* planned recording stop was right back in Chicago. It no doubt would have been simpler and cheaper to record remotely in Chicago first, if the Atlanta sessions hadn't been set up in advance.

The sessions there proved to be historic for more reasons than one. At first, things weren't going all that well for Ralph Peer and his crew in Atlanta, in terms of drawing new talent; Warner's Seven Aces were recorded as planned, and Peer also recorded Birmingham-based blues singer Lucille Bogan, who would soon emerge as queen of blues records so sexually explicit that they still carry parental advisory warnings in the twenty-first century. On this occasion, though, they recorded her singing the relatively tame "The Pawn Shop Blues," which was the first blues record ever recorded in the South. There was a churchy quartet from Morehouse College, and more vaudeville blues, from Fanny Goosby. The lack of additional "finds" to justify the first-time location recording effort, which had no doubt been talked up to Peer's bosses back in New York and at the Chicago convention, too, had to have been palpable. They were running out of options.

Brockman then proposed a solution—recording that local fiddler he'd recalled, Fiddlin' John Carson, who had been publicized on WSB radio locally and who—unlike Texan Eck Robertson, whom Victor Talking Machine had recorded fiddling the summer before in New York but paid little attention to and had not released on record—also *sang*.

Carson sang narrative ballads old and new, topical songs, fast square dance tunes with lyrics, and old sentimental parlor songs. He had been playing dances since his childhood in northern Georgia, been a fiddlers' convention prizewinner, and worked for textile mills and railroads. He had already been playing for gatherings in Atlanta, where he'd lived for decades, since 1900—including political rallies staged by everyone from the Communist Party to the Ku Klux Klan. A gig was a gig for a scrambling semiprofessional, which was about as professional as a musician like Carson could hope to be—until the session with Peer and Brockman.

By all accounts, including his own, Ralph Peer was initially dubious about this utterly untested recording proposition, but Brockman volunteered that he could sell at least five hundred Fiddlin' John records just around Atlanta, so with little to lose, on June 19, 1923, they had John Carson come in. They recorded two sides for his first record—"The Little Old Log Cabin in the Lane" (a hoary minstrel number long played by both black and white string-band musicians) and "The Old Hen Cackled and the Rooster's Going to Crow." Fiddlin' John's "Little Old Log Cabin" might surprise contemporary listeners with its deliberate pace, particularly in the sawing fiddling, but its story, as the lyric informs us, is related by a man "old and feeble" and waiting for death to call him to "a better home." Faster fiddle breakdowns such as "Arkansas Traveler" would soon follow, but not on this very first hillbilly single. "The Old Hen," a novelty number intended in part to show off Carson's entertaining ability to imitate barnyard birds on his fiddle, also offered signs, despite the recording quality, of the first country star's versatility with fiddle *tones*—and that his music just might have some range.

Since this episode was a key foundation moment in the birth of the genre that came to be known conversationally as "hillbilly," and eventually as "country music," there are, once again, multiple versions of what happened next, some of which are clearly colored by the assumption that the Southerner Brockman must have understood the music and its prospects better than Ralph Peer, the uninterested "New York city slicker." In truth, the cosmopolitan Atlanta urbanite Brockman would eventually admit that he hadn't known any more about rural string-band music than Missourian Peer had, nor had he much cared about it previously himself.

Brockman told the groundbreaking researchers Ed Kahn and Archie Green decades later that, as he remembered it, Peer had found the music "plu-perfect awful," a phrase that has stuck in many minds and is repeated in many accounts, perhaps the most famous sentence that people understand Ralph Peer to have uttered, and one that supposedly demonstrated his sheer distaste for old-time country music. There is, however, not the slightest evidence that he ever uttered it. It's a memorable phrase, but it was clearly Brockman's own colorful characterization of what he took to be Peer's initial reaction. (He never even claimed that Peer "said" it.) Peer—also long after the fact—was explicit about what he did find "awful" about the "very difficult recording proposition," and it was hardly Fiddlin' John's playing or singing that day:

> The problem was, you've recorded through a large horn. Now, if somebody else had been playing the fiddle, you could have had two horns, one for the fiddle and one for the voice—which is what we did quite normally. But you couldn't do this; here's this fellow playing the fiddle down here and his voice up *here*, and you've got to get it all into that one horn; you've got to "bounce it up" in some way. Well, there was no way to bounce it up, so the first recordings were really bad. . . . We picked up all the reverberations from the wall.

That the high school boy who had written in such clear detail about the making of light bulb filaments should have been a stickler for quality

sounds sixteen years later and could describe the problem is hardly surprising—and, of course, the Okeh label was prideful about sound quality in any case. "When the wax recordings got back to New York and
they were processed," Peer told radio interviewer Don Owens, "I listened
to these two items and, believe me, they were terrible." Brockman assured
Peer that the five hundred copies could be sold locally anyway; Peer
recalled that first short run as having been a thousand, which he rushed
back down to Brockman: "I took the precaution of eliminating the cata-
logue number from the label, as I could not believe that such a bad
recording could be used."

Since no surviving copies of this unnumbered short-run recording
have been found by collectors, some scholars have questioned whether
they existed, but both Peer and Brockman reported that they did, and
they agreed also on the immediate aftereffects: "The shipment arrived in
Atlanta on a Thursday morning," Peer recalled, "and by ten A.M. Friday
morning Mr. Brockman had me on the telephone to request that I send
ten thousand more records by express—immediately." While he had
mixed feelings about manufacturing thousands more of what he considered a badly recorded product, he was inevitably delighted to see that
demand was there, and to meet it. He then arranged to have Fiddlin'
John come to New York to record more sides in the home-base studio.
"We just had to learn the hard way," Peer said later. "We made these
experiments, and in the end, we were able to do Fiddlin' John pretty
well."

The ad Okeh placed in the *Atlanta Constitution* on August 3, just
seven weeks after the recording date, included Warner's Seven Aces, the
black Morehouse College Quartet, and Carson's first record all together,
no genre or racial distinctions made, and all presented explicitly as local
radio favorites available on records.

Fiddlin' John was soon the very first example of a hillbilly music star,
and he recorded dozens of varied numbers for Okeh over the following
years, initially all produced by Ralph Peer. His success enticed Okeh and,
before long, other record labels to look at this untapped white, Southern,
down-home market. This specialized audience was about the *last* ethnic
population segment the recording industry identified as a targetable
group in that day, some of it genuinely rural, but more of it made up of

people like Carson himself, who'd long since left for the city but remained emotionally tied to their families' older ways of life. It didn't hurt either that, ten years before the major Roosevelt era push for rural electrification, this potential audience still had considerably more crank-up Victrolas for playing records than they did radios, even battery-powered radios. That lag in radio adoption helped the new genre get established.

Soon after the Atlanta session, another fellow out of the Southern mills, Henry Whitter, from the town of Fries in southern Virginia, showed up at Okeh's door in New York; he had actually written to Ralph Peer earlier asking for a chance to record. In the wake of the encouraging success with Carson, Peer had Whitter, primarily a harmonica player but also, it turned out, a singer (if a less consistently appealing one than Carson), come in and record. Peer perceived that the Fiddlin' John record was not just a one-off novelty, or Carson an isolated novelty performer. There was joint marketing potential of the two artists together, and possibilities for finding more music and music makers that would appeal to their shared audience—which is what identifying and establishing an ongoing commercial genre is. This one consisted, like race and others, of music made by that population for that population—old rural tunes and new ones along the same lines. Peer began actively to promote the new series, experiment with its borderlines, and look for other opportunities in it.

This new field was given its first, forward-looking name in an ad touting Carson and Whitter together, placed by Okeh in *Talking Machine World* of June 15, 1924, which, in retrospect, amounts to the genre's birth announcement. As the ad had it, these "mountaineers" they'd discovered, with their quaint "Old Time pieces," had set off a new craze for (and here it comes) "*Hill Country Music* . . . another new field discovered, originated and made possible by the manufacturers of Okeh Records."

Peer soon set up a separate record line for the format, which was referred to as "Old Familiar Tunes" in the first series catalog, published in 1925, designed for record dealers who could reach that audience. Columbia and Vocalion quickly jumped in to pursue this new market as well, providing further validation for the idea, and for most practical purposes, fledgling country music was born. How wide an audience it could keep, what it might include, and whether it would last, however, were all far from certain.

One aspect of Okeh's Peer-led promotion of these new artists was significant: though Carson, for instance, had been an urban dweller and a working live music professional for decades, he was portrayed as a picturesque old backwoods mountaineer just in from the hills. An obviously label-provided news item in the December *Talking Machine World* smacks of direct participation by Ralph Peer, since he'd make a habit of seeing to it that just such accounts regularly appeared in papers. The short article notes that while Carson was in New York City to record again, "there were several things that did not meet his approval; too much city and not enough 'country' to suit his tastes." Henry Whitter was described to the press as "a real hill country type." With Ralph Peer's active involvement, the positioning of "hill country" artists as authentic rustics uncomfortable with big-city ways was now under way—and it wouldn't stop.

Overcoming the initial technical challenges Peer's unit encountered on the first location session was largely a matter of gaining more experience working with the equipment—learning about optimum placement of the microphones and the musicians, for example. Recordings made using remote professional equipment were certainly not better than those made in the main home studio, but they would not be noticeably inferior, either; listeners rarely had reason to notice any difference. From the Atlanta session onward, regular location recording along the same logistical lines as the Atlanta sessions were basic to Peer's artist and genre development plans, with the South, Midwest, and Great Lakes areas particular targets for multiple location visits. His recording unit proceeded on to Chicago to record next, as planned, immediately after Atlanta, and location recording became a regular feature on the label's schedule. Competitors would soon follow suit, each with their own jerry-built, carefully guarded approaches to getting the remote recording equipment "right."

The practice immediately made a very substantial difference in the quality of talent and expanding scope of music that Peer could identify, record, and market through both the Race and Old Familiar Tunes music lines for which he was responsible. Between 1923 and the end of 1926 his recording crew went repeatedly to Atlanta, to Charlotte and Asheville, to Dallas and San Antonio, to New Orleans, to Kansas City and St. Louis, to Detroit, and to Cincinnati, with stops to record some of the same artists again back in New York and Chicago as well, often, but not always, led by Ralph Peer personally.

In keeping with his regular practice, as he'd established working on the race recordings, Peer's country finds and the sorts of recordings accepted for the Old Familiar Tunes series broadened as he went about defining the field. In Asheville, North Carolina, in 1924, he recorded Bascom Lamar Lunsford, a lordly gentleman lawyer from the town of Mars Hill, in northern North Carolina, who played a key role in bringing a sense of cultural importance to old mountain songs and their makers—and in the development of commercial folk music. Peer recorded him singing his now-celebrated "I Wish I Was a Mole in the Ground," for example; the two would maintain a significant correspondence for years.

More commercially significant for Peer, and for the course of country music, was the arrival at the New York Okeh offices of another young man, carpenter Ernest V. Stoneman from Galax, Virginia, another small town not far from his acquaintance Henry Whitter's Fries. By autumn 1924, it was becoming common for ambitious rural singers just to show up, asking about recording, and Stoneman, with an autoharp and harmonica on a rack in tow, arrived certain he could outsing Whitter anytime. Stoneman was a singer, a songwriter, an instrumentalist, and head of a large, talented, and eventually celebrated musical family. (The last survivors of his and wife Hattie's twenty-three children—daughters Patsy, Donna, and Roni, would still be performing in the twenty-first century.) Stoneman was a then-relatively-rare sort of "hillbilly" performer who was not only well organized as a professional and had a strong business sense, but possessed considerable understanding of modern technologies, despite the sometimes primitive conditions of the family's rural life. Deservedly, his reputation as one of early country music's most important and influential figures has only increased over time.

From the first, the relationship between Ralph S. Peer and Ernest V. Stoneman was characterized by straight talk and mutual professional respect, each finding that the other would go the extra mile for a musical result. When it was decided that the two songs cut at Stoneman's first session at Okeh were good but had been sung too fast to be released, Ernest wrote to Peer saying that he would pay his own way back to New

York from his Virginia home and redo those sides for nothing, if he could only record and be paid for two more in addition. The pair struck that deal, and one of the redone, improved recordings proved to be one of the great hits of the era, the somewhat belated disaster ballad "The Titanic."

Peer signed Stoneman to a five-year contract, the beginnings not just of a star's career, but also, as we will see, of an important working relationship with a man Peer quickly saw as a potential session leader, scout, and trustee. You could, it should be noted, also find Stoneman records recorded for Edison early on. As Peer recalled, "A recording artist worked for everybody—Victor, Columbia, and ourselves. . . . There were exclusive contracts, but Victor . . . and Columbia were so overpowering they didn't see any reason to tie up artists; they just let them do whatever they could." Okeh seemed to look the other way as well, in practice. Stoneman would still be making records in the age of stereo. Various members of his huge family and their friends recorded dozens of sides for Peer in varied configurations, and rose from working-class obscurity to a degree of fame and wealth in the process.

Peer's broadening of the allegedly "old familiar" sounds continued apace with the signing of the raucous Virginia-based outfit fronted by Al Hopkins, whose modernizing, raggy piano on numbers such as "Whoa! Mule" and "Old Joe Clark" quickly ended any supposition that this field would forever be limited to ancient narrative ballads and string-band music. Hopkins's outfit was a band in need of a name when they recorded with Peer in New York in January 1925. "We're nothing but a bunch of hillbillies from North Carolina and Virginia; call us anything," Hopkins is reported to have commented, to which Ralph Peer responded by naming the group the Hill Billies. It would always be a tag some took as funny or even with pride, as Hopkins did, and others found insulting, but before long nearly everyone was referring not just to that band, but to the whole field, casually, if unofficially, as hillbilly music.

Peer also recorded several of the very first, too-often-forgotten women of country at this time, including the speedy guitarist and vocalist Roba Stanley, who can sound like an energetic predecessor to later star Rose Maddox on her own version of "Whoa Mule!" (1924) and "Single Life" (1925), in which she informs us gleefully how "I am single and no man's wife, and no man can control me." It's another example among many of Ralph Peer preferring feisty, self-defining women on record, as he clearly did in life. (Having recorded "Single Life" with Ms. Stanley certainly was in his memory when he suggested that Sara Carter take a stab at "Single Girl, Married Girl" a few years later.) Peer also OK'd the first recorded appearances of Fiddlin' John Carson's talented and often hilarious teenage daughter Rosa Lee Carson, initially as a backup guitarist. She soon emerged as "Moonshine Kate," the first female hillbilly artist to make an impression by image and comic material both, and she developed her own stage act to match them.

Among the men Peer recorded for Okeh in the mid-1920s was Texas-raised and operatically trained Vernon Dalhart, a prime example of the New York studio singer of all sorts of popular material who, famously, took on some hillbilly style songs. His "The Prisoner's Song (If I Had the Wings of an Angel)," as recorded by Victor in 1924, backed by what was essentially a "cover" version of "The Wreck of the Southern Old 97" record that Peer had cut with Henry Whitter the year before, was unquestionably the first country record, and one of just a few of that era of any sort to ultimately sell over a million copies. (The "Old 97" record, as we'll see, was to become an issue in a tangled lawsuit.)

Well liked, Dalhart recorded for virtually every label around, under various names, and Okeh was no exception, another version of "The Prisoner's Song" included. As Tobe Little, he recorded multiple sessions with Ralph Peer, adding to the increasingly popular prisoner and disaster song cycle the success of his Victor single had sparked—"The Fate of the Shenandoah" and "Chain Gang Song," for two. Carson Robison, another talented New York studio singer with a long career ahead of him, joined Dalhart on some of the sides.

While there was no single region within the South to head to if you wanted to find new talent and material for the Old Familiar Tunes line, the Carolina and Virginia mills, and especially the state border area between them, continued to be prime sources for substantial hillbilly talent, especially as news of Henry Whitter's success in being signed by this man Ralph Peer as a recording artist got around. Whitter introduced to Peer his gruff and noticeably Southern-sounding mill buddy Kelly Harrell (like Stoneman, from nearby Galax), and then backed him on harmonica. The clear-dictioned Harrell, well known as an entertainer locally, was adept at delivering tall tales like "I Was Born 10,000 Years Ago" and jealous-lover songs like "Blue-Eyed Ella," which would provide the tune and structure for Woody Guthrie's "The Philadelphia Lawyer."

Whitter, Harrell, Stoneman, and Lunsford were all among those who sweated through August 1925 auditions and sessions conducted by Peer, Hibbard, Brockman, and Okeh salesman George Jeffers (Peer's future brother-in-law) in a makeshift studio set up in the enclosed, sweltering, turret-like roof garden of Asheville, North Carolina's George Vanderbilt Hotel. As the *Asheville Citizen* reported in a series of articles, "There is a lot of respiration and perspiration connected with the making of phonograph records." The paper's stories detailed the working of the location recording equipment and, unlike some items that Peer got placed in local papers later in the 1920s, when the usefulness of local publicity was more apparent to him, these reports were hardly designed to encourage more auditioning: "The first test is said to be one of the severest experiences the singer or player ever has to undergo," the paper informed local readers. The artists recorded, even the experienced ones, struck the reporters as visibly nervous, though the August heat may have had something to do with that.

Peer's ongoing work within the hillbilly arena led to his increasing acceptance as part of the culture; he was even asked to be a judge at the 1925 Old Time Fiddlers Convention in Knoxville, Tennessee. Fiddlers' conventions were good places to encounter country talent.

Peer's development of the blues catalog, meanwhile, remained focused primarily on the eye- and ear-catching vaudeville blues women who'd demonstrated star-level success. He recorded three particularly lively ones in those years who, like Ernest Stoneman, would still be appearing live and on records forty or fifty years later—Victoria Spivey, Sippie Wallace, and Alberta Hunter (who'd recorded elsewhere but now moved to Okeh).

Peer first crossed paths with the celebrated, funny, bawdy, and long-lasting vaudeville duo Butterbeans & Susie (husband and wife Jodie and Susie Edwards) during a return stand in Atlanta, when they happened to be playing a theater on the black vaudeville circuit at the same time he was in town to record. They sought him out, and he was not only charmed by their singing and banter, but taken with their professionalism. In those same sessions, Peer's unit recorded new sides with Bascom Lamar Lunsford, Fiddlin' John, and Sara Martin. Even as marketing lines were tending to be segregated into perceived audience targets by race, the Old Familiar Tunes and race aspects of Ralph Peer's working life in popular roots music became increasingly inseparable.

Some acts that he recorded in these Okeh years seemed to defy attempts to classify them. In some cases these were holdovers from older vaudeville or even lingering blackface minstrelsy days when lines of marketing demarcation had been much less clear—or worried over. For example, Charles Anderson, generally forgotten today, was a seasoned African American trooper known for female impersonation (a commonplace in his time), and since he sang some blues and also was an excellent yodeler of a sort, he was promoted as "the Yodeler Blues Singer." Among his first recordings for Peer were his 1923 take on the already old song "Sleep, Baby, Sleep," which would be the first number "America's Blue Yodeler," Jimmie Rodgers, would record in 1927—though in a style very different from Anderson's, which suggested a mother singing to her child.

During sessions at Asheville in August 1924, Peer also supervised the very first recordings of the once obscure, now nearly legendary, white blackface minstrel performer Emmett Miller, on "Anytime (You're Feeling Lonely)," "Big Bad Bill," and, yes, "Lovesick Blues," in its second recording ever, with yodel-style voice breaks and syllable extensions. (The first recording of the Broadway-derived song was by Elsie Clark, recorded for Okeh in 1922.) It was impossible to simply call these jazz or hillbilly or blues records, though a jazz band became Okeh's chosen backup for Miller in later sessions that did not involve Ralph Peer. There is no serious evidence that Miller directly influenced Jimmie Rodgers or vice versa; nor do they sound much alike, but Anderson, Miller, and the then-unrecorded Rodgers all took part in novelty vaudeville traditions involving voice breaks and memorable stylings. Peer valued them all enough to give them a shot at recording, though Rodgers's career and winning, promotable image would become a more important focus for him and have the greatest impact by far on popular roots music.

Out on the edge where blues and jazz overlapped (and were not necessarily even distinguished yet) was the nonpareil-smooth, forward-looking singer and fluid guitar picker Lonnie Johnson, who met and was recorded by Peer in November 1925 when he won a recording date as the prize for winning the talent contest at the Booker T. Washington Theatre in St. Louis—for eighteen weeks running. Peer recorded Johnson with a jazz band backing ("Won't Don't Blues"), in a remarkable pairing with James P. Johnson on piano ("Sun to Sun Blues"), and also solo (on the hit "Mr. Johnson's Blues"). Lonnie Johnson's signing, coupled with the popular recording success of Blind Lemon Jefferson for Paramount Records that quickly followed, were milestones in the soon-decisive prominence of guitar-playing male singers in the blues arena.

Location recording also paid rich rewards for Peer in jazz. Some of the recordings wound up released in the race line, as jazz per se, others, considered more accessible to a broader and whiter audience, were classified as "hot dance" pop, but all were milestones in what, it must be remembered, was still very much an underrecorded arena. As with blues, the African American musicians who'd been the central, originating formulators of jazz had been particularly underrepresented. Victor had first recorded the white Original Dixieland Jass Band in 1917, the same year studio vocalists Arthur Collins and Byron Harlan (the same Byron Harlan who did those "rural interpretations" for Okeh) recorded "That Funny Jas Band from Dixieland." In general, jazz historians suggest, those earliest "jas" or "jass" referencing records, including some 1917 sides by Wilbur Sweatman, who was African American, were barely distinguished in tempo or attack from earlier ragtime records. Some jazz historians point to a few recordings by W. C. Handy and Ford Dabney of the same years as the first jazz records to be rhythmically and stylistically credible. In any case, Peer and company now began homing in on what was different, available, attractive, and untapped in the early jazz field.

That follow-up Chicago stop for Peer and Hibbard's traveling crew, just days after that first location session in Atlanta (June 1923), was in a temporary studio set up in their regional distributor's offices, where they proceeded to record the first New Orleans star, Joe "King" Oliver and his Creole Jazz Band, with one Louis Armstrong on cornet, virtually singing the blues through that instrument. Among the laidback sides were "Sobbin' Blues," pulsing even as it cries, and "Where Did You Stay Last

Night?" credited to Armstrong and pianist Lil Hardin, also in the band, as composers. (Oliver had recorded nine sides for Gennett Records in Richmond, Indiana, a few weeks earlier, in April, including "Dippermouth Blues," which had given Oliver an endlessly imitated solo and Satchmo a secondary nickname.)

When Peer's recording crew returned to Chicago that October, Ralph Peer added to the race line the bands of both his old acquaintance W. C. Handy and of Jelly Roll Morton. Signing Morton was a mark of Peer's willingness to reach back to a crucial jazz founder who was between peaks of fame but could still be considered fresh, since he had never been heard on record. Peer was not then, and never would be, interested in "documenting" historic or fading styles for the sake of doing so, for history, the impetus behind Alan Lomax's Library of Congress recordings of Morton sixteen years later. He was focused on what was new and enticing, and regional jazz was both novel and promotable.

Peer and Okeh's marketing staff quickly began to exploit the arrival of his unit in cities where they were to record, with such events as a "live" public, auditorium recording session in Detroit of Finzel's Arcadia Orchestra, reportedly attended by 5,000, and a Chicago parade, with the cooperation of the black fraternal Elks Clubs convention, which put King Oliver, Mamie Smith, and "placards mentioning colored artists who can be heard on Okeh Records" before a reported thirty thousand people, quite a feat of promotion in any era.

In the summer of 1923, Ralph Peer returned home to Kansas City, though it couldn't have felt much like a homecoming after his divorce and his parents' relocation to Virginia. This visit was about business; he headed right into African American district nightclubs, apparently without qualms or trepidations, at a time when racial tensions were dangerously on the rise. The neighborhood was becoming a base for some of the key, regional "territory band" players who would move jazz forward to the regional music-turned-pop concoction that would come to be called swing—Lester Young, Count Basie, Hot Lips Page, and Jimmy Rushing, no less. Peer checked out and, in effect, auditioned a six-piece outfit recommended to him by the local African American music promoter Winston Holmes (a sometime scout for Okeh), the band of pianist Bennie Moten—which was in the course of evolving from its local, Missouri ragtime roots toward some of the most cutting-edge jazz of the era.

Impressed, Peer immediately arranged to have Moten, along with Ada Brown and Mary Bradford, two blues singers who were working the same neighborhood clubs, record for Okeh at a scheduled location stand in St. Louis, with Moten also providing backing for the singers. The eight initial Moten sides recorded, such as "Crawdad Blues" and his hit "South," were built on well-played but familiar blues and ragtime ideas. By the time Bennie Moten and his Kansas City Orchestra recorded a second set with Peer the following year, at home in Kansas City, they'd begun to move to a rawer, stomping "riffing" style heard on sides such as "Sister Honky Tonk." That attack set that band and Kansas City jazz in general apart in rhythm and feel from the more orchestrated, sophisticated big-band style Fletcher Henderson was developing in New York. Both Moten's and Henderson's innovations proved to be important popularizing jazz milestones.

Peer continued to mine regional jazz roots, in March 1924 finally reaching what today seems an inevitable stop, New Orleans, though no one at all had yet gone there to record jazz, or anywhere else in the Deep South, for that matter. His unit set up to record at the former home of the Junius Hart Piano House at 123 Carondolet Street. Some jazz chroniclers have rated Peer's New Orleans Okeh sessions as historic, yet also a missed opportunity. His usual scouting method—asking people in the area about good and successful local musicians, lining them up, and recording them—was not infallible. Some early jazz artists there were missed, and others, such as Morton, Oliver, and Armstrong, as he well knew, had already scattered in pursuit of greener pastures. The outfits that Peer did record in his first and second visits tended to be roadhouse bands that featured driving dance music, as the earlier sessions elsewhere had stressed small group blues. Jazz was still very much a developing concept as a distinct entity separate from the sound of the day's so-called hot dance bands, the pop outfits that took no solo breaks and didn't improvise.

The true jazz bands Peer now recorded included locally popular units led by cornetists Johnny De Droit and Johnny Bayersdorffer on the first visit, and the New Orleans Rhythm Kings and Oscar "Papa" Celestin's Original Tuxedo Orchestra on the second. (Papa Celestin was black and had previously been a mentor and employer to both Oliver and Armstrong; the others were white outfits.) Peer's unit would also record local blues vocalists Ruth Green and Lela Bolden.

In 1969 Johnny De Droit recalled that the first sessions at the old piano company site—in comic contrast to the stories of overheated Asheville—took place when it was so cold that they had to place clarinets on the radiator, and featured a recording engineer who'd "found out that New Orleans was a joy town, so he was loaded all the time," all of which may or may not have contributed to the fast and easy friendship De Droit developed with Ralph Peer. During later sessions out of New York, they would travel out into New Jersey together by trolley, to play golf. "He played a fair game of golf," De Droit recalled, "but he thought he played a better one!" When Peer's secretary at Okeh kidded De Droit about having lost the second nine holes to her boss, De Droit confided (or boasted) "that he could beat Mr. Peer with one club." Papa Celestin, in a 1960 interview, recalled Ralph Peer heading his session, as well, though offering no details other than recalling him as "a nice guy."

That summer, back in New York, Peer approved the recording of a highly capable jazz outfit put together by his Okeh A&R associate—Clarence Williams' Blue Five. This significant small group, on its own and while backing some new Sara Martin records, included iconic New Orleans clarinetist Sidney Bechet, and on some sides, such as "Coal Cart Blues" and the well-recalled "Cake Walking Babies from Home," Louis Armstrong. Louis was now married to the smart and ambitious Lil Hardin, and she'd encouraged him to take a big career step—out of King Oliver's Chicago band and into Henderson's in New York, where he'd potentially be more noticed. What happened next was another one of those epic turning points in musical history.

Lil Hardin Armstrong, next in the line of go-getters Ralph Peer would trust and turn to for ideas, pressed him to record Louis with a small group, under Louis's name, as Clarence Williams was doing with the Blue Five. Peer agreed, signing Louis to do just that as soon as he returned to Chicago to put together a band. Louis quickly headed back there, at Lil's insistence, greeted by banners welcoming home "the World's Greatest Trumpet Player." Louis himself then brought together three fellow New Orleans veterans—Johnny Dodds on clarinet, Johnny St. Cyr on banjo, and Kid Ory on trombone, with Lil on piano, adding up to Louis Armstrong and His Hot Five. Their recordings (some augmented by Lonnie Johnson on guitar), and variants Armstrong went on to make with a slightly modified and expanded lineup as the Hot Seven, offered landmark drive, improvisation, extraordinary solos, crying blues, and what was for many the added surprise that Louis Armstrong was a brilliant innovator in scat-singing and vocals. They are universally accepted as among the seminal recordings of jazz history, and of American musical history.

As Brian Harker stresses in his recent book on the sessions, for Peer, for the musicians involved, and for many listeners of the time, these Armstrong "Hot" bands were not generally seen as milestone acts at first, but simply very good extensions of hot dance music and vaudeville entertainment, and of jazz both hot and sweet. In the course of musical history, considering the impact, the Hot Five sessions came to be understood as milestones.

Ralph Peer, boasting years later, blurted out some ill-considered words to describe his involvement with the project ("I *invented* Louis Armstrong") and claimed a decisive role in selecting the musicians employed, which was almost certainly overstated. There are no independent records regarding anyone in particular he may have suggested to Armstrong for the sessions (something it wouldn't have been unusual for him to do) or whether he made such recommendations at all. Considering that he and Armstrong were not particularly close personally, and that underlings such as Okeh's Chicago manager of the time, E. A. Fearn, and pianist Richard M. Jones (playing a supervisory role similar to Clarence Williams's), were involved with the recording sessions, some early jazz chroniclers questioned whether Peer had been involved at all. In some histories, the question was simply finessed, suggesting that we *couldn't* know who at Okeh gave the green light to the Hot Five project. But there's simply no question about that; as the company was set up, it had to have been Peer. (Lil would check in with Ralph Peer again before a later, famous Hollywood session at RCA Victor.) He didn't "invent" Louis Armstrong, and arguably nobody else did either, but he played that very significant role in his emergence as a bandleader and solo star; he cleared the path for Armstrong's solo stardom. That's not a contribution to overestimate—or to underestimate.

Peer's reputation was rising, beyond the boundaries of the music business itself. In the summer of 1925, most likely while he was conducting sessions at Asheville in late August, the pioneering academic music analyst and sociologist Guy Benton Johnson called on Peer, while researching the next in a series of groundbreaking books he coauthored with his mentor at the University of North Carolina, Professor Howard Odum. Remarkably for its day, the book, *Negro Workaday Songs*, published the following year, included an analysis of blues recordings and record labels' varied output, and of the effect recording was having on the blues idiom—which had, of course, only been recorded at that point for six years. In a memorandum entitled "Notes on 'the Blues'" written after he spoke with Peer, Johnson noted, "Mr. R.S. Peer of the General Phonograph Corporation (The Okeh Company) gives some interesting information concerning the Negro blues. He has perhaps done more in this field than all others combined. His organization sells in the neighborhood of three to four million records a year, practically the entire number going to colored folks."

Peer told him of his continuing puzzlement that blues record sales were consistently lower among residents of a "strange East Coast hiatus" between Savannah, Georgia, and Norfolk, Virginia, and noted that blues records were more successful when the songs were both composed and sung by "Negro artists." The academic Johnson found particularly interesting a question Ralph Peer was pondering, the question of musical connections between the different roots music lines he was handling— some thirty years before those interactions and two-way borrowings were systematically studied: "Mr. Peer raises the interesting question of the relation of blues to certain native American music like the 'Hill Billy' music, such as the Rovin' Gambler old ballads . . . whether there is not an accent note in which all the music is 'blued.'" Peer, as always, had one eye on sales response, but he was also listening carefully.

So here, then, was Ralph S. Peer, later in 1925, having made major contributions to the twentieth century's mass entertainment markets, and to the establishment of paths for regional roots music to extend into popular music. This would have been noteworthy and still recalled today if his A&R career had stopped right there. Okeh took into account the full set of accomplishments under his belt—development of blues and gospel within the race records line, establishing the new Old Familiar Tunes hillbilly market, introducing seminal and popular jazz to records, organizing and executing the new concept of location recording, while still maintaining his role in keeping up relations with the distribution chain and retailers, and empowered him further. He was now referred to in the industry simply as Okeh's "director of record production."

The situation in the recording industry as a whole was still quite challenging, and pressures were mounting; it was a time of corporate buyouts and label mergers, and a large opening was left at Okeh when Peer's boss Fuhri chose to return to Columbia Records. And so on December 15, 1925, the front-page headline story in the *Talking Machine World* trade journal made it official, announcing yet another Ralph Peer promotion: "R.S. Peer Made Okeh General Sales Manager—Promotion of Popular Member of Staff."

Peer was thirty-three, and he certainly had gained much of the corporate influence and outright power he could have desired and imagined for himself as that ambitious teenager in Kansas City. The money was good, the equivalent of a six-figure salary today, and he viewed some of the new challenges on the horizon as invigorating. For instance, there were talented A&R competitors at work, recording roots music on location and working to popularize it, as he was, men he openly admired. Frank Walker over at Columbia Records, working with Fuhri after his move there, had found acts such as Gid Tanner and the Skillet Lickers for their hillbilly line, and Bessie Smith, no less, for blues. And a Brit who loved American roots music, "Uncle" Art Satherley, was doing similar work for Paramount, where he'd recorded Blind Lemon Jefferson and Ma Rainey, and would soon work in hillbilly as well. Ralph Peer didn't mind that validating level of competition one bit, but some things were bothering him.

He didn't much like the way Okeh had treated the question of song copyrights, for one thing. At first, some of the in-house executives and regular music scouts bought songs themselves, outright, keeping all the related performance rights and mechanical rights proceeds and working to see that songs they owned were recorded. Fred Hager, Clarence Williams, and even outsider Perry Bradford had all set up publishing companies for themselves, buying songs that they were going to record along with all of the rights to them. Polk Brockman, down in Atlanta, had gone even further, attempting to combine artist touring management with song publishing—again, including buying out all rights to the composers' songs. Peer had not gone into anything like that himself, but he had suggested a step Okeh initiated—that the *record company* would buy and own the full song copyrights for songs they recorded, an added incentive for the company to promote the songs, as well as a revenue stream.

Now he'd come to see that idea as both troubling and shortsighted, too: "It was the custom that the fellow who came in with his own composition," he later recalled, "we'd take them over. . . . [It] wasn't a square deal, because you can't give them any publisher service and if you need sheet music you can't print it very well or you won't, because it's too much bother." Songwriters were not receiving their share of the songs, and the record company wasn't pressing for any further use of the songs beyond their own, on other record labels or in live performances (the "publisher service" Peer referred to), which were missed opportunities, and unfair to the writers.

As he took that new headline-making executive promotion, Ralph Peer was pondering these things, as well as a new string of mergers and acquisitions that were consolidating the recording industry, the value he'd already proved he had, and what he might do next. It wouldn't be what anyone was expecting.

3

To Victor, On to Bristol, and the Making of Giants, 1926–1927

RECORDING INDUSTRY READERS of the January 15, 1926, issue of the lavish trade publication the *Talking Machine World* were greeted with an excited, if typical and unremarkable, front-page news story in which Okeh Records' freshly promoted general sales manager, Ralph S. Peer, announced the introduction of Truetone, a higher-fidelity acoustic recording process designed to limit distortion in louder musical passages. Further inside, they encountered a lengthy report on the annual year-end dinner and sales conference of James K. Polk, Inc., the Atlanta phonograph products wholesaler and Okeh distributor. Among those present were Peer and the dinner's toastmaster, Polk Brockman. Nothing suggested that anything out of the ordinary was afoot for Ralph Peer or for Okeh Records. That would change quickly.

The following month's issue, of February 15, featured a front-page story on Otto Heineman's appointment of a *new* general sales manager for General Phonograph's Okeh label, one Allen W. Fritzsche, previously the head of phonograph needle sales. A terse final sentence reported a fait accompli, in the quickly assumed past tense: "R.S. Peer, formerly general sales manager of the record division, had resigned from the company's staff."

It wasn't until October that what lay behind these surprising events became evident, when Columbia Phonograph acquired Okeh. General Phonograph had not been able to license any of the fast-developing variations of the superior new electrical recording technologies from any of their developers, and saw a bleak future ahead for itself in selling records, despite Okeh's acoustic recording glories. Okeh's strong hand in the race and hillbilly music markets, which Peer had been so central in developing, proved a principal attraction for Columbia. As so often happens in such media buyouts, both Heineman and Fritzsche quickly found that they were reporting to the management of their new Columbia parent.

Ambitious and increasingly restless, that was not the subordinate position, the competitive situation, or the direction that Ralph Peer envisioned for himself. He'd seen the situation developing, and that was certainly a factor in his sudden departure from Okeh after seven epochal years and multiple promotions. The dual grind of being at once a hands-on sales executive constantly tending to record dealers and a key A&R man for the label was wearing thin, too; Peer would never wear that particular combination of hats again.

He had begun having arguments with Heineman, untypical occurrences earlier, and in a final disagreement just after the turn of 1926, told him uncategorically, "I'm tired of this anyway; so let's call it a day." Peer recalled, "He couldn't imagine anybody quitting a job like that, and, nevertheless, I just left and walked out. . . . I was making about $16,000 a year [at least $200,000 in today's money], (for) a young man, much too much money. I sort of got a big head. . . . So I quit!"

There were still no personal obligations to give Peer pause, but his home life, too, was on the verge of change. A few months earlier his widowed mother, Ann, had returned from a trip to Bermuda on the S.S. *Fort Saint George* with Anita Jeffers Glander, a neighbor in East Orange, and the sister of the Okeh sales representative George Jeffers who'd been joining Peer on location recording trips. Born only days before Ralph, Anita had previously been married to German émigré Richard Glander, a naturalized US citizen and an international purchasing agent for Heineman. As had been the case with Sadie Hildebrand, Anita lived near Peer and had connections to him through work. The records don't indicate that Ralph was traveling to or from Bermuda along with his mother and the woman who'd prove to be his second wife, but the Ralph-Anita connection was growing. He married her little more than a year and a half after that trip, in May 1927—in a much-changed life situation. With her brash Charleston era flapper style, relatively outgoing way with people compared to Sadie's, and eagerness to travel across the United States and abroad, Anita Peer would prove to be a comfortable match, companion, and coworker (officially, his corporate secretary) during the heart of Peer's "Victor years" just ahead. She was an intense, wisecracking personality who left strong impressions.

Peer's choice of spouses over his lifetime, three in all, who in succession had increasingly formidable intellects with increasingly cosmopolitan outlooks, evidences a surprising and telling temperament departure from the standard 1920s "man in charge" model he otherwise aspired to, one with implications for his career in music as well. In this generation, and particularly for executives of his level, life and work partnerships rarely went hand in hand, and wives were openly valued for a style of supportiveness indistinguishable from pliancy. Peer's trusted marriage partners, by contrast, but entirely in keeping with his preferences in musical acts and working partners, were smart, strong, ambitious, and self-defining—the sorts of people he'd habitually refer to as "live wires." He was inclined more toward active, contributing partners than dutiful underlings; what's more, as a natural introvert who had to expend energy overcoming his own reticences, extroverted wives would increasingly take leading roles in his social encounters.

What would be Ralph Peer's next working home was not immediately clear. Incongruously, on leaving Okeh, he had temporarily considered sticking with the sales executive work and walking away from the music, which, in practice, he would never really do. He briefly promoted a concept for the national distribution and sales of apple pies, no less, a new and untried idea, if also a reminder that his father had, early on, sold confections back in corporate baking center Kansas City, but he couldn't convince large-scale bakeries to even try to compete with the nation's mothers in that particularly hallowed arena of home-based (and home-baked) Americana.

"Getting kind of nervous" about his employment situation, and likely thinking about that potential second marriage, Peer then approached the biggest recording company of them all, the Victor Talking Machine Company, a firm that was well aware of his successes at Okeh in the popular roots music arenas in which they'd never seriously and consistently ventured themselves. He realized that after Victor's breakout, one-off success with studio singer Vernon Dalhart's million-selling "The Prisoner's Song"/ "Wreck of the Old 97" record in 1924, the odds were good that they wanted more hits along those lines. It seemed the most promising, logical place to turn.

"I had what they wanted," Peer recalled. "They couldn't get into the hillbilly business; they didn't know how to do it . . . [but] they were trying to hire me for about $5000 a year [$80 a week plus expenses—less than a third of his previous salary] . . . and they found it very difficult to talk to me, because of the tremendous salary that I would expect. . . . I was sensible enough not to go to work for them, *just* to go to work. I couldn't make a deal, so we didn't get any place."

Not at first. Not long afterward, however, Peer approached the executives at Victor Talking Machine again, executives in the employ of the label's very new, more experimentally inclined owners, a consortium of banks, including New York houses Speyer & Company and J. & W. Seligman & Co., which had taken the firm public. They ran the label from December 1925 until it was acquired by RCA just over three years later, retaining most executives, including symphonic music–favoring musical directors, from the established Victor Talking Machine. This was Peer's first, experimental probe of a new proposition, an unprecedented, even revolutionary one that seems to have been improvised to get a "yes" from them, built on insights from his own experiences in the music business, including how song ownership had been handled at Okeh.

"I went back to New York one night," he recalled, "rather discouraged, because it seemed to be an impenetrable wall, and I sat down and wrote a three-paragraph letter that said I'd considered the matter very carefully and that essentially this was a business of recording new copyrights, and I would be willing to go to work for them *for nothing*—with the understanding that there would be no objection if I controlled these copyrights."

Ralph Peer was audaciously proposing he be allowed to "control," in lieu of salary, the mechanical song copyrights he was referring to as the heart of moneymaking in the record business, that two cents per record paid to the song copyright holder for its initial and subsequent recordings under the law.

Record companies (and motion picture companies turning to sound) were increasingly going into the music publishing business themselves, following the line of thinking that had initially been Peer's at Okeh. Whether or not they were making the most of performance rights licensing possibilities—placing songs in revues, shows, performers' repertories, and early broadcasts—they were not making much of the mechanical rights that could accrue on songs recorded. Record company publishing arms weren't aggressively setting aside the accumulating two cents per side due, which the parent firm easily could view as simply an accounting record-keeping question. They very rarely shared any mechanical royalties that did accrue with songwriters, or actively promoted further recording of the songs by others. It is not hard to fathom their lack of enthusiasm for promoting strong songs to what they viewed as competing labels and recording acts. If, as Peer proposed, though, he were to be a contracted talent scout and producer, a representative of Victor and consultant paid via income from mechanicals but *not* an outright employee, he would not have that reluctance.

In effect, what Peer was really wagering as he approached Victor Talking Machine in 1926 with little to lose was that with strong new, copyrightable songs, hillbilly, blues, and gospel recordings could be much more broadly popular than they yet had been, and so could their performers, properly handled, so the record sales in those areas could be much greater. That would, of course, also yield a lot of income for him as the holder of the mechanical copyrights of the new songs on the records.

While the resource-rich Victor Talking Machine had been the first label on earth to define and exploit the development and publicity-driven buildup of a recording star, with the firm's long-standing focus on selling the record player as a tool for cultural uplift and music appreciation, a sort of home encyclopedia of sound, they hadn't applied that promotional experience to artists in any roots music field—hillbilly music, blues, gospel, or regional jazz—or very much to any popular music at all, for that matter. Even before World War I, though, they had demonstrated what star-building might do for their upscale, high-priced Red Seal classical label, and the key singer on it, the exceptional Enrico Caruso.

As David Suisman noted of the advertising and promotion campaign they had designed to promote the great tenor's records in *Selling Sounds: The Commercial Revolution in American Music*, "Victor promised that every one of its 103 recordings of Caruso offered consumers 'not only his art, but his personality.' The break from a musical culture based on sheet music could not have been clearer. . . . What Victor was advertising was the performance and the performer himself."

The combination of Caruso's personal charisma and Victor's deliberate star-making campaign had proved potent. The singer's charm and power, the "performer himself," were apparent on record to a broad popular audience, evidenced in that affecting sob heard on record right along with the man's huge voice. The marketing campaign, which included consumer and trade magazine ads, identified the voice heard on the record with the star's manly, forceful personality, and the music he performed with conspicuous classiness that could conveniently be acquired at your local record dealer. The ads, in a sign of things to come, were buttressed with publicist-fed newspaper and magazine articles about the drama of Caruso's real and purported offstage life, personal habits, and fast-accumulating wealth.

Ironically, one way Peer had persuaded Okeh to build up its hillbilly line in the first place was by suggesting that the expenses entailed and disc price involved could be contained; the records wouldn't, he had suggested, "need to have the same quality as a Caruso."

Behind Peer's "pay me with mechanical rights" wild-card proposition to Victor were his own then-unique insights about the possibilities for expansion: if a hit record sold the artist identified with it, and a promoted, hit-making personality like Caruso could set up the song for further placement with other artists in operatic recordings, the same pattern could hold for specialized, previously marginalized roots music and its audiences. Both the artists and their songs, if handled properly, could be more broadly popular.

Peer saw that, but at first Victor Talking Machine did not. They simply saw what looked like a can't-lose proposition in having him identify and record some performers for their underdeveloped hillbilly and race catalogs, and they underestimated considerably what that might mean in total sales and dollars for the company—and, particularly, for him. As Peer would later tell jazz chronicler and photographer Duncan Schiedt, "a couple of members" of the Victor A&R board had calculated that if their new roots record sideline sold as they were projecting, he might make the equivalent of $100,000 a year in today's dollars as publisher and consultant—less, in fact, than he'd been making at Okeh. In practice, the record sales in his lines would quickly reach the utterly unexpected level of hundreds of thousands of copies per month, with Peer's income exploding accordingly. Victor's conservative A&R board simply didn't appreciate what they were getting into.

Peer later recalled that a few days after sending the initial proposition letter, "I got a letter saying that they accepted my offer; please get in touch with Mr. Nat Shilkret at their New York recording laboratory." A contemporary of Peer's and already a longtime industry acquaintance, Shilkret, Victor's principal musical director, undoubtedly played a decisive role in acceptance of the "copyright control in lieu of salary" offer that brought Peer to the label, although he was keenly aware that the arrangement had no precedent.

The Victor executive A&R board Peer had approached had long been comprised of men from the classical music world; often, they were orchestra conductors, a factor that both reflected the label's emphasis on high-toned "serious" music and helped to perpetuate it. Shilkret had those credentials himself; he'd been a celebrated child prodigy clarinetist and pianist and played for top symphony orchestras by age twelve. In 1924, though, he had gone on to serve as the head of Victor Taking Machine's "light music" division. This was the popular music unit that was then producing Shilkret's own hot dance orchestra, the bestselling dance band of Paul Whiteman and His Orchestra (which recorded "Rhapsody in Blue" with George Gershwin on piano that year, and saw million sellers in "Whispering" and "Three O'Clock in the Morning"), as well as Fred Waring's Pennsylvanians, and the phenomenally popular crooner Gene Austin, whose 1927 recording of "My Blue Heaven" would be the all-time bestselling US single until Bing Crosby's "White Christmas" came along fifteen years later.

Significantly, Nat Shilkret was also more comfortable with American roots music than any executive at Victor had ever been. He was, as he told *Phonograph Monthly Review* not long after he contracted Ralph Peer, "a lover of folk music . . . of thirty-five nationalities." In 1922 he'd presided over what are generally cited as the first country music recordings ever, instrumentals by fiddlers Eck Robertson and Henry Gilliland, though Victor was slow to release those sides. When the Vernon Dalhart "The Prisoner's Song"/"Wreck of the Old 97" record exploded, the first hit of such proportions aimed at the white rural and small-town Southern audience, Shilkret understood the possibility not just for a follow-up novelty or two, but for an ongoing line of business. In 1925, inspired by the enormous success of Dalhart's "Wreck of the Old 97" disaster ballad in particular (a song first recorded by Peer's artist Henry Whitter at Okeh), Shilkret had traveled to Staunton, Virginia, to purchase a set of similar disaster-commemorating and current-event story songs from C. B. Obaugh, a fellow who'd written suggesting that he knew hundreds of hillbilly songs in that vein of potential use. That wasn't quite the case, as it turned out, but Obaugh did lead Shilkret to his parents' home in West Virginia, where a local fiddler and friends of the family provided fifty-two event-story songs and a dozen dance tunes for twenty dollars apiece, and Victor had such versatile urban vaudevillians as Frank Crumit, Frankie Marvin, and Carson Robison record those songs. Still, the label was not successfully competing in signing and developing truly down-home performers for the Old Familiar Tunes rural market, and Nat Shilkret knew who could fix that.

According to Shilkret's own memoir, the deal struck with Ralph Peer was not the one he had been most inclined to suggest, which would simply have been increasing, even doubling, if necessary, Victor's salary offer. He'd had Walter Clark, the label's manager of A&R, meet with Peer, who persuaded Clark to assign him a mechanical royalty of just one cent per side that he would divide with songwriters, not the full two cents. Clark was not "too experienced in the record business" at the time, Shilkret noted, and since the total mechanical royalty rate remained and would remain for many decades two cents per side by law, Clark saw Peer's offer of controlling just one cent as a great bargain, with the company holding onto the other penny per side. "When I heard of this," Shilkret recalled, "I was stunned! No one on the musical staff had been offered a [mechanical] royalty for his arrangements or compositions, and here was a man collecting royalties with *other* men's compositions!"

It wasn't as if they'd done much in pursuit of the two cents per record, shared or otherwise, themselves. For a huge, slow-to-change organization like Victor Talking Machine, late in deciding to get into the downscale hillbilly, blues, gospel, and regional jazz markets in a serious way at all, promoting *additional* use of the new material elsewhere had been very far from a top priority. In practice, lack of song promotion to other labels, or any further promotion and "servicing" of a song, was especially limiting for songwriting roots music artists, since they had few additional income opportunities, with their pay from performances and performance rights to their songs typically limited, and sales potential of any sheet music virtually ruled out by their audience's widespread inability to read it. Mechanical royalties could matter to roots music songwriters—matter a great deal.

While Victor's initial interest in contracting Peer as a full-time consultant was his obvious facility for developing a hillbilly line for them (which they would refer to variously in their catalogs of the era as the "Old Time Melodies of the Sunny South" line, "Old Time Fiddlin' Tunes," "Old Familiar Tunes and Novelties," and "Native American Melodies"), the big firm nevertheless put him to work in A&R across the whole developing spectrum of popular American roots music once he was in place, and they would have been foolish to do otherwise.

A number of performers with whom he had ongoing relationships quickly and loyally followed him from Okeh to Victor. The relative sales clout of Victor as the number one label was well understood, and virtually all of those performers would soon see higher Victor-style sales levels, not just in how large sales of a hit could be, but in the baseline sales of their average records. Many of them would also express loyalty to Peer himself, an understanding of his appreciation of them, and the desire to continue to work with him. In the hillbilly markets, Ernest Stoneman and family, Kelly Harrell, and Henry Whitter all followed him to the big label; in jazz, Fats Waller (initially, as a member of Thomas Morris and His Seven Hot Babies), Bennie Moten, Johnny Dodds, and Jelly Roll Morton all came along; in blues, Mamie Smith; and in spoken-word gospel preaching, the very popular Reverend J. M. Gates.

Under the terms of his contract with Victor, a three-pronged "record, publish, and manage" approach became Peer's new standard, self-invented procedure for doing business. "I couldn't bother Victor with a thing like putting hillbilly artists under contract; they wouldn't have *signed* such a contract," he recalled, because "anything less than $5000 they wouldn't be bothered with. So I had them all sign artist management contracts with me personally . . . and it worked out all right . . . [although] I never made any money out of those contracts, *as* manager."

When Peer found a new recording talent for Victor, he would immediately sign the artist to an exclusive personal management contract, in which, as the agreements said, "the Manager agrees to book the Artist to make phonograph records," for a year at a time, sometimes with a stated minimum of selections to be recorded, with the artist getting fifty dollars plus expenses per recording. That was no paltry sum, as it might seem to be, thinking of fifty dollars in twenty-first-century terms, but that was over $600 per side in today's money, and for virtually any roots music performer of the day, it was not at all bad. It was also, at Victor's insistence, twice what was paid at Okeh, for example. For down-home artists, that per-side payback and the work itself compared very well with such alternative (and otherwise, often inevitable) work as heavy lifting on a truck farm.

The publishing of the songs recorded, which Peer now insisted all be distinctive enough unto themselves to be copyrighted as fresh under law, was initially by United Publishing, an essentially "paper" firm he set up for the purpose. This whole concept was novel, and it had lasting implications. The artist Peer looked for to record, he later explained, has "either got to write his own music, or you've got to get it for him, and *then* you take him to a record company . . . which essentially is the method which I invented and which I take credit for." Hot new songs were lined up and matched with a performer before that artist was signed—and with song-originating artists much preferred when encountered.

"I always insisted on getting artists who could write their own music," Peer noted, in 1959, with some pride. "The point that I never recorded an established selection—the record business is *founded* on that today. . . . The stuff comes from the writers, direct. . . . [It] stems back to that decision, which I had to make. Nobody else made it."

His idea of making distinctive copyrightable new material so central was not simply some intuitive shot in the dark, nor was it merely a potentially clever way to make a lot of money—though it was that, too. (Adding up the income from mechanical royalties, the publisher's share of performance royalties, smatterings of sheet music publishing, and such, Peer estimated he was soon making $50,000 a month.) The context of Peer's fateful "decision" to go in that direction was his early realization that the major media of the day—the record companies, the largest urban radio stations, the rising radio networks, the motion picture studios producing the new music-hungry talkies—were going to be calling most of the shots as to what songs were needed. The heyday of the Tin Pan Alley–based old-boy network of sheet music factories pumping out "a fast one," "a slow one," "a love song," "another waltz" on demand was essentially over, and Peer knew it. (The old-line publishing firms themselves, such as the founders of the ASCAP performance rights collection organization, were not finished, of course; some adapted and others were absorbed by motion picture companies and then reflected those interests.) In short, songwriters needed to be able to meet the demands of the new media outlets.

For the roots music recording artists who wrote songs, the performers so favored by Peer, the attractions of his new business model did not stop with the higher per-record pay rate. While publishers didn't have to share the mechanical returns with songwriters, and few did, "in control" of the mechanicals he saw to it that the songwriters were in fact contracted to receive royalties, and, more unusually still, he actually *sent* the money when it accrued. Never once, as so many in publishing firms and many involved with record companies would notoriously do over the years, did he buy 100 percent of the copyrights outright, a buyout, with the mechanical royalty "eaten whole." Nor would he even once stick his name on a song as a coauthor, claiming some piece of the separate writer's share of performance royalties, as so many would. Few of the hillbilly or blues artists would ever have been offered a royalty at all, let alone a deal like this.

"I never, never bought a copyright; that's one of the precepts from which I started in the publishing business," Peer stressed, citing competitive, frankly practical, not some saintly, altruistic reasons. "I couldn't see how I could come back to these people, [since then] . . . somebody else would get in and offer a royalty. So I said I will always conform to the standard publishing practice; in those days [when they chose to] the publishers paid twenty-five percent of the mechanical royalties [i.e., a half cent per side sold of the two cents total]; I knew all this from being in the record business [first]." It's also quite probable, as his son Ralph I. Peer (usually referred to as Ralph Peer II) suggests, that there was no practical way for his father to have considered going the song buyout route in any case, for the sheer outlay of capital it would have entailed.

For the many hillbilly, blues, jug band, gospel, and jazz performers that Peer would record at Victor beginning in the late 1920s who sold five thousand records or fewer (and perhaps fewer still, when the world Depression dampened the music business a few years later), the standard half-cent mechanical royalty share he provided couldn't add up to all that much over the initial per-side payment. It was more a tantalizing prospect than a life-altering windfall, and some would forever be puzzled where the big money was, when their records simply hadn't sold well and the songs had not been picked up by others to record.

But for those who recorded with him, wrote copyrightable songs, sold tens of thousands or even hundreds of thousands of records, and saw other artists recording the songs as well, the returns to the artist quickly became huge. To take the most obvious example, star-to-be Jimmie Rodgers's quarterly royalty statements soon earned, even early in his recording career, very substantial royalties from songs such as "Blue Yodel (T for Texas)," "Waiting for a Train," or his version of "In the Jailhouse Now"—not just from his own huge hit Victor recordings, but on lucrative mechanical returns on those songs as recorded by Frankie Marvin, Riley Puckett, Gene Autry, and Frank Luther, among others, from records that were selling tens of thousands on labels such as Plaza, Pathé, Cameo, and Columbia.

One catch in working with new song material with strong connections to musical roots was that, in practice, the rules for what constituted the distinctive versions of songs, the copyrightable versions that Peer was looking for, were subject to interpretation and, on more than one occasion, to legal disputes over competing claims of effective authorship. If the uninitiated often take a copyright credit on a song as a pure acknowledgment of authorship history, of artistry, as what "ought to be" a perfectly reliable statement of "who actually created that song," it has always been something quite different to the music industry—a claim of song rights ownership.

The music business sees a song as a property. The right to use a parcel of land's street address as a tenant, or even current ownership of a house (heavily mortgaged perhaps), doesn't suggest to anyone that the current occupant built the place, let alone was its architect. Given how the typically rough-and-tumble music business often works, a clearer metaphor would be gold prospecting: claims get made, especially when a previously obscure song becomes a moneymaking hit, and competing claims—like claims for plots of land along a gold rush stream—hold when someone can and will defend them. Instead of pistols, music copyright claims usually are settled through lawyers. Many lawyers.

Copyright law in the United States and beyond as it was operating in Peer's A&R years, when his publishing concerns were founded, and long since, has recognized original *versions* of songs culled from the public domain as distinctive and copyrightable works. It's the same principle that applies with today's open-source software, for instance; while it's generally shared and free of charge, it is perfectly legal and sometimes viable to own and charge for an original variation unique and strong enough, with enough value added, that people *want* to turn to it repeatedly and specifically—and are willing to pay for it. This aspect of copyright law simply says that if people are singing Lead Belly's lyrics and tune for "Midnight Special," or Jimmie Rodgers's version of "In the Jailhouse Now," though there are others around, that *counts* for something—for the publisher of that version, for Lead Belly or Jimmie Rodgers, and, for a length of time set by law, for their heirs or estate. There are versions and versions; if you do use a songwriter's variant of the old song, you pay appropriately. You don't have to use that one.

Peer noted of the repertoire of his backwoods 1920s clients and performers G. B. Grayson and Henry Whitter: "These men, being what they were, didn't get the words from a book or from anybody else; they heard them and then they would forget part of them, and they'd make up their own version. These are all *versions*."

As fledgling and limited in activity as United Publishing was as he began recording artists for Victor in 1926, the establishment of that publishing enterprise immediately increased Peer's involvement in song rights disputes—and that would prove not entirely a negative development. While most music industry copyright arguments are minor, unpublicized, lack drama, and are settled reasonably amicably with agreements, when the stakes are high and the rights ownership or song origins are ambiguous enough, they can turn into epic battles. And since Ralph Peer specialized in songs that had connections in musical traditions to older songs updated or changed into new versions, rights and origins questions inevitably arose regularly. As he would remark in reminiscing about a dispute that arose during those first months working with Victor, "I've had a *lot* of arguments about copyrights. . . . We've had many of these things come up."

The issue that emerged was ownership of the rights to a disaster ballad about a factory fire written by the topical country and gospel songwriter Reverend Andrew Jenkins, a friend of Peer's; the song's publisher was another. Peer, in fact, had *no* business interest in that specific dispute, but he could now use the substantial resources at Victor to look into the matter for his friends—a revealingly generous use of his capabilities. Jenkins (who would before long write "Ben Dewberry's Last Run" for Jimmie Rodgers) had leaned heavily on an earlier tune, probably unconsciously, one attached to a then quite obscure forty-year-old ballad about President James Garfield's assassination, "The Ballad of Charles Guiteau." Peer and staff found that the tune was actually older still, and crucially—from a practical standpoint—that nobody was around to claim it. Jenkins's claim to his fire song was unassailable.

The inspired aspect of the episode was what Peer did next, as the brand new A&R man at Victor; he had his early hillbilly star Kelly Harrell record the forgotten Guiteau ballad, simply because it struck him as a pretty *good* old song that nobody remembered. Harrell's March 1927 recording became the first of a ballad that has remained familiar ever since.

Here was a commercial record producer reviving an old, published topical broadside of dubious originality, and reintroducing it into the nascent commercial country market and, eventually, into commercial folk music—an act of both preservation and revival. Nothing in that line of events conforms with anyone's romantic ideas about "oral transmission" and the so-called "folk process," but that's what happened, as it would many times again in the commercial development and exploitation of traditional music rooted in place, regional cultures, and history. Academic folklorists and roving song collectors of that day often operated under an assumption that would linger in some circles—that popular music, particularly recorded and broadcast music, was inevitably diluting and hastening the *demise* of traditional regional sounds and culture. That attitude was going to evolve, and Peer's efforts would be a factor.

By the time he was contracted by Victor, his own thinking about what might be done with hillbilly tunes and acts had had time to evolve, too. He had already found that rewardingly elastic range of acceptable, successful styles in the race line at Okeh, with strong potential for marketing records from all across that spectrum, from sophisticated jazz to down-home blues, bawdy vaudeville to sacred music. He'd come to believe that as expansive a range, broader than he'd yet tried, could be identified and made to work in the music made by and for Southern rural and small-town whites—a range that might veer closer to mainstream pop music.

There were practical issues to come to grips with. When Ernest Stoneman reported to Victor's Camden, New Jersey, headquarters in 1926, ready to record a set of fresh sacred numbers he and Peer had planned as the Stonemans' first Victor sides, there was some surprising news. As Stoneman recalled, "Mr. Peer came in and said, 'Well, they pulled a fast one on us, Ernest. They want you to do the Powers family's records over again, with an electric microphone. We think we can improve on them, and they like your group, so what do you want to do about it?'" (The Powers Family had been one of Victor's few early rural acts; they had recorded such familiar, traditional tunes as "Cripple Creek," "Ida Red," and "Old Joe Clark" back in 1924–25, mainly as instrumentals, with the earlier, lower-fidelity acoustic recording equipment.)

The surprise demand from the Victor higher-ups reflected several facts of Ralph Peer's new recording life with the leading recording company. He did not have ultimate, sole say as to what record would be produced, or when, for all of Victor's dependency on his development of artists and the recording repertoire in the roots fields. He was going to have to handle relationships with care, especially with the label's A&R

board, and to pick his fights. ("At that early age," he later commented, "I had the sense to conform to whatever the company wanted.")

Popular recording acts were still, with rare exceptions, considered interchangeable by the industry, since the song and arrangement continued to be viewed as more important for sales than the performer, despite the experience with Caruso. Earlier Victor executives had gone so far as to have their house favorite, Carson Robison, "ghost" Charlie Powers's vocals on those original Powers Family recordings, simply preferring that sound. Now, with Stoneman and his vocal-emphasizing ensemble close at hand, the thinking went, they might just as well be the ones to lay down the updated, better-recorded versions of the same songs, and under their own names. They were simply after better-sounding records of the old songs.

Stoneman hadn't expected to need a banjo for the sacred song session he and Peer had planned, but he did for this material, for his band's picker, Bolen Frost. Peer had Stoneman go across the bridge from Camden to Philadelphia to pick up a fine Weymann Keystone State Special banjo made there, a model that cost a whopping $150, equal to several thousand today, a gesture that further cemented their relationship. ("It was some banjo!" Ernest enthused.)

By the Spring of 1927, Peer was back recording on location, supervising Victor recording expeditions in Memphis, Atlanta, and New Orleans, mainly of rural, little-known, if eventually celebrated African American acts such as Will Shade's Memphis Jug Band and songster Richard "Rabbit" Brown (of "James Alley Blues" fame). He also began to record hillbilly string bands, outfits similar to those he had worked with at Okeh, including Dock Walsh's Carolina Tar Heels (Peer named the group) and the relatively smooth-sounding Georgia Yellow Hammers, who, for the record, he'd record again in Charlotte, North Carolina, later in the year on "G Rag," with the African American Andrew Baxter on fiddle, an early racially integrated recording.

More suggestive of Peer's thinking at that time were some of the records he recorded at Victor's headquarters in Camden, New Jersey, in early 1927—rurally tinged but clearly contemporary sides by the Johnson Brothers, Paul and Charles, all released labeled "mountaineer song with guitar." The Johnsons, who originally hailed from western North

Carolina or nearby eastern Tennessee, sang in a rhythmic, sometimes slick patter style that spoke of working vaudeville experience, not of farm labor and square dances, and they brought fresh and varied material to record. In just one precursor of things to come, their recordings made with Peer at Camden prominently featured Paul's steel guitar playing, on the likes of their pure urban vaudeville novelty "Alecazander," which married steel guitar and bird whistles, and "Careless Love," established at the time as a jazz/blues standard, now hauled by the Johnsons and Ralph Peer into the early hillbilly field with Hawaiian steel. Other songs they recorded in those initial sessions included "Henry Judd Gray," an original topical ballad about the fresh, notorious, headline-making Ruth Snyder murder case, the new sentimental Tin Pan Alley–meets–Tennessee ballad "Down in Happy Valley," a prison song, and "Dream of a Miner's Child," later, a bluegrass standard.

This was an expansive new definition of what "mountaineer song with guitar" meant. While the Johnsons were entirely capable of playing traditional string band music, the sort that someone might label "from the folk tradition," old-time sounds were *not* the emphasis on these records—with implications for the future of commercial "hillbilly" music and how Ralph Peer was beginning to envision it.

Obscure as they are today, this modernizing brother act was the one that Peer singled out to show off at a Rotary Club lunch at the local YMCA during the episode that would be the most regularly referenced of his fifty-year musical career, his series of recording sessions at the Tennessee-Virginia border town of Bristol. ("Mountaineers Making Records Here Give Program; Peer Speaks" noted the headline in the *Bristol Herald Courier* the following morning—July 29, 1927.)

The Victor label backed their first full-scale recording expedition specifically targeting hillbilly music in a big way. "They asked me for recommendations," Peer recalled, "and I said, 'Well, I should make a trip to Southern territory and find places where I can record.' . . . They appropriated $60,000 for a trip . . . and they thought that was peanuts. I could have done it for half that!" (That would be, by commonly used translation methods, at least three-quarters of a million dollars in today's money.)

There are myriad stories about the events of that week, since it proved to be a watershed time for American music; many are fanciful. There is, after all, an understandable and common impulse to embrace genesis stories that are uncomplicated, colorful, and satisfyingly romantic. In the romanticized terms in which the Bristol sessions are often discussed, it's easy to picture Ralph Sylvester Peer wandering across the countryside in search of undiscovered rural talent, in the style of the "song catchers" and folk music collectors featured in school social studies curricula, then chancing upon the idyllic, rural village of Bristol where, thanks to star-crossed fortune and a newspaper advertisement he places, in walk the Carter Family and Jimmie Rodgers, happenstances marking the "birth" of country music—though he, and by now others, had, of course, been recording that music more or less systematically since 1923.

For Peer himself, such common characterizations were sources of amusement: "That was the first recording trip for Victor, and the first stop was Bristol . . . [but] I had had all my experience, of course, from handling the Okeh situation." This most famed of location recording trips represented, for him, both the chance to implement ideas that had not been practical until that moment and to show Victor what he could do.

If Okeh had not had the resources or demonstrated the inclination to engage themselves in any sort of massive campaign to turn a Fiddlin' John Carson or Ernest V. Stoneman into household names in the early 1920s, factors were coming together that could make such an effort conceivable for regional music performers signed on at Victor. There could be a new level of down-home stars, with new levels of popularity for their songs. Producing hit-making hillbilly stars, some country Carusos, Peer understood by now, was going to require both singers with strong individual stamps to leave an impression as they performed them, and the right songs to match. If, as a later Nashville music-marketing slogan would remind us, it "all begins with a song," it could also pretty much end right there, too, if the song and the right performer weren't promoted in tandem. Promotion possibilities were changing right along with technology.

The previous November, NBC, the National Broadcasting Company arm of David Sarnoff's RCA, the Radio Corporation of America, had linked a fast-growing network of local radio stations to its home station in New York and gone on the air with live network programming. If the record industry initially perceived national network radio as a threat (you bought a radio once and had a steady stream of music, free of charge, without buying any records), it wouldn't be very long before the potential was better understood for promoting charming singing personalities on the radio, and selling more of their records as a consequence. It was no coincidence that in just a matter of months the names RCA and Victor would be permanently fused, with RCA Victor records an arm of the same corporation as NBC broadcasting.

Meanwhile, in Hollywood in that summer of 1927, Warner Brothers had signed vaudeville star Al Jolson to star in the first feature film with both synchronized dialogue sound and singing musical numbers as central components, *The Jazz Singer*. Jolson began filming his part ("Wait a minute; you ain't heard nothing yet!") precisely two weeks before the Bristol sessions commenced. Movie studios making musical talkies quickly enlarged their positions in song publishing from that point, to own more songs they'd spread around on film. The Hollywood fantasy factories had already done the most to foster the concept of personality-based stardom. It may seem that audiences hardly needed to be reminded who Rudolph Valentino or Gloria Swanson or Charlie Chaplin were, but they had been anyway—constantly. Here came sound film, making the sense of connection to individual stars, and a sense of intimacy with them, exponentially potent for audiences. And rising new media (cheaper, faster photojournalism was yet another; radio news and sound newsreels were oncoming) were making Charles Lindbergh, whose transatlantic flight, like Jolson's sound filming, had occurred just a few weeks before Bristol, and Babe Ruth, who was on his way to hitting his longtime-record sixty home runs that same summer, into Americans more broadly famous than any had ever been before.

A truly central new development that lay behind the lasting impact and significance of Peer's Bristol sessions was the new technical ability to take higher-fidelity, electrical recording technology out of the big-city studios, where it had been having substantial impact on recording quality and the music recorded for two years, out on location. This technology allowed Peer to quickly set up elaborate equipment in storefronts or hotels as he had done with the acoustic equipment for Okeh. These first-rate sound studios could produce crisp, professional-sounding Victor singles that would make any newfound personalities discovered on location sound clear, accessible, and personable to masses of listeners.

Victor had moved out of the "shout into the cone" era in early 1925, implementing an electrical recording system developed by Western Electric for telephones and sound-ready motion picture theaters, adapted for standard-sized 78 rpm record recording at their Camden, New Jersey, studios. They were releasing notably higher-fidelity Orthophonic recordings and record players that matched them by that summer. Within two years, nearly all record companies had made the switch to electrical recording, and along with that change had come a shift in pop music tastes, from booming, large vaudeville hall– and opera house–filling acts, such as Irish tenor John McCormack, toward modern, era-defining crooners—such relaxed, novel singers as Gene Austin, "Whispering" Jack Smith, Nick Lucas, and Rudy Vallee, singers whose intimate, low-key styles perfectly suited higher-fidelity recording. Indeed, they couldn't have been effectively recorded before the new electrical technology's arrival.

Electrical microphones' very first use on hillbilly location sessions may well have been some sides recorded in March 1927 in Atlanta by Peer's competitor, Frank Walker, at Columbia Records—releases stamped with a telltale *W* used to denote discs recorded with Westinghouse carbon microphones—but Peer's Bristol recordings would have more lasting effects. Peer was bringing the new quality recording technologies into location recording of hillbilly acts, explicitly interested in identifying distinctive down-home performers who sang as simply, intimately, and truly as they and their neighbors talked. He was going to find some— and songs that matched.

In his 1955 letter to folklorist John Greenway, Peer elaborated on this, explicitly: "I made it a rule not to use any artist for recording who could not compose his own repertoire. This rather radical departure from the traditions of the recording industry 'paid off' in a big way. By this device it was possible to popularize new artists, because the public liked a new song—or to popularize a new song, because the public liked a certain artist. These same principles operate to this day, with the result that thousands of *future* folkloric songs have been created."

The Johnson Brothers' varied set performed at the Bristol Kiwanis luncheon, the local *Herald Courier* noted, included the familiar "Turkey in the Straw" hoedown, but also a new Hawaiian number and several of their recently recorded, original vaudeville-patter-and-steel-guitar songs. This accumulating range of sounds was no accident, since Ralph Peer was to use this time and place, under these circumstances, to push forward his central agenda—bringing the novelty and potency of regional roots music to a broader popular-music audience.

"Mr. Peer," *Herald Courier*'s July 29 report on the Kiwanis lunch noted, "gave an interesting talk, telling why his company had selected Bristol as the town to make mountain records, and describing the latest methods used by the Victor Company in recording records."

Why Bristol at all? Peer answered that question in different ways in different situations. At the time, he made the flattering suggestion to the local newspapers, no doubt repeated in his luncheon speech, that musical "experts" had ascertained that "in no section of the south have the pre-war melodies and old mountaineer songs been better preserved than in the mountains of East Tennessee and Southwest Virginia . . . and [that] it was primarily for this reason that the Victor company chose Bristol as an operating base." On the other hand, asked why he'd gone there years later, he simply responded, "I can't tell you why; . . . it just seemed to be a likely spot."

It is conceivable, as country music historian Charles K. Wolfe speculated, that Victor executives were aware of the research in the area conducted by British folksong collector Cecil Sharp during World War I. Sharp had come hither looking for Appalachian versions of old British ballads. He'd found some, of course, and exaggerated their prominence by failing to note the other sorts of music commonly encountered, while furthering the spurious notion that there were isolated Appalachian peasants scattered through the area who still spoke like "old-fashioned, seventeenth-century Englishmen." (There weren't.)

The immediate impetus for the choice of the Tennessee/Virginia border town, which was not in the country or even a rural backwater, but a fast-growing, modernizing smaller city, was not really a mystery. It was chosen because his client, friend, and trusted musical advisor Ernest V. Stoneman thought it would be a good idea.

Charlotte, North Carolina, and Savannah, Georgia, had already been selected as well-located urban centers for Peer's first hillbilly recording excursion for Victor, places still not "over-mined"; Bristol was the last added to that list. From previous scouting, Peer knew that the Appalachian town could be easily reached from the nearby hills and valleys of Virginia, Tennessee, and North Carolina, and that a good many acts he'd already worked with, including Stoneman, Henry Whitter (who would record several new harmonica sides at Bristol), and the Hill Billies' fiddler, Charlie Bowman, had all come from the region. Ernest Stoneman, as he later related to his daughter Patsy, suggested that there were appealing rural talents in the area that could be lined up to be recorded, performers he knew who might not have ways or time to get to the more distant cities. Peer took the suggestion, and the most specific result was that the first days of recording at Bristol were dominated by acts featuring or introduced to Ralph Peer by Stoneman himself.

"Mr. Peer wrote me a letter," Ernest recalled. "[He asked me] to go out in the mountains and hunt up people that have got something on the ball, that we can use, and go to Galax and rent a room for an audition and have them come in there. . . . I don't know how many places I did go and listened at 'em and let 'em rehearse, so I could kind of tell whether he'd want them or not. . . . I done my best for everybody I could. . . . I took ever so many down there, but he didn't want nobody but Eck Dunford. . . . [Mr. Peer turned down] some pretty good music, but they didn't seem to be interested; they were bands, but the trouble of it was, they couldn't none of them sing. He liked Uncle Eck's old voice . . . [and] he wanted *songs*; Uncle Eck had a whole bunch."

Eck Dunford, a remote relative of Mrs. Stoneman, indeed had songs, and that was quick to grab fledgling publisher Ralph Peer's attention. Peer's predilection for favoring appealing, distinctive song-singing vocalists for Victor hillbilly recordings, and throughout his work for them, was not so much a consequence of his new role as a song publisher, however, but of his bet that in hillbilly recording, as elsewhere on records, the era of singing star personality dominance was at hand. So while the preference flummoxed Ernest Stoneman, Peer had reasons to be more interested in a distinctive personality with new songs and patter such as Uncle Eck than in one more instrumentals-only string band, however accomplished.

Ralph Peer's father,
Abram B. Peer.

Ralph Peer's mother,
Ann Sylvester Peer.

At the Peer family's East Bloomfield, New York, farm, turn of the twentieth century: grandmother Hannah Peer, grandfather Benjamin, Ralph (about age eight), and mother Ann.

"At Home Day" ad, 1912.

White doorway at right: Peer Supply Company talking machine and sewing machine shop, Independence, Missouri, 1909; with apartments the Peers lived in upstairs. JACKSON COUNTY (MO.) HISTORICAL SOCIETY ARCHIVES

Ralph Peer at twenty, 1912, while
working for Columbia Phonograph.

Sadie Hildebrand
Peer, early 1920s.

Ralph Peer,
1918.

NEGRO RECORDS

A booming field discovered,
developed and led by OKeh

A LARGE demand always existed for records by negro artists—particularly in the South. But it remained for OKeh alone to first recognize and appreciate the possibilities that this field had to offer, and, as pioneers in the field, to release the first Negro Record. Since then, each succeeding year has shown a remarkably rapid increase in the popularity of OKeh Negro Records until today they are nationally famous.

SARA MARTIN
(Exclusive OKeh Artist)

MAMIE SMITH
(Exclusive OKeh Artist)

We are proud of this fruitful field which we discovered and developed. "The Original Race Records" are the best and most popular records of their kind today. Every effort is made to release promptly the latest hits that have the greatest appeal to those who buy Negro Records. These hits are recorded only by Negro artists whose fame and popularity are unquestionably established. Sara Martin, Mamie Smith, Eva Taylor, Esther Bigeou, Lucile Bogan, Clarence Williams and Handy's Orchestra are but a few of the famous colored artists whose talents are available on OKeh Records.

The growing tendency on the part of white people to hear their favorite "blues" sung or played by famous colored "blues" artists, added to the already immense demand by the colored race for such records, has made the Negro Record field more fertile than ever before. OKeh dealers are amply assured of getting their full share of this booming demand, for they alone have the privilege of offering to their customers "The Original Race Records."

CLARENCE WILLIAMS
(Exclusive OKeh Artist)

OKeh Records

The Records of Quality

**General
Phonograph Corporation**
OTTO HEINEMAN, President
25 West 45th St.   New York

Okeh race records ad, *Talking Machine World*, August 1923. TALKING MACHINE WORLD

Okeh country music birth announcement, *Talking Machine World*, June 1924. TALKING MACHINE WORLD

Ralph Peer (standing, second from right) and Polk Brockman (seated at right), Atlanta, 1926.

TALKING MACHINE WORLD

Ralph and Anita Peer at the Carter family's home, Maces Springs, Virginia, 1928.

Ralph Peer, RCA Victor
years, in Havana, 1931.

Monmouth Beach, New Jersey, 1932: Jimmie, Carrie, and daughter Anita Rodgers at left; Ralph and Anita Peer and her nephew at right. (Man in rear unidentified.)

Ralph Peer and Monique Iversen, S.S. *Sandy Hook*, off New Jersey coast, 1934.

Stoneman had also mentioned a new song, "The Wreck of the Virginian," that he'd heard, by the singing, fiddling topical songwriter Blind Alfred Reed, commemorating a nearby fatal train wreck of just a few weeks before. Since you could hardly go wrong with songs on that subject at the time, Peer wrote to the talented, often sharply satirical balladeer and invited him to come to Bristol as well. Several more local acts that proved that, for all of the new emphasis on potential singing stars, string band hoedown styles were not entirely finished quite yet—the Shelor Family (ancestors of Sammy Shelor, the bluegrass banjo star of over sixty years later), and a banjo-fiddle duo, J. P. Nester and Norman Edmonds—were signed on to record at Bristol at the suggestion of a Victor dealer from the region, Walter Howlett of Hillsville, Virginia.

Peer next proceeded to check out the working situation in Bristol for himself, nine days before the recording trip, as was duly noted in a July 13 report in the evening *Herald Courier* ("Representatives of Victor Talking Machine Co. to Make Records Here"). Looking into the locations for potential recording in advance had already become his standard procedure. "The preliminary trip is to stir up local interest and find out if there actually is anything," he explained. At Bristol "I stopped in at the hotel and began to get acquainted with the people. I also went to the Victor dealer in the town [and] told him what I was up to."

The successful Bristol Victrola dealer, then and for decades to come, was the loquacious Cecil McLister. Peer first met with him at the Clark-Jones-Sheeley instrument and record store (later, simply McLister Music) on Bristol's main thoroughfare, during that preliminary visit, and according to McLister himself, "two or three times" total before the recording session began. A self-proclaimed lover of "good music" like those on Victor's classical Red Seal records, McLister also played mandolin and fiddle for local square dances. He helped identify the available downtown Bristol warehouse space useful for the recording sessions, introduced Peer to the local press, and, more famously, brought to his attention the then-unknown Carter Family.

For several years, fruit-tree salesman and aspiring recording artist Alvin Pleasant Carter (to be forever known as A.P.), along with his brother Ezra (known as Eck), husband of guitarist Maybelle Carter, had been coming into town from Maces Springs, aside Clinch Mountain, twenty miles away, and stopping into McLister's store to buy records—virtually since the earliest hillbilly stars had begun appearing on disc. A.P. and his singing wife, Sara, had auditioned for a Brunswick Records talent scout the year before, but *that* scout had been fixated on fiddlers and had seen little potential for a hillbilly act with a female singer up front. While Sara and Maybelle Carter (Sara's remote cousin, as well as her sister-in-law) recalled years later that it was an "ad" in the local paper that alerted them that Victor would be showing up to record, a story since endlessly repeated, it was almost certainly that initial news report on Peer's visit that led them to ask McLister about the upcoming sessions in the first place. (The only relevant ad to appear in the local papers concerned the coming to town of a Victor "recording machine" when the Victor crew arrived, not a call for talent; perhaps that ad simply reminded them that the sessions they'd heard about were on.)

A few days before the sessions began, Peer arrived at the Galax, Virginia, home of the once impoverished, now financially comfortable Ernest and Hattie Stoneman, along with his new bride, Anita. She would make enough of an impression on the musical families who came to the Bristol sessions that Maybelle and Eck Carter would name their daughter Anita after her, and a short-lived daughter of the Stonemans, Anna Juanita, known as Nita, would be named for her as well. (Jimmie and Carrie Rodgers's daughter, coincidentally named Anita also, was not; she'd been born six years before the Rodgers and Peer families met.)

Patsy Stoneman, though she was just two that year, recalls the Peers' succession of visits to the Galax house, which began with that one, and offers a sense of what those stay-over visits meant to the Stoneman family—and of Peer's demeanor when he got there:

> Mr. Peer was the kind of a man you could *be* friendly with, because he looked and acted like he thought something of you. We were a bunch of hillbillies and he was a big city Yankee, but he never looked down on any of us; you could tell that. Daddy respected him because he respected Daddy. You wouldn't think that he was just your boss—though, in fact, he had our future in his hands.
>
> Now, Daddy had gone to get a guitar while he was in New York, and I thought it was the best thing that had happened since

water. I wanted to get up and play it, though I couldn't play, but I'd get the first finger and *chunk-a, chunk-a, chunk* it. Mr. Peer patted me on the head, watching me doing it, and Daddy laughed; he would pat us kids over the head. Mr. Peer wasn't cold at all, like he can look in some of those posed pictures.

We had a great big dining room table, and a cook and a maid, and—believe it or not—electricity, and a telephone, and the Peers would come eat at our house. When they'd come, it was 'the people from New York' we'd refer to; 'the people from New York's coming.' We had a great big buffet in the dining room, and we'd dress up the house when they'd come. There would be a lot of picking and singing and talking, and a lot of family around, so Daddy and Mr. Peer would also go off in the side room and talk. That was business time.

In a 1961 interview, Ernest Stoneman recalled the Peer crew's arriving at Bristol "with a couple of recording engineers and about twenty-five trunks of stuff. . . . They put carpet on the floor, and to get the right acoustics they'd haul the carpet up with a big wooden block in the middle of it and make like a tent; this would kill the noise, the echo in the building."

The engineers were Edward Eckhardt and Fred Lynch; traveling with two engineers rather than one was a luxury provided by Victor that Peer had never experienced before. The blankets, he would note later, actually didn't buffer the "room tone" sounds all that well. In part to minimize intimidation of the new recording artists by the bulky, unfamiliar electrical technology, those blankets also masked all of the equipment but the microphone. Bristol's *Herald Courier*, then charmingly but accurately promoting itself as "A Model Semi-Metropolitan Newspaper," reported on July 24, the day the vague "recording machine will be here" Victor ad also appeared, that "Ralph S. Peer and two engineers from the recording department of Victor Records . . . have leased the old Taylor-Christian building on State Street, and are fitting it up as a studio at this time." That former home of the Taylor-Christian Hat Company, at number 408 State Street, was on the Tennessee side of the main town thoroughfare, the street that separates Bristol, Tennessee, from Bristol, Virginia.

The sessions began the next morning, at 8:30 AM Monday, July 25, and went on all day, with Ernest Stoneman and varied homegrown musical backup—vocal duets and trios with combinations of Hattie's sister Irma Frost, neighbors Kahle Brewer and Walter Mooney, and Eck Dunford—and in the afternoon, all of them together as Ernest Stoneman & His Dixie Mountaineers, recording a half dozen of those hymns they'd planned to record the previous year, organ and fiddles adding to the underlying guitar and harmonica sound. Hattie Stoneman and another Stoneman neighbor, Tom Leonard, joined in on the group recordings. As musicologist Jocelyn Neal has noted, the hymns, and even the first song recorded at Bristol, the sentimental ballad "Dying Girl's Farewell," had been culled from commonly used paperbound hymnals long used by evangelicals in the region, such as John B. Vaughan's *Windows of Heaven* series, and simplified by Ernest, in arrangements notated by Hattie Stoneman and sister Irma, both of whom were musically trained.

They had all known these songs, designed for harmony singing, for years. The original songwriters were in fact credited on the records. Ralph Peer's notes on the songs were detailed enough to suggest that the hymn books themselves were on hand at the session. That not one of the new Stoneman recordings could be credited to him as a composer would begin, before long, to have a limiting effect on Ernest's working relationship with Peer. "Daddy didn't claim anything he didn't know was his," Patsy Stoneman would explain. "He was too honest for his own good. He'd tell where he got the song from, so you couldn't very well publish it."

When Stoneman family members returned to recording that Wednesday, Uncle Eck would record the untraceable old rhythm song "Skip to Ma Lou, My Darling," which, as the local paper noted at the time, had already been "one of the favorites at every country dance held in this section for half a century." It had never, however, been recorded before, and Dunford's energetic version helped put it on the permanent map, far beyond that "section." His unusual verses, involving redbirds and bluebirds and pigpens, were not those commonly known today, and Peer soon saw to it that Dunford's version was copyrighted.

The first truly pioneering Bristol session recordings were set down on the Tuesday between the Stoneman family dates, in the form of a half dozen sides by Ernest Phipps and His Holiness Quartet, backed by

fiddles and guitars. Unlike more culturally mainstream, generally familiar hymns, the emerging, raucous, spirited quartet sounds of the
Southern-based Pentecostal Holiness denominations had never yet been
recorded. It is not documented how Peer and Phipps, an evangelist out
of Kentucky, first crossed paths, but there had to have been an audition,
and on hearing the far-from-genteel quartet, Ralph Peer had to have
said, "Yes, let's make some records of *that*."

The six sides Peer recorded with them that morning—fast, spirited,
and in 4/4 time—plus the additional stomping, handclapping six he
would record with baritone Phipps and company when returning to
Bristol the following year, broadened the vocabulary of recorded American music. Such pioneering recordings as "Do Lord, Remember Me,"
"Old Ship of Zion," and "A Little Talk with Jesus" were the opening salvo
of what would come to be called southern gospel, driving music that has
had an evolving life of its own to this day. It would be such a central part
of the musical vocabulary and experience of such artists as Elvis Presley
and Jerry Lee Lewis thirty years later that it would also prove to be a key
building block of rock 'n' roll.

This was obvious to no one at the time. Peer realized that the music
might move people and, at least as important from a record company's
perspective, then or later, that the sound was novel, and so the records
might sell; it was a gamble worth taking. He'd have Ernest Stoneman and
friends record the two-sided down-home comedy sketch "Old Time
Corn Shuckin'" that Wednesday morning for an equal and opposite
sales-oriented reason—imitation, because Gid Tanner and the Skillet
Lickers, the highly successful and influential string band produced by
Frank Walker, was having success with the sketch "A Fiddler's Convention in Georgia," recorded in Atlanta in April. There have never been
better reasons to produce a commercial record than that it is utterly
unlike anything anybody has heard before—or that it is just like what
people are already buying.

It might seem, then, that Peer would have been very pleased with
how things were going at Bristol that first week, and he had those
pop-ready Johnson Brothers, the satirical Blind Alfred Reed, and another
distinctive sacred-song vocalist, Alfred Karnes, set to record by week's
end. In fact, he was not convinced that they had yet come up with

material strong enough to meet Victor's high expectations, and so with stimulating more acts to show up to audition in mind, he invited the editor of the *Herald Courier*'s competitor, the afternoon *Bristol News Bulletin*, introduced to him by McLister, to be on hand for the Wednesday morning session as it unfolded.

This reporter (who had no byline in the resulting article; he may have been the paper's general editor, Walter Crockett) described the making of Eck Dunford's "Skip to Ma Lou, My Darling" recording and, with excited precision that suggests prompting by Peer, also of "What Will I Do, for My Money's All Gone," a Dunford song recorded with Ernest and Hattie Stoneman and Galax ukulele player Iver Edwards backing him up. "It is a plaintive mountain song expressing wonder over what the singer will do when all his money runs out," the paper duly reported. "The synchronizing is perfect. . . . Bodies swaying, feet beating in perfect rhythm. It is calculated to go over big when offered to the public."

The article, headlined "Mountain Songs Recorded Here by Victor Co.," appeared very prominently in that afternoon's paper. Peer could not quite recall the editor's name, years later, vaguely remembering the name Lynn. (J. W. Lynn was actually the city's mayor, chief banker, and chamber of commerce chief at the time, and was very likely encountered, but not as a reporter.) Peer did recall, "When I asked him if he would print something in the paper about what I was going to do, he took the left hand column on the front page; he really gave it the works." That editor, he also reported years later, laughing, had additional incentive for the prominent placement of the story.

This fellow seemed to me to be quite an intelligent man. We got talking, and just then there was news on the financial pages that RCA was going to buy the Victor Talking Machine Company, so it seems this fellow dabbled in the stock market a little bit, and he began questioning me. . . . There really wasn't any secret about it, [but] the news hadn't gotten around. So I said to him 'There's gonna be something happening in the next few days and it wouldn't be a bad idea if you had a little of this.' . . . Sure enough, before Saturday came around there was a big jump, and he made quite a bit of money out of it. I can't say that was the reason for it, but when I asked him if he would print something in the paper about what I was trying to do, he takes the left hand column on the front page!

However large a role was played by what would come to be considered insider trading just a few years later, as new regulations came into play after the Wall Street crash (though it was perfectly legal at the time), the *News Bulletin* article was important for attracting acts to Bristol and locking in appointments with some stragglers, who'd likely heard about the sessions but had not yet shown up to audition. The specific enticement, it's universally agreed, was the article's final paragraph, which blithely related the sort of money Ernest Stoneman and company were making: "The quartette costs the Victor company close to $200 per day—Stoneman receiving $100, and each of the assistants $25. . . . He received from the company over $3600 last year as his share of the proceeds on his records."

"After you read this," Peer reminisced later, "if you knew how to play 'C' on the piano you were going to become a millionaire. So this worked *very well*! He told them I was staying at such and such a hotel and I got all kinds of mail as a result of that." He would also recall being "deluged with long-distance calls from the surrounding mountain region."

Perhaps, but the practical result of the celebrated article was the addition of no more than a half dozen acts to those already scheduled or recorded that first week. The latecomers were mainly acts rarely recalled today—including the Alcoa Quartet, a formal, quite practiced a cappella gospel group that had recorded previously for Columbia; Red Snodgrass's Alabamians, never mentioned as an Appalachian find since they were an anomalous local jazz combo and the resulting recording was never issued; the very capable if not particularly distinctive West Virginia Coon Hunters string band; and the Tennessee Mountaineers, a twenty-member church choir.

If the additional acts had stopped there, the Bristol sessions might simply have come to seem just one more Ralph Peer location recording stand among many, rarely revisited, despite their significance as a starting point for Victor's new commitment to actively seeking roots music artists in remote locations and recording them well. But the newcomers who came in to audition for recording in the wake of the "you, too, can be rich like Ernest Stoneman" article did not stop there, for in came, with that extra reminder, the original Carter Family and an obscure, recently cobbled-together group who'd driven to Bristol from Asheville, North Carolina, the Jimmie Rodgers Entertainers.

Because the Carters and Jimmie Rodgers turned out to be performers credited—and rightly so—as foundation acts for decades of music to come, these sessions would come to be seen by many as "the Big Bang of Country Music" (as historian Nolan Porterfield put it), and, in Johnny Cash's formulation, "the single most important event in the history of country music." Widespread mythologizing of Bristol would grow right along with the reputations and legends of these performers. So would jealous possessiveness of the story and accounts flavored by the teller's region, class, and social/political ideology, attitudes toward the music business and the country genre, individual and family credit taking, and applied mixtures of them all, coloring more than eighty years of retellings and commentary.

Depictions of Ralph Peer's relations with the musicians recorded and the music they made have been particularly ripe for restyling—both from populist, culturally conservative perspectives, portraying Peer as the archetypal "slicker," from New York (naturally), tempting simple country families into the evils of show business with minimal payback and the promise of fame; and from more urbane, ideological perspectives, portraying Peer as a sort of remote corporate imperialist breezing through to exploit pure, noncommercial, rural folk artists. These sorts of characterizations are often accompanied by the suggestion that Peer had no particular experience with, taste, or feel for the down-home music he recorded, let alone the artists involved—a fundamentally nonsensical assertion, given Peer's steady, ongoing involvement with developing such acts, his success in doing it, and the personal relations he had with those he chose to trust and concentrate on, as he had Ernest Stoneman.

That scout from Brunswick Records had turned down the Carter Family for being an act led by female vocals rather than A.P.'s fiddle, but Ralph Peer, and therefore the Victor Talking Machine Company, said yes for precisely the same reasons. Peer later noted: "As soon as I heard Sara's voice—that was it. . . . So many people would come in and they'd be a quartet; they'd sing well but there was nothing outstanding and I knew I was wasting my time. But soon as I heard *her* voice, I began to build around it—and all the first recordings were on that basis."

The Carters' principal biographers (residents, incidentally, of New York and Connecticut) would much later ask, in a disingenuous remark loaded with assumptions about region, class, and musical appreciation, "How could Ralph Peer and the boys in New York have the ear to recognize the amplitude of that keening pitch?" Peer, in fact, had precisely the experience, the inclination (based on his own reading of the importance of vocals), and the *job* to pick up on Sara Carter's singing. As he would explain, "I'd done this so many times; I was trained to watch for the one voice."

That "one voice," in this case, struck a very attractive balance between the assertive, occasionally declamatory vocal style familiar to audiences from church, the intimacy of family singing at home on the porch and in the parlor, and narrative storytelling when there was a story to be told. Sara Carter sang involvingly and effectively, employing the rhythms and emphasis people much like the Carters used in everyday speech, and her searing, sometimes swooping vocal style could work putting over a relatively varied array of songs. Her feisty personality stuck to shellac and came through. Those were attributes Ralph Peer should not have missed—and he didn't.

Still, shopkeeper Cecil McLister suggested to several interviewers that Peer (unlike himself) had not been inclined to put out the Carters' initial recordings at all, that he hadn't realized the power of their music and delayed releasing any. In fact, their first single was released only a few weeks later than the very first Bristol recordings to reach the stores, a meaningless timing distinction and from today's perspective, an astonishingly fast production process in any case—though the three-month wait likely made the Carters, so new to all of this, nervous at the time.

Peer, clearly recognizing what he had at hand, immediately recorded six songs with them (for three two-sided records) on Monday night and Tuesday morning of the second week of the sessions. The Carters were the *only* new secular recording act with whom he recorded that many. (Six were also recorded with Ernest Phipps and His Holiness Quartet and the distinctive, forcefully rhythmic guitar-playing gospel singer

Alfred G. Karnes, reminders of Peer's interest in getting the under-recorded white sacred song singers on record.)

As for his building these first Carter Family recordings around Sara's voice, on the second day of recording, the predictably unpredictable A.P. had not shown up at the studio ("Mr. Carter not in this selection" the logs for those two numbers would read), and Peer went ahead and recorded Sara and Maybelle without him.

Sara, singing and playing autoharp, and A.P., singing and sometimes playing that fiddle, had been performing together at local church gatherings, schoolhouse community socials, family events, and such since they'd met and soon after married in 1915. Sara's cousin Maybelle Addington Carter, born in 1909 (eighteen years later than A.P. and eleven later than Sara) and pregnant at the time of the sessions, had joined the act only the year before, after marrying A.P.'s brother Eck. Maybelle's innovative, blues-influenced guitar style, including the rhythmic, adaptable "Carter scratch," which enabled simultaneous rhythm and melody picking, was an important modernizing aspect of the trio's music that would prove influential for country music, commercial folk music, and rock alike. Ralph Peer would only rarely mention it over the years in describing the Carters' strengths, which was no doubt a practical effect of his own focus on singer personalities, which was Sara's department, and on supplying new song material, which was mainly A.P.'s.

Peer's glib description of the Carters' arrival for their audition that morning, offered in an interview over thirty years later, has rubbed some commentators the wrong way—either as a misleading overstatement of their "hillbilly" appearance and background or as condescending in tone: "They wander in; they're a little ahead of time. They'd come about twenty-five miles, through a lot of mud. It seems to me like it was [in] an old car. And he's dressed in overalls and the women are country women from way back there—calico clothes on, and the children are very poorly dressed. . . . Later, I called them 'hillbillies,' and that's what they looked like. At any rate, they were backwoods people and they were not accustomed to being in town."

Ralph Peer, like many music industry veterans, was sometimes flippant when relating show-business stories and, at times, when speaking to other executives or observers from the more advantaged classes, talked about the down-home performers he worked with, whatever their ethnic background, as if they were amusing underlings. In this case, though, the circumstances of the interview clarify his tone. The interviewer, writer Lil Borgeson, was a latter-day friend and former neighbor of Sara Carter, and well aware of how far the Carters had traveled from that humble start; Peer's description of his first sight of them had about it the ring of "Can you believe that?" and Mrs. Borgeson's reaction, on tape, was knowing laughter.

The three Carters, by their own accounts, had taken A.P. and Sara's young children, Gladys and Joe, in hand, and indeed rushed to make it to the date, on a summer day that was more than usually hot and sticky. They had forged a river in a borrowed car to get to Bristol from Maces Springs, so mud and dishevelment very likely *were* in the picture. Given the conditions, they'd not really dressed up for the occasion, as some of the other auditioning artists had. Exactly how badly off A.P. and Sara and Maybelle and Eck were before musical success came their way has been described by observers in varying terms over the years, some emphasizing their "good, solid people" respectability, others their hard, challenging scrambling just to get by, but no one, however well they knew the Carters' circumstances, has suggested that they'd been doing *well*, for all of their notable dignity. (Bristol's Cecil McLister recalled, "They lived in a two-room house for a long, long time; one room didn't even have a floor, just a dirt floor in it. But after they begin to get some revenue from their records, they got more land and built better houses.")

The Carters had been assembling a large repertoire for their community performances for a dozen years. It included songs that they'd known from childhood, learned from neighbors and friends. Some of those proved to be aging, published, sentimental Tin Pan Alley ballads and heart songs, but they weren't necessarily aware of those song origins, nor had they had any reason, before meeting Ralph Peer, to check into the question. Some songs they sang were first learned from hymn collections, and some, no doubt, from records, since they'd been snapping up whatever early hillbilly recordings they could. Because the same local audiences tended to follow them from appearance to appearance, they'd kept expanding their song list to avoid too much repetition—intriguing for Peer in itself.

With the old, acquired songs, it was A.P.'s practice, as he would explain to researcher Ed Kahn, to "change tunes to get them in their style." He also wrote "a little music" from time to time, marking down his tunes in the old, simplified shape-note style in which he'd been trained to sing as a boy. Then all three Carters would modify the notes and words he'd written to better work for them as performers—and they would consistently do that well. This ability and experience can be credited, in part, to the rural harmony singing tradition of each one finding the right spot in an arrangement, but it was also a testament to this particular trio's notable professional capabilities. They likely underestimated those abilities themselves at first, but they would serve the three of them, and chief song developer A.P. in particular, very well, as Ralph Peer's focus on new songs and versions of songs that could be copyrighted became clear. And it did from the first day they met. The Carters, Peer would recall fondly, "had plenty of repertoire. They had an incredible memory; if they heard somebody singing a song forty years before, they could sing that song for you!"

A.P. had presented a number of songs at their morning audition, and Peer picked the ones he wanted them to record, beginning that same evening. The very first, "Bury Me Under the Weeping Willow," was one the Carter women had known all their lives, but had been arranged for the trio by A.P. and would be copyrighted as such. It would become an all-time country standard, and later a bluegrass standard as well.

Much the same could be said about the staying power of the fourth and last song Ralph Peer lined up to be recorded that first evening, "The Storms Are on the Ocean," an adaptation of A.P.'s that emerged on record in a dramatically original form, one with historic implications. The two minute, fifty-one second length, perfect for a popular recording, which Peer had stressed was vital, was markedly shorter than the old ballads from which it was partly derived—the epic "The Lass of Roch Royal," centuries old, as collected in many lengthy variations by nineteenth-century folklorist Francis James Child, or "A True Lover's Farewell," a well-known variant documented in Appalachia just eleven years earlier. The British "Roch Royal" songs were themselves variations of the traditional "Lord Gregory" story that contained the musical questions "Who will shoe my pretty little foot, and who will glove my hand?

Who will comb my yellow hair?" And so on. (The answer is usually a member of the family who will handle all that while the lover is gone.)

Through the "folk process" of centuries-long song concatenation, "whispering down the lane" mistakes and improvements, local and singer-specific variations and updatings, this was the lyric for "True Lover's Farewell" presented by Mrs. Rosie Hensley of Carmen, North Carolina, to British folklorist Cecil Sharp, in August 1916, as typical of their Appalachian region. Given what was about to be done with it, it is useful to recall:

O Fare you well, my own true love, so fare you well for a while;
I'm going away, but I'm coming back, if I go ten thousand mile.

If I prove false to you, my love, the earth may melt and burn,
The sea may freeze and the earth may burn, if I no more return.

Ten thousand miles, my own true love, ten thousand miles or more;
The rocks may melt and the sea may burn, if I never no more return.

And who will shoe your pretty little feet, or who will glove your hand,
Or who will kiss your red rosy cheek, when I'm in the foreign land?

My father will shoe my pretty little feet, my mother will glove my hand,
And you can kiss my red rosy cheek, when you return again.

O don't you see yon little turtle dove, a-skipping from vine to vine,
A-mourning the loss of its own true love just as I mourn for mine?

Don't you see yon pretty little girl a-spinning on yonder wheel?
Ten thousand gay, gold guineas would I give, to feel just like she feels.

The Carters' quite distinct version would update the language to sharper, more direct, contemporary American (eschewing the "guineas" and "yons" if not the pretty little feet) and specifically regional ("a'goin'," for example, and *mourning*, not turtle doves), further simplifying and regularizing the meter, and using that "sea that may freeze" line in an entirely new and fresh way, not as a passing reference, nor as part of a symmetrical answer to a question, but as a catchy, repeating *pop chorus*.

That was an idea that particularly excited Ralph Peer, who, some historians have suggested, may have pressed A.P. for this specific innovation at the morning audition, considering it a way to broaden the Carters' acceptance and to nudge the traditional into the realm of pop. In any event, it was precisely the modernizing, popularizing sort of element—a "hook" in later terms—that he was looking for. It was a chorus with its own rolling rhythm, its own tune, snappy internal rhyme, and catch phrase, which became the song's title:

> *I'm a'going away to leave you love, I'm a'going away for a while;*
> *But I'll return to you sometime, if I go ten thousand miles.*

> (Chorus, repeated after each verse:)
> *The storms are on the ocean; the heavens may cease to be;*
> *This world may lose its motion, love, if I prove false to thee.*

> *Oh who will dress your pretty little feet, oh who will glove your hand;*
> *Oh who will kiss your rosy red cheeks, when I'm in the far off land?*

> (Chorus. Guitar break.)

> *Oh, Papa will dress my pretty little feet, and mama will glove my hand;*
> *You can kiss my rosy red cheeks, when you (I) return again.*

> (Chorus. Guitar break.)

> *Oh, have you seen those mournful doves, Flying from pine to pine;*
> *A'mourning for their own true love, just like I mourn for mine.*

> (Chorus.)

> *I'll never go back on the ocean, love, I'll never go back on the sea;*
> *I'll never go back for the blue-eyed girl, till she goes back on me.*

> (Chorus.)

Having that verse-chorus structure was the very definition of a "popular song" at the time, quite literally, and not at all the norm for hillbilly ballad storytelling. No one could seriously argue that "The Storms Are on the Ocean," recorded again and again by a variety of musical performers ever since in this form, was not in a fundamental way the Carters' own—and a turning point for popular roots music.

The pace of the record is driving throughout, Maybelle's guitar picking and the vocals alike, the latter almost breathlessly so. Atypically, A.P.'s low vocals are nearly as prominent as Sara's higher lead; he sings "I" as she sings "you" in that third verse. It's all quite polished. The record's pace and the song's structure add up to nothing less than a contemporary musical leap forward into roots pop. There is just enough of the folk sound and background still lurking in the song as recorded, and in others to come from the original Carter Family act, that their music would be accepted by the commercial folk song revival of thirty to forty years later. There would always be those who would revere the Carters precisely for their connections to utterly local, homemade music, and to "just folks" amateurism, but that characterization is both limited and myopic, and does an injustice to their knowing, skilled artistry. Their very first day of recording with Ralph Peer was the historic moment when he drew the Carters *out* of traditional and amateur music, into the realm of pop music with a rooted, regional background and tone.

That corner of popular roots music would prove to have tremendous, lasting potential, one genuine starting point for the commercial country music that lay ahead, music dominated by songs with regional, rooted references—and verses with catchy choruses. The Carters' ability to deliver such music consistently, in changing times and conditions and changing personal relations as well, was a mark of their consummate professionalism.

The milestone became all the more pronounced because Peer saw to it that Victor made the B-side of their "The Storms Are on the Ocean" record a song Sara and Maybelle recorded the next morning. The pairing proved to be a remarkable hit. When A.P. failed to show up for that next session (he may have been out looking for a new tire for the car), it could not have been that surprising to the Carter women. He'd long been capable of taking off to find work and staying away for months without communication back home, much to Sara's annoyance. He would even fade away from the microphone in the middle of a song and begin wandering around the room, backing off recording in midstream. (Noting that behavior during the first day of recording, Ralph Peer is reported to have pulled A.P. aside and teased, "You didn't do very much!")

Alvin Pleasant "Doc" Carter had his peculiarities, and there's little doubt that the tensions they could cause were on display for Ralph Peer. Sara Carter (and at that point, Maybelle, too) wanted little more from recording than to make some relatively easy money compared to farm work, and they were content to go on performing locally at those churches and neighborhood socials. A.P. not only had ambitions, the born wanderer in him was perfectly happy taking off in search of new song material, as often and as long as he needed to make the act work. Instead of writing off A.P. as a potential problem for this new recording group, however, Peer saw as major assets his focused ambition and his clear ideas about what the Carters might sing, how to provide their songs, and (working closely with the women) how they'd perform them. The man was worthy of confidence and trust.

There was a concealed personal factor at work as well, a degree of quiet, empathetic identification with A.P. and his "work versus home" situation, across the apparent social divide, since Peer's own first marriage had foundered over exactly the issues he was witnessing complicating life for A.P. and Sara. If Ralph Peer had stuck with a homebound marriage to Sadie, he'd not have been there at Bristol himself, or, odds are, working with a global recording company in the capacity he was. He had every reason to understand A.P.'s itch to go where he needed to, when he needed to, but also to be sensitive to Sara's irritation and sense of entrapment in a marriage in which she and the children were regularly being abandoned without warning. Peer would play a continuing role in keeping the Carters' differences from their audience, which, given the majority of music the act would record—home-, family-, and church-centered—and active promotion of all of that by Peer and Victor, would understandably respond to them as icons of country domesticity.

Both A.P. and Sara, in separate interviews at different times, recalled that "Mr. Peer" had cautioned them not to tell people too much about their personal lives because "it wasn't good for business." The exact, double family relation of Maybelle to Sara and family (both cousin and sister-in-law) was even kept vague; they were simply the Carter Family, by some means or other, accent on *family*. This vagueness worked well enough that almost forty years later, when Pete Seeger was interviewing Maybelle's daughter June Carter on his public television program, she had to clarify for him that, no, Maybelle was not Sara's daughter and Aunt Sara, therefore, her grandmother!

This careful handling of the Carters' domesticated image was another aspect of the Carters being a modern commercial act, not "just" down-home folks. But it also signified a fact about them—well understood by Ralph Peer instinctively—that their musical identity, as their public image, was by necessity relatively *fixed*. The subjects they might sing about had limits, as did their comfort zone ("The Program is Morally Good," their circulars would announce) and so would the instrumentation and produc-tion choices that could work to the advantage of their music. There was just so far they could be or would be modernized, but there would still be novelty and evolution and stretches in their music along the way, if within those limits, as was seen even by their second session at Bristol.

With A.P. absent that next morning and Sara irritated, Peer, the orig-inal model A&R man, did exactly what a good A&R man would always do—he came up with the right song to record with the singer on hand, right then, in that situation. (We'll never know if he'd have turned to it otherwise.) This was *not* a typical Carter Family domestic presentation, and a song that they had not performed much, though it had been among the list of possible songs to record that A.P. had brought to Bristol and brought up at the audition; he later reported having learned it from his own mother. The reason for their usual hesitation to perform it was simple enough: Sara plain didn't like it.

"Single Girl, Married Girl" was a startling rural complaint, and a vivid description of the liberties a young woman gives up in marriage and motherhood. In concept, it was not unlike the familiar "I Wish I Were a Single Girl Again" or the "Single Life" song Peer had recorded with Roba Stanley earlier, but it was still more pointed. No one, Peer included, could know then that it was to be Sara who would bolt from the marriage, leaving both a nonplussed A.P. and the kids behind when she left, but it was a song that she really had a handle on, which may well have been the very source of her discomfort with it.

"I didn't want to sing that song," she recalled years later. "I didn't like it, and I told Mr. Peer 'I don't like that; I'd rather not sing that.' And he says, 'Aw, I want you to sing that.' So I sang the 'Single Girl,' sang it as a solo. . . . It wasn't long before [the records] came out, you know, and when we got our first royalty, why the 'Single Girl, Married Girl' had sold the most—the very one that I didn't want to sing! . . . There are some songs we'd sing that I liked, and some I didn't like, but mostly the ones I didn't like seem like the ones that sold the most." (She wouldn't think much of one they'd record at Victor studios in Camden the following May, either—"Keep on the Sunnyside," one of the Carters' all-time standards.) If there's any doubt that Ralph Peer's turn to that song that day was based on the performers' mood, circumstance, and his own A&R instinct, the other song he had her record that morning was "The Wandering Boy," a mother's lament for a son who just keeps wandering away.

At Bristol, Ralph Peer began to form a bond with the original Carter Family, to the point that he'd stick with them as their active manager and producer longer than any other act, even when he'd stopped focusing on managerial work and when their sales had passed their peak. In turn, they would stick with him when enticed in other directions. The Carters would come up with material to perform, record, and publish that would be widely accepted and have lasting impact—and it wasn't just A.P. who made it happen; Sara and Maybelle both knew songs that could work and, like him, sometimes would write their own. Peer would give them a good deal of leeway in that regard, letting them, as A.P. recalled, "record what they wanted," as long as they were fresh, copyrightable songs they hadn't "learned from records or the radio."

Peer had found, in this trio, a major commercial act with whom Southern rural and small-town audiences could instantly identify, one capable of recording a moderately modernized version of old-time rural sounds, potentially broadening the scope of the emerging country field's audience, and generating copyrightable songs that could and did last while doing it.

Ralph Peer's Bristol sessions had, with the combination of this historic find and the expanded recording of new sacred music, become significantly more than just one more set of location recordings he would supervise among many. The results, no doubt, would have been pleasing enough to the people upstairs at Victor, given the Carters' sales to come, if the sessions had stopped right there. But there was to be a topper, a performer who arrived on August 3, for the moment at least fronting the squabbling quartet the Jimmie Rodgers Entertainers.

The charismatic thirty-year-old Meridian, Mississippi–raised vaudevillian and former railway worker had been looking for some route to making show business his full-time profession since he was twelve; Ralph Peer was to be the connection Rodgers had long been looking for. Peer didn't have to "invent" Jimmie Rodgers but, as would soon be clear, Rodgers was remarkably close to the sort of performer he would have conjured if he could.

If Ralph Peer's assignment was to put Victor on the map with the hillbilly music audience, beginning with those rural and small-town white Southerners who had record players (preferably Victrolas), Rodgers not only took the label there, he would take it to the front of the country record sales pack, and add down-home elements to the Victor pop roster as well. Peer wanted a performer who'd take newly recorded, published songs out to that audience live, promoting them further, and this was an entertainer who would do so constantly, almost obsessively— even risking his fragile health in maintaining the pace. (The sometimes-fragile Rodgers had been diagnosed as suffering with a serious case of tuberculosis three years earlier.)

If Peer wanted a Caruso-sized personality who would bring that personality to the records and leave a strong impression, Rodgers was one of the largest personalities that records, let alone hillbilly music, had seen or would see. He brought a strong personal stamp to all he did, and yet was capable of assuming multiple appealing personas—railway brakeman and hobo, blues man and cowboy, Southerner and Westerner, ladies' man and family man, outlaw and successful "just folks" star—and getting them all to shine on record. Peer was looking for a performer who could thrive within the rising, fast-changing new media—and in short order, Jimmie Rodgers would comfortably appear on radio, make himself available for press interviews and photo sessions, and appear in the new short musical sound films, clear precursors of music videos, just as talkies were beginning to change the music business.

Rodgers, anxious and willing to please, would and could say yes to an expansive set of ideas for musical settings that Ralph Peer would bring to his records, handling a range of sounds, backing, and song sophistication levels within the roots-pop continuum, well beyond anything Peer had attempted with the Johnson Brothers or would attempt with the Carters. ("He could," Peer noted later, "record *anything*.") In a little over five years, Rodgers, with Ralph Peer managing, producing, and encouraging the sonic variations, would record with jazz bands, blues artists, jug bands, Hawaiian steel guitar players, and proto–western swing musicians, and introduce musical forms ranging from confessional sagas of a lone guitar slinging singer-songwriter to rhythmic, yodeling blues that spoke to the heartfelt concerns of down-home audiences (white and black alike), risqué novelties, and "rough and rowdy" songs that prefigured rock 'n' roll, with a potency that often spoke to audiences across the globe.

Together they would expand the very notion of what the "hillbilly-pop continuum" might include, and how far the resulting music might travel. Jimmie Rodgers would prove ready to write songs, alter old ones distinctively enough to be copyrighted, and find other appealing writers to work with to maintain a steady supply of fresh song material for him to record—Ralph Peer's priorities.

Rodgers's intimate, modern singing style was right and ripe for the higher fidelity of the new electrical recording era. It was marked by his natural, dramatic vocal stresses, determined by the individual lyric's emotional sense, not by the song's set meter, as had been the case with most traditional rural singing, and by his soon-famous yodel, with its breathy intimacy that registered as sexy at the time, putting him more in line with contemporary pop crooning stars such as Gene Austin than with previous hillbilly singers.

At Bristol, and in the weeks that followed, Ralph Peer and Jimmie Rodgers found each other. Since Jimmie would emerge as a key figure in the acceptance and extension of American vernacular music, becoming a new, precedent-setting sort of roots music star and, for many, a heroic, mythic figure, virtually every aspect of Peer's first encounter with him has been told and retold, with significant disagreement on some of the details; no one saw any reason to be taking notes at the time.

Peer likely first heard tell of Rodgers in a letter from Bascom Lamar Lunsford, the courtly North Carolina balladeer and impresario whom, as we've seen, Peer had recorded for Okeh in 1924 and 1925; their correspondence had continued. That spring, Lunsford had heard several local Rodgers appearances on the new Asheville radio station WWNC, including appearances by the Jimmie Rodgers Entertainers in May. The Entertainers, who had only banded together a few weeks before, when they'd met at a Rotary convention at Johnson City, Tennessee, not far from Bristol, consisted of Jimmie on lead vocals, and a young string band—the Grant Brothers (Claude on guitar and Jack on mandolin) and banjoist Jack Pierce—previously known as the Tenneva Ramblers, the name reflecting their home near that Tennessee-Virginia border. Lunsford met Rodgers soon after; in any case, by June 13, the Asheville radio station managers swiftly turned to Lunsford himself and his relatively genteel folk singing to replace the Jimmie Rodgers Entertainers' short-lived, low-paying radio program. Lunsford would recall sending that talent alert letter to Peer then, with the Bristol sessions just weeks away.

According to Rodgers's wife, Carrie, Jimmie was sending letters to both the Brunswick and Victor labels in the same weeks, heralding and overstating his limited Asheville radio "success," so the name could have surfaced in the Victor offices in that way as well. Moreover, since the Entertainers had played on a bill that featured none other than the Johnson Brothers back at Johnson City late in June, they very likely heard about Peer's oncoming recording sessions from the Johnsons at that point.

In any event, the arrival of the group at the sessions appears not to have been a complete surprise. Ralph Peer himself would vaguely recall sending Rodgers a letter saying, yes, he would record him on a given date, but his memory was even hazier about how the singer had gotten in touch asking for the chance. The consensus is that their first direct contact was made when Jimmie popped into Bristol with Entertainers member Jack Pierce, who was busy talking his father, a barber in town, into getting him a new used car, reliable transportation the band badly needed. Staying at the local boardinghouse run by Pierce's mother, the pair ran into musicians who said the Victor recording sessions were ongoing; they then met Ralph Peer at the temporary studio set up just across the street, and, as Claude Grant reported, Peer said, "Bring the whole bunch in and I'll listen to you; no promises."

The whole bunch arrived on August 3; the audition was immediate—and apparently tense. There was squabbling about who would have top billing on the records if the audition panned out, and about ongoing money issues. At sessions a day later, Jimmie Rodgers and the Tenneva Ramblers were both recorded, but as discrete acts—first Jimmie solo, then the band. Rambler Claude Grant recalled his brother and Rodgers having an argument, after which Jimmie went to Peer and asked to be recorded solo. Carrie Rodgers, in her memoir, presents Jimmie as the wounded party who discovered the Ramblers were set to record for Ralph Peer without him, then desperately, heroically going in and convincing Peer that he should also record on his own.

In fact, none of these things would have made much difference to Ralph Peer if the Entertainers as constituted had seemed viable to him, but it was obvious to all concerned that there was a fundamental awkwardness to the makeup of the recently cobbled together act. While the Tenneva Ramblers had expanded their repertoire somewhat to handle a few modern tunes, they were basically a hoedown dance-oriented rural string band, while Jimmie Rodgers had been fundamentally a personable, idiosyncratic solo singer of hot Tin Pan Alley and vaudeville novelties of the "How Come You Do Me Like You Do (Do Do)?" and "The Man on the Flying Trapeze" sort, some sentimental ballads, and some notably novel turns on the blues that included verse-punctuating yodels. He'd performed all of those at tent shows, at medicine shows, in any situation he could find with a chance of payment—for years by that point.

Peer never bought that the Jimmie Rodgers Entertainers were really a band at all, and made a quick decision. "I liked him the first time I saw him," Peer recalled of Rodgers himself. "He came in there and was obviously trying to put something over on me. . . . They were going to be the recording artists and he was going to sing with them. Well, he *couldn't* sing with them! . . . He was an individualist. He had his own style [and] it wouldn't fit with a bunch of fiddles. [So] I busted that up. In fact, the records would have been no good if Jimmie had sung with this group, because he was singing nigger blues and they were doing old time fiddle music; it's oil and water, and they don't mix."

(And yes, there he goes, in 1959, using the repugnant *n* word again, interchangeably in that conversation with "Negro," the generally accepted term of the time. In this case, it should also be mentioned that so-called "nigger blues," like "old time fiddle music," was a genre name regularly used for lowdown twelve-bar blues after—unbelievably—one George O'Connor, lifelong white man, had put one of the first blues on record under that very title, for Columbia, in 1916.)

"In order that nobody's feelings would be hurt," Peer continued, "I recorded the string band, gave them four selections. . . . I knew that would be useful to Victor, anyway. . . . Then I got Jimmie back alone and recorded him."

The lone living survivor of the Bristol sessions at this writing is Georgia Warren, age ninety-six in 2011 when asked to comment, and in August 1927 a twelve-year-old member of the large Tennessee Mountaineers church choir that auditioned the same day as Rodgers and recorded with Peer a few days later. She recalled some initial tension between Ralph Peer and Jimmie Rodgers on their first meeting: "Mr. Peer was nice to me, but I heard the argument, you know—Jimmie Rodgers and Mr. Peer. I was there. And Jimmie left. I don't know what they's arguing about—but he did come back!"

If recalled accurately, the youngster was likely witnessing an animated discussion not about billing or being allowed to record separately from the string band, but about the material Rodgers was and wasn't prepared to sing. Peer would later write: "We ran into a snag almost immediately because, in order to earn a living in Asheville, he was singing mostly songs originated by New York publishers—the current hits," which were, of course, not what Peer was looking for. "I did feel sorry for Jimmie on the first go round," he recalled. "He was quite ill at the time. . . . The man really had guts. I said to myself, 'I'd like to help this fellow all I can,' [but] when I told Jimmie what I needed to put him over as a recording artist, [he said that] if I would give him a week, he could have a dozen songs ready for recording. He just wasn't prepared for this sort of thing. He did just a few selections."

There have been multiple theories as to why one of his soon famous "Blue Yodels" was not among those few selections recorded at Rodgers's first, short session. Author Nick Tosches's widely circulated suggestion that Jimmie was still figuring out how to perform a novel style he'd only recently picked up from blackface minstrel Emmett Miller doesn't bear serious examination, since, as contemporaries noted and pre-Bristol handbills confirm, Rodgers had been performing his own blue yodeling vocal trick, quite distinctive from Miller's, for years (a distinction Peer surely would have recognized, since he had, of course, recorded Miller himself). Carrie Rodgers reported Jimmie's explanation to her that he'd held back his strongest suit strategically, so he'd have something really exciting to offer once he was under contract, but that smacks of a face-saving husbandly excuse being repeated.

Rodgers's lack of readiness for recording was surely, once again, the simple, understandable answer. Like so many blues singers and rural balladeers Peer had encountered previously, Jimmie had never had to take the material he'd performed live and edit it down for the length limits of a record, or to supply blues that had not just catchy verses live audiences would respond to, but clear themes or story lines that would distinguish one record from the next—what Ralph Peer "needed to put him over as a recording artist." The celebrated Mississippi blues talent scout H. C. Speir had turned Jimmie away earlier for precisely the same reason—not having enough material actually ready to record. At this point Jimmie Rodgers was less able to adapt songs virtually on the spot than A. P. Carter was.

These were the circumstances under which Rodgers stepped up to the mic at Bristol on August 4 and recorded multiple takes of his first two sides—the post–World War I, vaguely antiwar ballad "The Soldier's Sweetheart," with original lyrics Rodgers had put to an older tune, and "Sleep, Baby, Sleep," which contained some of his distinctive yodeling but was not representative of his "yodeling blues" specialty.

It is telling, regarding Ralph Peer's recognition of Rodgers's potential, that recording "Sleep, Baby, Sleep" went directly against his stated general principle of avoiding previously recorded songs with no chance of being copyrighted. That one had been a favorite of vaudeville performers black and white alike for decades, and had been recorded as early as 1902; Peer had produced at least one version himself. But it was what Jimmie had ready to record, and in this case Peer looked the other way and accepted it.

While he would later call Rodgers one of his "safest" Bristol bets, Peer was likely as much taken with Jimmie's sheer gall, would-be cunning, and clear ambition as by anything musical he'd yet shown. Rodgers had had an early, little-noted marriage that hadn't worked out, and as for being a traveler—if A. P. Carter was a habitual roamer, Jimmie Rodgers was an inveterate rambler. Ralph Peer could relate, and immediately empathized with Jimmie, seeing that, though far from healthy, he was fighting to find a way to support his family. Rodgers's wife and young daughter, unbeknownst to Peer, had been holed up in the rooming house nearby at Bristol, with no permanent residence at the time.

As Jimmie Rodgers's initial Victor single, which did reasonably well, was released a month before the Carters' first, Rodgers and family were relocating to Washington, DC, and became anxious waiting to reap the imagined grand-scale rewards of being a Victor recording artist. Rodgers took matters into his own hands, checking into an expensive New York hotel, and Peer received a call from him, in which Jimmie announced that he was ready for his next session. If the executive liked the performer's self-promoting gall, here it was in spades. He had Rodgers meet him at Victor's Camden studios on November 30, where they proceeded to record four tunes Jimmie had very ready—about a trainman (he'd immediately be promoted as "The Singing Brakeman"), a mountain home, and one that was the first of those yodeling blues with a theme that could stick, his career-making, bad-ass standard-to-be "T for Texas," which Peer retitled "Blue Yodel" for the record release. A small town Mississippi white man's frisky, knowing, and distinctively credible handling of the blues, it would prove to be a sales phenomenon.

The record launched the fabled career of the man eventually referred to as "the Father of Country Music," but it wasn't, in fact, marketed though Victor's hillbilly catalog, but as "mainstream" pop, with Rodgers's distinctive Mississippi accent and down-home references intact—a perfect realization of the direction Ralph Peer meant rooted pop music to take. Victor would soon include Jimmie Rodgers in an industry trade ad, hawking him not as a hillbilly singer, but as a key part of their stable of headliners with tremendous followings in the "popular field," right along with Helen Kane, Fred Waring, Frank Crumit, and crooner Gene Austin, of "My Blue Heaven" fame, noting that Jimmie "can pack 'em in with his guitar and down-South yodel any time."

By the time Peer returned to Bristol for a late October 1928 set of recording sessions, the *Herald Courier* noted of Rodgers (who had other places to be), "Now he is drawing over $15,000 a year and is on a circuit booked for twelve weeks making over half a thousand a week [the big-time Loews Orpheum circuit, as arranged by Peer as his manager]. He produces a record every month for the Victor Company and is Gene Austin's keenest rival."

Clearly Ralph Peer had been available to them for interviews once again. His relationship with Jimmie Rodgers remained uniquely close and strong, professionally and personally, throughout the remainder of Rodgers's historic, paradigmatic stand as a roots music star and hero—the mere five and a half years more of life and work America's Blue Yodeler had after Bristol. It's telling that while Ralph Peer would be forever most comfortable dealing with coworkers and even friends while wearing a suit and tie, and being seen in that formal executive mode, there would be, in this one case, shared trips to the New Jersey seashore by the Peer and Rodgers families, with most, Ralph Peer included, photographed in swimsuits.

Jimmie Rodgers, not inclined toward polite deference, would not be one more rural artist referring always to "Mr. Peer"; he always addressed his manager, producer, publisher, and career collaborator as "Ralph," and Peer is never known to have flinched at that. The autographed personal photo of Peer that Jimmie kept was signed, "To a great artist, a loyal friend, a great Pal, Jimmie Rodgers—Ralph Peer." In May 1953, in private correspondence with a sponsor of the huge Jimmie Rodgers festivals that celebrated Rodgers's lasting impact, Peer used words to describe this particular client and pal not used for any other, ever—though there were many more illustrious names and friends to come: "my protégé." Rodgers made good on what Ralph Peer wanted a broad swath of popular music to be and what, time would tell, the Bristol sessions were about.

Before Bristol, there had been a nearly total separation between the down-home music made on porches and in churches, square dance halls, and saloons, especially in the South, and the broadly accepted music put on records with professional sheen, as made by highly polished orchestras and trained vocalists for a more sophisticated population across the United States and around the globe. There had been some intermediate attempts to narrow that gap. First, the recording companies had maintained the familiar gloss by having New York pros record down-home songs; then, in the initial breakthrough idea Peer had defined and worked on at Okeh, they had looked for homespun performers of quality (in blues, hillbilly, gospel, regional jazz; in regional roots music in general) and began to record *them*, specifically for the same populations from which they had emerged.

Finding all of the attributes that were embodied in Jimmie Rodgers, and seeing the strong potential the Carter Family presented as well, Ralph Peer felt empowered, consciously, though partly by instinct, to attempt to usher in a crucial new concept for the future growth of American music—the meaningful and serious intermingling of region- and tradition-based roots music with modern pop. The yawning roots/pop gap, Peer saw, could be bridged with creative individuals who maintained their "up from the people" regional identities and accents in performances, on records, and in songwriting, but who also were entirely capable of being ambitious, polished, and focused professionals themselves, enough so to speak to a broader audience—in many cases, more capable of handling popular success than those New York studio pros, who'd rarely performed outside of the studio walls, had ever been.

You had to be able to identify people like that, whether they were performers first, or songwriters, or business partners, and you had to be sure of yourself enough to trust them with the power you would hand them. Working with them, you had to have the savvy to avoid polishing away or hiding the very attributes that made the performers and their music attractive, while looking for ways to extend their reach. These were necessary preconditions for the rise of country music, and in that sense, the town of Bristol's self-identification as the "birthplace" of that modern music has merit.

But the forward-looking roots and pop wedding at which Peer officiated resonated beyond the birthing of the commercial country "section"; it was the basis of making cowboy songs pop hits, helping transform territory jazz into the pop of the swing era, of taking blues toward R&B, making gospel sounds the root of much Southern-tinged pop, and eventually, to the making and marketing of the conglomeration that was rock 'n' roll. By analogy and extension, the marriage of pop and regional music from places outside US borders might and would impact the global pop marketplace as well—and the life and business of Ralph Sylvester Peer. He would have a direct hand in all of those further developments.

4

Reaching Out from the Roots: Southern Music, 1927–1933

BECAUSE HE DISCOVERED MAJOR TALENTS on his recording expeditions who'd been regional artists with some connections to musical traditions, Ralph Peer's A&R work of the 1920s and '30s has sometimes been conflated with that of the roving song chroniclers of his time and later. He has regularly been mistaken for a folklorist himself, or taken to task for a lack of "pure" devotion to traditional music outside of its commercial utility—as if that were his job or were somehow required to have been his aim. How his seminal song-establishing A&R and publishing work *did* relate to the musical preservation work of academic folklorists and song collector-promoters such as John and Alan Lomax is not a simple question with a simple answer, but what is unquestionable is that they were two markedly different sorts of endeavors, performed by professionals with essentially different motivations, outlooks, and goals.

Peer and such friendly commercial A&R competitors as Frank Walker, Art Satherley, and Dave Kapp, who were soon engaged in important work similar to his own, were looking for novel song material that would sell. They had no particular interest in preserving traditional music purely for its own sake, and they rarely suggested otherwise. Whether the needed novelty was derived from a song so old or obscure that no one around remembered it, as with Peer's resurrection of the Charlie Guiteau ballad, or from a new version of older material, or something dashed off this afternoon in the *style* of old-time regional songs, made no difference to them at all, as long as the result seemed reasonably likely to appeal to the public.

The contrast with folklorists had been stark; the academics had long been interested in documenting and preserving varying occurrences of old songs, especially lyric variations—the more ancient the better—but at around the time Ralph Peer was born, Texas song collector John Avery Lomax began modifying that pattern, considering relatively spry cowboy and hillbilly ballads and blues as worthy of documentation. Literary-minded folklorists had paid little attention to performance styles at all, or worried over the appeal of performances before recording when they occasionally recorded rather than taking notes, as any record-minded A&R talent scout would, since they were documenting songs, not selling performances. The folklorist/A&R distinction over interest in performance began to blur in the 1930s as well, as John Lomax's son Alan and his generation of folk song enthusiasts documented traditional music performing styles and promoted engaging practitioners of them, hoping that the performers and their songs would reach more people and generate musical, and even social and political, impact. (Woody Guthrie would emerge as a national recording artist in that context.) The song collecting and recording industry "sides" now shared interests in seeking success for roots music stars, despite their differing motivations. Their attitudes often remained quite different; roving song collectors typically assumed that pop music, particularly as recorded and broadcast, was inevitably going to dilute and hasten the demise of traditional regional sounds and culture, and they often showed distaste for it.

Clashes between preservationists and commercial popularizers like Peer over who—if anyone—had rights to successful versions of old songs arose quickly, but with surprising twists. An epic, relevant battle began in 1927, in Ralph Peer's first year of working with Victor Talking Machine, that would go on for over twelve years, over clashing claims to the authorship of "The Wreck of the Old 97," with Peer and company turning to a noted folklorist/collector for supporting expert testimony.

The actual wreck on that "mighty rough" line of track "from Monroe to Spencer" Virginia had occurred in 1903, and multiple people had been moved to versify about it, including two local performers, Fred

Lewey and Charles Noell. They used a pair of existing tunes and verses from older songs in their somewhat different tellings of the story—"The Ship That Never Returned" (by Henry Clay Work, of "My Grandfather's Clock" fame) and a related song, "The Parted Lover," the latter being the source for the familiar but seemingly tacked-on, moralizing ending about "never speaking harsh words to your true loving husband." Work's "The Ship That Never Returned" had been repeatedly parodied since the 1880s, and the tune had gotten around; it was still happening as late as the Kingston Trio's 1959 hit "M.T.A.," a parody partly written by John Lomax's daughter Bess.

There is no question that the first recording of the Old 97 song was by Ralph Peer's early Okeh hillbilly performer Henry Whitter, in 1923, as "The Wreck of the Southern Old 97," under Peer's direction. Whitter had heard a version years before sung by a friend of Lewey and Noell's, and adapted it, in ways that would later be well described in an excellent piece of musical criticism offered by an appellate court judge: "With the dramatic instinct of a real musician, Whitter shortened Noell's song and made it more 'peppy' by changing a few words, and quickening the time of the music of the song known as 'The Ship That Never Returned.'"

Henry Whitter's adaptation, with modifications that conformed quite well to the Ralph Peer model for taking old ballads pop, hadn't set the world on fire, but it was heard (or more precisely, misheard) by Vernon Dalhart, in whose hands in 1924 it would become one-half, along with "The Prisoner's Song," of the million-selling Victor single that sparked that label's serious interest in down-home Southern music. Massive sales brought other alleged composers of the song out of the woodwork, as so often happens, including one who sparked the epic court battle, David Graves George, who suddenly perceived that Dalhart's million seller was derived from a train wreck song he'd written years before. Henry Whitter had sold the rights to *his* Old 97 adaptation to a publishing company owned by Okeh executives such as Fred Hager (not by Ralph Peer, who'd had no publishing involvement at that time), so that wasn't a question. The immediate question was whether Whitter's verses that appeared in Dalhart's huge hit were penned by Lewey and Noell or by Mr. George.

To look into that, Victor turned to the somewhat eccentric Robert Winslow Gordon, who'd founded the Library of Congress's folk music archive and preceded the Lomaxes in working there. One of the first to try to build a nonacademic career as a folk song finder and promulgator, Gordon had offered himself to Victor as a consulting history detective earlier, but they'd turned him down. They hired him in 1927, though, the change of heart induced by an enthusiastic thumbs-up from Ralph Peer, who'd known of Gordon and liked his work for several years. Gordon had an ongoing column, Old Songs That Men Have Sung, in the popular men's magazine *Adventure*, in which he published lyrics to old "outdoor work ballads" and talked about their history. That reach into pop culture had not endeared him to academics, but it had to Peer. Bascom Lamar Lunsford had become one of Gordon's regular, acknowledged song sources by late 1925, the column crediting him for it in print and directing readers to seek out Lunsford's recording of "I Wish I Was a Mole in the Ground." ("You can hear Mr. Lunsford himself sing that if you will get hold of an Okeh phonograph record 40155," Gordon had written.) This was excellent and well-targeted ongoing publicity for which Ralph Peer understandably congratulated Lunsford, in a January 1926 letter on Okeh/General Phonograph letterhead, while adding as a coda, "I am glad to note this interest in the old time music." Ralph Peer valued Robert Gordon.

Hired, Gordon provided modern, sophisticated testimony about the Old 97 song in court, examining the exact wording in song versions for previous influence, and presenting visual aids that proved that Vernon Dalhart had used the Henry Whitter recording as his source. (He'd mistakenly rendered Whitter's phrase "lost his airbrakes" as "lost his average," which meant nothing at all.) Gordon then proved that those "airbrakes" were derived from Lewey and Noell's lyric, as were specific names and places in the song. He even arranged for a forensic chemist to analyze the paper and ink used on Mr. George's ballad, supposedly written down within ten days of the Old 97 wreck, revealing that it couldn't have been on that paper in 1903; it was likely brand new.

The judge on hand apparently couldn't follow these "modern" arguments, for all of their potency, and proceeded to award George $65,295.56 in damages against Victor for infringement, and for selling all those records—a huge sum higher than the cost of Peer's entire Bristol sessions expedition that same year. An appellate court later overturned the judgment, on the reasonable grounds that serious evidence had been ignored and that George had never proved authorship; it would take multiple legal decisions more, two by the US Supreme Court, before, twelve years later, Victor officially and finally was found not to owe David Graves George a cent. Many alternative, legitimate versions of "The Wreck of the Old 97" have been copyrighted since (Johnny Cash's, for example), but the standard original arrangement and lyric remain assigned to Lewey, Noell, and Work, thanks to that joint effort of Peer's team, folklorist Gordon, and lawyers.

By 1931, when John Lomax sought support for expanding the work of the Archive of American Folk Song at the US Library of Congress in Washington, he cited the rapid rise of the hillbilly and race record lines in commercial recording as a reason for proceeding with the documentary work—not, as might earlier have been expected, because the popular records' rise threatened the survival of the old oral culture, but because, Lomax argued, recordings such as Peer's underscored the music's *importance* to American culture, an argument that brought positive funding results for his work.

Within months of Bristol, Ralph Peer was enjoying some very substantial positive funding results of his own. As he recalled later, under the terms of his agreement with Victor assigning mechanical royalties to him, including mechanical royalties from other labels' recordings of Rodgers-composed songs, for example, and whatever publishing royalties the songs earned for performance and in print versions, he took in "close to a quarter of a million dollars" for the second quarter of 1928 alone. Whether that figure was exact or not, he was certainly making money well beyond the level anyone had predicted, much of it going to him directly through his as-yet-unincorporated and only marginally operational United Publishing business. The extraordinary cash flow was a potential embarrassment for him, if of a sort many in the music business would be happy to learn to live with; it seemed *too* conspicuous, a potential red flag and point of contention with Victor executives, though they hadn't initially been paying close attention.

The idea came to him that it might be wise to establish multiple operating corporations to spread the totals around—more window dressing than a substantive change, but less blatant. He now formally incorporated

United Publishing (with wife, Anita, its owner, on paper), Ralph S. Peer, Inc. as an artist management company (based at 145 West Forty-Fifth Street, near Times Square), and the firm that would come to be the core of his business interests for the thirty-two years that lie ahead for him—Southern Music Publishing Company. Southern was initially located at the nearby Paramount Building, at 1501 Broadway.

The incorporation document for Peer's Southern Music, dated January 31, 1928, is a multipage encyclopedia of possible future directions for a firm in the music business born at that time, some of them no doubt legal ground-covering boilerplate, others reflecting some of Ralph Peer's thinking on what conceivably might lie ahead. Southern Music Publishing might, the birth document states, publish, print, and sell sheet music, scores, and music books; buy and sell copyrights; manufacture, buy, and sell recording equipment, records, record players, radios, and cabinets, and also "apparatus for the simultaneous broadcasting of sound and still and/or motion pictures in any and all developments of the said method" [i.e., television]; operate commercial broadcasting stations, theaters, or a motion picture distribution company, produce shows, manage performers and bands, act as a booking agent, and more.

There is no reason to believe Ralph Peer seriously considered starting his own record label, equipment manufacturing company, or motion picture studio, but he would never again work outright for anybody else's, either. At the outset, Southern Music Publishing was little more than another copyright placeholder; it was well into 1929 before Southern was truly operating as a publishing unit, with song pluggers working to place songs, a small business staff, and the like, but under modified terms.

Two months after Southern Music's founding, on April 4, 1928, a working agreement with Victor stipulated that Peer would provide his services "in obtaining talent for the use of the company for its various catalogs, in assisting in the selection of the repertoire to be used . . . and assisting in selling said selections" (doing the same A&R work), while assigning to the record company copyright control of the songs he would record. Victor could decide what to do with those copyrights, including whether to put out the recording involved at all, and the rights to license live performances of the songs, but Peer, on through most of 1928, would receive the standard two cent mechanical royalty for each side "of every record manufactured and sold . . . throughout the world." (He could still pass on that standard cut of the mechanical royalty to the songwriter, and he did.) His still-mounting mechanical royalty bonanza remained a source of contention, no matter how many on-paper companies he filtered them through.

"I could split these royalty statements four ways as I collected the copyrights," he explained, "but the people I was dealing with were not stupid at all, and they brought pressure on me to do something." Under those circumstances, Peer made Victor yet another audacious proposition that autumn—rather than remaining a licenser of songs to Victor, he would actually cede ownership of Southern to *them*, a setup that would be closer to what Shilkret had wanted from the first.

Peer first suggested that he and Victor might co-own Southern Music Publishing 50/50, sharing the profits equally—not just from mechanicals, but on *all* future song copyright revenue streams recorded by Victor, for which Southern would be the general publisher. This was a variation on his "label owns a publishing company" idea back at Okeh, and it might well have expanded his business overall in practice, extending his reach beyond the hillbilly and race catalog songs he recorded to more broadly popular new songs likely to provide sheet music publishing value and performance licensing royalties as well. He would always have one eye on that bigger popular market. They didn't go for it. He countered with a deal under which he'd be paid on a percentage-of-profits basis but remain in place as "President and Director" of Southern; they didn't accept that either.

The new arrangement they did agree to, which made both Shilkret and the Victor board of directors more comfortable, since performance royalties and sheet music royalties would be Victor's, as well as final decisions on where and when to place songs, went into effect on December 2, 1928, and remained so for four years, into the time when Victor Talking Machine itself had been acquired by David Sarnoff's RCA. Victor would own the fledgling Southern Music Publishing outright, and Peer, while continuing with his artist and copyrightable song repertoire work as before, would be paid on a more constrained basis, not on the net "per record sold" mechanical royalties, but on a piece of Southern's profits. Victor saw to it that there were still incentives for him to keep finding hot new songs to record; he was to be paid half of the unit's annual profits up to $50,000, and 35 percent of profits beyond that on songs he obtained for the company—in practice, new songs from and for the artists he'd record—but just 12.5 percent falling off to 7.5 on profits "derived from selections which may be secured by the Company other than through the efforts of said Peer."

For those key years, then, the record company and its corporate owners were the ones with control over Southern Music Publishing, buying and selling copyrights, pushing other labels to record Southern songs Peer had come up with—or not—and deciding on performance uses. As their roots music A&R man, Ralph Peer would be treated more like a conventional employee; they assigned in-house recording directors to whom he had to report on his recording expeditions and sessions, men he had to persuade to release the records, artist-by-artist and, at times, virtually song-by-song.

The new truth was, whatever power in the recording industry Peer actually achieved during this peak period of A&R work, and whatever payment, came from his own ability to find the right artist with the right song and arrangement and put them together on records. He needed new hits, and he needed to sustain good and trusting relations with both the hotter artists he was responsible for and the executives to whom he had to report. While Peer would often boast of his control of song copyrights as a key element of his success, over time, much of that career success would actually come from *yielding* considerable autonomy to the artists and underlings he worked with, not from controlling them. And for now, his situation at Victor offered not a portrait of a man in "control" of much of the business at all, but of a hired consultant needing to produce results for the company.

At first, Peer's go-to "Record Sales" executive was Loren L. Watson, who'd been a talent scout and occasional record producer in the Memphis area for Vocalion and Paramount Records, then headed Victor's jazz department. When in late 1930 Watson's own growing role became controversial among power-jealous RCA Victor executives, he was replaced by an old friend of Peer's from the Okeh days, a virtual Peer protégé who first came over to Victor as an accountant—Eli Oberstein. ("I knew he was a live wire," Peer recalled.)

In ongoing correspondence through 1932, Peer's relations with both men and the corporation they worked for was clearly casual, friendly, and focused on their common interest—identifying artists and producing recordings of strong songs that would sell records for Victor. The January 1929 acquisition of Victor Talking Machine by David Sarnoff's rising Radio Corporation of America brought remarkably little change in those working relationships; for once, key personnel *did* remain in place, as is so often promised in major corporate takeovers and so rarely adhered to.

The young RCA of the late 1920s was a glamour stock, running up in price and hoopla in proportions equivalent to those of the Internet or mobile communications explosions (and bubbles) of our time. Sarnoff's acquisition of Victor Records was just one part of his ambitious new media agenda that included establishing RKO Radio Pictures in the movies, furthering Victor's sound-for-film technology, setting up an unmatched network of NBC Radio broadcasting stations (in fact, *two* national networks, NBC Red and NBC Blue), and investing heavily in R&D on that outer-edge technology starting to be referred to as "television."

With a strong hand in all of these technologies and business units, and RCA Victor alliances and extensions in place across the globe, there were supposed to be, as twenty-first-century observers need hardly be told, "synergies"—the sorts of synergies that Ralph Peer understood and could use, as he'd already experienced recording known radio artists at Okeh and promoting recorded artists with live shows and broadcasts. His immediate goal for his performers and their music—broadening their reach—was already becoming evident by the time of the Bristol sessions, and was very much in line with the formidable multimedia goals of Sarnoff's dynamic and generally admired technology company—more in synch than they could have been with crusty old Victor Talking Machine.

In 1923 the "old" Victor had timidly suggested, but not demanded, that their record dealers time sales events to artists' radio appearances, as well as live local shows. For RCA Victor, there was now some regional success with that strategy. As a manager, Peer would see that a promotable artist like Jimmie Rodgers would show up for in-store autograph signings or radio appearances in the long line of towns and cities in which he appeared.

It would take until the mid-1930s for the full power of broadcast and movie appearances to augment sales of both records and live performance tickets to become clear. By then, recording roots performers capable of "going popular," such as Fats Waller or Gene Autry (who began as a Rodgers imitator and recorded plenty of Peer-published songs, though he was never recorded or managed by Peer), would be stars on-screen and on the air, with regular radio broadcasts out of Chicago.

In the short term, though, much as digital media would be at the turn of this century, the new media of the day were often seen as threatening by the established music industry—radio a threat to record sales, since you only had to buy one radio and then your music came into the home endlessly, and movie musicals to live performance, since for the price of a ticket you no longer had to wait to see the performer on infrequent vaudeville stops in your town.

Movie musicals and changing economic times would indeed combine to finish off live vaudeville, but very few hillbilly or blues or hardcore jazz performers, even those who'd had substantial vaudeville touring success, could make a quick leap to the broadly targeted musical talkies, as pop recording and stage stars such as Bing Crosby and Al Jolson did. During the very first year of the new RCA-Victor combine, however, the soundtrack unit contracted with Columbia Pictures to produce twenty-six Columbia Victor Gems, sound shorts in which popular singers entertained. Ralph Peer arranged for Jimmie Rodgers to star in one of them, shot at Victor's Camden, New Jersey, studio, the now-famous short *The Singing Brakeman*, in which he performs "Waiting for a Train," "Daddy and Home," and "Blue Yodel (T for Texas)," another indication of how Peer and Victor viewed Rodgers's strong potential for broad appeal. Audiences savored the sight of Jimmie performing his train whistle imitation, looking wistful thinking of Daddy, talking with ladies at the train depot—and taking a close-up. The Peer-developed blues star Mamie Smith appeared in another of the Columbia Victor Gems, singing about jailhouses.

As for internationalization, soon a central Ralph Peer preoccupation, releases by such popular RCA Victor artists as Rodgers, Waller, and, eventually, the Carter Family sold well as far away as Australia, India, and Japan. It was not simply serendipity that in 1932 the popular London show band Jack Hylton and His Orchestra recorded and performed Jimmie Rodgers's version of "In the Jailhouse Now" as a pop-jazz tune; both RCA Victor and Peer were working to make such international adoptions happen. It was exactly the sort of roots-to-pop movement and border busting that Ralph Peer wanted to encourage.

Peer is not known ever to have turned down any new media or marketing opportunity that arose for the acts he signed; he tended to be enthusiastic about them. It's certainly no coincidence, for one example, that Victor marketers introduced, very tentatively, a photo album–like leatherette cover that could hold five or six 78 records, an idea moved over to the "light" music arena from their classical and operetta lines, where they'd introduced them to market entire long works or to collect Caruso 78s. One was created for holding a collection of Jimmie Rodgers releases, with intimate liner note biographical information that appears to be Peer written or suggested.

As he explained to Rodgers himself in a letter of August 18, 1931, "Victor is preparing a special Jimmie Rodgers album which the dealer can give away with every sale of ten Rodgers records or some such scheme. The album will be very attractive, containing a special article on your life history. The jobbers will buy this a little below cost and use it as an advertising proposition to increase the sale of Rodgers records." *America's Blue Yodeler*, as the handsome if record-free 1931 album jacket was called, marked the first arrival of the idea of having *albums* by a popular artist, years ahead of its time—though, of course, the term "album" was more literal than we'd think of it later, since it was not a set collection of recordings.

A second, more celebrated experiment was related to this "buy an album's worth" ploy in its purpose. After Rodgers's "T for Texas" was released as "Blue Yodel" at Peer's suggestion, the point being to emphasize its most notable qualities, Peer and RCA Victor went on to title a dozen more "blue yodels" just that, with the famous "numbers" attached—"Blue Yodel No. 2," "No. 3," and so forth—in today's jargon, "branding." While the singles chosen for numbering weren't always particularly distinguishable from other Rodgers blues recordings that weren't, the message was clear: if you liked the earlier blue yodel, here's another one that you don't yet own but should; you'd like it. Meanwhile,

Peer succeeded in encouraging Victor's Southern Music to actively promote use of the songs to the growing numbers of Rodgers imitators, effectively stimulating a "blue yodeling" craze. As it happened, after the initial blue yodel releases, people and artists recording the songs found it a lot easier to recall and distinguish "California Blues" than its official title, "Blue Yodel No. 4," so the numbering practice did not become a recording commonplace.

Through these peak A&R years with Victor and RCA Victor, Peer's work and travel were ceaseless. From 1926 through 1933, using essentially the same transportable, temporary warehouse or hotel setup he used at Bristol, he could be found running recording sessions in familiar cities he'd used as location recording sites for Okeh—New Orleans and Atlanta, Dallas and Chicago, and with new recording stands in Memphis, Louisville, Houston, and Hollywood, plus, of course, back in New York and Camden. (Memphis was used as a site often enough that they rented a facility there that they could return to as needed.) It was common for artists he recorded regularly to be called to Camden for one set of sessions, meet him in some other town a few months later, and record closer to their homes when he came through.

For a man whose place in music history is often over-condensed and reduced to that of a promulgator of "market segmentation," or even "segregation" because of his role in developing the discrete hillbilly and race music arenas, Ralph Peer could rarely compartmentalize his own roles or areas of musical responsibility at all—not in the course of a session, or in the course of some days. "I had to run the recording end of it, and then I had to decide what was to be issued, and then I had to sell the sales department on what I'd already done," he recalled—which gives a sense of his ongoing duties, even in his new, less autonomous situation, but doesn't quite capture the flavor of doing all of those things in multiple popular roots music genres at once.

The back-to-back, even overlapping quality of Peer's work is not clarified by typically compartmentalized genre discographies or histories, which report on one musical field at a time. His trips piggybacked discoveries and signings, cross-genre. The 1927 sessions that followed immediately after Bristol, at Savannah, during which Peer recorded cowboy singer Carl T. Sprague ("Rounded Up in Glory"), also included

high-spirited jazz pianist Sugar Underwood ("Dew Drop Alley Stomp").
The Atlanta stop, where he recorded Henry Whitter with his ingratiating
new fiddle-playing partner G. B. Grayson on classics such as "Train 45,"
also marked Peer's first sessions with the great, nuanced blues singer
Blind Willie McTell ("Mama T'aint Long Fo' Day").

In Savannah, Peer went to a beachfront nightclub one evening and
found the orchestra of Blue Steele, "the Dean of Dixieland," playing a
new pop song written by his sax player, "Girl of My Dreams," and saw in
it possible regional *roots* potential, another indication of how imprecise
these definitions could be.

"I thought, well, I'll record this fellow because he's in a small-time
deal and he's [only] worked in Southern cities," Peer recalled. "I thought
this would fit into my hillbilly catalog. . . . Well, of course, 'Girl of My
Dreams' hit and sold 250,000 records or something, [although] it wasn't
a very good orchestra. And then, two or three years later, Gene Austin
did it and sold a million records! . . . There was another instance of *only
recording material that was local in nature*. I could have had this fellow
record some popular song of the day from Broadway, but instead of that,
I followed the precept of '*Always the Amateur Stuff*.'"

Peer also continued to develop new underserved roots genres. Keeping things regional and novel, a year later, he would produce only the
second Cajun record ever released, the gleefully hard-driving and genre
tone-setting "Mama, Where You At?" by Maius LaFleur and Leo Soileau.
He had them staying at the same hotel as Jimmie Rodgers; it was the
same week of sessions that produced Rodgers's "My Carolina Sunshine
Girl" and "Waiting for a Train." (Peer would never see that act intact
again; a little over a week later, LaFleur was shot dead in an altercation
having to do with a truck.) During that same stand, Peer recorded Blind
Willie McTell singing his celebrated and lasting "Statesboro Blues."

This is how Peer's sessions and life now would go. The November
1929 sessions at the Women's Club in Atlanta, for instance, in which
Jimmie Rodgers recorded "Mississippi River Blues" and the jazzy
"Nobody Knows But Me," was part of the same recording stand at which
the Carter Family first recorded "Wabash Cannonball," and "Jimmy
Brown the Newsboy," and where both Rodgers and his sister-in-law Elsie
McWilliams, who was on hand as songwriting backup for Jimmie, met

the Carters for the first time. And on the same day and at the same place Peer recorded "Anniversary Blue Yodel (Blue Yodel No. 7)" with Jimmie, he recorded "Drive Away Blues" with Blind Willie. There's no record as to whether McTell and Rodgers chatted, but it would not have been at all unlikely.

Peer's recording ventures in Memphis the following May yielded in short order "Cocaine Habit," "Fourth Street Mess Around," and "Papa's Got Your Bath Water On" from the raucous Memphis Jug Band, an outfit Peer loved, and also new standards-to-be from those determinedly non-raucous Carters, including two of their substantial hits, "Worried Man Blues" ("It takes a worried man to sing a worried song . . ."), and "When the World's on Fire"—a gospel song that would provide the basic melody and guitar strum for Woody Guthrie's "This Land Is Your Land."

Peer's ongoing search for new genre development did not stop with the early Cajun recordings. Back at Okeh, by 1924, he and Clarence Williams had recorded some of the earliest examples of American pop blues adaptations of Jamaican and Trinidadian music, calypso included, employing immigrant performers who'd established some New York vaudeville and even Broadway credits, and whom Okeh had initially recorded as West Indian artists solely for the West Indian audience back home. The interplay of Caribbean and local African American music in New York, even as the populist black nationalist movement led by Jamaican Marcus Garvey was at a peak of influence in Harlem, was a harbinger of future hemispheric musical interactions in which Peer would take part. Among those he worked with was the sly and highly influential singer Sam Manning, who followed him to RCA Victor, now recording, with backing by Donald Heywood's West Indian Band, "Touch Me All About, But Don't Touch Me Dey," a title typical of the comic, suggestive material found to be acceptable when sung with a Jamaican accent. Peer would have opportunity to feel prescient about predicting in the 1920s that calypso like Manning's, as both tropical and topical, could extend its audience and return to North American, even global popularity regularly, in cycles.

Another case of genre expansion: Soon after Peer left Okeh, in June 1926, African American artists he'd worked with there who'd been emerging as talent scouts in their own right, including Sara Martin, arranged to make the very first fiery black Pentecostal gospel recordings with the innovative vocalist and pianist Arizona Dranes, freshly developing music that would go on to play such a key role in future American musical developments. Not to be outdone, the following February, in a particularly dramatic instance of Peer's seeking out the novel and stepping up to competitive challenges, he was on the lookout for what he referred to as "holy roller" music. ("This thing kept preying on my mind," he'd note.)

He stopped at the small town of Bethel, South Carolina, and, no more intimidated by racial barriers that generally prevented a white man from going into a black church than he had been going into black nightclubs in Kansas City, he quickly convinced a large part of a church choir to get onto a bus. They all drove to Atlanta, where he recorded them as the Big Bethel Choir, getting the previously unheard dynamic holiness *group* sound on record with "Hand Me Down the Silver Trumpet, Gabriel."

What artists came out of all of Peer's seeking, signing, and recording in his first six years as A&R scout for Victor? In that central hillbilly line development effort, there's no doubt that bringing Jimmie Rodgers, the Carter Family, and Blind Alfred Reed to the roster would have seemed enough. After Bristol, he added Grayson and Whitter as a duo, Harry "Mac" McClintock (the "Haywire Mac" of "Big Rock Candy Mountain" fame), cowboy singers Carl Sprague, Jules Verne Allen, and Stuart Hamblen (the latter would later become a major gospel songwriter), future star and longtime Peer songwriting client-to-be Jimmie Davis (in his early, sexually suggestive blue yodel mode), and such important, if less-generally-remembered, country acts as the Carolina Twins (Fletcher and Foster), the harmonizing yodelers Fleming & Townshend, Hoyt "Floyd" Ming, topical songwriter and Rodgers acolyte Dwight Butcher, and the entertaining banjo and guitar duo the Allen Brothers.

The Allens, who hailed from Chattanooga, mixed current event–based songs (their "Jake Walk Blues" concerned the epidemic of paralysis of poor folks who'd drunk adulterated Jamaican ginger tonic) and sometimes suggestive, often funny hillbilly blues that proved very appealing to audiences, and also to Ralph Peer, who'd heard a few sides they'd recorded for Columbia and invited them by letter to record for RCA Victor.

Famously, they had been so adroit with blues material that Columbia, apparently mistakenly, had released one of their records on its race label. Their "A New Salty Dog," as recorded with Peer, would be one of the better sellers of the era and later become, with some variations, a bluegrass standard. Lee Allen, who added jazzy kazoo to many of the fast-paced sides Peer recorded with him and brother Austin, recalled for historian Charles Wolfe how Peer insisted they stick to their knitting:

> Peer was a very nice man, a very fine man. . . . He was *the* man—we were under contract; we'd sign for our rights and his rights. . . . We'd get to record once a year, and at that time, that paid very good. When we went into New York and went into his office, he would set up a place for us to play so he could hear [the songs we had ready] and he would decide on the ones he wanted to have. He wouldn't accept some that we wanted to do; he wanted to stay in the blues . . . if he thought it wasn't blue or in the blues, why, he'd object to having it recorded; he'd just say, "I believe if you stay in one line of stuff, you'll do better." [But] most of the stuff that was current events, why, he would release it. . . . If we thought we had a good thing ourselves, then we'd let Ralph Peer decide that—and if he thought it wasn't good—usually, he *did*—he'd record it, whether it ever was released or not.

The blues artists Ralph Peer recorded in this same period for RCA Victor's race records line tended to be, by design, *not* more of the vaudeville-seasoned women, but fresher rural blues and jug band artists—overwhelmingly male, and almost all with their first recordings—in marked contrast to his Okeh years. The commercial success of Blind Lemon Jefferson on Paramount Records, beginning in 1926, underscored the new opportunities for bluesmen with guitars. The general switch in emphasis reflected, once again, the relatively stronger sales of records among rural audiences, and their tastes; many fans of vaudeville blues and jazz were, at least for the time being, moving on to following the radio. The extraordinary list of artists Peer recorded for the RCA Victor race line included Will Shade's Memphis Jug Band, Gus Cannon's Jug Stompers, Frank Stokes, Jim Jackson, Furry Lewis, Willie McTell,

Memphis Minnie, Tommy Johnson, Booker ("Bukka") T. Washington White, Sleepy John Estes, and Yank Rachell, a list of historic proportions, and in the important if lesser-known names category, Richard "Rabbit" Brown ("James Alley Blues"), Blind Willie Reynolds (the same singer as the Blind *Joe* Reynolds of "Outside Woman Blues" fame), Ishman Bracey, Clifford Gibson, Luke Jordan, Will Weldon, and Walter Davis.

In jazz, Peer had been the first to record Fats Waller as a soloist, pulling him out of backup bands for the famed solo organ sides he recorded at Camden; he also recorded the modernizing, revamped, and era-defining Bennie Moten orchestra (which now included Count Basie, "walking bass" innovator Walter Page, and jazz blues vocalist Jimmy Rushing), Fletcher Henderson (with Roy Eldridge, Coleman Hawkins, Ben Webster and Chu Berry in his orchestra), Johnny Dodds, Jimmie Lunceford, Eddie Condon, and relatively late in their careers, Jelly Roll Morton and, again, King Oliver.

This is, to anyone even passingly familiar with American music of the period and its influence ever since, an astonishing array of artists in all three of these occasionally overlapping arenas. Many of them, of course, were genre-shaping giants. It would take—and in a number of cases there have been—whole or multiple volumes dedicated to many of them to do them justice musically and biographically. But those among them who recorded time and time again, who had impact over time, had in common the full set of Ralph Peer requirements—that willingness to seek sound variations for novelty on records (and for musical innovation beyond that), the ability to keep coming up with fresh songs that could be copyrighted, personalities that led to additional public interest, and, not least, a degree of self-motivation and determination that lay behind possessing and acting on all of those at once.

Bennie Moten, for example, whose recording career had been fostered by Peer from the beginning and who followed him to Victor, was in the process of adding essential musicians from the old, now-celebrated Kansas City Blue Devils to move from the riffing innovations of the twenties to the swinging rhythms we now associate with the thirties and forties. That was fortuitous—but it was also just the sort of creative tendency Peer saw in Moten when he recorded more than a few passing sides with him in the first place. The Moten and Fletcher Henderson bands Peer was recording were by this point setting the pace in defining swing, regularizing rhythms, and working up set arrangements, at the beginning of the period in which formerly regional, specialized-interest jazz music exploded into the central general popular music of America and the Western world.

Peer continued to record and manage Jimmie Rodgers in this same time frame, often matching him with musicians and sounds that shaped his voluminous output, with jazz bands, proto-western swing bands, and even Hawaiian steel players. The Hawaiians included such leading lights as Lani McIntire and Charles Kama, who would have songwriting and recording careers of their own—another line of regional roots-based American pop. Peer would record 112 Jimmie Rodgers sides in five and a half years, roughly equal to the output of the Beatles and Rolling Stones at their commercial peaks; the sheer output and sonic variety is why we know Rodgers's music as we do.

Elsie McWilliams, the gung ho, musically trained sister of Rodgers's wife, Carrie, had been drafted by Rodgers to supply customized song material as soon as his regular recording sessions for Victor began and he realized how many fresh songs he was going to need to keep up the steady stream of recordings Peer and the label had in mind for him. Credited and sometimes, by her own choice, uncredited, McWilliams had a hand in writing close to forty of the songs Rodgers recorded. Ralph Peer quickly came to value her contributions, and brought her along for a number of sessions on the road so she could demonstrate her new compositions for Jimmie, who did not read music—and, sometimes, to come up with material for him on the spot. Peer even presented her with a portable Victrola for use on the road, in case she had to listen to new records or song demos when summoned for some emergency songwriting at remote locations.

Elsie was, for instance, on hand in Dallas, in August 1929, as Rodgers was about to be backed by Hawaiian steel guitarist Joe Kaipo. She recalled, "Boy, it was hot. It had a ceiling fan and it had a desk fan there, but I was just burning up. . . . They were talking about Hawaii. . . . Mr. Peer had told them 'I'll have to take Jimmie down for a recording date in Hawaii some time,' and Jimmie said 'Oh yeah; I'll find me a hula-hula girl and bring her home with me' . . . and (one of the men) said 'Well, everybody does!' That night, I was sweating and couldn't lay on my bed, it was so hot, and I got up and wrote 'Everybody Does It in Hawaii.'" The next morning, Peer heard Kaipo toying with a tune he'd written and suggested to Elsie, "Get some words to it and we'll let Jimmie sing it and record it." Within a few hours, having heard it just once, McWilliams had written the words in shorthand for what became Rodgers's "Tuck Away My Lonesome Blues."

Peer's sessions with Jimmie Rodgers, for all of their variety, had a set pattern to them. Rodgers would meet with Peer before each recording session, often in hotel rooms or in some studio space where the assembled backup musicians were out of earshot, and go over each song Jimmie had in mind to record, to see if any lyrics and rhythms needed to be straightened out for the sake of lyric simplicity or rhythm, or if they needed to send—quickly—for additional, varied musical backing. This was typical of the more hands-on side of Peer's A&R approach.

"My policy," Peer explained, "was always to try to expand each artist, by adding new accompaniment, or adding a vocalist, or what-have-you. Finding new stuff month after month was not easy!"

Peer couldn't help but take to the jug bands of Louisville and Memphis—down-home, folk jazz and novelty hokum bands closely associated with blues venues and players. It was in these outfits' very nature to come up with great entertaining variations in music, songs, instrumentation, and lineups, just what Peer liked to see. Memphis Jug Band leader Will Shade became another of the trusted allies Peer regularly identified and came to rely on for lining up sessions, material, and performers. An African American harmonica and guitar player and vocalist, Shade would sometimes be logged in at sessions as outright coproducer. ("Mr. Peer and Will Shade Present," the logs would read. No "Mr." for Will Shade—but a job; he was responsible for hiring the always-changing lineup of the Jug Band, which scored with such hits as "Stealin', Stealin'" and "K.C. Moan.") Peer had occasionally provided whiskey for the sessions, beginning in 1927, which always helped matters, but that was hardly the total reward. He put Shade on retainer, providing a twenty-five-dollar weekly advance on his composer royalties, a sum large enough that he could buy a house and even some RCA Victor stock. For Will Shade, as for the

Stonemans, the Carters, and Jimmie Rodgers, the relationship with Peer changed his life—at least for a while.

It will forever be difficult to determine when precisely Peer was "in the room" or not at many of the Okeh recording sessions he had been responsible for, since he had multiple jobs to do at the time and could approve a day's recordings and leave it to the engineer to record them. It is generally safer, though, to place him right there, and hands-on, at the hillbilly and race sessions of those early RCA Victor A&R years. There has long been speculation as to how involved he was with various records and musicians, particularly in the race records sessions, and the answer, unequivocally in this period, is very much so.

In the case of the important and varied May 1930 sessions at Memphis, for example, the detailed notes that Peer sent back from the sessions to executive Loren Watson at RCA Victor's New York headquarters have survived. They are full of chatty commentary on what he had recorded, which ones he believed should be the next records released, and how to market them. However much he chose to give people the impression, later in life, that the more rooted parts of his musical world were a sort of necessary burden he'd put up with until he could get into more sophisticated music, his excited, involved, and knowing private commentary when he was at work in roots music regularly betrays tremendous relish for both the music and its makers, and with that side of the music business.

Of newcomer Bukka White (recorded on this first outing as Washington White), Peer would report, "This is a new artist brought to Memphis by Ralph Lembo of Itta Benna, Mississippi. . . . The four blues selections are very good cornfield type and should have a big sale in the delta country. 'The Panama Limited' is a train piece played on the guitar and it should be coupled with 'The New Frisco Train.' 'I Am In the Heavenly Way' and 'The Promise True and Grand' [and two other numbers] are sacred selections done in Holy Roller style. We have nothing else like this, and I recommend a quick release of one of these records."

There is more than business calculation going on there; there's excitement. White himself recalled, of those first sessions he'd ever taken part in, "I never forget that [long as] I live. I was singing church songs, you know, and he paid me good. Yeah; he really paid me good. 'I Am in the

Heavenly Way,' I used to sing in the church. . . . My grandfather was a bishop, and my daddy was a musician, and that church stuff was too slow for me, so I cut out and went on my daddy's side! And I been sliding ever since."

Peer would interact with the performers even in relatively obscure acts, enough to send along translating explanations to New York of what the local, very down-home terminology referred to. Regarding the fiddle-driven hillbilly instrumentalists the Grinnel Giggers, whom he recorded during these sessions, he explained, "This is a string band from Manila, Arkansas. . . . A grinnel is a local species of fish and a gigger is one who gigs or spears said fish!"

In a June 6, 1930, side note to Loren Watson, at the close of those sessions, Peer demonstrated how attuned and responsive to consumer trends he could be, if also how cold-blooded, when necessary, as a tightening recording industry and changing tastes now demanded. (The rural audience, black and white alike, was, thus far at least, still less likely to be distracted by radio from buying records.)

He'd been set to do some new recordings with the entertaining, shrewd black vaudevillian Jim Jackson, who'd recorded the insinuating "I'm Wild About My Lovin'" and the hilarious "I Heard the Voice of a Pork Chop" with Victor two years before and who, as a semiofficial scout, had sent other performers in Peer's direction, including Sleepy John Estes. After meeting with Jackson once more at that point, he had second thoughts about recording him again, at least for the time being, with interest in uptown vaudeville blues markedly fading:

"Practically all of the Race business down here is with the country Negroes, and I would classify Jim as a little too high-brow for that class. Under the circumstances, I am dropping the idea of using him for the present. . . . Jim does not have any worthwhile [new] material and I am not convinced that he is now of enough importance to justify teaching him new stuff." Ralph Peer had had to make the quick determination that Jim Jackson was now too hip for a rapidly shrinking, more rural, country blues–favoring room.

Peer's experience working multiple roots music genres could pay off in unanticipated, unpredictable ways. He'd already seen the regular success hillbilly singers had had with topical songs for some time, so when he had Memphis Minnie in the studio with Will Shade's jug band outfit during those same Memphis sessions (very likely introduced to Peer and RCA Victor by Shade, who was a friend), he encouraged her to record "Meningitis Blues." Minnie would later describe having suffered from meningitis herself before writing the song, and likely brought it up at the session; understanding the strength of topical songs, Peer was enthusiastic about getting the song on record, and talked up rushing it out quickly in his note back to headquarters. ("As you probably know, there is a meningitis epidemic in this part of the country . . .") It was the same day and same location at which he had the hillbilly Allen Brothers record their topical "Jake Walk Blues" to mark that other regional epidemic.

Another seemingly unlikely artist for such material whom he encouraged to record topical songs was Fats Waller, who had never done so before Ralph Peer made the suggestion. In 1927 the sudden death from tuberculosis of African American Broadway star Florence Mills came as a major shock to the Harlem community and to her fans on both sides of the Atlantic. Peer suggested Fats take up the theme, which he did, in the song "Florence," recorded by Juanita Chapelle, again in "Bye Bye Florence," recorded by Bert Howell (both with Fats on keyboards), and on "Memories of Florence," an instrumental Waller recorded himself.

Peer also looked for musical synergies between the acts he recorded and managed, some of which surprised audiences, though they had little reason to be aware of the background. For example, "Everybody Does It in Hawaii," Elsie McWilliams's lightly suggestive pop change-up for Jimmie Rodgers, "happened" to be recorded by King Oliver in late 1929— with early steel guitar wizard Roy Smeck taking a solo. Most famously and strikingly, performers he was recording for race records would show up, credited or uncredited, on recordings by hillbilly artists recording in the same sessions. Guitarists Ed Schaffer and Oscar Woods, the Shreveport Home Wreckers, backed Jimmie Davis on multiple records at sessions in Memphis and Dallas during which the Wreckers were also recorded. Blues guitarist and singer Clifford Gibson and the Louisville Jug Band featuring Clifford Hayes (who'd recorded for Peer at Okeh) both backed Jimmie Rodgers during his 1931 Louisville sessions—at which Peer was also recording those acts themselves. And he'd use virtually the same arrangement and musicians on "Please Don't Holler,

Mama," with bluesman Ben Ferguson as he used with Rodgers and the jug band on "My Good Gal's Gone Blues."

Peer gave his artists considerable leeway, as well as aid, in lining up their instrumental backing, but this pattern of what we might call session "economy of presence," with musicians at hand being put together regardless of race, strongly suggests active producer involvement in these pairings—practical and perhaps even offhanded calls that also represent cracks in the long-standing racial segregation of recording sessions. The same pairings might just as easily have been forbidden, whatever the cost. The most famous integrated combination Peer recorded, however—Father of Country Music Jimmie Rodgers with foundational jazz giant Louis Armstrong and his wife Lil Hardin, on "Blue Yodel No. 9" in 1930—clearly happened as more than a convenience. The greatest likelihood (since there is no precise testimony on this matter) is that Peer saw that Louis, with whom he'd had that role in raising from band member to front man, was headlining at the Cotton Club in Los Angeles, actively pursuing pop stardom and some sort of Hollywood career, and he got in touch with Lil, with whom he'd always had more of a working relationship, about the casually approached but historic session with Rodgers, who was in Hollywood for recording sessions himself.

This is not at all to suggest that Ralph Peer was any sort of political or social activist concerning racial integration in music, in the sense that, say, producer John Hammond was in fostering integrated outfits by design at Columbia in the late 1930s; such activism was not his style, nor particularly reflective of his socially open but business-oriented politics. But presented with situations where it looked like the music and combination of players would work, he said yes, and openly so. Saying yes as he did was audacious for a time when, for example, white jazz guitarist Eddie Lang was working with black blues and jazz guitarist Lonnie Johnson under the assumed blues name Blind Willie Dunn, an apparently all-black pair of ax aces being considered more likely to be accepted than a racially mixed one.

Jazzman Eddie Condon, just relocated to New York from Chicago (white, and later a promulgator of the popular, throwback Dixieland jazz style), recalled approaching Ralph Peer in 1928 with the idea of recording a racially integrated band that included musicians he'd caught at the

Small's Paradise club in Harlem and, after a little persuasion, getting the simple, straightforward positive response from Peer, "This will be for Victor; I hope it's good." When sides such as "That's a Serious Thing" resulted, Peer called them "excellent . . . an interesting experiment." Peer would then record Condon (on banjo), Jack Teagarden on trombone, and young Gene Krupa on drums behind Fats Waller on "Lookin' Good but Feelin' Bad" the following year. With those steps from Peer and Victor, the door to racially mixed sessions had been pried open, at least a bit, and other labels took notice.

Ralph Peer's experimental pairings were not limited to the interracial. There is no doubt about the background of one—the well-remembered comedy record pairing of the Carter Family and Jimmie Rodgers. Peer and the marketing team at RCA Victor recognized that the audiences of his two personally managed acts—one home-and-hearth church people and one rambunctious bad boy—were partly different, however much they overlapped, and decided to put them together for potential audience expansion of both. A note from Eli Oberstein to Peer dated Christmas Eve 1930 reminded him of the increasing urgency of getting on with what was clearly a previously discussed proposition: "I hope that some day you will be able to get Jimmy (sic) Rodgers together with the Carter family before Jimmy quits this earth. . . ."

The records, awkward but much loved, were recorded at Louisville the following summer, emphasizing that the Carters were Virginia mountain folk and Jimmie a Texan (which by then he was, having moved there in part because of the deteriorating health Oberstein refers to) and a cowboy (which he wasn't, except by occasional costume and material choice), a sort of lighthearted first meeting of country and western. The Sara Carter–Jimmie Rodgers duet on "T for Texas" that concludes the "Carter Family and Jimmie Rodgers in Texas" sketch, Jimmie's only recorded duet with anyone, was a particular highlight. Steel guitarist and blue yodeler Cliff Carlisle, present at the time, later recalled the lighthearted atmosphere Peer maintained during the sessions: "A.P. made that big mistake on that record, on that one take. Recorded half a day and then cussed on it; he thought they had it turned off, and they didn't. Peer liked to died, man!"

In practice, Ralph Peer was far more personally involved with artist management of the Carters and Rodgers than with any other of his acts. In these years, A. P. Carter wrote some songs outright, and regularly combed the countryside for song material to adapt for the family act to record. All of the Carters, and A.P. especially, came up with songs and performances that would have a huge impact, not just on sales but in terms of influencing musicians to come, songs that would see renewed life after the folk music revival of the 1950s and '60s. From 1928 to 1932, all recorded by Ralph Peer, came "Keep on the Sunnyside," "Wild-wood Flower," "I'm Thinking Tonight of My Blue Eyes," "The Foggy Mountain Top," "Wabash Cannonball," "Lonesome Valley," and "Worried Man Blues," and there were more to come on that order.

If the three Carters maintained their reluctance to tour, they proved quite willing to take long excursions from Maces Springs for recording purposes—to Camden, Atlanta, Memphis, Charlotte, Louisville, and then to New York City. There was cross-cultural comedy in some of the first Peers-meet-Carters encounters after Bristol. A.P. and Sara's daughter Gladys recalled her family's frantic preparation for the first stopover by Ralph and Anita Peer at the "Carter Fold" home place, quite reminiscent of the Stoneman family's Peer visit story. With just two days notice of the impending visit, there was much killing of chickens and sunning of feather beds, intended both to welcome and impress the Peers. In that short time, A.P., with his usual determination, managed to construct and paint a whole new garage to house the Peers' car during the stay—which turned out to be too short to use, since he built it the size of a Model-T Ford, the only size he could visualize, and the Peers arrived in a Cadillac. They all ate at Maybelle's place, by the Carters' choice, because she was the only one with a matching set of dishes.

"The Peers learned what red-eye gravy was," Gladys recalled, "and they loved our country hams. They loaded us kids down with toys and those fancy chocolate candies . . . and bless Mrs. Peer, her pretty new dress had chocolate smears and little fingerprints all over. . . . The Carters were left with a new recording date, and more money than they had ever received at one time in their lives. . . . Anyway, after the Peers left, daddy bought our first new [not used] car." It was a Chevy.

Anita Peer also features prominently in Gladys's narrative of the Carters' first trip to Manhattan, in 1933, for a one-off radio broadcast on NBC, not long after the birth of Maybelle's daughter Anita, named for Mrs. Peer. (The Carters were favorites of Anita Peer's in return; "The Storms Are on the Ocean" was reportedly her favorite of their songs.) Thanks to the miracle of mechanical royalties, Maybelle and Sara were wearing fox stoles. Peer sent a chauffeur for them to New Jersey, where they waited. He also provided tickets to a Broadway show, and they went on to visit the new Empire State Building, the zoo, and Coney Island, with Anita taking them to drink champagne and to try on stylish hats. Agonizingly, she didn't, however, take them for any meals, Gladys recalled, because "these New York people, who we were hoping would treat us to a dinner at noon as we like to eat, [all of their cash on hand was being spent on a car repair] had their dinner from nine o'clock at night until midnight."

Peer demonstrated continuing trust in the Carters' ability to come up with new material, and rarely involved himself in that process. In 1964 Sara would detail for researcher Ed Kahn the background of many of the songs the Carters were then recording. The origins varied greatly, from lyrics sent through the mail by strangers and set to music by A.P. ("The Winding Stream") to a number written by Maybelle, some by Sara herself, but credited on record, as they all were, to A.P., who was nevertheless always scrupulous, whatever the label read, about dividing the income among the three of them. Some were A.P. adaptations of songs from old gospel songbooks and sheet music; some were in fact original to him. A good many were songs A.P. had found in his regional rounds accompanied by slide guitar–playing African American bluesman Lesley Riddle, whom he'd met on one of those rounds in late 1927, and who became his traveling companion and human recorder of songs heard on their song searches together.

The settings Peer would gladly accept for their recordings had range. There were Sara vocal solos, vocal duets and occasional trios, and a few A.P. vocal solos. Riddle's influence on Maybelle's guitar playing (on her freshly acquired top-of-the line *f*-hole Gibson) becomes evident in the increasing sophistication of the Carter Family recordings in these years, in the likes of the driving "The Cannon-Ball," the slide guitar that accompanies the winning harmonies and yodels on "Foggy Mountain Top," and the relatively complex, rhythmic pick on "When I'm Gone." Meanwhile, without any obvious or specific pressure from Peer, their variety of material expanded to include the likes of the light "Chewing Gum" and "If One Won't, Another One Will," and the topical "Cyclone of Rye Cove." The Carters were increasingly sophisticated about where the music they could do best intersected with what Ralph Peer was looking for.

There were some musical disagreements. In later years, Maybelle recalled wanting to do more takes of some recordings than Peer would approve, to "make it perfect," laughing ruefully that "they'd" always choose the one with instrumental mistakes. Her complaint—not an unusual one, then or much later, when musicians of perfectionist inclination speak of record producers who've said "that's done; lets move on" faster than they'd like—must reflect at least in part Peer the A&R man containing session costs, as he was tasked to do. It is also further evidence of his personal ranking of an involving vocal and an overall sense of spontaneity as most important in making popular roots music records work.

It would be anachronistic to even try to identify a "Ralph Peer sound." The latter-day conception of a "producer" with a trademark style was not yet in practice, or even imagined, but Peer certainly had strong opinions about what worked and would sell, and the privileging of strong personality presence and sonic novelty remained among them. The instrumental perfection that Maybelle Carter wished for was a very secondary question, as critics of some of the guitar work and backing band choices heard on released Jimmie Rodgers records also would note.

Unsurprisingly, Peer played a very active role in taking Rodgers's recorded sounds and subject matter further afield than the Carters'. He encouraged those wide-ranging sonic turns that appeared in Rodgers's records, introduced him to new songwriters, such as future cowboy songwriting heavyweight Billy Hill, who had approached him with useful ideas, and went out of his way to ease Rodgers's collaboration with Elsie McWilliams, once he saw how well it worked. (Peer would also arrange for alternate, broadening sounds for Jimmie's records—the Hawaiian and orchestral backup, for instance.)

In 2007 guitarist and songwriter Hoyt "Slim" Bryant, who lived to be older than one hundred after bringing a new level of jazz-influenced sophistication into country guitar playing in the 1920s and '30s, recalled for this author Ralph Peer's active involvement in putting those guitar sounds on Rodgers's records such as "No Hard Times" and "Whippin' That Old T.B.," and then tapping him to be a sort of translator between Rodgers's more down-home musicians and New York orchestral backup in sessions there:

> Mr. Peer saw the possibility there. He was right there in the room, waiting for everything to go on, one thing after another, and if you hit on something he didn't like, he would say so, [like on] the ones we did in New Jersey, strictly right along the country music line. The ones we did in New York—he changed it; that was Ralph Peer who did that. He says to me, "Can you play with these New York musicians?" And I says "Mr. Peer, I can play with anybody." I was putting my best foot forward, you know. I think that he knew what I was doing. I won't call it "upgrading" the music; he just wanted to change it a little bit, and this is why he added two violins and a clarinet and me and made a little orchestra out of it. He told me that at that recording studio, we would be reading music, the sheet music. They *didn't* have bona fide "arrangements," but we ran over the tunes two or three times and a simple arrangement came to us.

And that was the genesis of the sound of such memorable, forward-looking summer 1932 Rodgers recordings as "Miss the Mississippi and You," "Prairie Lullaby," and "Sweet Mama Hurry Home."

Bryant, like Carlisle, also spoke of the jovial "take it as it comes" atmosphere Peer could maintain in the recording studio—tested when a song music copyist, hired to write down what was actually played during a Rodgers session, had some issues:

> He had a man settin' at the piano taking these tunes down, and writing the music down to them. And right in the middle of one of the records, he had a shelf of booze sitting on the piano, too, and the booze fell off on the floor and ruined the record. And Peer just laughed! We did the record over again.

I liked Peer; in fact, after Jimmie died he took over a lot of my songs, and he was still the same guy. I never heard him get rowed up about anything, you know. We did seven books of our music, and we withheld publishing rights on them all when we recorded them—the right to publish the words and the music. And Peer was good to let us do that; he collected a royalty off of the record company and paid us and Jimmie and whoever the writer was.

For all of his encouragement of sonic variation, Peer would later come to the conclusion that the sonic variety he had pressed for in the interest of novelty, some of which may even have made Jimmie Rodgers uncomfortable and less spontaneous in practice, was not as key for sales as he'd once believed: "The accompaniment didn't have as much to do with it as I thought it did at the time. . . . Truly, it was the *ideas* of the song . . . that put the thing over; even if it was badly done it would be a big seller." The conclusion could be taken with a grain of salt, however. By that point, Peer had become a full-time publisher, no longer an A&R man, and may have been thinking about the importance of the sound of a record a lot less in general.

Ralph Peer generally afforded Rodgers plenty of leeway to bring in or request musicians of his own choice to back him in recording. ("What accompanists will you want for your next work?" Peer asked in an April 1930 note.) That was not so very different from what he provided his trusted leaders of jug bands and jazz groups. He'd also arrange with Jimmie by mail where and when they might get together to record next, coordinating location recording, when possible, with Rodgers's busy touring schedule. And he did not hesitate to offer musical advice as his record producer: "I hope that you have been working on some new numbers and will have some good ones ready the next time," he suggested in October 1931. "Avoid the ballads, as they are not going at all. . . . I will appreciate it if you will try and figure out some more sketches similar to those we made with the Carter Family. . . . Take care of yourself and let me hear from you as much as possible. . . . Ralph."

There was, however, a fundamentally different quality to Peer's working relationship with his star Singing Brakeman compared with any of his other clients, even the Carters. Peer demonstrated occasionally paternalistic but generally quite concerned involvement with Jimmie's ongoing, overlapping personal and professional issues, much on display in a steady string of correspondence between them. The tone—encouragement, reassurance, and scolding included—would seem utterly typical to anyone who's witnessed relations between managers and their touring meal ticket stars of much more recent vintage. The often rascally Jimmie Rodgers, no less typically—even archetypically—sent back notes and telegrams from the road notably short on details of what he was actually doing out there (and with whom), but rarely shy about asking to have more money sent, then still more money, or requesting that Peer help him get his long-lost first wife Stella's lawyers off of his back, since they were pressing *him* for money.

Attempting to manage the era's favorite bad-boy rounder from a distance had its lighter side. In August 1930 Peer received a letter from a Mr. Finhorn, a New Orleans lawyer representing an aggrieved A. B. Simon, to whom Rodgers had apparently handed a problematic check at a large local hotel—to cover some roulette chips, according to Jimmie, and for debts having nothing to with gambling according to Simon. Jimmie claimed he'd been drunk and confused and swindled into writing a check at all, but Finhorn was reporting to Peer that twenty witnesses could testify that he'd been sober; Jimmie was being accused of knowing what he was doing.

It seems that Rodgers had gotten creative and told one of those "witnesses," Mark Boasburg (a notorious bookie who'd done jail time), that he had funds to make the check good on deposit, back home in Texas, at the Bank of Kerrville—all very reasonable, except that there was no Bank of Kerrville. Simon was demanding his money. Ralph Peer, of course, could only surmise what had taken place, and wrote to Rodgers, with a tone that is pure artist manager. "Jimmie . . . *if* this check was given for a gambling debt, I do not think the amount can be collected. As I do not know the entire circumstances, I do not know how to advise you. It seems to me that the best course is to do nothing at all. It will be impossible for these people to collect, as you have no assets in the state of Louisiana. I am assuming that you were actually swindled out of the money and that this is not an honest indebtedness."

When things were flush for Rodgers, before the Great Depression began to take a devastating toll on the entire recording industry, Peer had even been advising Jimmie on buying and selling shares of stock in RCA Victor, General Electric, and RKO Pictures. Down-home Jimmie had become a stockholder. By 1932, however, Rodgers, in declining health, was also nearly bankrupt—a result, in part, of Jimmie and wife Carrie's fast-and-loose star-style spending, their low savings, and Jimmie's tendency to be an easy touch for other musicians and hangers-on. By then, though, the context for Jimmie and Peer alike was the previously burgeoning recording industry's virtual collapse.

Rodgers's fairly dependable sales in the high-flying half-million-copy neighborhood were over; five to ten thousand copies sold had become the new "good," and as early as spring 1930 Peer would need to reassure Jimmie that "on a percentage basis your stuff is selling at least as well as anybody else's. In other words, you are still at the top of the heap, but the heap isn't so big." By that November, Peer's tone had darkened further: "The next royalty statements will be just too bad, but you will still not starve to death. Stop spending so much money—you worry me because you won't build up a reserve. Business is still very much in the dumps. It can't get worse so it must get better." A recording industry that had seen total US sales of $74 million in 1929 took in $46 million in 1930, $17 million in 1931, and was down—and nearly out—with just $5.5 million in 1933. It would not truly snap back until the late 1930s.

Ralph Peer was, to state the obvious, a more practiced manager of finances than Jimmie Rodgers, and he was able to help Jimmie deal with his financial straits by means of a "loan" agreement of August 30, 1932, under which Peer laid out some $5,500 toward the mortgage for the Rodgerses' rising Blue Yodeler's Paradise mansion in Kerrville, Texas, with little expectation of ever being paid back. The secured mortgage not only kept a large new roof over the Rodgers family's heads, but served as collateral so Jimmie could pay off the personal first marriage debt as well.

While the implication has generally been overlooked, it's certain that Ralph Peer, with his pay tied to levels of song use in RCA Victor records sold, now had substantially less income coming in himself than he'd had in the glory days before 1930. The label's record sales division had much less coming in overall, of course, and was cutting back on personnel, on expenses like rent on that building they'd regularly used for recording in Memphis (now dropped), and, devastatingly for many recording artists,

on the number of recording dates and releases. As year-end 1930 correspondence from record division sales manager Eli Oberstein to Peer
noted flatly, "We are not selling sufficient Race Records to cover our
expenses." Less than three weeks later, Oberstein noted, "I am trying to
put out only sure stuff on the Hill-billy list. I have cut our list down to
five records and am limiting my sacred and fiddling records to one every
third list."

These were seriously difficult times. Letters to the RCA offices and
directly to Peer began to arrive from everyone from Noah Lewis of Cannon's Jug Stompers to Clifford Gibson, Blind Willie McTell, and some of
the hillbilly artists, all pleading to have more sessions or at least to see
unreleased sides already recorded put out. The answer had to be no. Peer
sent Noah Lewis ten dollars out of his own pocket, with regrets.

In August 1930 Henry Whitter wrote to Peer announcing the death
of his musical partner G. B. Grayson in an accident. Clearly afraid that
his own recording contract was about to die along with his partner, he
suggested in the same letter a replacement he already had lined up, radio
personality and banjoist Fisher Hendley. Peer approved that new pairing
for his longtime client, despite the current sales climate, and a new, if less
successful, recording team was born. When Peer tried to help out another
historic Okeh-era friend a few months later, however, Oberstein
responded, "I cannot see any use for Fiddling John Carson." That may
have just been straight business talk, but under all of the obvious business pressures, some subtle shifts in the tone between Oberstein and Peer
were now detectable, too.

By early 1932 RCA Victor was dropping all but its most productive
artists, sticking with that "sure stuff," and taking fewer risks by means of
shorter-term contract commitments; they had little choice in the matter.
Faced with that pressure, Peer, in moves that have been widely misunder-
stood ever since, found a way to help out Jimmie Rodgers and the Carter
Family, using an approach that would be commonplace later. Instead of
having them wait forever for small mechanical royalty payback that,
given the drastically reduced sales being experienced, might never come
at all, he saw to it that Rodgers was paid $250 a side and A.P. Carter
$100 a side up front—in the Carters' case "payable in ten days," though
it was unlikely that the difference between the old per-side rates and the

new considerably larger advances was ever going to be recouped through record sales.

The new agreements guaranteed fewer sides per year for the artists, as few as four in the Carters' case, but Peer never held either act to that few recordings even at any one session, let alone per year. He might have better explained the changes; Rodgers would ask him by letter where his royalties were, not understanding that he, in effect, already had in his pocket any that might happen to be forthcoming, in the form of the larger advances. That the Carters were supposedly forced by Ralph Peer to agree to a dastardly "no more royalties" contract has appeared in print regularly, since some chroniclers took a naïve misunderstanding of the situation by A.P. as writ—when, in fact, Peer was seeing to it that they got more cash in hand quickly than they would have under the original contract. (For the record, the Carters' mechanical royalties for the whole first quarter of 1934 proved to be just $69.94; that's the payment level he was sparing them from.)

In May 1932 Ralph Peer reached both his often-attention-focusing fortieth birthday and the fifth anniversary of his marriage to Anita. They were still living in East Orange, childless, in a two-story corner house shared with Anita's parents, Harry and Elizabeth Jeffers. Anita had been no stay-at-home; she had accompanied Ralph on voyages to France, Spain, Cuba, and England, as well as to places like the Carter family's home fold, but their lifestyle together was not particularly more lavish than that typical of upper-middle-class couples of the time. With pay from record sales on which Peer's income had been depending near collapse for everyone, everywhere, and with even the mighty RCA Victor record unit severely damaged by the sharp downturn, events conspired to change his focus.

Peer's ticket out of the declining state of affairs in recording, somewhat ironically, was a result of the relative *strength* of David Sarnoff's multimedia empire. The rise of radio was hardly all bad news for the Radio Corporation of America as a whole, which now included NBC and a large piece of the RKO motion picture studio. The incoming Roosevelt administration intended to take a closer look at monopolizing practices than Hoover's had, however. Sarnoff, now happily presiding over a Depression-challenged yet growing empire from the recently opened RCA Building tower at 30 Rockefeller Center, was concerned that as a major media *consumer* of songs, in films, on records, and on the air, continuing as a song publisher at the same time might bring unwanted federal scrutiny. The concern was not irrational; in the future, there would in fact be, for example, federal intervention to split the film- and music-oriented talent-marketing agency MCA from its holdings as a talent-buying film production company—Universal Pictures—as both a concentration of power, and unfair competition for other talent sellers. It was certainly not clear as 1933 approached where new lines might be drawn, and Southern Music was certainly a much smaller business unit in Sarnoff's empire than the others, negligible by comparison with NBC or RKO, or even RCA Victor.

"Mr. Sarnoff," Peer recalled, "woke up to the fact that Southern Music owned copyrights, and licensed copyrights—and on the other hand, RKO Radio Pictures . . . were *buying* synchronizing rights [the rights to use songs in films] from publishers. . . . He had heard of the Justice Department in Washington, and he was just a little afraid that he shouldn't be on both sides of the fence! He was a very astute man."

And so with larger issues to worry about, on November 1, 1932, precisely one week before the election of Franklin D. Roosevelt to the White House, the astute RCA Victor Company offered the Southern Music Publishing Company, Inc. to Ralph Sylvester Peer in its entirety, for the current book value of the company—$31,000, payable in increments over the next two years. Peer accepted; control over Southern reverted to him, and with Southern the copyright holder of so many recorded songs, so did the revenue from mechanical rights and from the songs' live performance rights, shared with their songwriters—but no longer with the record company.

Earlier that year, a lighthearted "Soulful Silhouettes" profile of Peer in the musicians' business magazine the *Metronome* noted that he "hates publicity, grapefruit, and mufflers," has a favorite saying, "You never know till you try," and "is bothered by people saying 'You look like Herbert Hoover'—and he actually does."

Maybe he did, but in November 1932, Ralph Peer, the music publisher, had himself a new deal.

5

Breaking Loose, Branching
Out, Starting Over,
1933–1940

RALPH PEER HAD TO BEGIN THINKING like a publisher. He was already thinking that way early in 1933, when he heard from the husband-and-wife songwriting team of William and Mary Goodwin of Tempe, Arizona. In 1905 they had registered the copyright for a song titled "An Arizona Home." It began, familiarly, as "Oh, give me a home where the Buffalo roam" and had a chorus that went "A home! A home! Where the deer and the antelope play." It had been published, with little effect, by the St. Louis firm Balmer & Weber, but after several publishing acquisitions, it was published and copyrighted by Peer's Southern Music. Peer and his staff hadn't even been much aware of them or their song until then.

As difficult as it is to imagine, "Home on the Range" as the world has come to know it had remained relatively obscure until just then; there had been a few recordings of it, but the song was not yet regularly sung in schoolrooms, turned to as a patriotic anthem, or considered an archetypal example of Americana. Then, on November 8, 1932, a group of reporters had sung the song on FDR's New York doorstep on that night of his election, since he'd claimed it was his favorite song. Maybe it even was; at any rate, interest in the song immediately exploded. Bing Crosby had a hit version, and so did Metropolitan Opera baritone Lawrence Tibbett. In Chicago, blue yodeler turning cowboy singer Gene Autry was performing it on the radio. Kay Francis sang it to Edward G. Robinson in the feature film *I Loved a Woman*. In part, the song spread so quickly because it was understood to be in the public domain.

The Goodwins were claiming to have been the song's true authors. It appears to have occurred to Peer that, whatever financial gain there might be in it for Southern (potentially a large one if the Goodwins' claim held up), battling for these obscure clients would be a strong public indicator to songwriters of how far he was willing to go for them. He understood that their story was potentially credible, because virtually all versions of "Home on the Range" in circulation were derived from the one John Lomax had included in his book *Cowboy Songs, and Other Frontier Ballads* in 1909—published after the Goodwins' song had appeared as copyrighted sheet music.

On March 27, 1933, Ralph Peer wrote to Lomax directly, asking how he viewed the Goodwins' song, and Lomax replied: "I had thought, until receipt of your letter, that my version of 'Home on the Range' was the first published of that song, both the words and music."

Later, Peer went on the record about his reaction to the very different folklorist mind-set about these matters, primed to finding public domain tomes beyond the reach of copyright, and he did so bluntly: "It amuses me—the people like Lomax who . . . started going around. . . . They hear one of these songs, and it's always 'legendary.' And I've always taken the position, 'Well, I don't know whether it's legendary or not. Now you *prove* it; I've got a contract on it.' . . . You'd be amazed the number of times that nobody's been able to bring anything to show that it was 'legendary.' They just *assume* that it is."

He well knew that if a court held that later variations on a song were in essential ways derived from an earlier published, copyrighted version, the publisher and the songwriters were entitled to be paid for its performance. This looked like a "Now you *prove* it" case in point, and a question worth pursuing.

On June 7, 1934, Peer's Southern Music filed suit in New York's US District Court seeking a half million dollars in damages against some twenty-nine defendants who'd made recent commercial use of the song.

They included First National Pictures (owned by Warner Brothers), Sar-noff's NBC (in a sort of new declaration of Peer independence), CBS Radio, and such old-line Tin Pan Alley– and ASCAP-aligned music pub-lishing firms as Carl Fischer, Schirmer, Edward B. Marks, Sam Fox, and Mills Music. Remarkably, pending settlement of the issue, "Home on the Range" was temporarily banned from use on the airwaves. The media defendants turned to the Music Publishers' Protective Association (MPAA), the long-established trade group, which hired powerhouse New York lawyer Samuel Moanfeldt to lead an investigation to bolster their defense.

Teams of lawyers and detectives moseyed west to find the origins of the song. As Moanfeldt recalled, "I interviewed a great number of people . . . ex-cowboys, people who were employed as cooks in cowboy camps, ex-stage coach drivers and buffalo hunters." He got written statements from many that they'd known the song before 1890, and then, to top it off, a song was reprinted just at that time (1934), "Colorado Home," said to have been sung in Leadville saloons and vaudeville houses in the 1880s and '90s in the mining town's wild heyday, with an opening verse and chorus essentially the same as the Goodwins.' A copy of the Kirwin, Kansas *Chief* from February 26, 1876, eventually surfaced with the poem "Western Home" by a Dr. Bruce Higley reproduced on the front page; Moanfeldt soon had detailed affidavits from Higley's surviving friends affirming that he'd written the words, and that the tune was soon added by another local, Dan Kelley. That songwriting pair has been credited with the song ever since, and the suit Ralph Peer had taken the lead in initiating collapsed without ever going to court.

There was no bonanza for Peer and Southern in that one. "Western Home" proved old enough that it actually was in the public domain; the Goodwins never did explain where exactly they'd heard the previously existing song elements. That the song only took off after the chorus evolved into the catchier, poppier "Home, home on the range" is some-thing Ralph Peer, roots pop specialist, might have predicted.

The "Home on the Range" case, for all of its prominence in the press at the time, was not the first thing on Ralph Peer's mind, however; his future as an A&R man for RCA Victor was. In a note early in 1933, he warned A. P. Carter: "I will have to make the next recording either in

Camden or New York, as nobody will go to the expense of sending out a recording expedition." It was a sign not just of cutbacks, but of ongoing, systematic curbing of what he could do. With his reemergence as a music publisher, the stage was being set for him to end—by choice—his dramatic and fruitful, but often frustrating years as a record-producing A&R man and talent scout.

"I never was able to really get what I wanted out of Victor—a close connection with the popular department," Peer suggested in retrospect. However pop Peer's roots music recordings became, the Victor A&R board never saw any advantage in extending his reach into that broad arena, and an increasingly ambitious Eli Oberstein began treating Peer as an obstacle in his own career path. The former Peer protégé had begun doing some limited record producing and talent signing for RCA in 1930, and now wanted to do more, make more, and to have final say about more, without interference from anyone else.

In early 1931 the combative Oberstein attempted to shoot down any pop promotion of the successful, slightly jazzy orchestrations of Peer's friend Archie Bleyer, which were being adopted by a number of jazz musicians. (A generation later, Bleyer would head Cadence Records and produce the Everly Brothers.) In a memo to Southern, Oberstein noted firmly, and seemingly acidly, that "undoubtedly Archie Bleyer will help sell 'hot' tunes [a phrase still suggesting "pop," not jazz] to musicians, but musicians do not buy records, and unless the tunes he turns out can be sold to the record buying public, we will not be interested in making any of his material." A handwritten comment added to the memo by Ralph added: "No reason, though, why tune should not be published." And, at that point, Bleyer's soon lucrative "Business in F" was. Having continued as a principal discoverer of new songs that the firm he'd founded published, and with staff members such as chief accountant Robert S. Gilmore (known as "Bob" or "Gill") working there right through the Victor purchase and sell-back, Peer had never entirely lost influence at Southern Music Publishing.

Oberstein's lengthy memoranda to Peer began to head for the jugular in the months leading up to the late 1932 Southern sell-back, as he pointedly rejected practices as fundamental to Ralph Peer's point of view and livelihood as favoring new copyrights over recycling old ones. "Our jobbers," he said in one memo, "will not buy unknown tunes—likewise our dealers . . . and unless we can do something to bring a record to their attention, we find that the record is unprofitable."

Facing the record market's collapse, the dealers would likely have been happy to see *any* new records doing very much at all, however known or unknown the song. Oberstein saw to it that established hit songs were placed on the B-side of records in the jazz line all through 1931, effectively cutting the opportunities for Ralph Peer to introduce new material there. Peer would later contend that Oberstein also spread deliberate misinformation within RCA about his expense account spending at that time: "He had a carefully planned campaign to supplant me."

In fact, after the turn of 1933 Peer would supervise no further recording sessions besides the last, tragic one with Jimmie Rodgers in New York that May, and three sessions with the Carter Family at Camden, one in June and two more the following year. With the returns to RCA Victor from new Southern Music–published songs eliminated, Peer's position within A&R was weaker, and Oberstein could quietly block him from producing anyone but that very short list of artists he was actively managing. "Theoretically, I continued with it," Peer would note, "but practically, he pushed me out as soon as he could."

As jolting to Ralph Peer as this might have seemed, there is no direct evidence or even a strong suggestion that giving up on A&R and supervising recording sessions seemed a deprivation to him, however much he had enjoyed it over the years before. His diminished clout at RCA Victor and the active opposition were factors, but those might just as easily have been reasons for him to look for A&R job possibilities elsewhere. He never did. No one could predict confidently at the time when record sales would begin to recover or if, facing the rise of broadcasting, they ever would. Pressures were building, and not for the first or last time, Ralph S. Peer had unnoticed escape valves at the ready. Inadvertently, RCA Victor had been supplying them.

All the way back in 1928, based on his early recording successes for them, Victor Talking Machine had asked Peer to investigate another, previously little-explored competitive problem they were having—their relative failure to export records to Mexico and to Latin America in general, despite their commercial successes elsewhere around the globe.

"Because I'd solved the hillbilly position, and their distributors were so well-pleased with that," he recalled, "they thought, 'Well, maybe Peer can help us about Mexico.' . . . I never did understand how they got this idea, because I'd never been in Mexico, I didn't speak any foreign language, I'd never talked to anybody about the subject, and had no ideas about Latin American music. . . . I got on a train and went."

He would come to see this unexpected cross-border excursion, generally unknown to those who associate him only with recording his celebrated roster of American hillbilly and blues artists at that time, as fated, as a chain of positive accidents and coincidences that made it feel, as he put it, like God was "sitting on my shoulder." Ralph Peer would arguably make more life-changing connections, and come to more career-shaping realizations as a direct result of that 1928 trip south of the border (so reminiscent of his earlier fact-finding mission to Virginia to gauge African American interest in buying records by black artists), than from any of the countless trips he would make in his life.

He identified Victor's basic problem within two weeks: Wagner & Levine, a music publisher ("Wagner" was pronounced "Vogner," German-style), had effective control over the locally composed "real Mexican selections," and they were supplying just one US label, Okeh's sister label Aeolian, with all of their best instrumental tunes. Victor, Peer then suggested, needed to open a branch of Southern Music in Mexico City, find and sign regional writers with good songs, and simply apply the same recording ideas they had implemented at Bristol. As early as his first trip to Mexico, he was suggesting that the popularizing approaches he was envisioning as workable for American roots music could work well beyond the American South—emphasizing vocal numbers that could be attached to strong singers with clear regional identities, strong personalities who could reach beyond their region, especially singing songwriters, and recording them. The way to sell more records across the regions of a slowly but truly modernizing Mexico was the way they were doing the same thing within the United States.

Following the Bristol pattern of first checking the possibilities, then returning to record local talent, Peer was soon back in Mexico City for a recording "excursion" there. ("We just operated like I did with the hillbilly," he recalled.) As we've seen, Peer's usual practice was to take advice from local record dealers, but that couldn't apply in this market that the label had not been able to develop. One of the first people he would get to know in Mexico, however, was Victor's ambitious, if still obscure, wealthy young radio set distributor, Emilio Azcárraga Sr., who spoke English (he'd spent his high school years in the United States), and who would prove a lifelong friend and contact of importance. He pointed Ralph Peer toward some acts to record on his unique cross-border trip, and bought a strong minority interest in the Mexican division of Southern Music when it was founded that would make him a lasting, key partner once all of Southern came back into Peer's control.

There was no reason for either RCA Victor or Ralph Peer to foresee it then, beyond spotting the man's drive and business talent, and, not entirely incidentally, his relation by marriage to a Monterrey banking family, but Azcárraga would go on to become the single most powerful man in Mexican broadcasting—first radio, then television, too, a sort of elite homegrown version of David Sarnoff, only more so, since Azcárraga's broadcasting empire would later be described as "the size of NBC, CBS and ABC combined." He would prove to be an invaluable career ally for Ralph S. Peer.

For personal communication while in Mexico City, Peer brought along a translator, a Mr. Solis, first name unknown, who was from El Paso. (Peer had met people in that Texas town during recording sessions there, which had involved artists such as cowboy singer Jules Allen and early cowgirl singer Billie Maxwell.) Solis was as new to Mexico City as Peer was, but asking around about places to check out, he was pointed toward a coffeehouse. There, Peer found an obscure piano player at work doing original material of a sort popular in Vera Cruz but considered novel everywhere else in the country, including the big city. The songs were mainly romantic, melancholy ballads—boleros of a sort that actually originated in nineteenth-century Cuba. This was Agustín Lara.

Lara may not be a household name in every English-speaking household today, but throughout the Spanish-speaking world he is considered not less than one of the most important Latin American songwriters and composers of the twentieth century. For Mexicans, Lara is a national hero and a legend of the romantic, rough-hewn, scar-faced, up-from-down vagabond variety, with, as one recent commentator noted, a macho-but-sensitive male Mexican identity "rooted in the past but thoroughly modern at the same time." Commonly referred to as "El Flaco de Oro" (roughly—The Golden "Beanpole" or "Thin Man") he would appear on radio and in musical films and marry the nation's most famous female movie star, Maria Félix. Eventually, he became celebrated enough to be portrayed in a feature film dramatizing his life, and to be lionized for the young in comic books; there are monumental statues of Lara as far away as Spain. People everywhere are likely to be familiar with a number of his globally popular songs; "Solamente Una Vez," "Granada," and "Maria Bonita" were among the six hundred he would write. That they would become popular around the world was in no small part a result of what would be a long-standing, close relationship with Ralph Peer.

When Peer met Lara and recorded him—he alone accounted for a third of all of the sides the RCA Victor team recorded in the Mexico City excursion—the Mexican singer-songwriter was run-down, sick from a variety of serious illnesses, and barely had a foothold in the music business. There are clear-enough parallels with Jimmie Rodgers, his exact contemporary, but Lara was more sophisticated in background and more of a self-consciously bohemian rebel. He was the son of a middle-class doctor, and classically trained, but had bolted from the family's bourgeois life plan for him and was playing piano in brothels by the age of thirteen. He'd picked up a broad range of musical styles in various dives in the years since, including those boleros, which he'd only just begun writing when he met and was recorded by Peer.

From Ralph Peer's standpoint, colored by his own experiences with broadening acceptance of American roots music artists, this was an easy call. Lara was charismatic and, since he suggested so in songs, taken by all to be regionally rooted in the Mexican state of Vera Cruz, a steamy region romanticized for its stand against foreign invaders. (He was actually born in Mexico City, according to later myth-busting biographers.) He was a composer of compelling story songs and, as would quickly become clear, very media-friendly. His music featured styles and sometimes rhythms picked up from Cuba, a novelty, and there was and would continue to be fascination with Cuban music and its exciting, "exotic" Afro-Cuban rhythms and lyric styles, and with Caribbean music in general, throughout Mexico. It was a Mexican equivalent to Jimmie

Rodgers's success in bringing blues to white audiences who hadn't yet much heard them.

Peer saw to it that Lara got money to see a doctor, and even agreed to go against his general royalties policy to sign him. Lara didn't trust and may not yet have understood the whole idea of seeing royalties arrive at some later date, so he initially insisted that his songs be bought outright—for what Peer would recall as twenty-five pesos apiece, equivalent to the fifty-dollar initial payment paid in the United States.

To Peer, at that point, Agustín Lara looked to be a strong songwriter who had all the makings of a rooted pop star—within Mexico. This was an unlikely find that seemed to be one more piece of unexplainable good luck: "Lara didn't write Mexican music; he wrote Cuban music! How could I step into this thing where the radio business was just about to get started—and Lara would become the principal artist?" It would be, not so coincidentally, Azcárraga who quickly got Mexican radio going just at that point, and put Lara on the air as a featured regular within a few months. So there was broadcasting across the nation to back the Victor records. "Within a very short time," Peer recalled, "Mexico was completely bolero conscious; everybody started to write boleros; it just changed the country."

Ralph Peer could reasonably be described as newly "completely bolero conscious" himself. One thing he did while in that condition was see to it that, a few months after the Mexico City sessions, Southern Music opened a publishing office there as well, as he'd recommended. ("I found an orchestra leader and set him up in a room with a desk.") Within months, Victor had other artists recording Lara tunes, notably his "Claveliot," by Trio Garnica Ascencio. Later in 1929 he'd see to it that both Lara and Tito Guízar, a handsome opera-trained Mexican singer who'd also taken part in the Mexico City recording sessions, would record Lara songs for RCA Victor in New York and make live appearances there during their stay. Within a few years Guízar—who told his conservative parents that he was going to New York to attend medical school—would not only become Mexico's leading homegrown singing cowboy movie star, but a successful radio show host in Los Angeles. By the 1940s, he would be one of the first Mexican musical performers to become a regular in Hollywood films, singing Lara's "Granada" and

"Solamente Una Vez," the latter as "You Belong to My Heart," the hit English-language version that would be published and fostered by Peer, in the 1948 Roy Rogers movie *The Gay Ranchero*. By that point, Guízar would also be godfather to Ralph Peer's son.

In bringing Lara and Guízar to New York to record and perform live, Peer was clearly beginning to experiment with the possibilities for expanding Mexican music north of the border. That thinking gelled after an incident that occurred as he stopped in San Antonio on an early return trip from Mexico, apparently around the time of his August 1929 Dallas sessions with Jimmie Rodgers, the one where they recorded "Train Whistle Blues," and "Everybody Does It in Hawaii." Peer went up to the roof garden of his hotel on his first night there and encountered an orchestra playing the infectious Cuban hit "The Peanut Vendor." If that was appealing to people in Texas, maybe the new catalog of tunes acquired south of the border could be as well. "It was the first time I'd heard it" he recalled, "and I was pretty much taken with it, and I got thinking, 'Maybe I've really got something here; maybe I can popularize these Mexican selections in the United States.'"

"The Peanut Vendor," the widely familiar song that features the shout "Pea-NUTS! Pea-NUTS" and irresistible Cuban rhythms, was a bolero with a rumba beat, credited to songwriter Moisés Simons as "El Manisero." It had become a hit in Cuba the year before, as recorded by Rita Montaner, and reached the States a few months later, as published by Edward B. Marks, one of the old-line Tin Pan Alley publishers whom Peer admired most. Marks had had some success selling American songs in Latin America before World War I, and worked to take advantage of the global tango craze of that era. He recalled in his own 1934 memoir, "In putting across 'El Manisero'—'The Peanut Vendor'—I had to get danceable arrangements and singable translations to put them over in the United States."

L. Wolfe Gilbert, composer of "Waiting for the Robert E. Lee," wrote the lyric translation for Marks; he would later be a close Ralph Peer associate. The very first of the many successful pop American recordings of that translated "The Peanut Vendor" version was by Peer's pop act of the Okeh years, Vincent Lopez. There would be over 150 recordings of the song to come, and what had to have been most striking for Peer was that it sold over a million copies in sheet music form, as the translated song sparked the rumba craze in the United States and elsewhere. There were soon a great many orchestras and singers performing that one, on rooftops and elsewhere, and they were buying published arrangements. This was a very interesting sort of formerly regional music.

There was a strong link between the wider success of Latin songs and dance-craze rhythms associated with them, as with the tango and now the rumba, and to some degree that would always be so. Peer and Eli Oberstein very privately congratulated each other in correspondence of 1931 for "stealing a march" on RCA Victor's pop music department by getting hit rumba numbers out on their race/jazz list—an understandable internal turf battle, at a time when Latin music was both starting to have some breakthrough pop moments and also beginning to influence jazz in New York; the boundary lines were truly fuzzy. There were novelty aspects to the success of "The Peanut Vendor," but it raised the possibility of transporting and, if necessary, translating compelling Latin vocal numbers across international lines, which no one was doing in any systematic, focused way.

By the time Peer had Southern Music back in his hands in 1932, he had a good many Latin American songs in the catalog that he'd taken on in Southern's last RCA Victor years, and he began to focus on the opportunities and practical issues in that arena. Within a short time of his new, intense focus on publishing, branches of Southern Music were solidly in place in London, Paris, Mexico City, Havana, and Buenos Aires.

As Peer put it, simply and directly, in a summer 1959 autobiographical sketch, "On a trip to Mexico [in 1928] I conceived the idea of an organized chain of music publishing houses to cover the principal countries of the world." By his own estimation, that was—all things considered—the idea of his lifetime.

As it happened, cross-border Latin music marketing, region to far-flung region, was just one door RCA had inadvertently opened to Peer and his future publishing empire with the 1928–29 Mexico City "side show" trips. For the recording sessions there, he'd needed a musical director, and it was most likely Nat Shilkret who assigned that job to Leroy Shield. Generally called "Roy" by his friends, Shield was working out of Chicago as a musical director on both early NBC radio broadcasts and on some recording dates staged in that city, including jazz sessions that Peer had overseen. The Mexico trip had further cemented their friendship, and then in 1930, Shield left RCA Victor for a new job—one that wouldn't have existed until that point—as in-house composer and musical director of the Hal Roach motion picture studio.

Early in the summer of 1930, Ralph Peer had Jimmie Rodgers in Hollywood for a set of varied, remarkable sessions that included the recordings with Louis Armstrong and sides with engaging, varied backing by Bob Sawyer's jazz band and Lani McIntire's Hawaiian band, sessions in which Rodgers also introduced outlaw songs such as "Moonlight and Skies" and "Pistol Packin' Papa." There was also what may seem an incongruous biographical moment.

As reported by Carrie Rodgers, on a break, Peer took Jimmie to the Hal Roach Studios for lunch with Mr. Roach and a visit to meet Laurel & Hardy. There were soon some notions floating around about how well it might work to pair Jimmie Rodgers on-screen with Will Rogers, the hugely popular comedian and folk hero with whom Jimmie went on a fundraising tour for distressed farmers the following winter. Quite compatible, they might have emerged as an early down-home singer-and-comedian predecessor team to Bing Crosby and Bob Hope, but by that point nobody really expected that Jimmie, increasingly slowed by the tuberculosis, would regain enough physical strength for the proposition to become a working reality. If he had had more time than he turned out to have, he certainly would have been, at the least, the sort of musical guest whom star and friend Gene Autry regularly featured in his singing-cowboy pictures just a few years later.

Searching for film possibilities for Jimmie Rodgers was not why Peer and his singing star happened to be visiting the Hal Roach Studios, however. The independent, feisty Roach was only the second studio head after the Warner brothers to commit fully to sound pictures, and they'd contracted to use RCA's motion picture sound system to do it. The Rodgers recording sessions were held in a huge sound facility RCA Victor had just opened in Hollywood with film work like that in mind. During the course of negotiating those recent corporate arrangements with Roach, Roy Shield had jumped to the studio side of the new media ship, much as established media professionals would take risky leaps toward new Internet-based media or mobile communication start-ups at the turn of the twenty-first century—for better or worse.

The role Shield would play for Hal Roach was a brand-new one; he would be an in-house composer not just of songs (though the Roach Studios' Laurel & Hardy and Our Gang/Little Rascals movies would have plenty of those, sung by Stan and Ollie, "Alfalfa the Crooner," and others), but of the newfangled incidental music used throughout *all* of the pictures, around and behind dialogue. And that was a very interesting topic of discussion for Roy Shield, Hal Roach, and Ralph S. Peer.

Through the silent era, just a handful of publishers had specialized in scores and scene-by-scene musical cue sheets for music played in the theaters along with the films. By the 1920s there were predictable battles over collecting payment for publishers and composers for use of the music, with ASCAP understandably trying to collect live performance royalties, and film studios and theater owners attempting to skirt paying by turning to more so-called "untaxed" public domain music. It may seem ironic, aware as we are of the post–World War II movie-theater-versus-television battles, but at that point independent theater owners were even supporting the brand-new mid-1920s National Association of Broadcasters organization, because the new radio station operators shared their concerns about music costs, and were, like the theaters, already attempting to get by with material not licensed for performance use by ASCAP. It was a battle that would play out again and again under various auspices as media evolved, and it still does, but a brief truce was reached in 1926, just before talkies came into force, with the movie exhibitors agreeing to become ASCAP licensees and pay for use of music, a major new source of income for the composer and publisher association. Extending the truce, the Music Publishers' Protective Association (the same trade group later involved in the "Home on the Range" investigation) signed a deal in December 1927 in which movie exhibitors agreed to pay publishers for the songs used in sound films.

Systems were then put in place to pay music publishers for music mass-replicated on movie soundtracks, some of which were on discs, in a system fostered by AT&T's Western Electric and Warner Brothers' Vitaphone, others distributed as "optical sound" embedded right on the film, in the photophone system developed by General Electric and fostered by RCA. The latter would eventually become the norm. Warner set up a new licensing agency, Electrical Research Products, Inc. (ERPI) on New York's West Fifty-Seventh Street to collect fees for use of their system, and for licensing the music recorded on it, as "synchronization fees," a new and continuous source of income from copyrighted songs. After some predictable self-seeking format fights, the RCA system was brought under the same fee-collection aegis, and ASCAP agreed to use the setup, finding ERPI simple and useful to work with as a central "synch" licensing agency.

Hollywood studio hiring of salaried, in-house songwriters fluctuated with studio fortunes through the Depression years, and by the time Peer and Jimmie Rodgers visited Hal Roach Studios in 1930, many former Hollywood tunesmiths had already been sent packing. Yet there still was and would be the need for incidental music—fresh background music, not just repetitive stock tunes; Roy Shields was providing Roach those new tunes. The studio's Anglo-American team Laurel & Hardy, who'd successfully transitioned from silent to sound comedies, were excellent examples of stars with international appeal, and in keeping with the practice of the time, there were multiple foreign-language versions of their shorts and features produced for European markets—entire pictures redone with foreign casts and the box office stars Stan and Ollie speaking the necessary French, Spanish, Italian, or German phonetically for the export versions.

The incidental music needed to travel abroad, too, and in that niche was an entirely new enterprise that Peer worked out with Roy Shields and Hal Roach, one he was able to fully execute when he resumed control of Southern Music in 1932. This was not a business Roach wanted to involve his own firm in, since they had no experience with anything like it; licensing the music composed for Roach films internationally became both an important new business for Peer and the entree into the potentially lucrative new sound-centered Hollywood he'd been looking for. By the mid-1930s, licensing songs to Europe for multimedia use would be a growing business for him—some from Southern Music Publishing's American roots catalog, some from his emerging Latin music catalog, and many more musical snippets from Hal Roach pictures.

Peer would explain, "I began to collect large royalties from film performance in foreign countries, and using that money, that's the way I started a branch in England and I had a company in France." These were early outposts of what would emerge within a few years as that global music publishing enterprise he'd dreamed of—and one of the ways that Peer, deprived of the gusher of mechanical royalties from records as record sales plummeted, would become financially strong again.

A final accounting from RCA Victor made just days before Southern returned to Peer's control listed key songs being handed over to him that had already seen revenue-generating, screen-related ERPI uses in 1932, while Peer was still concentrating for the most part on his hillbilly and blues sessions. They included Bleyer's "Business in F," "A Una Ola," by Maria Grever, who was based in New York but was another key early Latin American songwriter Peer had signed up, the Cuban "Buche y Pluma," actually composed by yet another important Latin writer already in the stable, Puerto Rico native Rafael Hernández, and, oh yes—a couple of little pop numbers called "Georgia on My Mind" and "Rockin' Chair."

The last two were another legacy of Ralph Peer's friendship with Roy Shield: the premier American pop and jazz songwriter Hoagy Carmichael was now published by Southern Music. Peer was in Chicago in early 1929 when Shield informed him that he was "bringing up a fellow named Hoagy Carmichael, who has the dance orchestra at the University of Indiana; he's got some wonderful stuff; you might want to pick it up." Carmichael quickly signed a contract. "He and I got along pretty well together," Peer recalled. That was not surprising.

A sometime law student, piano player Carmichael was already composing melodies, with or without lyrics, that had found some limited acceptance in jazz circles, songs that were uniquely deft in digesting broad lyrical and sonic elements from the history of American music, from old minstrel songs and vaudeville, to blues, hillbilly ballads, and gospel sounds in particular, and drawing them all into a universal and original style of very American, sometimes Southern-tinged pop. (Carmichael would, for the record, summarize his own key influences as the American roots music of "Negroes and the hill-whites and the fever-shaking crackers.")

At the 1929 session with Roy Shield that Peer attended, Carmichael recorded an instrumental version of his lazy standard-to-be, "Rockin' Chair," best known as "Rockin' Chair's Got Me." There, for an impressed Peer to see, was a performer and songwriter (and it would only later be clear, a singer, too) on the verge of edging into the big-time popular music field from small-circle jazz roots, a sophisticate who was steeped in the very sorts of American music on which he'd been focusing. This looked like "roots meets pop" for the mainstream.

Pop "hot bands" led by Red Nichols and Paul Whiteman had already recorded Hoagy's "Washboard Blues." He'd made several instrumental records for the Gennett label, and had an unusual tune by the name of "Stardust" that seemed to be going nowhere. In early 1930, smart, ambitious, frustrated, and dissatisfied with his current publisher Irving Mills's paltry song placements, Carmichael signed with Peer's Southern Music. ("Stardust" would become a smash a year later, but it turned out to be a Mills copyright, after some initial confusion about the matter was sorted out.) Carmichael began a highly productive period, relocating to New York—though he would always be, at heart, a midwesterner from Indiana; the midwestern traits he shared with Ralph Peer were points of personal connection and recognition.

"Dad was a Bloomington guy," his son Hoagy Bix Carmichael explains. "He'd known flapper types—and then coming to New York, he knew Ralph right away; I think there was that symbiotic 'I've met guys like you before' reaction going on."

Peer and Shield arranged for Carmichael to have a New York recording date at Victor on May 21, 1930, with backing musicians that included jazz fiddler Joe Venuti and guitarist Eddie Lang (friends of both Carmichael and his close buddy, cornetist Bix Beiderbecke, the source of Hoagy Bix's middle name), and three young virtual unknowns—Tommy Dorsey, Gene Krupa, and Benny Goodman. The session included a finished version of "Rockin' Chair" and the first recording ever of another new song Hoagy had been working up recently, "Georgia on My Mind," the now universally known minstrel and gospel-influenced elegy to a place that Carmichael had never been at the time. (Peer recorded "Georgia" with Hoagy Carmichael just three days before recording the Carter Family performing "It Takes a Worried Man" in Memphis.) That autumn,

Peer introduced Carmichael to Sidney Arodin, a New Orleans clarinetist who had an infectious tune that called out to be sung; with some tweaking of the melody and creation of a lyric by Hoagy, they had "(Up a) Lazy River," another American pop standard-to-be.

The crux of all this for Ralph Peer was that however bleak the recording industry's prospects were, and however urgently Eli Oberstein wanted to clear him out of the way in A&R at RCA Victor, he already had been handed heady new potential markets in Latin, in American pop, and in globalizing Hollywood tunes. He began to look at his situation from the standpoint of a music publishing company operator—which, by default, was exactly what he was.

"I was always trying to get away from the hillbilly and into the legitimate music publishing field," he recalled, thirty years later, "because the big profit in music publishing has come from selling sheet music, not the records, [and] you can't sell it on hillbilly stuff. . . . I did make good money out of the royalties on . . . Jimmie Rodgers, the Carter Family, and so forth, and I kept on with that as much as I could. As long as I was operating as an individual . . . that was wonderful . . . [but from] the minute I organized as music publishing and I began [having two or three] song pluggers and all that sort of thing, this amount of money meant nothing. . . . What I was doing, unconsciously, was to take the profits out of the hillbilly and race business and [spending] the money trying to get established as a pop publisher."

One step he'd already taken, which would look prophetic in retrospect, was getting the Southern Music Publishing operation to relocate north to Forty-Ninth Street and Broadway in the autumn of 1931. The site had been planned as a skyscraper but downsized just before construction, as so much in Depression America had to be, to eleven well-situated stories; this was the Brill Building. Ralph Peer's Southern Music, a year before he fully controlled it again, would become the first industry tenant of the Times Square tower that would become a pop-music business icon.

In just the first months of 1933, Adolf Hitler seized power in Germany, Franklin Delano Roosevelt was inaugurated as president, Prohibition reached its end, and New Deal Tennessee Valley Authority legislation was passed to bring rural electrification to the American South. The changes in the wider world in which the music business would be operating could not have been more dramatic. For his part, Ralph Peer now had the de facto beginnings of his global publishing network. The deteriorating situation in Europe would impact virtually all of those plans, but that was not yet clear to almost anyone.

Of Peer's key career choices made during this time, his son Ralph Peer II suggests, "A decision was made, first, that if he was going to be a manager of individual acts, he was going to have to have a set number of acts at most—three or ten—that he could truly devote his attention to and be successful, but if he wanted to expand his business relationships to other countries, to other genres of music, he was not going to be *able* to give that amount of personal attention to these people. He couldn't do it successfully. So that was a big transition."

This was the context in which Jimmie Rodgers, one of Peer's few remaining contracted management clients, and the one who still had more of Ralph Peer's time and attention than any other, got on a boat in Galveston headed to New York to record again that May, knowing that the tuberculosis was getting to him—but then, his health had been bad for years; this was not necessarily so different. (He told Peer, by phone, that he was feeling well; he failed to mention that he was to be accompanied by a nurse.) While RCA Victor remained uninterested in paying for remote sessions, Peer had made it clear that in Rodgers's case he was willing to go wherever Jimmie needed to be to record. Yet Rodgers himself was insisting that he was coming to New York with a pile of new songs ready—pressing to make what money he could since, unlike so many, the record company was keeping him on the roster.

The Depression-pressed RCA Victor was at this point renegotiating the few recording contracts they chose to maintain, and Jimmie would write to wife Carrie that his own new terms looked favorable, even without the jacked-up, higher advances he'd recently been receiving. Ralph Peer had gotten him a new deal in which he would be switched from the higher retail-priced RCA Victor label to the lower-priced Bluebird line, which would likely mean more record sales, yet he was going to get the same royalty and original per-side mechanical rate that he'd had for the songs. As it turned out, by the time Carrie received that letter a few days later, America's Blue Yodeler would be dead.

Rodgers arrived in New York with nine songs, one of which the notebook he carried listed as "Why Don't Women Let Me Be Blues," the song that would emerge as "Jimmie Rodgers' Last Blue Yodel." Work in the Twenty-Fourth Street Manhattan studio, which began on May 17, was halting. (Rodgers would report this to Carrie in that last letter, laughing it off with "But you know how slow Ralph is.") Jimmie took a break of several days for some fresh seaside air at Cape Cod and returned to the studio on May 24—for the last session, at which he had to rest on a cot between takes.

Near midnight on the night of May 25–26, management of the Taft Hotel, where Jimmie was staying, called the Southern Music phone number they'd been given for immediate help; Rodgers was in trouble, hemorrhaging badly. The employee who quickly arrived at the seventh-floor room was Fernando Castro, who had recently been appointed head of Southern's emerging Latin American division and who would work for the Peer organization for decades. That night, Jimmie Rodgers, not yet thirty-six years old, died in Fernando Castro's arms. It could not have been lost on Ralph Peer, when he heard the details of that scene the next morning, that the artist who was so central to the period of his own life just ending had died held upright by a representative of a central focus of the next. Tragically and decidedly, a page had been turned.

Peer took charge of shipping Jimmie Rodgers's body back to Meridian for burial; between New York and Mississippi, thousands lined the tracks as the train went by to salute a man who'd become a hero to so many he'd spoken to, and for. In less than five years, Rodgers had shaped one modern pop and down-home roots music fusion that would later lead to his recognition as "the Father of Country Music"; he'd introduced an approach to blues that brought it to a broad audience without minstrelsy or racial condescension; he'd pointed toward the direction of commercial cowboy music just ahead; he'd fashioned models for both the solo, confessional singer-songwriter with guitar and for the rough and rowdy outlaw who would emerge again in the rock 'n' roll era. Ralph Peer, as his manager, producer, mentor, and publisher, had had a strong, direct hand in making all of those achievements real, in enabling them, and to a significant degree, shaping them. To the list of dramatic events altering Peer's life and work at that time, we can add the loss of an exemplar of his ideas of what a popular roots music artist might be—and the loss of a unique friend.

The decision to walk away from recording work could not have come lightly; he had had great fun there, and great recordings had been set down, but those experiences were drawing to a close. Some of the very American pop composers he was spending more time with proved to be of the "live wire" variety he favored, too, and he paid them personal attention.

Fats Waller, like Hoagy Carmichael, had simply been selling off rights to songs to publisher Irving Mills for quick cash—in his case, to such priceless yet lucrative originals as "Ain't Misbehavin'" and "(What Did I Do to Be So) Black and Blue." His publishing relationship with Southern began in 1928, when Peer published and recorded songs from the Broadway show *Keep Shufflin'*, in which Fats and James P. Johnson played duets. It was natural that the A&R man who'd first seen in him a star recording soloist (if principally as a jazz organist) and was known to offer to pay actual royalties to songwriters, favoring those with star potential, looked like a better bet as a publisher.

Waller stuck around knowing also that Ralph Peer would go to such lengths for him as, on one occasion, rising from bed in East Orange at two o'clock in the morning, driving to Fats's overnight gig at the bootlegger-run Connie's Inn in Harlem by 5 AM, passing out two bottles of gin he'd had in the car when he got there, then chauffeuring Fats and "four or five others, all of them sleeping like logs" down to a three-and-a-half-hour Camden recording date that morning. (Driving back and forth over the Hudson had only been made possible by the opening of the Holland Tunnel in 1927, and the George Washington Bridge in 1931.) Showing up for recording dates was something the good-natured but incorrigible Waller could as easily forget to do then as in the early "no show" Okeh days; Ralph Peer got him there.

Peer admired Waller's masterful backing of singers almost as much as his keyboard work. "He was patient, affable and jolly, putting them at ease and drawing out the best in them," he told Duncan Schiedt. Peer was also on hand, along with a host of jamming jazz greats, at Waller's apartment for his surprise birthday party of 1932. At that point Fats had a regular live radio show featuring his patter and singing, which proved to be the bridge between his soloing instrumental work and his emerging career as a charming pop singer. And so for a few years, as long as he ever stayed with anyone, Waller remained on Peer's publishing roster, sending notes to ASCAP that instructed them to "send that next hundred dollars to Southern Music Publishing."

Waller's nearly equally talented frequent writing collaborator Andy Razaf was writing scores for revues at Connie's Inn at the time, and Peer would have run into him there as well. Southern published a number of Razaf songs in this period, most notably "That's What I Like 'Bout the South," the comic jive-talk hit recorded by Bob Wills in 1942 and made famous as pop circa 1947 by Nashville bandleader and singer Phil Harris, but first introduced by Cab Calloway at Harlem's Cotton Club in 1933. (Harris would suggest he'd written the number himself until firmly reminded by Razaf and Peer's Southern organization to set the record and the royalty payments straight.) The closing of Connie's Inn in May 1933, the same month that Jimmie Rodgers died, a casualty of the Depression and the repeal of Prohibition both, marked the de facto end of that period of Harlem nightlife.

By 1934 things were tight and foreboding in the music business even for those who'd had a few hits. Hoagy Carmichael, with his stream of live jazz gigs decreasing, and with the early death of his closest friend, Bix Beiderbecke, having kicked the romance out of playing that music, took a day job right inside Southern Music, as one of Ralph Peer's in-house song pluggers. That put Carmichael right there in the Brill Building offices, and there was a piano for song demonstrations. As his son Hoagy Bix Carmichael notes, "While Dad was working as a sort of song plugger there, call it what you like, they jammed right in there, and wrote right in there. There were songwriting shenanigans going on."

Among the songs Carmichael came up with at that time, and almost certainly in that place, was one that was specifically suggested by Ralph Peer, entirely in keeping with the way he thought, a copyrightable and clean version of "Barnacle Bill the Sailor." (Peer had tried the same trick with a version by Frank Luther and Carson Robison in 1928; this one had more impact.) *This* actually was a "folk song" if there'd ever been one—the sort guys in bars and at frat house "smokers," as pledge mixers were then known, made up verses for, with lines as "top this" filthy as they could invent. Catchy as the song was, it was utterly unplayable on the radio in any form anyone knew, so Carmichael took up Peer's idea, somewhat reluctantly at first, and altered the tune, and delivered an acceptable lyric. If you know the song today, having heard it featured in a *Popeye* cartoon of the era, for instance, that's where it came from. (Jimmie Rodgers might have been equally at home with it; the gap between the territories of the "hillbilly" singer pressing into pop and the "pop" singer taking off with down-home influences was no chasm.)

Another new Carmichael cowrite proved crucial to keeping Peer's Southern Music Publishing in the black. It was not as if song publishers were necessarily in dramatically better shape in the depths of the Depression than record companies; there had been few recent hits substantial enough to build a business. A year or two earlier, however, RCA Victor's plugger-executive at Southern, Eddie Woods, had introduced Hoagy to a possible up-and-coming collaborator from the Savannah area, ten years younger than he, another pop-oriented writer who was deeply steeped in Southern roots music, black and white, and another one who also—oddly enough for a tunesmith of that day—could *sing*, one Johnny Mercer.

They came up with a laid-back song that, in the twenty-first century, may well grate as a racially condescending return to some of the worst attitudes of minstrelsy, but was very much accepted at the time as some winning, sassy scolding by a black mother to an ornery child—"Lazybones." When it turned out that young Mercer was under contract to another publisher, which prevented publishing the writing duo together, Peer bought out the contract, put his song-plugging staff to work on it, and the result—with a melody by Carmichael and lyric by Mercer—sold over 350,000 copies in three months; there were hit recordings of the song by both the racially conscious Paul Robeson and by Louis Armstrong. (Carmichael would be filmed singing it himself a few years later.) With Southern's working, growing connections in Mexico, thousands of copies sold *there*, too. "Lazybones," Peer noted, "was the first hit after the worst slump that had ever occurred in the music business; this was *the* hit."

On the face of it, Ralph Peer had quickly assembled a fledgling stable of songwriters that could have spelled major success for his new pop enterprise, singers who played off forms of American roots music he well understood, and most of whom were among the first successful singer-songwriters in pop, at a time when most mainstream popular songwriters were not expected to be marketable performers at all. Within a few years, Waller, Carmichael, and Mercer would all be seen on-screen regularly and emerge as celebrities with successful singing careers. Peer's notion that appealing roots-influenced performers sold songs and appealing "rootsy" songs sold performers was holding; these particular working relationships with Peer and Southern, however, didn't last.

Fats Waller remained a Peer friend to the end of his too-short life in 1943, but he never stuck with any one publisher for long. Carmichael and Mercer, in practice, were virtually *too* perfect as examples of the ambitious, business-savvy musical idea generators Peer sought for them to stay put. Mercer soon headed for Hollywood and eventually became a founder of Capitol Records, in addition to establishing a legendary writing career and his own vocal successes.

Carmichael would later have his own publishing company, too, following Irving Berlin's model. Never having been entirely in love with any nonmusicians in the music business, he kept looking for what he took to be better deals. "I thought Ralph Peer was a good businessman," he commented in his memoir. "He was, and he profited much more out of the deal than I." Hoagy would nevertheless have reason to regret leaving Southern as his publisher to go to work for Paramount Pictures in 1935. He would write great pop songs there in quick order ("The Nearness of You," "Heart and Soul," "Two Sleepy People") but under fully sold "work for hire" terms that meant that no long-term royalties came to him from these standards-to-be. His son comments, today, "I wish those *were* Peer songs! At least Dad was with Peer when 'Georgia on My Mind' came out, and thank God for that." Carmichael and Peer would remain friends for the rest of Ralph Peer's life.

Peer later characterized his efforts to become a substantial player in the competitive mainstream pop field, demanding as it was of time, focus, personnel, and expense, as "hopeless." It was, for an independent publisher, too much like "hitting the ball where they *are*." While there would always be pop songs in the mix of what Southern and Peer's other imprints published from this point on, "pure pop" and Broadway never did become Ralph Peer's publishing mainstay. And given ASCAP's grandfathered "point system" rules for allocating performance revenues, under which the old-line founding firms were paid at the highest rate, other publishers with the most song performances secondarily, then everybody else less, it could take decades of building up a songwriting roster for a relative newcomer to compete—which is why Peer could see his attempts to enter the pop music mainstream in a serious way as having "failed."

We do have the provocative period reminder, however, that the 1934 edition of Southern Music's original Carter Family's song folio features ads on the back for Southern's Hoagy Carmichael songbook. How many people purchased both, we can't be sure. The Carters were still being actively and directly managed, published, and recorded by Ralph Peer, under new terms agreed to at the time of the Southern buyback, and still under contract with RCA Victor Records, but there were issues.

The act that represented the very image of rural domesticity for so many was privately being pulled apart by domestic tensions. Sara Carter was tiring of A. P. Carter's constant absence on song-hunting trips, and his remoteness and lack of involvement in everyday farm and family life when he did come home. A.P.'s more fun-loving, naturally affectionate, and *present* cousin, Coy Bayes, had increasingly been attracting her attention, until the worried extended family forced Coy to leave the area entirely. A despondent Sara absented herself from the farm and her children, moving in with relatives. A.P. and Sara were now very much separated, as Peer would learn when he brought up getting music and the family members together for recording in April 1933; Sara was refusing to join in, preferring to avoid A.P. altogether.

This threat to the act's existence was clearly causing considerable concern in the pressed Peer household that fated month, just weeks before Jimmie Rodgers's death. With the new aspects of Southern's business only beginning to develop, it couldn't have been otherwise. In a move that has no documented precedent, Anita Peer wrote to Sara Carter on May 3, noting that her husband was "quite disturbed" over the seeming impossibility of getting A.P., Sara, and Maybelle in the same room. She went on to say, in her characteristically blunt but chatty and personal way:

Of course, it is really none of my business, but I just wondered if there was anything I could do to help things along. I realize that it would be distinctly awkward for both you and A.P. to work together again, but on the other hand, the 'Carter Family' has become well known and there is a chance to make some more money, even in these days of depression. Let me know if there is anything I can do. I have been divorced once myself, as I think I told you, so I can sympathize with you perfectly. . . . Even if you never live together again you could get together for professional purposes like the movie stars do. Practically all of them are divorced, or should be. . . . We are anxious to see you, and to make some more records. . . .

Mrs. Peer's practical if somewhat cynical appeal to financial sense seems to have done the trick; there would be three more recording sessions by the Carters for RCA Victor, all at Camden. The session of June 17, 1933, produced "Gold Watch and Chain" and the very first, unissued version of "Will the Circle Be Unbroken?" (a particularly pointed question given the circumstances under which it was being sung). They had two more sessions with Ralph Peer in 1934, the first in May, which yielded such selections brought in by A.P. as "I'll Be All Smiles Tonight" and "You've Been Fooling Me Baby," both straightforward indicators of his collapsed marital situation, and the second at the tail end of Peer's A&R contract, in December, with twenty sides recorded, including "March Winds Goin' to Blow My Blues Away" and A.P.'s self-explanatory "Are You Tired of Me, Darling?"

Soon after, predictably, Eli Oberstein attempted to stir the waters, working to break off the Carters' relationship with Peer, while continuing their contract with RCA Victor/Bluebird. A March 26, 1935, letter that Oberstein sent to A.P. survives, in which he suggests that Ralph Peer no longer has a working contract with the Carters, that Peer is only trying to take advantage of them, and that he, by contrast, would see to it that they were paid more. ("I intend to have you record for the Victor Company as in the past and will do everything possible to keep you happy. . . . P.S.: I do not believe that Mr. Peer would sue you for recording for us, as, if he is damaged, he will be damaged by us and not by you. . . .")

That last openly acknowledged "damaged by us" is certainly a reasonable indication of the level of goodwill at which Oberstein was working by that point—none at all. He wanted Peer out of their "circle." While nothing appears to have legally prevented A. P. Carter (or Sara, or Maybelle) from signing with RCA Victor for the years just ahead, or working out some arrangement where Peer and Southern would be their publisher but they'd sign with the record company on their own, they quickly opted to stick strictly with Ralph Peer as both their manager and publisher. They trusted the man.

Peer was now determined to bring an end to the whole conflict. He not only stayed on as the Carters' manager after he had given that up for everyone else—until the 1937–38 season—he proceeded to move them away from RCA Victor and Oberstein, at first, for multiple sessions through 1935, to ARC Records, the American Recording Company, for what would be one of the Carter Family's busiest recording periods, with newer versions of their earliest hits joined by new A. P. Carter copyrights. (ARC had been cobbled together from close to a dozen small-to-medium-sized label imprints, by 1934 including, ironically enough, both the old Columbia Phonograph and Okeh; in 1938, the whole conglomeration would be purchased by CBS, the previously unrelated Columbia Broadcasting System, and reemerge as the more modern Columbia Records label.)

Peer then arranged an improved deal for the Carters the following year at the upstart Decca Records, a new American offshoot of Decca of the UK being run by his old friend Dave Kapp. There they recorded exclusively new material, including "Hello, Stranger," "No Depression in Heaven," and "My Dixie Darling," in clean, relatively modern-sounding renditions. As Sara and A.P. headed toward their divorce, which became official near the end of the year, Peer stayed as far away from the personal fallout as he could. He asked Sara, discreetly, in a letter of December 15, 1936: "What are your plans now as to A.P.? He has written me that you are suing for divorce. . . . He apparently wanted me to exert some pressure upon you, but I told him that this was a matter which people have to settle for themselves, and something in which I did not want to interfere. Some time during this Spring, we will have to record again for Decca. . . . From a business standpoint, it is important that the Carter

Family should not be too badly broken up." The unspoken emphasis was on the *too*.

Sara Carter almost certainly did not know at that point just how fraught Peer's comment that marital situations were matters that people "have to settle for themselves" surely was for *him* just then; few did.

No later than 1932, in the course of his work with RCA, Ralph Peer had met Monique Hildborg Iversen, fifteen years younger than he, from a Danish family but born and raised in England. They may have crossed paths without documented consequences the year before, as mutual friends of singer Tito Guízar, but she was now very much in Peer's vicinity. She was busy inventing a unique position for herself at RCA's fledgling NBC Radio network, as their authority, representative, and negotiator in developing international broadcasting relationships and, via transatlantic shortwave radio, global news and program exchanges. She'd been recommended to NBC by the network's celebrated adventurer-broadcaster and newsman Floyd Gibbons, whom she'd met in the course of her often-dizzying social rounds. Iversen had studied at the universities of London, Heidelberg, Munich, Lausanne, and Paris.

A striking light blonde who had only been in the United States for three years, she was being pursued by diplomats, wealthy businessmen, artists, and at least one US senator. Her job was cutting-edge enough that she was being profiled in publications in both the United States and Europe; that it was an intriguing, energetic young woman holding the position was unprecedented, and naturally added to the mystique. The German-language New York daily *New York Herald* noted in the summer of 1932, "Millions of listeners on both sides of the ocean owe the little lady a debt of thanks for what the radio brings to their ears."

At twenty-five, Monique was a cultured sophisticate, an experienced international traveler versed in world politics and business who spoke accent-free English, French, German, and Spanish and who, when she felt like it, also sang pop songs, which she could accompany on a ukulele. She had briefly looked into career possibilities as a radio singer or film starlet; she would always have a theatrical side, but her work would be in global business.

At midlife, Ralph Sylvester Peer, the ambitious and status-conscious shopkeeper's son from Independence, Missouri, saw the global, new-era business prospects before him and yearned for a lifestyle that matched them, one where he could mingle as easily with the mighty and cultured of world society as he had with the down-home and marginalized, where his simultaneous urges for globe-trotting and for quiet, classy elegance when home might be matched or bettered, including perhaps the family life that two marriages had not produced. In Monique Iversen, his aspirations had a face.

As her provocative early essays and other writings testify, Monique might easily have been a serious author if that had become her focus, and she kept detailed diaries that chronicled her developing relationship with the still-married Peer. A family photo shows the two of them together on the New York area–based day-trip steamer the S.S. *Sandy Hook*, both looking quite pleased to be on board, in July 1934. The two of them would sail to France and Naples the following winter. By April 1935, in the course of a diary entry that makes it clear that their affair had been consummated, that she was in love with him, and that they were speaking of a future together that would include having children, she describes one drive through New Jersey with Ralph: "I have never felt so completely happy, satisfied and natural in all my life."

Ralph Peer, though associates seemed to take no note of it, was clearly separated from his wife, Anita, for extended periods by this time, as he traveled to South America without her while she vacationed in England, for example. No correspondence or commentary from Anita Peer from this time has surfaced, if there was any, but based on her written comments years later, it's clear that she was aware of the new situation before long, was infuriated, and had no intention of simply fading from Peer's life.

Still, he made no legal moves to end that marriage at that point, nor did she, outspokenly resistant even to discuss the possibility. Monique would express increasing frustration with the lack of motion in that direction as time dragged on—and it did. Peer may have had some unspoken qualms about proceeding with a second divorce, or a possible third marriage, and Anita's determination to leave things status quo legally made it all the more difficult. His main explanation to Monique for his hesitation and indecisiveness on this matter so crucial to him, however, was that money had become tight, not a situation in which to start a new household. Yet this was after "Lazybones" had become a hit in multiple recorded versions, and there were company funds to support that trip to England, however much Peer was or wasn't taking in personally, so Ms. Iversen had her doubts.

"If he doesn't show me a definite plan of action before leaving for South America," she wrote in that same April as her diary entry on being so happy, "I will think he is rotten. . . . His actions simply do not make sense."

In August, Peer attempted to reassure her of his serious intentions over breakfast at New York's Essex House: "I am going to do everything possible to marry you," she reported him telling her. "And when you doubt, take a pencil and write down all the advantages I will gain by marrying you: your love, affection, companionship, stability, the home and children I crave, and all the things I've wanted and never had."

That summer 1935 diary quotation seems as forthright a statement of what Ralph Peer wanted in his own life and still aspired to at forty-two as any on record—but given that he would keep talking this way for several years to come, there were times when, reasonably enough, Monique was convinced that it was all just talk, or some cruel sort of game. Ralph Peer's tendency toward closed-mouthed reticence persisted; there were multiple occasions where she met with him expecting to hear some word of new action concerning Anita or even new statements of affection from him. To her great frustration, though, through walks and rides through Central Park, over successions of dinners at some of New York's better-known restaurants, and over more than a few breakfasts, she heard little talk from him at all, or talk only of business.

The business that was occupying so much of his attention was evolving. By the mid-1930s, the whole entertainment industry was beginning to pick up again, slowly but surely, though the Western economies remained in the doldrums. Commentators on the movie, music, and broadcasting businesses have often suggested that the mass audience had reached a point where they were so hungry for the emotional release of music and movies that they'd stretch to spend precious nickels and dimes (and other currencies) on them. American popular music moved in a direction that was more rhythmic and dance-friendly, both more matter-of-fact in its roots music lyrics and more gushingly romantic in popular song—a trend that would be very much in play by the World War II years.

Peer had played a real if limited role in fostering the transformation of specialized audience jazz into the pop form of the swing era, as publisher and A&R man for innovators Fletcher Henderson and Bennie Moten, and in publishing set band orchestrations (a necessary prerequisite for big band swing). But since, as we've seen, mainstream pop markets seemed prohibitively walled off in practice for his publishing firm, he could only take limited advantage of that history and those connections.

On the other hand, Peer had his plans for a global publishing enterprise to develop, his new Latin American and film music–related businesses to try to stimulate, and his hillbilly catalog to build on as a publisher. Already, musical models he'd tried out with Jimmie Rodgers earlier were becoming the basis of new sorts of successful popular roots music. Multiple Jimmie Rodgers sides, including "Travellin' Blues," had employed future western swing musicians, in arrangements that leaned in that jazz-country hybrid direction. And ersatz cowboy songs such as "Prairie Lullaby" featured all of the ingredients that soon combined in Hollywood singing cowboy material.

Jimmie Davis and other acquaintances who met Ralph Peer in the Jimmie Rodgers years served as his connections to the growing Texas-based western end of what, for a while, was called country and western music. Exactly how much hands-on songwriting Davis himself ever did is debatable; there's no doubt that he was willing to buy songs from others over the years and add his name to the credits—or that he knew when he had a good song to "adopt" or writer to work with. While Peer never engaged in that practice himself, he considered such dealings by his songwriting performers, if done legitimately as a purchase, not as theft, but as *their* business, and he was capable of looking the other way.

Davis had a first large hit of his own with "Nobody's Darlin' but Mine" in 1934, his ticket out of the aging risqué blue yodel genre, and his first big song copyright for Peer. Davis's connections to the circle of Texas musicians that had worked with western swing pioneer Milton Brown and then Cliff Bruner after Brown's early death also proved highly fruitful. "It Makes No Difference Now," officially cowritten by Davis and a newcomer named Floyd Tillman, was not only a western swing hit for Bruner but would also prove a prototype for the new, worldly, and world-weary honky-tonk songs of the forties. A notable songwriter and distinctive vocalist who split the vocal difference between the charming if limited-range style of Rodgers acolyte Ernest Tubb and the emphatic phrase-bending of the as-yet-unborn Bob Dylan, Tillman would be published by Ralph Peer for years to come. Another singer-songwriter from the Milton Brown–Cliff Bruner Texas camp, Ted Daffan, came up with what's considered the first song in the sturdy truck-driving song genre, "Truck Drivers' Blues," also recorded by Bruner, and he too joined the Peer songwriting stable, with larger hits to come. (Peer's predilection for performing songwriters continued.)

As much as jug band music before it, western swing, first based mainly in Texas and Oklahoma, then migrating to California, was an American roots music amalgamation—of jazz, blues, and hillbilly, Mexican, Texas Czech Bohemian, and Hawaiian music, all presented as danceable pop with regional Southwestern flavor. Little wonder that this became an area of Ralph Peer's focus. Before long, Bob Wills and Tommy Duncan, the biggest stars in the field, were published by him as well, as was their steel player, Leon McAuliffe—whose seminal "Steel Guitar Rag" was, in fact, an adaptation of Sylvester Weaver's "Guitar Rag," recorded by Peer more than a decade earlier.

Jimmie Davis put an exclamation point on this transitional period when "hillbilly" music evolved into an increasingly gone-to-town flavor of country with the song forever most associated with him, that sweet standard of all country standards, "You Are My Sunshine." Versions of the song were recorded months before Davis got hold of it—he'd bought it from Paul Rice, who'd already recorded it with the Rice Brothers Gang, and the Rices, in turn, had used an already existing lyric themselves. But Davis "made" the song and ran with it, and Ralph Peer published it. It would prove a phenomenon, a hit also for Gene Autry, and sung by everyone from Bing Crosby to the Carter Family.

Meanwhile, Peer was still managing the Carters, who continued to work hard well after A.P. and Sara's divorce became official, though A.P. was not as prolific as he had been in coming up with new material. (Monique's diaries include references to the Carters coming to New

York; whether they were aware that she was there in the background through the late thirties is not certain.) There was a last Carter Family session for Decca in Charlotte in June 1938, and then Peer learned of a potential deal for them that could solve their problem of promoting themselves without wanting to tour (or in Sara's case, even to be around much) while reassuring him that they would be secure—in fact, in some ways, do better than ever—as he moved out of artist management entirely.

A Chicago ad man, Harry O'Neill, proposed buying time for a client patent medicine company on the enormously powerful, 500,000-watt Del Rio, Texas/Villa Acuña, Mexico "border blaster" radio station XERA, owned by the infamous medical quack Dr. John R. Brinkley, for a twice-daily Carter Family show that would potentially be heard across all of North America, at a starting salary that then seemed huge to them—$4,000 a year, the equivalent of over $65,000 a year today, an amount that could go very far indeed during the Depression. After several meetings with those involved, Peer decided that he liked the idea, as did the Carters. The far-reaching broadcasts were likely to promote record sales again (and did), and they had already done similar programs as on-disc transcriptions for radio distribution out of studios in New York, so he knew they could be comfortable with the format, as they did. The Carter Family act, which now began to expand to include Maybelle's daughters and Sara and A.P.'s children, reached new heights of fame and managed to stay together as a musical entity, despite Sara's marriage to Coy Bayes in 1939, until XERA went off the air in March 1941. They were famously photographed by *Life* magazine for a major story scheduled for late that year that was put aside because of the attack on Pearl Harbor.

The Texas-Mexico musical border seemed permeable in multiple ways; there was an increasing overlap between crooning pop cowboy music and Mexican tunes both on records and in films, and this, of course, had to be good news for Ralph Peer. For example, Gene Autry would have a hit, in 1941, with Lorenzo Barcelata's "Maria Elena"—which had been published by Peer back in 1932. His concept of bringing Latin American songs across the border and taking them around the globe was showing signs of taking hold. A craze for Latin music—rhythmic, romantic, and a little exotic—lurked just ahead. The early international successes of Peer-published songs such as "Maria Elena," "Green Eyes" (by Adolfo Utrera and Nilo Menéndez, 1931), and Lara's "Granada" were only preludes to a flood at the end of the decade.

In 1937 there was Pepe Guízar's "Guadalajara," perhaps the most celebrated mariachi number of them all, a song that would first be heard in the United States in the hands of border crossers such as Tito Guízar and Desi Arnaz, and eventually by everyone from Nat King Cole to Elvis Presley. In 1939 alone, Peer published internationally the infectious samba "Brazil" by Ary Barroso; "Babalú," an explosive paean to a Santeria deity by Margarita Lecuona, first a success in Cuba for singer Miguelito Valdés and soon a lasting American theme for Desi Arnaz; "Frenesi" (the very word suggesting a frenzy), by Alberto Domínguez, soon after a swing hit by Artie Shaw; and "Perfidia," also by Domínguez, a US hit for Xavier Cugat. English lyrics were supplied in all of those cases for vocalists wanting to sing them; Helen O'Connell would have a 1941 English-language hit single with "Green Eyes" on one side and "Maria Elena" on the other. The notable stardom of Arnaz, Cugat, and soon Carmen Miranda as well indicated that Latin-flavored North American pop was on its way.

But then, so was war. The international nature of Ralph Peer and Monique Iversen's interests (and in her case, also her Anglo-Danish background) made them acutely aware and wary of developments in Germany. Given her job, she'd had to begin balancing keeping lines of radio broadcast communications open to that country with the bleak reality of the Nazis' hardening grip, from the very first months of the Hitler regime. Her diaries are full of knowledgeable and moving accounts of the dark events unfolding in Europe. Meanwhile, all American music publishers and film companies were faced with increasing German restrictions on any use of so-called "non-Aryan" material, and Peer's efforts to form that organized chain of global publishing houses was running up against unmistakably deteriorating conditions, with the outbreak of the Spanish Civil War in 1936 and Japan's invasion of China in 1937.

Peer had gone to some extraordinary lengths to promote more cross-border musical travel and appearances. In the early thirties, he'd introduced to the United States Mexican singers, such as the operatic "tenor of the Americas" Alfonso Ortiz Tirado, in a US tour of a Mexican production, and others who sang Latin American songs, but seen that there was limited commercial follow-up. There had, it turned out, been little ongoing incentive for Central and South American record labels or music publishers, including even those in which he might own a share or be working with, to build the cross-border market, let alone back global appearances of their artists. ASCAP had never had any interest in representing Latin material, and there was no other performance rights agency to collect for use of Latin songs in the United States. It was more profitable just to have artists stay home.

Peer would focus on that problem and begin to consider some ideas about what could be done about it. The idea that he soon began to experiment with—that if "your" sort of music wasn't being performed much because there was no one willing to collect performance royalties for it, you could start up an organization to fill the gap yourself—would soon have a profound impact on the intersection of roots music and pop in the United States and around the world, and on the music all would hear after the war.

Early in 1939 Monique relocated to Mexico City, after multiple trips there with Ralph, this time to enroll as a student of local history, music, and literature. In the spring, Peer came to an agreement with broadcaster and friend Emilio Azcárraga on the terms of a new jointly owned Mexican-based music publishing venture. Ralph and Monique would travel together, back and forth from New York (never from East Orange) to Havana and Cuernavaca, and they would check in with both Hoagy Carmichael and Fats Waller, who both were performing in London, during one last peacetime trip across the Atlantic. The Soviets and Germans divided Poland between them at the end of September.

On November 8, 1939, Ralph Peer finally came to divorce settlement terms with Anita Peer. He would pay her $350 per month until her death, and the East Orange house became hers alone; she "renounced all claims" to his publishing businesses. She would keep the name Anita Peer for the rest of her life and, like Sadie Peer before her, never remarried. Anita's considerable show-business experience would be put to continuing use, however—as number two in the publicity department for the international *Holiday on Ice* skating shows. On the very day of their divorce decree, the new Southern Music, Mexico was incorporated.

Reporters interview Ralph and Monique, Mexico City, 1943.

Peer with Mexican
musical hero
Agustín Lara.

Walt Disney, Ralph Peer, and "José Carioca," 1942.

With Consuelo Velázquez,
composer of "Bésame Mucho."

The Peers with Tito Guízar and his wife at the christening of Ralph Peer II, 1944.

The Peers with Governor and Mrs. Jimmie Davis, Baton Rouge, 1945.

Ralph Peer with prized camellias, 1950s.

The Park Hill estate, Hollywood Boulevard, mid-1960s.

Ralph Peer II, Monique, Peer, and his mother, Ann, at White Firs, Lake Tahoe, 1954.

Peer-Southern twenty-fifth anniversary party for. R. B. (Bob) Gilmore (to Peer's left) and Dorothy Morrison (to his right), Hotel Astor, New York, 1954.

Presenting the 1955 Ralph Peer Award to Tennessee Ernie Ford, along with Tennessee governor Frank Clement.

Sheet music for "The Great Pretender," in Swedish.

(From left) Vaughn Horton and Roy Horton reunite with core Peer-Southern country songwriters Ted Daffan and Floyd Tillman.
COURTESY OF PEERMUSIC

Murray Deutch with Buddy Holly and the Crickets, at Peer-Southern's Brill Building headquarters, 1957. COURTESY OF JOHN BEECHER

Ralph and Monique Peer with chronicler Lil Borgeson, at Park Hill, 1959.

Two months later, on January 11, 1940, Ralph Sylvester Peer and Monique Hildborg Thora Alexandria Iversen were married in San Antonio, Texas, looking at Mexico City as their main home base. Latin music was not about to be quite as disturbed by events on other continents as most flavors; indeed it soon became part of the US Good Neighbor policy to promote Latin-Allied ties on cultural matters as a buttress against fascism, and they would do their part.

Meanwhile, lasting recognition for what Ralph Peer had contributed during his active A&R years took an important step forward. In that same year Alan Lomax, in part to buttress and further American culture in the face of the same fascist threat, compiled a "List of American Folk Songs on Commercial Records" for the US Library of Congress. He smartly culled 350 key selections from more than three thousand early race and hillbilly records that he listened to so that, as he put it, "the interested musician or student of American society may explore this unknown body of Americana with readiness. . . . I have come away from this listening experience with the certainty that American folk music, while certain folklore specialists have been mourning its decline, has been growing in new directions. . . ."

The younger, forward-looking Lomax was beginning the process of taking stock of commercial recordings of country music, blues, gospel, and regional jazz and calling attention to them as documentation of American musical history—even though documentation had not been their producers' point—with an accounting that would have continuing impact in future revivals of the music of the 1920s and '30s. Of Alan Lomax's list of important records, dozens had been recorded by Ralph Peer at Victor and its affiliated labels. He didn't have the earliest, relevant Okeh records available to him at the time, or there would have been dozens more included from Peer's A&R output.

At the time, however, the unavoidable fact was that there was a world war on, and that the United States was going to be involved before long, too. Ralph and Monique Peer relocated to Mexico City for the beginning of the next vital era in Ralph Peer's personal and musical life.

6

Crossing Borders: The War, Latin Music, and the Media, 1940–1945

"UNLESS YOU HAVE THE FACULTY of changing with the times, you don't get any place," Ralph Peer commented, looking back at this tumultuous period. As the songwriter Tommy Duncan sang with Bob Wills and His Texas Playboys in 1940, in a song of the same name Peer published, "Time changes everything." The lingering Depression and the world war—already real and deadly for Europe and Asia, looming for the United States—were indeed changing just about everything. International entertainment marketers such as the movie studios, the largest record labels, and music publishers such as Peer himself were already facing the loss of access to war-torn markets, business hopes and plans that were dissolving or forced to be indefinitely postponed, and working relationships that were becoming volatile.

American recorded music and sheet music sales, which had just started to recover in the mid-1930s, were walloped once again by the substantial recession of 1937–38. The movies, on the other hand, were edging into a renewed interest in musicals, often lavish color musicals, and there would be opportunities to place songs in them, numbers in line with evolving swing era tastes. Broadcasting looked like more of a lucrative port in the musical storm than ever, with radio doing relatively well and television apparently ready to arrive soon.

NBC's *Let's Dance* radio show, for example, had elevated Benny Goodman to the level of national swing star. More jazz bands were turning to arranged, published straight-ahead rhythm songs of the style pioneered by Fletcher Henderson and Don Redman (who was also published by Peer), and finding popular hits doing so—a necessary component for transformation of the adventurous, improvisational regional jazz of 1920s New Orleans or Kansas City, sold in the recording companies' race records lines, into the mainstream pop that swing became. In Peer's early days with Okeh, and even with RCA Victor into the early 1930s, there were conscious efforts to differentiate pop "hot dance tunes" from jazz records; in the big band swing era, the commercial impetus was to blur any such distinction.

Most of Peer's catalog, dominated as it was by hillbilly, blues, jazz, and Latin songs, was not at all the stuff of everyday national or big urban station broadcasting interest. One significant reason was that the performance rights–handling organization ASCAP, which broadcasters turned to for both easy one-stop song licensing of songs played live on the air and a validation of musical "class," still had little to no interest in representing any of those. ASCAP's old-line publishers and composers still tended to view the roots music spectrum as illiterate, beneath them, and, more important, unprofitable, since there were the known limitations on sheet music sales, or possibilities for promotion on Broadway, upscale nightclub revues, and so on. Overwhelmingly, broadcasters didn't even want to touch the music, and that made hillbilly, blues, or gospel all the more difficult to bring out of genre ghettoization.

There was, on the other hand, a new opportunity for record labels and song sellers alike in the fast rise of a new technology—the jukebox. Millions of records were now needed to fill the glowing boxes, and new songs to put on those records; this was a new mass market not identical to home record sales, one that could address different audiences in targeted neighborhoods and venues. Plenty of bars and restaurants were installing jukeboxes rather than hiring live musicians, and this would soon cause major conflicts.

Publisher Ralph Peer had to deal with song placement in these changing circumstances. He had to connect dots between songs, performers, and the people they worked for, to reach out to the people who were making song decisions. In that regard, his working relationship with Emilio Azcárraga Sr., his junior publishing partner in Mexico, was indeed lucky; by 1940 Azcárraga was the emerging broadcasting titan in the country. Without his old built-in connection to NBC Radio that he'd had working with RCA, Peer had to build and maintain broadcasting relationships, just as he did movie studio relationships, multinational business relationships, and, in some cases, even political relationships.

As a practical matter, these relationship-building efforts, most often unpublicized and behind the scenes, dominated the rest of Ralph S. Peer's professional life—indeed, they *are* the things, though few outside of the music business are aware of them or have to be, that music publishers do all day. They add up to that "constant activity" Peer described as key to publishers' success, and they took, as they still take, energy and stamina— for an independent, international publisher, something like the stamina of pop performers on a never-ending world tour. There would be constant rounds of luncheons, parties, and cocktail receptions thrown for (and by) the right music makers or film producers or dignitaries.

A substantial difference from this point on was that Monique Peer was at his side, as extroverted as he could be reserved, able to connect with a wide variety of people, multilingual, and with gusto for travel, relationship building, and entertaining that seemed to outmatch his own, which was real enough. In her, he had a partner who would push him further toward public recognition and personal publicity than he'd ventured himself, not unlike the way Lil Hardin Armstrong had pushed Louis to the foreground years before. In the general news reports and interview features in which Peer began popping up much more frequently—in Mexico, down the length of South America, in Hollywood and New York—there was often mention of Monique. South of the border, where she often did most of the talking, even as he picked up some working Spanish, there was regular focus on her glamour and perceptiveness. If Sadie Peer was, in effect, Ralph's hometown wife, and Anita Peer his brasher national wife, Monique Peer was his third act—his lasting, flamboyant but diplomatic global wife. ("That one stuck," he would joke, years later.)

Elisabeth Waldo came to know the Peers in Mexico City at this time. A child prodigy classical violinist from Washington State who'd been encouraged and fostered by Jascha Heifetz and Leopold Stokowski, she'd found herself utterly taken by mariachi and older Mexican music while on tour there as a teenager. She'd met Emilio Azcárraga Sr., who arranged for her to work on the regular Mexico City radio broadcasts of Agustín Lara, and, since she was fast developing as a composer herself, he was also her connection to the Peers, and to a significant publishing relationship with them that would last for decades.

"Ralph seemed serious, and Monique was very outgoing," she recalls. "She spoke Spanish very well, but he understood the Spanish well enough, and he had a great sense of what composers he wanted to sign up."

The late Diane Disney Miller, the elder daughter of Walt Disney, who, as we will see, had many chances to spend time with the Peers during the course of World War II and after, told this author in March 2010, "There was a flair about Monique. Mrs. Peer struck me, as a little girl, as kind of a warm, wonderful character. She was very dramatic—expressive; I thought of her as artistic. And Mr. Peer always had a smile on his face, at least, when I saw him."

It's doubtful that the smile was always there. Working partnerships could end for an independent as quickly as they arose. For instance, Peer's first important Hollywood publishing relationship, with Hal Roach, had come to an unexpected halt in late 1935, when Roach suddenly switched from Southern Music to Robbins Music for publishing. The reason was instructive: Roach's films were distributed by Metro-Goldwyn-Mayer by that point, and Nicholas Schenck, one of the studio's owners, had come to own a substantial stake in Robbins Music as well; pressure to switch had not been difficult to exert.

Characteristically, Peer would retain his personal friendship with Hal Roach in any case, even when it was far from convenient. Just a few weeks before the Pearl Harbor attack, the Peers had Roach and his daughter accompany them to an anti-fascist "victory ball" at the new, already celebrated Ciro's nightclub in Hollywood. As Monique noted in her diary, that proved to be a "major faux pas," since, unbeknownst to the Peers at the time, Roach had recently gone into a tone-deaf and highly untimely movie production partnership with Benito Mussolini's son Vittorio.

The unpredictable world of 1940 marked a turning point for Ralph Peer's business life. The wider world now kept encountering *him*. By planning and by circumstance, he was in a position to act on some extraordinary opportunities, and to exert considerable leverage, in new working relationships with individuals and organizations whose interests suddenly paralleled his. His direct involvement in the growing battle between broadcasters and established music publishers would change not just his own business situation, but the face of popular music—the reach of popular roots music most dramatically.

Back in 1935 the large, often old music publishers that had come to be owned by the film studios, such as the Warner Brothers–owned Chappell-Harms and Witmark, the Fox-owned Crawford Music, and the MGM-controlled Robbins Music, had already begun to dominate the ASCAP song performance rights organization. They had noticed the relative health of radio broadcasting versus all of the other Depression-era music-consuming sectors; it was now the single most important outlet for their music. As their agreements with the networks and network-affiliated radio stations came up for negotiation that year, they began to raise the royalty rates the broadcasters had to pay for use of their songs—knowing full well that those songs, from Broadway shows, movies, and other mainstream popular music sources, were virtually the only ones radio saw as prestigious and would use. The royalty shakedown had the broadcasters bristling; the NBC and CBS networks were the dominant parties.

Ralph Peer was bristling himself just then, about the iron wall the motion picture studio–owned publishers maintained to limit royalty payment rates to newer and less-connected ASCAP publishers—to any firms, such as his, not one of the old Tin Pan Alley founding firms or their Hollywood-dominated successors. The actual dispersal of the song performance royalties ASCAP collected remained heavily and openly weighted toward the grandfathered firms, and the powerful movie studios threatened to leave the organization if there was any softening of these practices that now so favored them.

Privately, Peer would tell Monique of his intention to write to the US Federal Trade Commission regarding the difficult position of "independent music publishers versus film corporations which finance music companies." He was no doubt thinking of the recent example and experience of multimedia RCA's return of Southern Music to him in the face of antitrust concerns. Perhaps the film interests—both suppliers of songs as publishers and markets for songs as movie-making studios, as RCA had been—might experience some of the same.

All of that was taking place while Peer was in the process of disengaging from his consulting work with RCA Victor, but was still just inside and connected enough there to be made aware of RCA's corporate displeasure with ASCAP's demands on their NBC radio networks. As a music publishing authority they knew, he presented to NBC a massive document spelling out his view of the situation, and what was bound to ensue after a new contract was signed. He suggested to them that since "ASCAP was a monopoly . . . they would gradually bring more and more pressure" and that as a broadcast network, NBC should be ready for it. He suggested that what the networks really ought to do in response was set up their *own* music publishing companies—publishers, by implication, either powerful enough to force ASCAP's hand on rates, or which, alternatively, could together collect royalties without belonging to ASCAP. (The report itself has not survived.)

Four years later, Peer's prognostication that ASCAP would consistently exert more pressure on the networks had proved quite correct. One early broadcaster response was to develop lists of "tax free" songs for airplay—public domain songs that, since no performance royalties were involved, were of no interest to ASCAP. ASCAP dominance of the air was such that in the autumn of 1939, 83 percent of all tunes played on the NBC and CBS national radio networks were ASCAP signatory publishers' songs.

A significant response was first proposed by Sydney Kaye, a leading copyright attorney who represented CBS and was a friend of Peer's, as were a good many copyright lawyers by then. (Peer's own lawyer, Arthur Fishbein, had become the attorney for Southern Music in 1931, and would remain so throughout Peer's life and beyond.) Kaye advised radio's National Association of Broadcasters to obtain rights to use more songs that were not from ASCAP-affiliated publishers—not just songs from the public domain, as they'd been doing, but also from smaller publishers unaligned with ASCAP, and from overseas sources. Kaye then went much further. In perfect parallel with the ASCAP-avoiding strategy Peer had been suggesting (though not by establishing broadcaster-owned publishing firms as he'd suggested), Kaye advised establishing a new, rival nonprofit performance rights fee-collecting organization (commonly referred to as a PRO, a performance rights organization) funded by substantial broadcaster contributions. There had to be some way to collect and pay those non-ASCAP song sources if they were to be strong enough to stay alive and dependable.

On February 15, 1940, less than a month after Ralph and Monique Peer were married, their friend Sydney Kaye opened the doors on the new organization, Broadcast Music Inc.—BMI—in Manhattan, with just five employees. It was no coincidence that those doors opened just as all of the broadcasters' ASCAP contracts were up for negotiation again, five years having passed since 1935. This time, ASCAP shamelessly demanded an instant doubling of their previous royalties from the networks, to 7.5 percent of advertising revenues. Strikingly, they also offered a lower sliding-scale rate for individual US radio affiliates and independent stations, a differentiation designed to divide the stations from the networks and weaken the networks' position.

With the ASCAP contract unsigned by the broadcasters, BMI went about signing up the stations themselves, as they were free to do, while ramping up their list—now a catalog—of "nontaxable" music, with fresh arrangements of public domain songs that broadcasters could turn to instead of ASCAP's formidable hits, augmented by some others from the catalogs of small publishers that had never affiliated with ASCAP. By that September, BMI's five-employee staff had grown to 220, many of them busy sending affiliated stations both sheet music that could be played live on the air and disc transcriptions of recorded non-ASCAP "live" music programs. (The Carter Family radio transcriptions, including performances of songs that were precisely the sort of Southern-published material that had never been accepted for ASCAP affiliation, were among those.) A radio war was on; Ralph Peer would play a crucial role in that war.

A central and what then seemed an unanswerable ASCAP response to BMI's assault was that they alone had the "quality," prestigious songs that radio listeners really cared about—not that no-account, lowdown hillbilly and blues and foreign stuff. Seeing the possibility for expansion of the music he focused on into the mainstream media realm, Peer stepped up to bolster BMI's response to that claim; BMI management would often call it the crucial act enabling its birth. He supplied the fledgling organization an early lifeline by incorporating a new publishing firm, Peer International, as a BMI signatory, and assigning much of his existing catalog, which, as hillbilly, blues, and Latin material, had never had ASCAP collecting for it or promoting it, to BMI. He knew those songs could give a major boost to the fledgling performance rights society, and they did.

Nearly simultaneously, he launched his own south of the border–based nonprofit American Performing Rights Society (APRS) affiliated with BMI, specifically to ease the path for Latin American songs into North America and beyond. It was at once his own demonstration of the "if the structure's not there, then start it" idea, as BMI itself was, and an answer to the underdevelopment of rights societies in Latin America he'd noted as early as 1928. As his son Ralph Peer II elaborates, setting up APRS was also insurance that if the whole BMI experiment didn't pan out, as no one could yet be sure it would, a Latin American–based global performing rights society would be in place in any case.

ASCAP, rather than cutting their own deal with Peer's fledgling APRS outfit for importing Latin songs into the United States, refused to deal with it at all, but when, to retaliate, they looked into signing up other Latin American music publishing firms that didn't have relationships with Ralph Peer, they quickly discovered that by this point there virtually *weren't any*. Peer began supplying radio, through his BMI-affiliated firm, the formidable catalog of Latin tunes to which he held world rights, as well as more of the existing Southern Music Publishing catalog by switching some songs, such as Hoagy Carmichael's "(Up a) Lazy River," to BMI. (Southern Music's more pop catalog remained ASCAP affiliated, for the most part, still as a lower-ranked firm.). The E. B. Marks publishing firm, which had had that very early South American experience and success, followed suit, and switched from being primarily an ASCAP to primarily a BMI signatory house. These were voluntary, contractual agreements, and publishers could choose where to make them.

The songs available for airplay were getting stronger, and the results could not be missed. By late in the year, the "mainstream" ASCAP tunes on the American airwaves dropped to just 25 percent from the monopolizing 83 percent, and BMI began attracting more songwriters and publishers by beginning a practice ASCAP would not take up until the 1950s—counting disc jockey plays of *records* on the air as "songs played" when figuring royalties due (ASCAP was counting only live performances of the songs). By late December 1940 there were no ASCAP songs at all being played on the NBC, CBS, and Mutual radio networks, which then had some five hundred affiliated stations, large and small, between them—*none*. Broadcaster-owned RCA Victor and Columbia Records began the soon-familiar practice of listing songs on record labels as ASCAP or BMI affiliated—initially so the stations would know which song was affiliated with which organization and stick to the "right" ones.

On December 27 the *Los Angeles Times* interviewed Ralph Peer, who was in Hollywood to "confer with the radio industry," for an article headlined "Popularity of Latin Music Held Due to ASCAP Fight," in which he spelled out the new situation, tossing in a short dissertation on Latin music:

"Deprived of good domestic songs," he noted, "the public naturally took up the Mexican ones that had quality. . . . Today, the song 'Frenesi' is the top seller in music stores; it was written by Alberto Dominquez. The tango tunes, being strictly Argentine, are not so popular as the rumbas, which may be Mexican or Cuban. Also the congas, strictly Cuban, are popular." Peer, apparently with a straight face, called the ASCAP fight he'd had such a considerable hand in fomenting and abetting "regrettable," but added, as the report paraphrased him, "it only goes to show . . . that a free market should be maintained in creative work like songwriting." The new US love affair with Latin music that Peer was describing—and practically inventing—moved from radio to dance floors and local bands and on into the movies, having begun as a minority, often regional taste in the United States and generally unfamiliar outside of its home hemisphere. BMI affiliation of Peer's international Latin copyrights was changing airplay—and music sales.

More broadly, the significance of the establishment of the BMI performance rights society for popular music heard since 1940, which from that point came to be dominated by varying styles of popular roots music, simply cannot be overestimated. The impact was felt first in the United States, of course, where BMI went to work, but the effect would be worldwide, as the styles of American music that would boom as a result had international impact. The postwar explosion of American country and western music, of rhythm and blues, of rock 'n' roll, commercial folk, and later forms of "out from down home" regional music that have come along ever since all depended on this media revolution, on the breaking of "mainstream" music's domination of the US airwaves.

One logical extension of what Peer and Okeh had been doing in Atlanta back in 1923—recording acts on location that had been promoted on live local radio—would be the rise, twenty-five years later, of scrappy independent record labels scattered around the United States that produced C&W, R&B, and regional/ethnic records and promoted them in their own areas. They were able to get their music played on the radio locally and sometimes, if they hit there, nationally and internationally. Those would, overwhelmingly, be popular roots music genre songs published by BMI affiliates. The long-standing ASCAP focus on music written and orchestrated for uptown, so-called "class" audiences, by composers catering to those tastes alone, was quickly becoming inadequate, even archaic; eventually that organization would change its tune as well.

A handful of Southern Music's early roots music songwriters who had seen some sheet music or songbook publication, including Jimmie Rodgers, had had songs tenuously and informally affiliated with ASCAP simply by default, though the agency had had no particular interest in tracking or detailing the results. Southern had been low on the performance payment totem poll there, and the popular roots music songwriters in particular were of no ASCAP interest, but there'd been nowhere else for Peer to go to get performance royalties collected on public use—perhaps, in Rodgers's case, by some local performer who could read music.

On the brink of 1941, the Jimmie Rodgers catalog might well have seemed to offer limited future prospects; his songs were less recorded and performed across the 1938–48 decade than they would again be later, and virtually all of his records had gone out of circulation. Strongly suggesting that Ralph Peer foresaw, or at least hoped for, a revival of interest in the material in the context of a new era for country music on the air, as it received concerted BMI attention, he now transferred all of the Rodgers copyrights to BMI affiliation. Peer's longtime copyright department head and former secretary Dorothy Morrison recalled her Peer-Southern unit working late into the nights between Christmas 1940 and New Year's Eve, doing the paperwork that transferred songs by a number of songwriters, Rodgers included, from their nominal ASCAP affiliation to BMI, effective New Year's 1941. By that day, ASCAP music would be entirely off the air, both nationally *and* on US local radio stations, which, despite ASCAP's efforts to separate them from the network broadcasters, remained opposed to the established PRO's excessive royalty demands.

With that milestone, the radio war naturally reached another level, and headlines moved beyond the *Billboard* and *Variety* trade papers to the general news media, as the public couldn't help but notice the surprising changes afoot on-air. The January 15, 1941, *San Francisco Chronicle* featured a photo of a gleeful Ralph Peer, who was no doubt enjoying himself, toying with this subject and with reporters at the Mark Hopkins Hotel, as the accompanying article noted: "Just before taking off for Mexico, the tall, erudite Peer admitted great irritation over the ASCAP-BMI war. . . . Affiliated with both societies . . . no ASCAP enthusiast . . . [he] declares he has no ax to grind either way: 'The broadcasters will win if they *want* to win. What's more . . . the public seems perfectly satisfied with the type of music that's being presented over the air today.' New composers . . . he said, are being given their first chance, since BMI is encouraging mass production of music."

The *New York Times* would add an exclamation point to his comment on public acceptance of that "type of music," the formerly avoided, even denigrated American roots music and Latin music. On February 9, 1941, their report on the ASCAP-BMI battle concluded with the still-astonishing news that "the sale of sheet music of BMI tunes is far ahead of that for ASCAP music throughout the country. Radio has demonstrated for five weeks that there still can be music without ASCAP." There was still a question as to whether the BMI song supply could remain strong enough to compete once the radio boycott of ASCAP tunes was over—which it soon would be.

Peer made an additional relevant move that February, taking the helm of Melody Lane Music, a publishing company he acquired from old-line ragtime composer Abe Frankel, who'd long been published by Irving Berlin, among others, but had found only limited success trying to go it alone. Peer's Melody Lane Music division would be based in Los Angeles, on Vine Street, a block from the famed corner of Hollywood and Vine, right next door to the new BMI Los Angeles branch office, its express mission publishing pop songs that could appeal to the motion picture industry—BMI-affiliated pop.

After overseeing the opening of that new Hollywood office, Ralph and Monique Peer drove back to Mexico by way of Texas. In mid-March, after flying up to New York in a blizzard, they met with Richard Baer, a representative of reigning radio, theater, and film genius Orson Welles, whose *Citizen Kane* would open just a few weeks later. Welles was contemplating making a Nazi spy film in Mexico based on Arthur Calder-Marshall's novel *The Way to Santiago*, a political thriller, and knew where to go when contemplating an appropriate musical score. That planned picture never got made, but with the connection made, Peer and Welles would cross paths again shortly.

While in New York, the Peers also spent time with Agustín Lara, who was finding more international attention, and with the hot Spanish American bandleader Xavier Cugat, who was reaching new heights of stardom popularizing Latin music in the United States, rumbas in particular, on NBC Radio. (Rumba classes were soon all the rage in the Western world, courtesy of the Arthur Murray dance studios and Latin music's growing radio prominence.) Peer would establish an ongoing working relationship with Cugat—another star that sold the genre songs that would be picked up by others. The bandleader had also developed a close friendship with Peer's Latin American market specialist Fernando Castro, whom he would credit in his 1948 memoir for persuading him to record such Peer-published hits as "Maria Elena."

It would likely have been interesting to hear Ralph Peer's conversation with Cugat that day. In June, *Variety* reported that Warner Brothers music publishing had suddenly started up a Latin publishing company in which Cugat turned out to be a stockholder, noting also "Another outsider given stock in the setup is Fernando Castro, who has quit Southern Music Co. to become professional manager for the WB subsidiary." Castro, the fellow in whose arms Jimmie Rodgers had died, had moved on—briefly, it would turn out. Cugat would nevertheless continue to be a key performer of Peer-published songs, knowing hits when he heard them, whatever the source. It couldn't have been clearer now, though, that Warner and other film-controlled publishers coveted Peer's Latin music territory.

The Western hemisphere nation-hopping that would be part of Ralph and Monique Peer's regular routine and lifestyle over the next years was on in earnest. That spring they stopped in Cuba, Haiti, Puerto Rico, Trinidad, Peru, and Brazil, meeting with contacts and taking in fresh local music, such as Margarita Lecuona's Afro-Cuban conga group in Havana. Lecuona had come up with that staple of Caribbean exotica "Babalú" in 1939; published by Peer, it became globally famous, particularly in the hands of Desi Arnaz, and she had new songs to show.

Aware that they were going to be doing plenty of driving south, east, and west in North America, the Peers bought themselves a new car that spring, a two-tone Cadillac, gray, with a blue roof, and pontoon-like fenders. They picked it up at the same San Antonio dealer where Jimmie Rodgers had bought his many Cadillacs, and drove it through Memphis, Nashville, and Bristol on the way back to New York. They would drive it for years; it would get its first workout as they drove west, cross-country, after seeing Peer's family in upstate New York that summer, stopping to explore Yellowstone National Park and Mount Rushmore, American tourist destinations that Monique had never seen and that Peer had never managed to take in during previous business travels—a preview of their world travel together to come.

Soon it would be commonplace to see Xavier Cugat, Desi Arnaz, or Brazil's Carmen Miranda, who was just being introduced to the United States in 20th Century-Fox's *Down Argentine Way* and would soon be a friend of the Peers', featured in roles in major Hollywood musicals, performing Latin songs. This was precisely the sort of association Ralph Peer had long been hoping to make. That June report in *Variety* ("Latin Music Subsids Multiply") included comments he made while in Chile. "Peer said he found an increasing tie-up between films and music. His affiliate, Southern International, is the only publisher doing biz in the United States in this manner."

Before 1941 was over, Peer would have his long-desired major Hollywood connection, though not one that he might have anticipated. Laughable as Fox's *Down Argentine Way* was as a depiction of life in Argentina or anywhere else south of the US border, it was an early example of a movie theme that was being actively encouraged and financially supported by agencies of the US government—the story of upbeat, interdependent Latin American and North American solidarity.

Rockefeller family scion Nelson Rockefeller, while working at their Standard Oil subsidiary in Venezuela in the late 1930s, had become alarmed by blatant and rising Nazi influence across the region. One pertinent example: many theaters in Buenos Aires were now exhibiting nothing *but* propaganda-minded movies made by the Nazi-controlled UFA studio in Germany. He had proposed a counteroffensive to the Roosevelt administration, setting up an office to foster positive images of the United States and of US/Latin American relations and to counter Nazi cultural influence, through efforts described, unabashedly, as "economic warfare" and "psychological warfare." In the summer of 1940, Rockefeller was named head "coordinator" of this new agency, the Office of Inter-American Affairs (OIAA), as the office became an important arm of the United States's Good Neighbor policy. By October the Rockefeller office had contacted Roy Disney, financial head of the Walt Disney organization (and Walt's brother), about the possibility that the famed animation producer might perhaps work some light Latin themes into a cartoon short or two. The proposal had grown into something much larger, efforts that would prove important in Ralph Peer's life and work.

Walt Disney was at the height of his artistic acclaim; the groundbreaking success of the animation feature *Snow White and the Seven Dwarfs* in 1937 had led to even more ambitious features. *Pinocchio* had been released in February 1940 and the classical music–driven *Fantasia*, which involved collaboration with the likes of surrealist painter Salvador Dali and conductor Leopold Stokowski, was released in November of that same year. The studio was doing preliminary work on *Dumbo* and *Bambi*. Disney's "fun factory," however, was actually in trouble.

They were all very expensive projects, and even as the particularly Europe-friendly *Pinocchio* was being made, Disney's crucial market there was cut off by the war, just as Peer's was. Without global reach, there was little chance that any of these projects could break even, and financing was limited, but Walt Disney had ramped up his whole operation to meet this challenging production schedule before the predicament was clear. What had been a handful of old-line animators with whom he'd worked closely as they did work by hand was now truly a factory, based in Burbank, with some eight hundred employees. Some of those eight hundred still worked on whole sequences and ideas as animation artists traditionally had, others on repetitive pieces of assembly-line animation frames, and there was dissension in the ranks about exhausting working hours, lack of recognition, and relative pay among different levels of employees. In late May 1941 animators attempting to have the Screen Cartoonists Guild recognized as their union went out on strike, in a highly public and bitter confrontation that left Walt Disney both nonplussed by the shifting tone and incensed, inclined toward retaliation. The pro-labor Roosevelt administration officially recognized the strike as legitimate in July, and sent a mediator.

Roy Disney, recognizing that brother Walt was in no mood to make ending the confrontation any easier and likely to make it more difficult, reminded him of that other government agency proposal on the table—financial backing by Rockefeller's office of some Latin-themed films and the preparation for them. That older idea was now coupled with a proposed Walt Disney goodwill tour across South America, where he was generally held in particularly high esteem. Walt agreed to the trip, not simply to get away from the labor confrontation and controversy, or to get that needed federal financial backing, but with the idea, also, of bringing more credible versions of Latin American life to the screen, material that would be credible to people there as well as in the United States. He knew that a more accurate, believable job could bring more of a response, and was interested, just for a start, in getting right the cultural and natural specifics of individual countries rather than presenting some vague, fantasy Latin America.

In August, with US OIAA backing, Disney and a team of artists, writers, and musical researchers that came to be referred to internally as

El Grupo headed south for two and a half months, stopping in Rio, Sao Paulo, and Buenos Aires and, divided into smaller subgroups, across the countryside and small towns in Ecuador, Panama, Bolivia, and Chile. They made drawings of what they saw, filmed the local dances, clothes, architecture, flowers, and animals (this *was* a Disney group), and met with local animators and performers, all background for what would eventually emerge as the celebrated feature travelogue animation *Saludos Amigos*. (El Grupo's films that documented the local flora and fauna for animators' reference inspired the studio to begin producing its famed nature documentary features for the public soon after.)

Inevitably, Walt Disney was also looking for the right music to use in these Latin projects. From the earliest days of his career in animation, even the silent cartooning days, he had given music a central role, privileged it. Since sound had come in, entire cartoons had been built around songs, as was the case with the innovative Silly Symphonies series, "Who's Afraid of the Big Bad Wolf?" in *Three Little Pigs*, and the musical and visual sophistication of *Fantasia*. "When You Wish Upon a Star" from *Pinocchio* had just won the 1940 Oscar for best song, and later generations would grow up seeing his cartoons focused on music and its history, such as 1953's "Toot, Whistle, Plunk and Boom." Lining up songs for the south of the border feature (or shorts; that still wasn't certain) was a priority, and El Grupo and Disney himself scoured cities and towns for authentic local songs and instruments as assiduously as any folklorist or "Home on the Range" lawsuit attorney. What they found was that they were following a trail Ralph Peer had already traveled.

Within days of arriving in Rio, Disney himself had been struck by two catchy songs that were being played there constantly, even by the band in the hotel where they were staying—Ary Barroso's immensely hypnotic, rhythmic, and frankly sexy samba "Aquarela do Brasil," generally known in the United States simply as "Brazil," and the equally grabby but fast "Tico-Tico no Fubá," which had been written by Zequinha de Abreu back in 1917. Disney secured rights to the songs from their original Brazilian publisher, Irmãos Vitale, which informed him, apparently only after the fact, that rights to use them anywhere but at home in Brazil, by the way, were controlled by Peer. As ASCAP had already discovered, for international use of the enticing music of South America, you were going to encounter Ralph Peer.

On October 20, the same day that Walt Disney, his wife, Lilly, and some of El Grupo boarded a steamship to head home, Ned Washington, the Oscar-winning lyricist for "When You Wish Upon a Star," invited Peer to lunch in Los Angeles. It was by no means coincidental. Washington expressed interest in having the Peer organization publish the score for *Dumbo*, on which he was now at work. The subject of the Brazilian songs no doubt was mentioned, and although the Eddie Duchin orchestra had already recorded Peer's new version of "Brazil" with English lyrics by Bob Russell weeks earlier, and Cugat was about to do the same, Peer realized instantly that this could be the significant Hollywood opening he had long been looking for. Monique noted in her diary the next day that "Ralph spent all morning, and I spent all afternoon, waiting for Roy Disney to call." Southern Music never did get the call to publish that *Dumbo* score (that would go to Irving Berlin's publishing house), but Peer would indeed be hearing from Disney and company again just weeks later on matters Latin—by which time the Pearl Harbor attack had brought the United States into World War II.

That December, Walt Disney and his staff were sifting through the masses of potentially useful material they'd noted, drawn, and collected on the Latin American trip, and they invited relevant composers, including Barroso, to join them at the by-then-unionized Burbank studio as animation began. The decision was made to link together the animated shorts—set in Chile, Lake Titicaca, the Argentine pampas, and Rio— into one feature, with both "Aquarela do Brasil" (literally, "Watercolor of Brazil," a visual conceit that would be used in the film) and "Tico-Tico no Fubá" central in the film's climactic final sequence.

The first direct Ralph Peer–Walt Disney meeting appears to have occurred at this time. With negotiations on use of the songs settled, Peer was set to publish colorful sheet music emphasizing their use in *Saludos Amigos* upon the film's release in 1942. While the English-language lyrics the Peer-published version provided were not heard in the film itself, they offered a way for American and other English-language singers, professional and amateur alike, to perform the songs the Disney film put on the American map.

It's telling that Disney's features were then being distributed by RKO, and that Orson Welles was also under contract there. Nelson Rockefeller was a co-owner of the frequently bought and sold studio at the time, and its key releases were generally premiered at Radio City in Rockefeller Center. Negotiations with these RKO-related filmmakers brought Peer closer to that studio, with results. *Billboard* soon noted that "Ralph Peer, whose continuous stream of hits during 1941 has been truly sensational, has stepped into the charmed circle of picture publishers through acquiring the score from the RKO Kay Kyser picture *Playmates*." That musical, which featured that popular bandleader plus John Barrymore in his last film, had a score by Johnny Burke and Jimmy Van Heusen, and its song "Humpty Dumpty Heart" (not to be confused with the later honky-tonk number recorded by Hank Thompson) was a hit for both Bing Crosby and Glenn Miller.

The Peers and Jimmie Davis attended the Sugar Bowl game in New Orleans on New Year's Day 1942, with "You Are My Sunshine" money still pouring in, as it would for decades to come. Helen O'Connell's "Green Eyes" and Gene Autry's "Maria Elena" had been among the top sellers of 1941, in no small measure a result of the growing use of BMI music on the air—and of Ralph Peer's vision in operation. So were a series of hits that were prime examples of the narrowing gap between mainstream pop and the roots genres.

For example, June Hershey and Don Swander—the team that had written the FDR campaign theme song "Happy Days Are Here Again"—had signed with Peer's Melody Lane and come up with the standard-to-be "Deep in the Heart of Texas," which was a hit not by some guitar-slinging Texan singing cowboy, as might have been expected, or even by a western swing band, but by Perry Como singing with the Ted Weems Orchestra, and then by Bing Crosby with Woody Herman. (The Crosby version would be banned by the United Kingdom's BBC for daytime airplay, on the remarkable grounds that it was bound to cause wartime factory workers to stop work and clap their hands in time.)

The Dallas-based duo of Wiley Walker and Gene Sullivan, on the other hand, had written "When My Blue Moon Turns to Gold Again," also published by Ralph Peer, a longing love song with no specific regional or class reference of note in it. Walker and Sullivan would record it for Okeh, as cowhand material, and it went on to become a country, bluegrass, and rockabilly standard, as would Peer-Southern clients Bob Wills and Tommy Duncan's 1941 "Take Me Back to Tulsa," which *they'd* introduce to the world in a Hollywood movie.

Ralph and Monique Peer's first direct encounters with Rockefeller OIAA–backed film operations at work south of the border would not be with the Disney El Grupo, with whom they were already becoming familiar during postproduction of *Saludos Amigos* in Los Angeles, but with Orson Welles and his staff in Rio, in mid-February 1942. Welles was not shooting an international thriller; he was filming Rio's Carnivale for the legendary, eventually aborted documentary *It's All True*. (The politically liberal Welles was as willing to be involved as the conservative Disney with wartime Good Neighbor productions.)

After meeting with Welles's executive assistant, Richard Wilson, and Rockefeller's motion picture production chief John Hay "Jock" Whitney (the backer of the Technicolor process at the time, and later the publisher of the *New York Herald Tribune*), the Peers attended balls being filmed by the Welles crew—first the Carnivale ball at the popular Cassino da Urca, where Carmen Miranda had been discovered the year before, and, the following night, the upscale Vargas costume ball at the city's Teatro Municipal. The Peers met Welles himself at the society affair, where Monique came multicolorfully dressed *as* the song "Aquarelo do Brasil."

Welles became fascinated by the same samba music, and its relation to the rhythms of American jazz, that had enthralled Walt Disney, and he took up the theme in his film. But it was Disney's *Saludos Amigos*, and its "Aquarelo do Brasil"/"Tico-Tico no Fubá" pairing, that induced American performers—and amateur dancers—to take to the samba upon its release. "Brazil" was performed on radio's *Your Hit Parade*, presented by Lucky Strike, for sixteen consecutive weeks. For Ralph Peer, this level of popular success with songs from his Latin catalog had been a long time coming. As he would remind a Rio newspaper in 1945, "It was a *battle* to introduce the samba in my country. Even in 1926 people thought it was Chinese! In 1935, while in Rio, I learned to dance the samba, and after that I insisted. . . . It finally became a hit in 1940."

This was the period in which half or more of the Peers' year was spent in Central and South America and the Caribbean, and in Mexico in particular. New York and Los Angeles demanded most of their time when they were back in the United States, but they actually had no permanent American address. Approaching his fiftieth birthday in May 1942, Ralph Peer still needed to register for the World War II draft, and when he did, he listed his residence as Mexico City, with his US residence as the St. Regis Hotel in New York, and his domestic contact as Bob Gilmore, Southern Music Publishing's long-standing financial executive, at the company's Brill Building headquarters.

That spring, it became obvious to Peer—and everyone in American music—how important placement of songs in movies and on the air was becoming. The recording industry had been witnessing a notable but brief sales comeback. Helen O'Connell's hit version of "Green Eyes" recorded with the Jimmy Dorsey orchestra, for example, had sold 850,000 copies, but that high level of record sales success was about to become literally impossible. Washington severely limited the availability of shellac, a central ingredient in record making, in April, as necessary for the war effort; sales then *couldn't* be that high.

That was the big topic of industry discussion only until June 8, when record production was virtually shut down in its entirety for sixteen months. As broadcasters had challenged the role of ASCAP in the fast-changing music business, and organized animators had challenged the working conditions at Disney and other animation studios, now, under the aggressive leadership of James C. Petrillo, the American Federation of Musicians—the musicians' union—went out on strike, protesting the growing attention the record labels were paying to the jukebox phenomenon, which cut, from the union's standpoint, opportunities for working musicians to play live. No AFM musician would set foot in a recording studio through the end of September 1943, and the labels turned to recordings they'd hurriedly stockpiled before the strike for whatever few shellac-limited releases they could get out, or to a cappella recordings. Then, as in the modern digital era, a decrease in revenue from recordings focused music industry attention on song placement on-screen and in live performances.

Peer still found some opportunities for multimedia interplay. Oliver Wallace, British, and cowriter with Ned Washington of many Disney studio songs, came up with the well-remembered, satirical anti-Hitler blast "(Right in) Der Fuehrer's Face," described as a "Bright Two-Step" on its Bluebird Records label, as recorded by Spike Jones and His City Slickers just days before the strike began. An extended Disney cartoon version followed, starring Donald Duck in a nightmare "Nutzi" dreamland, and then popular sheet music, which pictured Donald tossing a tomato in Hitler's face on the cover, plus a "Buy War Bonds and Stamps for Victory" emblem—published by Peer's Southern Music.

Ralph Peer would become actively involved with one substantial Rockefeller OIAA project himself in that summer of '42. *Music of the New World* was an ambitious educational radio series broadcast across the United States and in Spanish and Portuguese on the Pan American Broadcasting network throughout the Americas; it began that October as part of what was called the *NBC Inter-American University of the Air.* With contributions by prominent academics and musicians, from 1942 through '44 the regularly scheduled programs wended their way through music of the continent—classical, folk, and occasionally even pop— from the pre-Columbian period forward and across the hemisphere. The music and lectures presented, for all of the collegiate trappings, occasionally sounded like the pro–Allied Forces political propaganda they were in part designed to be; Southern Music published all of the handbooks and guides for the series, on behalf of NBC.

The Peers spent most of that first wartime autumn back in Manhattan, in part because Monique suffered the first of several miscarriages, which left her exhausted for weeks, and which had to have been emotionally draining for them both, considering how central having a family was to their personal plans. They then switched from the St. Regis Hotel as their regular New York lodging of choice to the Westchester Country Club, the golf club they would return to from that point whenever they were in the city. The membership, which provided ample room to entertain guests while in the East as well as a getaway for themselves, suggests a tacit acceptance that when they did establish a permanent address, it was going to be out in California, closer to the motion picture industry—a relocation so many music industry professionals would make over time.

Ralph Peer's most important and established movie connection, the Disney organization, was rapidly developing a broad contracted relationship with branches of the US government, producing training films for the armed forces and animated public health and literacy films aimed at Central and South American audiences. Meanwhile, Ralph and Monique Peer were developing a lasting personal friendship with Walt and Lilly Disney.

Walt Disney had spent part of his childhood in Kansas City and returned there from Chicago to start his first animation business—indeed, to the very neighborhood, near the tennis courts, where Ralph and first wife Sadie were living, though he didn't meet Peer at the time. He came from a relatively modest background very similar to Ralph's, exhibited that same generational impulse to grow up and take charge quickly, the same determination to rise from middle-class beginnings into the upper echelons of society, and the same intense curiosity that was inseparable from his pleasures in life. Peer and Disney shared, too, of course, a marked willingness to act on large-scale ideas, to experiment. As Walt and Lilly Disney's daughter Diane Disney Miller, having often seen her parents casually socializing with the Peers at home and elsewhere, told this author in 2010: "Ralph's background was very much like my Dad's; they came from the same place, middle class and Midwestern, and they both had something they wanted to do—*to get it done*. And Dad liked interesting people."

Disney and the El Grupo team returned to Mexico twice in the months that followed, to research the literacy situation in the country for the related films Walt was making; to gather information, music, and new visual ideas for *The Three Caballeros*, his second Latin feature; and also, it would seem, to see Mexico as the Peers had been seeing it, because Ralph and Monique were their de facto hosts and near-constant guides around the country through both trips.

In mid-December 1942, in Mexico City, Walt explained and acted out for the Peers what would become the piñata party sequence for the new film, a complicated set of combined live and animated scenes in which the linchpin romantic musical number would just happen to be Lara's bolero "Solamente Una Vez," then still largely unknown outside of the Spanish-speaking Americas, where it was cherished. Unlike the Peer-copyrighted songs that appeared in *Saludos Amigos*, this one was actually sung in English in *The Three Caballeros*. Dora Luz, obviously at Peer's instigation, sang it with Ray Gilbert's English lyrics (quite different from Lara's Spanish ones) as "You Belong to My Heart."

Peer had come to believe firmly, in keeping with the earlier tango era experiences of publisher Edward Marks, that a lyric had to speak to the audience in the country it was brought to, as any pop lyric would. That meant in practice that, however much of the original language was retained in a partly or entirely imported song, the localized lyric would only occasionally be a close translation of the original. For his part, Lara, not an easy man to overwhelm, would say of the world recognition that resulted, when approached by Robbins Music to change publishers, "If I had another hundred years to live, they would be with Mr. Peer."

During this two-week tour, the Peers wined and dined the Disneys and such key El Grupo members as Disney's foreign-language soundtrack specialist Jack Cutting, the celebrated watercolor artist Mary Blair, and musical director Chuck Wolcott. Ralph and Monique then drove the Disneys to a festival in Mexico City that featured the religious dances of the "bird-men" of Papantla (flying on ropes descending from tree-high poles is involved), and to an equestrian show at the Rancho del Charro festival. As the Mexican magazine *Estampa* reported, just a few weeks later, back in Hollywood, the Peers threw a Mexican-style fiesta for the whole Disney El Grupo contingent, attended by their increasingly close friends Carmen Miranda and her sister Aurora (who would star in *The Three Caballeros*), and featuring music by a lineup of Mexican composers published by Peer.

The second 1943 Disney visit to Mexico, in October, centered particularly on research for the educational and health films on which his studio was working. This time, the Peers drove Walt and Lilly Disney toward Vera Cruz to see schools there, and over the mountains to schools and museums around Cuernavaca. Staying overnight at the large hotel Rancho Telva in nearby Taxco, Disney introduced Peer to a significant parrot that resided there; the talented bird proceeded to perform a full repertoire of popular Mexican songs. This was the parrot that had inspired his animators to create the suave Joe Carioca character for *Saludos Amigos*; Joe (sometimes "Jose") had a larger return role in *The Three Caballeros*.

The Peers and Disneys were often accompanied on their school visits by key El Grupo specialists and by the enthusiastic literacy activist Professor Enrique Lozada. Lozada was a special advisor to Rockefeller's office who was advocating an exchange program much like the future Peace Corps, and, to Disney's crew, also the use of eye-catching color film and Disney-style character animation in the educational films. He was something of a quirky absent-minded professor. He was supposed to lay the groundwork for these visits but had gone missing until the Disney team showed up. He was flummoxed, as Monique's diary would note, when the Peer's car had a flat heading back into Mexico City ("I am helpless as a baby!"), so Ralph proceeded to demonstrate for him how to change a tire. Back in the city, Monique wrote, "every dance they played, Enrique danced the tango anyway, with his famous death grip." Monique would provide breakfast for the Disneys and El Grupo at 5 AM on December 21, before they all flew back to Los Angeles.

The rarely interrupted rounds of parties the Peers attended in Mexico City at this time were an indication of how integrated into the social life of the wartime capital Ralph and Monique had become. Along with the Disney contingent, they attended a formal dinner at the lavish home of the US military attaché General Arthur Harris. (Harris was in fact involved in military intelligence.) The house just next door was that of the celebrated muralist and Marxist Diego Rivera, where Leon Trotsky had been residing until just before he was assassinated in 1940. Rivera and his on-again-off-again wife, painter Frida Kahlo, were traveling in the same circles as the Peers and the general; it was Rivera who suggested to Peer client Elisabeth Waldo that she look into the remnants of the historic music of the Aztecs and Mayans, a musical direction that would shape her future musical life.

"I have always proceeded on the theory," Peer explained to a staff member in Mexico City, "that to the extent of my ability I must make myself into a citizen of the country in which I am doing business. I strongly favor a policy of retaining all of the good things of Mexico for the Mexicans, and I could well understand the unsympathetic attitude of Mexican authors and composers towards a company devoted solely to foreign works."

That attitude was increasingly appreciated. In January 1943, as part of a feature story reiterating the history of his involvement in the country, he and his "distinguida esposa" were interviewed at length by *Estampa*, the popular Mexican magazine, as a noted authority on the growing acceptance of Mexican music around the world, and as an important advocate for it. A follow-up article would spell out how, for the first time ever, very significant amounts of performance royalty money were flowing into Mexico through Peer's efforts. ("An American. What a paradox!" the magazine commented.) Peer spoke of his interest in seeing that Hollywood films used more genuine Mexican songs and confirmed for them that "Mexico's musical success abroad exceeds anything we could imagine; its success is huge . . . even in countries . . . whose mentality is so different from yours."

If there was one song during the war years that best illustrated that point, it was a passionate romantic ballad Peer had picked up for global publication in 1940 and that exploded globally in 1943 at the height of the war, to an extent that word came through the London office and the Soviet embassy there that, in its wake, the Russians were inviting Peer to establish an office in Moscow to promote Mexican music—this while they had such other matters to occupy their thoughts as the Battle of Stalingrad.

The song was "Bésame Mucho," and it would be recorded by everyone from Jimmy Dorsey, with Bob Eberly and Kitty Kallen on vocals, to the Beatles, for their first audition tape in 1962. It was composed by Consuelo Velázquez, who was not yet twenty, and, as she would reveal to the many who asked, had not yet been kissed. She was another trained Mexican musician who, quietly rebelling against the career preordained for her, tried her hand at a pop song. It would turn out to be an all-time BMI seller, topping US charts for twelve weeks in 1944, as recorded by Bing Crosby, Fred Waring, and many others, establishing her reputation. Writing to Peer's son Ralph II in 2003, two years before her death, Ms. Velázquez recalled, "I was, in 1943 when I met your father [she'd previously been working with Peer's Mexico City publishing unit chief, Luis Martínez Serrano], a concert pianist who liked to write, almost secretly, the lyrics and melody of popular songs which I have always carried in my heart, perhaps because my father was a poet and I inherited it . . . but it was [Ralph Peer's] vision that helped me and my fellow Mexican composers to project our music internationally."

With all of Peer's focus on importing Mexican songs into the United States (and with the amount of time he resided in Mexico City, it must have felt at times more like *exporting* them back there, and beyond, by that point), Southern was still doing quite well at home with new hits in the country music field, songs that were suggestive of the directions country would take in its own postwar explosion. Credit for much of the organization's wartime country music success goes to the man Peer hired and had set up in a Chicago office to handle that genre and some pop as well, veteran vaudevillian Nat Vincent, an old friend of Jimmie Rodgers.

Vincent was a performing songwriter who'd cowritten the all-time standard "I'm Forever Blowing Bubbles" and was one-half of the cowboy duo the Happy Chappies of the 1930s. While discussing his possible hiring by Peer's Southern for the new Los Angeles office just before it opened, he and Peer discovered that they had been born just a few blocks apart from each other in Kansas City; their parents had not only known each other, the two of them had been christened by the same reverend. In addition, Monique was familiar with radio scripts that Vincent had submitted to NBC Radio. It was like hiring knowledgeable family.

"I was with Peer for twenty-two years," Nat Vincent recalled in the 1970s. "We were damned near brothers. . . . I got a very nice, beautiful salary and got a very beautiful drawing account for expenses; anything that I wanted to spend, I spent. . . . There was no argument about it."

Vincent was earning that money well, finding writers and placing songs. Oklahoman Johnny Bond, a sidekick of Gene Autry, had come up with the lean, airy and slightly Mexican-tinged western song "Cimarron." Country's biggest star of the moment, the Grand Ole Opry's traditionalist Roy Acuff, later himself co-owner of the field's largest publisher, Acuff-Rose, had a signature hit with the Peer-published proto-rockabilly rhythm number "Night Train to Memphis." And singing songwriter Ted Daffan scored twice, with his archetypal honky-tonk loss ballad, "Born to Lose" and the well-remembered wartime complaint "No Letter Today."

At the turn of 1944, the Peers' typical day down in Mexico City might include a late breakfast with Rafael Hernández, the Puerto Rican–born composer who lit up Mexico and then, through Peer's song-placement efforts, the world with "Lamento Borincano," which depicted the lives of poverty-stricken Puerto Ricans, and the exciting "El Cumbanchero," followed by a meeting with classical composer Manuel Ponce, a compadre of Andrés Segovia whose compositions would become basic in the Mexican guitar repertoire, soon to be published by Southern Music. They might then attend a luncheon where Agustín Lara was presented a "hero of radio" award. Soon after, at the beginning of a new stay in Hollywood, Peer would join his friend Jack Kapp, brother of Dave, and now head of Decca Records, in the studio with Bing Crosby, as the crooner cut another huge Mexican-born, Peer-published global hit, "Amor" (shortened from "Amor, Amor, Amor") as written by Gabriel Ruiz, with English-language lyrics by Sunny Skylar.

Two days after that Crosby recording session, on February 19, 1944, Monique Peer sent a chatty, typically frank letter back to Professor Lozada with the first hint of news that she, and no less Ralph, had long anticipated:

> Ralph and I have some exciting news to give you. As a result of our trip to Mexico, in July we are expecting a Baby. . . . Since our arrival in California, I have had to stay in bed all the time. I have now passed the dangerous period. . . . Considering the past unfortunate experiences I have had along this line, we are taking every precaution . . . on the Doctor's advice, Ralph and I have decided to stay in California until the Baby is born. . . . As a matter of fact, Ralph and I are trying to buy a house out here. Just as fate would have it, it is very important that Ralph be here for business reasons. . . . Ralph has been able to have included in a large majority of the musicals at least one Latin number.

That sums up quite neatly how the Peers' home base came to be Hollywood—closer to the moviemakers, closer than New York for quick drives or flights back to Mexico. The creative operations for Southern Music, Peer International, and Melody Lane that were based in Los Angeles all grew over time, but the Manhattan office would continue to be central corporate headquarters until the 1990s, New York being, of course, closer to the European operations Peer looked forward to resuming and to much of the music and broadcasting businesses. It wasn't as if the entire staff was suddenly on the move. But the songs were taking off more than ever before.

The romantic "Amor" was filmed for the MGM Technicolor musical *Broadway Rhythm*; the singer, Ginny Simms, a Texan band singer who'd sung with Kay Kyser, was briefly a star but is not so well remembered today. She sang it in Spanish, just before Crosby went into the studio to record the English-language version. Ralph Peer seemed frequently to be on the Metro lot now, meeting with director-producer Jack Cummings (Louis B. Mayer's nephew), or with international publicity chief Robert Vogel. In the course of the next year, it would become clear why.

The Esther Williams–Red Skelton musical *Bathing Beauty* would be a showcase for Peer's Latin songs—"Tico-Tico no Fubá" performed by the popular instrumentalist Ethel Smith on organ, no less, Pedro Gutíerrez's "Alma Llanera" sung by the hip-swinging Lina Romay with the Xavier Cugat orchestra, and Maria Grever's "Te Quiero Dijiste" performed by the dramatic Columbian baritone Carlos Ramirez. (The song would become "Magic Is the Moonlight" in its English-language version.)

That Technicolor "women in bathing suits plus music" extravaganza was quickly followed by another, *Two Girls and a Sailor*, which had Cugat and Ms. Romay returning to perform "Babalu" and "Rumba, Rumba," and Carlos Ramirez performing Lara's "Granada." The MGM musical unit, a strong Peer connection and outlet, continued into the postwar years. When a compilation album of Latin classics from Hollywood entitled *Maracas, Marimbas and Mambos* was put together years later, liner notes author Will Friedwald joked, "M-G-M invented Latin-American music. . . . You doubt me?" and then added, seriously, "The man who really put Latin-American music on the Tin Pan Alley map was neither a Latin nor even a performer, but the music publisher Ralph Peer."

After the war, Peer supplied songs for such MGM musicals as *Easy to Wed* (1946), *Fiesta* (1947), and *A Date with Judy* and *On an Island with You* (1948). In *Fiesta*, a studio chorus and a dancing Ricardo Montalbán introduced to the United States the infectious "La Bamba," an adaptation of a folk song the world would come to know more widely a decade later in the rock version by Richie Valens.

This was, without question, one of the truly upbeat periods in Ralph Peer's life. The Peers had been renting an apartment at the Palacio building on Fountain Avenue in Los Angeles, looking for houses in spurts, when the chance to own a dream home—a tidy, impressive, and fabled three-acre estate—came their way. This was not a kind of investment

Peer had ever made before; indeed, at flush times he tended to plow the income back into the business, not personal luxuries.

Built in the 1920s at 8159 Hollywood Boulevard, near Laurel Canyon, as the home of developer C. F. DeWitt, the DeWitt mansion is still considered a classic example of Los Angeles regional architecture, not the biggest or the most gaudy, but one of the most successful in making use of hacienda influences. Designed by Charles Kyson, the sprawling California Spanish mansion, with its massive fireplace, winding staircase, and wood-beamed ceilings, had long since appeared in *Architectural Digest*; Frank Lloyd Wright designed the house next door. It was a nice neighborhood. The estate included its own waterfall and grotto-style pool; the house's forty-five-foot living room was going to see a lot of entertaining.

The most recent owner had had a son eligible for the draft, and the family was looking to relocate to some farm property fast so the son would be deferred as an agricultural worker, which lowered the asking price further, at a time when property values were already low because of the war. The Peers renamed it Park Hill, after Monique's family's house in England. It was Ralph Peer's home base for the rest of his life and also the site where, once he found the time, he had the space to return to his youthful preoccupations of gardening and science.

In July, as the Disney studio was finalizing work on *The Three Caballeros*, Peer was on hand in the recording studio at Decca as Bing Crosby and the Andrews Sisters recorded its title song. Ralph and a very pregnant Monique moved into Park Hill and had a first meal there on August 2, 1944; among the very first visitors were the film's live-action star Aurora Miranda, Carmen's sister, and their mother, "Mama Miranda." (Carmen would attend a number of parties at Park Hill herself.) The first guests to sign the guest book were Walt and Lilly Disney and their daughters.

A few days later, on August 9, Ralph Peer's only child was born, baby Ralph Alejandro Iversen Peer, delivered by Cesarian section at Good Samaritan Hospital that morning, weighing eight pounds, ten ounces. Mother and son came home to Park Hill ten days later to be greeted by family, music and film industry friends, and longtime Peer organization employees such as Dorothy Morrison, who'd been with Peer since starting out as his secretary in the 1920s. Telegrams poured in with congratulations that tended to take a topical tone. BMI's Sydney Kaye telegrammed, "Eight pound ten ounces well over expected quota" referencing performance royalty rules. Songwriter Walter Donaldson suggested, "Now you know what I mean by My Blue Heaven." The Peers' attorney Arthur Fishbein noted that this new "partner" would "pay exorbitant nontaxable dividends to you and remaining stockholder Monique. Am ready and willing to take orders from the new member of Peer companies but only ask that he emulate you."

The Three Caballeros premiered in Mexico City in December, by which point the Southern Music songbook for the film was already in circulation; in addition to the dance tunes and "You Belong to My Heart," the combined live action/animated feature introduced audiences to Ary Barroso's lush ballad "Baía." The Peers and Disneys attended the New Year's Day 1945 Rose Bowl together, and were all present the next night as singer Tito Guízar, now a recognizable movie star in multiple countries, recorded ballads at RCA for his upcoming film at Republic Pictures, *Brazil*. The next morning, at the Paulist Fathers chapel in Westwood, Guízar stood as godfather as baby Ralph was christened.

Peer published other well-recalled pop hits as the war drew to a close—Lawrence Welk's popping bubbles theme-song-to-be "Champagne Time," and Russ Morgan's "You're Nobody Till Somebody Loves You," a hit later for the Mills Brothers and, eventually, for Dean Martin. By now, it was difficult to name a motion picture studio not turning to Peer and Southern Music for Latin songs for films—MGM still, but also Paramount, for example, where Dorothy Lamour sang Lara's "Buscandote" and four other numbers in *Masquerade in Mexico*, and Republic, where Tito Guízar starred in *Mexicana*, singing Roberto Livi and Bebu Silvetti's "De Corazón a Corazón," all in 1945.

As the end of the war in Europe became foreseeable, the interest in the firm's songs was palpable, and Peer, through the sometimes daring efforts of the organization's London chief, Thomas Ward, was able to begin renewing contacts across the continent, in some cases, well before hostilities ceased.

Peer would recall, "'Amor, Amor' was very big in England, and in the closing days of the German occupation, all the French people would turn on their radios to the British station and all they heard was 'Amor,

Amor,' at this crucial moment. I had this fellow in England named Thomas Ward who was a copyright expert . . . quite a live wire for an Englishman, who some way or another got himself onto the first plane that arrived in Paris from London bearing non-military people. . . . He went back to the remains of [a publishing firm we had commissioned in France], cooked up a little deal, and gave them a six-month contract to print the sheet music of 'Amor, Amor.' The only paper in Paris was black market paper; paper was manufactured in the eastern part of France, which was still in the hands of the Germans. But still, there was paper around . . . some of it was white, some of it was gray, any color, any thickness, and we printed 'Amor, Amor.' We eventually sold 750,000 copies."

After the war, Ward wrote a very detailed, sometimes suspenseful thirty-six-page single-spaced memoir detailing his adventures in reestablishing Peer-Southern links across Europe in the months that followed, depicting how he managed to get into Spain early despite Franco hostility, and the stream of cables he received from Peer during a futile attempt to persuade the existing Spanish performance rights society to work with APRS and BMI as its representatives in the United States. Ward connected with the new post-Mussolini Italian authorities to look into bootlegged versions of Peer songs that had been appearing in the country, and reconnected with the Benelux countries and Scandinavia in the fall of 1945.

"It was my practice," Ward later noted, "to report so fully that more than once I asked Mr. Peer if my letters were too long and too many. His answers left no doubt about his quite avid interest. . . . He telephoned me frequently from New York, Hollywood, and other places. My letters from him tended to alternate between the pat on the back and the kick in the pants." (As did letters from Peer to more than one employee, over the years.) Ward would continue to be a key Peer-Southern executive through the postwar years, as Peer's long-brewing vision of an international string of publishing companies working locally, interconnected globally, could be fulfilled.

In New York, in February 1945, Ralph and Monique caught a new Theater Guild production, as they generally caught significant new Broadway shows. This one, *Sing Out, Sweet Land*, provided food for thought. It starred Alfred Drake and was presented as "the saga of American folk music," and it included adaptations of such songs as "Little Mohee," "Frankie and Johnny," "Casey Jones," and even W. C. Handy's 1924 "Basement Blues." Monique commented in her diary, accurately, "Ralph made the original recordings of most of these songs. . . . Hillbilly singer very good." The singer was Burl Ives, who within a few years would be producing a string of new hit songs published by Peer, in an era in which popular revival and reuse of "old familiar tunes" would be much in vogue.

7

Going Global: Expansion, 1946–1951

In **1946, at age fifty-four,** Ralph Peer had more reasons to stay home than he'd ever had before—his Hollywood connections, the parties at Park Hill, the novelty of the first real home base he'd had in years, the toddler son on whom he doted and on whose rapid growth he'd report regularly to friends and colleagues. (An organ grinder with a monkey had been a feature of little Ralph's second birthday party.) In addition, he was becoming more serious about a hobby that had begun almost accidentally, but which he quickly discovered appealed to both his scientific and aesthetic sides and seemed attractively removed from the executive demands of his music business work: cultivating and collecting camellias.

Peer's lingering, lifelong interest in gardening, an interest that sometimes puzzled those who knew the businessman more than the man, found a focus in these shrubs with large, varied, colorful flowers. As he explained in 1959:

> We had purchased [the Park Hill estate] because of the wonderful evergreen trees, but soon we noticed that the deep shade under these trees would permit nothing to grow, even grass. A camellia nurseryman gave me the idea that camellias and azaleas could be grown in some of the barren area. I started with three small camellia

plants placed just outside the front gates . . . [that] thrived mightily, and I began an expansion of the camellia planting activities that continue to this day. Almost at once I took advantage of my travels abroad to learn more about camellias and to bring in varieties and species from the various countries I visited.

By the time Ralph Peer recalled this, he would have over three thousand camellia plants at Park Hill, including rare species he'd introduced into the Western world from Asia. The pastime that had begun as an isolated, solitary pursuit in childhood became still another continuous executive activity in middle age. The parallels between Peer's burgeoning camellia-centered undertakings and the path of his music career are striking—evolving as they would from focusing on a specialized area useful for the special needs of the home grounds to building up his catalog inventory; expanding the search for examples of rare, quality species on location across the globe; cultivating and expanding the global presence of the species he found; and rising as a promoter and an executive among its enthusiasts. The similarities suggest once again how much the temperament of the man lay behind the scope of his ventures. The hobby that might have been one more reason to stay home quickly became one more reason to travel—and there were many now.

Peer had hardly been alone in having had to postpone business plans in the face of World War II. In any list of the war's notable effects, after previously unimaginable mass death and destruction, the defeat of the Axis powers, and the last gasp of European colonialism, were infinite stories of plans deferred around the world in every walk of life. Peer's stalled vision, awaiting implementation since the late 1930s, was for a truly global network of publishing firms that could identify and publish engaging music from virtually anywhere, enabling him to export it in ways that might appeal anywhere else—flavorful regional music made not just popular, but globally popular. The bulk of the profits from his Latin, Hollywood, and country music successes of the years since leaving RCA Victor would go toward execution of that global plan.

For all of the influence Peer had established down the length of the Western Hemisphere, the war had essentially confined his activities there. With wartime obstacles passed, and with Monique a wife and partner as eager to take up the travel entailed in implementing the plan as he was, Peer's "constant activities" surged. In the decade that followed, as the Peers traveled to key music markets, places of personal interest and, on two occasions, around the world, Peer International and Southern Music (referred to in this era as "the Peer-Southern Organization") would establish new, working corporate units in Australia, Austria, Belgium, Brazil, Columbia, Cuba, the Dominican Republic, Germany, Italy, Japan, the Netherlands, New Zealand, Puerto Rico, South Africa, Spain, Sweden, and Switzerland, adding to the existing units in the United States, Argentina, Canada, Mexico, France, and Great Britain.

Over Christmas and New Year's 1946–47, Ralph and Monique Peer took their first trip together into barely recovered Europe, flying by way of Canada and the Azores; it was still necessary to make stops to fly transatlantic. They stopped in at the Peer-Southern office on London's fabled Denmark Street, touching base again with friends and music industry contacts there, then checked on the occasionally prickly executive Rolf Marbot's handling of the office in Paris. Marbot was actually a Polish Jew born Albrecht Marcuse, and he'd shown considerable courage in staying in place on the job through the war, as had Manuel Salinger, also Jewish, at the Barcelona office. The Peers saw Edith Piaf perform while in Paris, and then, combining business and tourism, proceeded through Geneva, Barcelona, Madrid, Lisbon, Milan, and Rome, including a visit to the Vatican, before heading home. (Their time in Latin America appears to have made Monique, already inclined that way, a more devout Roman Catholic.)

One incident from the trip made the papers; Jimmie Fidler's nationally syndicated column would report, "Ralph S. Peer, the music publishing tycoon who specializes in buying American rights to foreign tunes, is sizzling. During his recent European jaunt, he bought several dozen originals, and then made the mistake of crossing a strip of Russian-controlled Germany. The Soviets seized all his music manuscripts and won't return them until they've been 'decoded' to see if they are really music." Apparently, no secret codes were unearthed.

Corporate expansion such as Peer now projected is often fraught with challenges, even dangers; stories of high-flying enterprises that crash at just that stage of growth are never in short supply. Inevitably, his focus on building up the global reach of Peer-Southern meant that he would more and more have to rely on trustworthy, savvy professional managers to sign writers, place songs, and develop markets, even in his core musical fields—country and Latin. His firm no longer fit into one room in the Brill Building, as it had in the late 1920s; it would soon occupy a whole floor.

On March 26, 1948, as Southern Music marked its twentieth anniversary, Peer wrote to his executives in both the US and UK offices recalling the company's modest beginnings and its path since, acknowledging that cash was temporarily tight because of war disruptions, high postwar taxes, and investments he was making, and adding: "As the business grows, my personal participation necessarily becomes less. I take great pleasure in turning over my responsibilities to others because this is insurance for the future, and also because it makes available new and fresh ideas. . . ."

Another page was being turned; the aspects of the musical work in which he would most often play a hands-on role were narrowing. There were certainly new opportunities and challenges for Peer and his firm in the dramatically expansive postwar pop music arena, however; the music was increasingly derived from regional roots music—fruits of developments he had worked for, and of choices he had made.

The American GI presence in England, the rest of Europe, and the Pacific had sparked added global interest in the swinging and often down-home music they'd brought with them. As unlikely as it seemed at first, the Japanese branch of Peer-Southern, for example, would be expanded in 1951 because of rising taste for Latin music in Tokyo, an aftereffect of the American occupation. Back at home, the wartime intermingling of men and women in uniform from all US regions, especially in the many military bases located in the South, led to a leap in potential national interest in once regionally limited music. In 1944 that trend led the industry trade magazine *Billboard* to institute a new chart to track popular roots music, including hits in both "folk songs" (most of which would later be deemed "country," some commercial folk) and blues. By the end of the decade, the totality included would be so booming that the magazine would split folk and blues into two long-standing, better-understood and -implemented specialty pop music tracks—country and western, and rhythm and blues. The explosiveness of these fields was a direct result of the influence of BMI opening radio to rawer, rootsier styles, just as Peer had hoped. As it happened, his own strong focus on developing Latin music at Peer-Southern in the 1938–48 decade, while looking to maintain the firm's position in country and western, made his company a lesser player in the emerging R&B field. Eventually, he would address that arena again as well.

The dozens of small, regional record labels that were now emerging changed the terms of the pop music business. The proliferating new firms were ripe new outlets for placement of songs, and ever more likely to record multiple versions of hot titles with different artists, putting multiple versions on jukeboxes and on the air. While that was, of course, largely good news for publishers, performers, and songwriters alike, for publishers like Peer, it also meant that more domains needed to be tended to, more relationships fostered, and that more song placements needed to be made—by more staff.

Ralph Peer's particular need for a strong in-house executive team became all the more pressing as the booming genres he'd been dominating began to attract ambitious competitors. Until World War II, if a country performer or writer's songs were not being published by Southern, they were very probably distributed only in "it's yours for a dime" handouts at shows, and weren't truly published in any professional sense—including tending to further song placement and royalty promotion—at all. But that was no longer the situation.

Jean and Julian Aberbach—two Austrian-born brothers who had founded the French music publishing firm SEMI in the early 1930s then sold it in 1935 to Peer, who'd been their principal American client—entered the fray on their own. Jean had also worked as Ralph Peer's representative in Europe, placing country, Latin, jazz, and pop songs on the continent, and had learned some things in the process.

Having relocated to the United States (the Aberbachs were Jews who had fled from the Nazis), and seeing by 1942 that the advent of BMI could offer opportunities, Jean had approached his New World boss, Tin Pan Alley publishing legend Max Dreyfus of Chappell Music, to bankroll the brothers in a new BMI-signatory firm that would have a cowboy song and country music focus. Disdainful of down-home music, Dreyfus had turned them down. By 1945 they had accumulated the wherewithal to buy out an audio transcription firm on their own, refocus it on publishing, relocate it to Los Angeles, and rename it Hill & Range Songs. They scored an immediate hit with Spade Cooley's "Shame on You," and began an assault on the country markets from that western point of entry. The Aberbachs next persuaded Bob Wills, who was just coming off a massive Peer-published hit, the western swing classic "Stay All Night (Stay a Little Longer)," to switch publishers from Southern to Hill & Range, offering him something unprecedented—setting up a firm in Wills's own name in which he would own one half and they the other.

Publicly, Peer said nothing about the opening salvos by this encroaching new competitor; privately, he tended to dismiss the Aberbachs as a serious threat, initially underestimating their level of understanding of the American roots music markets. By early 1946, however, when Hill & Range attempted to lure away two stalwarts of his country songwriter roster, Floyd Tillman and Ted Daffan, and even succeeded in prying away several secondary, cowritten songs by the latter, that couldn't go unnoticed. The high stakes were fully apparent as Floyd Tillman's era-defining "I Love You So Much It Hurts" and "Slipping Around" became massive hits in the following months, as recorded by Tillman himself, by cowboy pop singer Jimmy Wakely, and by many others—lucrative Peer-Southern copyrights that might very easily have slipped away.

Peer's pursuit of the global network seems to have limited his immediate cash on hand that might have been offered to writers as big signing bonuses—an additional enticement Hill & Range was offering regularly. In addition, the Aberbachs' concept of a 50/50 deal in which performer-publishers would have the likes of a "Bob Wills Music" company among their personal credits, administered by Hill & Range, was proving to be a formidable attraction—an ego booster, and sometimes, at least, a very lucrative one for the performer involved, even if they weren't substantial songwriters themselves. (The Aberbachs would eventually set up and run jointly owned companies for Ernest Tubb, Eddy Arnold, and, most famously, Elvis Presley.)

This was a boat that Ralph Peer missed. It was a proposition that would have been a natural extension of the responsibilities he had placed on recording artists to gather material back in his A&R days, of his firm's history of administering functions for smaller companies internationally, of selling songs broadly for smaller firms where they couldn't, and of his early realization that he could compete against record or movie company–owned publishers by providing more and better services. But he didn't pounce on this new model, and he would have cause to regret it.

Hill & Range was not his only significant new country music publishing competitor. In 1942, once again, in direct response to the possibilities opened by the founding of BMI, veteran music industry performer, radio host, and songwriter Fred Rose, who'd known Peer casually since the 1920s, got financial backing from Grand Ole Opry star Roy Acuff and founded Acuff-Rose Publishing, the first music publishing company to establish itself in the Opry's Nashville, Tennessee, home—at the very time Acuff was having his big hit with the Peer stable's "Night Train to Memphis." Acuff and Rose were hoping that relationships built in Nashville through the Opry and its on-air home, WSM radio, would prove decisive; that it would actually turn out that way remained to be seen.

When a thin, charismatic young singer-songwriter named Hank Williams brought his songs to Acuff-Rose in 1946, Rose signed him and became his manager, his frequent song cowriter, and often his producer at the just-established MGM Records label. Though Peer had that excellent working relationship with the MGM film studio, he still had no interest in returning to A&R work when "Metro" decided to start a record label. By contrast, his one-time competitor in the early development of hillbilly, Frank Walker, who'd only recently succeeded Eli Oberstein as A&R chief at RCA Victor, was happy to move it on over to assume the label's presidency. Fred Rose would be MGM's unsalaried, Nashville-based A&R chief, and following the old Ralph Peer model, he received payment for his A&R work in the form of a share of the mechanical publishing royalties on the songs recorded. He quickly introduced the young Acuff-Rose singing songwriter Hank Williams to Frank Walker. Before the decade was out, with Nashville, Tennessee, clearly becoming the core home of the country music business, the Rose-Walker-Williams combination would make Acuff-Rose a growing power in country.

It would take several crucial years for Ralph Peer to respond directly to these developments, but Southern Music's history and preeminence in the field still had its rewards—as did the "hitting them where they're not" business philosophy. Peer began to publish a performing songwriter in 1946 who would change one significant face of popular roots music for all time, opening a new arena, a Kentuckian who revered both Jimmie Rodgers and the Carter Family, who'd started recording along with his brother at RCA Victor/Bluebird in 1936, with Oberstein producing. (One of the brothers' releases was actually the flip side of the "The Carter Family and Jimmie Rodgers in Texas.") He'd become a star of the Grand Ole Opry in 1940 with a frantic, driving, and furiously rendered version of Rodgers's Peer-published "Muleskinner Blues," a performance that, by his own definition, marked the birth of the bluegrass genre, a dynamic musical conversation between the traditional and the very up-to-date. This was, of course, Bill Monroe—an Opry star who was savvy about the potential money to be made in writing publishable songs, and who insisted on working with a publisher with a solid, established history of understanding the likes of himself.

As Monroe's son James would recall Bill telling him, "He knew about Peer-Southern, and had become friends with Peer; they knew each other even back into the Monroe Brothers time. Back in those days, people didn't know anything about publishing at all; my father said he couldn't find anybody in Tennessee who knew much about it, so he had to go find somebody who did! That's what I heard my father say."

In 1945, as Monroe began piecing together the classic Blue Grass Boys lineup, he switched to Columbia Records, where the British "Uncle" Art Satherley, whom Ralph Peer considered "a recording genius" and a friend, was in charge of production. The engaging guitarist and lead vocalist Lester Flatt would soon join the band, and then Earl Scruggs, whose epic banjo contributions to the music would be such that he's come to be considered the cofounder of bluegrass. Given Monroe's confidence in Ralph Peer as his publisher, the succession of epochal songs that the "Father of Bluegrass" produced in the following years would all be published by him, and they would be endlessly recorded and performed ever after—"Rocky Road Blues," "Kentucky Waltz," "Molly and Tenbrooks," "Blue Moon of Kentucky." Some would be cowritten by

Monroe and Lester Flatt ("Will You Be Loving Another Man," "Mother's Only Sleeping"), establishing a publishing relationship that would carry through to the Flatt & Scruggs era and the songs created by that band, making Peer-Southern the crucial publisher in the rise of the bluegrass field.

It soon got more complicated than that. As early as April 1947, Hill & Range had optimistically set up a potential Bill Monroe Music; the Aberbachs were no doubt attempting to convince "Big Mon" that somebody with an office in Tennessee might know something after all. No Monroe songs were actually published under that banner until 1951, though, and even then he continued to work with both houses, with many of his new songs still published by Peer-Southern under various pen names. Monroe was apparently intent on keeping happy connections with as many publishers as could possibly make him money.

By 1947, then, Peer was certainly aware that this was one more important (and shrewd) songwriter the Aberbachs were attempting to lure away. In-house, he expressed doubts that the veteran Nat Vincent was competing aggressively enough to fend off the raiding competition and to maintain songwriter relationships. It would take some months to find and add the right additional staffer to augment the effort, and, meanwhile, there was that global network to build, Ralph Peer's central preoccupation. While cash on hand seems still to have been tight, Peer could gloat, later on, that he had generally been able to use local royalties from his existing copyrights to establish new businesses in additional country after country. It was a time for relationship building across the world. "I make it my *business* to go on these trips abroad," he would note. "I get in touch with the recording executives, and try to know them."

And off they went. As Ralph and Monique Peer flew east from Los Angeles to begin their first around-the-world trip in September 1948, there was no explosive bluegrass breakdown soundtrack to be heard, but it would have felt appropriate. For alleged "peacetime," the globe they were about to circle was in turmoil and crisis; it was the time of Truman's Berlin Airlift in Europe, designed to reach Berliners cut off by Soviet troops, of the first Arab-Israeli war in the Middle East, of clashes between the new states of India and Pakistan, and of the civil war in China that would lead to the Maoist revolution within months. But take off into all of that they did. The younger Ralph accompanied them as far as New York, and then was taken back to Hollywood by a governess. (There was plenty of company back at home now; in addition to the nanny/governess, both grandmothers were on hand. Ralph's mother, Ann Peer, had moved into a full apartment in an outbuilding on the Park Hill grounds, and Monique's mother, Hilda Iversen, who had been living in New York after relocating from England, took up residence in a guest room at the main Park Hill house.)

After doing some business in Washington, the Peers flew Pan American to the United Kingdom in mid-October, where Peer met with Thomas Ward and his London staff, with Douglas Furber, the very English composer of "The Lambeth Walk," and conferenced with British Board of Trade delegates who were about to take part in a revision of the Berne Convention, the international literary and artistic copyright agreements. He pushed for a copyright treaty between the United Kingdom and Mexico while he was at it. In Paris, the following week, the Peers were invited by Maurice Chevalier to see his one-man show, in which he was singing half a dozen French Peer-published songs, including singer-songwriter Francis Lemarque's new "Le Tuer Affamé," the ballad of a long-suffering hit man who barely has time to eat between assassination jobs.

Having checked in with Peer-Southern's existing European connections, Ralph and Monique boarded a plane in Lisbon in October, heading south toward the Belgian Congo, on a globe-trekking route that would take them down to South Africa, then north to Egypt, on to India via Iraq, across Burma and Malaya to Australia and New Zealand, and then to Thailand, China, and Japan, before heading back to Los Angeles. Ralph documented the trip's nonbusiness aspects, particularly the camellia varieties they saw and natural and historic sights they encountered along the way, on sixteen-millimeter color home movie film; Monique maintained a detailed diary, recording their experiences and her thoughts on his Audograph dictation machine for later transcribing.

The mix of business and pleasure would have been exhausting for many of us; they'd, for example, follow the Congo River to its rapids by day, Ralph documenting the sights and camellia varieties, then meet with a representative of RCA International, or regional importers of Columbia or Decca Records, at night, followed by lengthy late-night letter-answering, as correspondence arrived from London and other offices.

Repeatedly, the global reach of the music Ralph Peer had been fostering for decades proved a point of contact not just with music industry people the Peers met by appointment, but with others encountered along the way. They were in South Africa's busy port city Durban as news came of Truman's "by a nose" defeat of Thomas E. Dewey in the US presidential election, attending a club where, interestingly enough during that nation's racial apartheid era, the band featured American blues, and, as Monique noted, "the most popular music to dance to were the Latin rhythms." (She offered the management some free, anonymous advice on beginning with slower rumbas and holding the conga for last if they wanted people to stay on the dance floor all night.)

In Cape Town, Peer met with a local Disney representative and with Ivan Silverbauer of the British Performing Rights Society, who joined them on a drive to the Cape of Good Hope. Arthur Harris, owner of a local record-pressing plant, filled them in on the continuing popularity of "American hillbilly music" in South Africa, a substantial percentage of which had been Peer-Southern copyrights, ever since the Jimmie Rodgers era.

In late November, they were in Egypt, and struggling through customs with endless questions about their film equipment, dictation recorder, and the film already shot. But the suspicious local chief of police at the ancient Luxor site at Thebes was suddenly all smiles when he saw "music publishers" on their passports; he turned out to be a lover of Latin music and then, as Monique chronicled, "when I told him . . . that we knew Carmen Miranda, he was ready to kiss my foot." The Peers would get to see the tombs of King Tut and Ramses II and the Temple of Karnak, after all, and were introduced to camel riding near the Great Pyramids. (Their camel rides, like their many interactions with the world's animals in the course of the trip, from monkeys to hippos to vipers and a talented sheep-herding dog in New Zealand, were captured on film for the entertainment of four-year-old son Ralph when they got home.)

The Peers obtained visas on December 3, 1948, to fly from Cairo toward the Indian subcontinent, taking off just as Dr. Ralph Bunche, the United Nations mediator, was arriving in the city to conduct Middle East peace talks. They touched down briefly in then relatively placid Basra, Iraq, on the way to Karachi, in the new state of Pakistan—where they were again greeted warily, this time because they intended to proceed into the new state of India as well. Staying overnight, they witnessed streets and former British military sites overrun with refugees after the recent partition. In Bombay, their guide around India was a Mr. Billimoria, of the large Eranee Brothers import-export house, which was involved in the music business. Together they toured Old Delhi, the Taj Mahal, the nearby Hindu temple of Vishnu-Shiva, and the gardens of the Royal Agri Horticultural Society. A number of young Hindu girls they were introduced to proved especially interested in stories of contemporary Hollywood, and in particular, once again, their friend and occasional houseguest, Latin music icon Carmen Miranda.

There was relatively little business talk on the subcontinent; within days Ralph and Monique proceeded to Rangoon, in the newly independent Burma, where there were ongoing government battles with Communist Party rebels just ten miles away, then on to Singapore via a flying boat for the mandatory drinks at Raffles, and to Surabaya, Java, where yet another war was on—this one between the Dutch government army troops and the Indonesian Republic. They arrived on the very night the Dutch recaptured the Indonesian capital. Their working destination for this leg of the trip was Australia; they were in Sydney on December 21 with music business to do.

There Peer called a meeting of the board of Southern Music Publishing Australasia, formed in late 1946, attended repeated business conferences, met with orchestras, and spent an Australian summertime Christmas Eve with Dudley Fegan, head of the Australian Record Company. It was during this visit that Peer first met and heard Tex Morton, a talented interpreter of Jimmie Rodgers's music, born in New Zealand, who'd been adapting some of the brakeman's musical ideas and lyrics for Australian settings, a key starting point for the lasting, popular "bush ballad" popular regional music genre there. The Peers, Monique noted in her diary, spent an evening with Morton and his guitar-playing partner, Johnny

Waikura, in "an old-fashioned hillbilly songfest." Peer signed Tex Morton as a songwriter and made connections for him needed for an attempted career in North America; the latter idea proved to be only a limited success, but Morton would become a legend at home.

After a brief sojourn in New Zealand with visits to Maori tribal towns, the Peers returned to Sydney, where they held a reception for some eighty music industry executives, broadcasters, government broadcasting regulators, and local musicians. Peer-Southern Australasia was formally established and would remain a very significant region for the organization. In what would prove a considerable personal bonus, in Sydney, Professor Eben Waterhouse, author of *Camellia Quest*, a book famous in that field, told the Peers about potential connections in Kunming, China, that might lead them to an extremely rare and much-sought-after variety of yellow camellia never seen in the United States. The tip would eventually pay off in one of Ralph Peer's best-known efforts in that arena.

Bangkok was the next stop. Evidence of bombing during the war was everywhere as they toured Thailand's palace and its celebrated Buddhist temples, attended Thai musical productions, and then flew on to Hong Kong. It was now late January 1949, and with its mélange of Nationalist and Communist higher-ups, black marketeers, and war refugees, Hong Kong was a center of considerable intrigue and drama, topped only by their next stop, Shanghai, where the Chinese civil war was ongoing and close at hand. Roving bands of gunmen of all varieties, their political allegiances often unannounced, were stopping buses. There were nightly blackouts to make air raids more difficult. In Allied Power–occupied Tokyo, the Peers met with a representative of JASRAC, Japan's performing rights society, who turned out also to be a nurseryman; he helped them pack up local varieties of camellias to take home. They were back in Los Angeles on February 20, some five months after taking off.

One of the major business accomplishments of the trip, a surprising one, perhaps, was Peer's finalization of agreements that made Peer-Southern the sole Western Hemisphere sales agent for a number of *classical* music publishers based in London and Paris, and publisher of classical music by firms in Rio and Mexico City outside of their home countries.

The trade paper *Billboard* reported this as "Southern Adds Longhair Dept." in August; officially, the unit would be referred to, less breezily, as the Serious Music Department, a name that itself was later modified to the less-argument-instigating Classical Department. The new unit, Peer would later admit, was partly set up as a tax-loss hedge at the time, but it was also a long-term investment that could "ultimately" be profitable. "I do not expect immediate financial returns," he joked. "You have to wait about fifty years!" It seems likely, however, that he was acting with the future of the firm and of his family beyond his own time in mind, and seriously so. The music also meant much to both Ralph and Monique Peer personally; their son Ralph II recalls being called into their bedroom, where the best radio resided, to hear Toscanini broadcasts.

That Southern Music's Latin American branches were involved with the classical division from the outset tells us something about its origin. Since a good many of the Latin songwriters and film score composers Southern published were classically trained, there was a relatively simple extension of musical vistas into "serious" classical compositions by some of those same composers.

Agustín Lara's violin player Elisabeth Waldo had introduced such composers as Oriol Rangel, from Colombia, and Carlos Chávez, an early advocate for electronic music and founder of the Mexican Symphony, to Southern Music and to Peer himself, functioning informally as a scout. By the late 1940s, while working as the violinist in Xavier Cugat's constantly touring pop band, she was simultaneously working to set up a string quartet that would play little-heard native music from out of Central and South America, and advocating for composers. "There were so many talents," she recalled, "and so many of them wound up with Peer. . . . When I met the Peers again, living at Park Hill, Ralph said, 'I hear you just got back from Mexico and all that touring. You should have been on my payroll, because I'm paying somebody else a huge amount to do what you did!'"

Ms. Waldo was by then too involved in her own composing and folklore work to take the job, but that "somebody else" Peer had hired and entrusted, Wladimir Lakond, immediately began to sign up an international cast of classical composers. Lakond, a musician and librettist himself, had held similar positions with several old-line publishing firms before, including E. B. Marks, and was well known as the translator of Tchaikovsky's diaries and Rimsky-Korsakov's memoirs. He would head the classical department for decades, bringing into the Peer-Southern tent works of Heitor Villa-Lobos, Manuel Ponce, Silvestre Revueltas, Virgil Thomson, Ned Rorem, David Diamond, and Turkey's national hero Ahmet Adnan Saygun. It would be a moment of particular pride for Ralph Peer personally and for the Serious Music Department as a unit when in 1958 an English-language version of a piece Peer dubbed "the most non-commercial thing I can think of," Saygun's "Yunus Emre," a national epic based on poems by the thirteenth-century poet of that name, transformed by the composer into an oratorio for voice and orchestra, was performed at the UN General Assembly, conducted by Leopold Stokowski. As early as March 1951, the League of Composers, promulgators of modern symphonic music, could stage an evening concert at Carnegie Hall consisting entirely of works by Southern Music composers.

Fittingly, several of the division's lasting contributions reflected Ralph Peer's career involvement with American roots music and were, in a real sense, further extensions of it. Elisabeth Waldo had become interested in the influence of Afro-Latino music in countries beyond Cuba and Brazil—in the less obvious places. She brought Afro-Hispanic mestizo–style music from Panama to the attention of a new mentor and musical partner, William Grant Still, sometimes referred to as "the Dean of American Negro Composers," the first African American to conduct a symphony orchestra, a successful Hollywood film soundtrack arranger, and a major classical composer. He'd also worked as an arranger for W. C. Handy and composed rhapsodies with James P. Johnson, both of whom had, of course, worked with Ralph Peer back in the 1920s, a second connection. Important Still compositions, including "Danzas de Panama," cowritten with Waldo, would be published by Southern.

Early on, Wladimir Lakond made history of his own, in seeing the value of the work of an obscure US composer who built his music on ingenious turns on American roots music, but who was spending most of his time as an executive in the insurance business—Charles Ives. Fostering Ives's music, Lakond would see to it that most of the now globally celebrated composer's works were published by Southern, and when the

Ives boom hit—not *fifty* years later, as Ralph Peer jokingly projected, but twenty years later in the late 1960s—the likes of his second symphony, his second string quartet, and "The Unanswered Question" would form another, perhaps unexpected part of Peer's legacy in American music.

More central to Ralph Peer's 1949 agenda was finding the right people to grow his core country music and Latin catalogs in the face of new competition. Some record production was just beginning to move to Nashville, starting with the WSM radio/Grand Ole Opry–connected Castle Recording Company, and publishing competitors Hill & Range and Acuff-Rose were both developing relationships with the record labels and producers that were coalescing there. Peer needed someone strong to work on Nashville country, and he found that person in Troy Martin. Still little-known today, he was a lifelong musician, songwriter, and song doctor out of Virginia who now took a room in Nashville's James Robertson Hotel and began to do country music business for Peer-Southern, matching artists with songs.

A poker-faced, imposing figure (some saw a resemblance to Nikita Khrushchev), Martin had already done publishing work for Gene Autry and was acting as a talent scout and occasional stand-in producer for Don Law, the American music-loving British-born A&R man. Based in Texas, Law had recorded both blues legend Robert Johnson and Bob Wills and had become, along with his former mentor Art Satherley, cohead of Columbia Records' country music unit. Peer had known Law almost as long as he'd known Satherley, and at first voiced no objection to Martin's two-sided arrangement, since he trusted Don Law. Law would refer to Troy Martin as "a big help to me in many ways; he sort of knew his way around, and got friendly . . . [and] he would give the impression that 'if you want to get to Don Law, you've got to go through [him].'"

That impression had its uses. Through the late 1940s and into the early 1950s, a succession of established and new country stars suddenly signed with or switched to the Columbia Records label, and, not coincidentally, began to be published by or recorded songs from Peer-Southern— all Troy Martin's handiwork. The list would still astonish any fan of country music of the era: Columbia's honky-tonk answer to Hank Williams, Lefty Frizzell; rising young star Carl Smith; newcomer Ray Price (whom Martin would introduce to Hank Williams); and Lester Flatt & Earl Scruggs. Songs such as "I Overlooked an Orchid," "If Teardrops Were Pennies," Frizzell's "I Love You a Thousand Ways" and "If You've Got the Money I've Got the Time" (quickly recorded by some fourteen artists), as well as his "If You're Ever Lonely, Darling," introduced by newcomer Ray Price, were all Peer-Southern copyrights.

To that list can be added a historic country anthem, Kitty Wells's "It Wasn't God Who Made Honky Tonk Angels," the breakthrough song that would come to be viewed as the long-awaited, self-determined female answer to country men's "blame the dame" songs. Its writer, J. D. Miller, had brought the song to Troy Martin's attention; it was obviously an answer song, responding to and closely derived from Hank Thompson's hit "The Wild Side of Life," so multiple record labels and publishers had been afraid to touch it, fearful of a lawsuit. Copyright rules as to how close to the song answered an answer song could get and not infringe were still vague, but would be made clearer as answer songs became more common in the 1950s. Ralph Peer, however, happened to have had experience with them for decades, at least as far back as early 1930s songs like Jimmie Davis's "Moonlight and Skies No. 2," which played off of the Jimmie Rodgers number. Peer and Martin realized that, somewhat comically, "The Wild Side of Life" copyright holder's claim was based not on the lyrics that "It Wasn't God Who Made Honky Tonk Angels" obviously shared with it, but on its hoary *tune*—previously used in Roy Acuff's "The Great Speckled Bird," for instance, and which Peer had published decades before even that, attached to the Carter Family's "Thinking Tonight of My Blue Eyes." Peer gave Martin the go-ahead, and Martin convinced Kitty Wells, who was contemplating giving up her struggling singing career, to record it for Decca, almost as a favor.

The rising Queen of Country Music's signature song would be a Peer copyright, and an unchallenged one—though, according to Troy Martin's assistant, Arnold Rogers, Martin had a secret compact, unbeknownst to Ralph Peer at the time, that sent royalties for a second song, "Back Street Affair," soon a hit for Webb Pierce, directly to Martin as a payoff for placing "Honky Tonk Angels."

The sometimes-slippery Martin's relationships had a tendency not to stick; a great singer and very capable songwriter like Lefty Frizzell, who was dealing with Peer-Southern through him, decided to take his publishing business elsewhere in short order, even though he'd had those early, most lasting songs published by Peer. On the other hand, Martin appears to have had a hand in Bill Monroe's decision to continue publishing songs with Southern Music under pseudonyms after turning also to Hill & Range. Both the benefits and hazards of relying on this increasingly powerful middleman were on display for Ralph Peer to see. Martin, it would turn out, was attempting to build his own publishing firm on the side, and the double-dealing did not sit well with Peer. In any case, Martin was more of a stop-gap Nashville connection than a lasting answer to staying competitive in country, and he would come and go from Peer-Southern several times in the years ahead, until Peer found a more trusted in-house song plugger to take the country reins in the mid-1950s—future Country Music Hall of Fame inductee Roy Horton.

Peer was not always as slow to respond to postwar competitive threats as he'd been in country music. Early in 1949 he took immediate, firm action when he found that the Aberbachs were attempting to horn in on the Cuban music market—a second arena they'd learned about while working with him. They'd convinced Ernesto Roca, Ralph Peer's very well-placed "man in Havana" since 1936, and still RCA Victor's recording supervisor there as well, to leave Southern and, in a deal reminiscent of their country star company setup, become half owner with them of a new publishing company, Rumbalero. The intrigue would be a headline story in US trade papers for months, referred to as "the Rumbalero War." ("Grip on Cuban Music Rights Is in Balance" trumpeted *Billboard*.)

Roca was well aware that the majority of Southern's sixty-plus Cuban composers' contracts would be up for grabs again in the months just ahead, and could be in play. Needing a new field general, Peer turned to another familiar insider, his old standby Fernando Castro, whose rehiring by Southern was announced with some fanfare. By the summer, the determined Castro could announce that he'd re-signed every one of the Cuban writers in question to new long-term contracts, noting that the Cuban songwriters "appreciate that Peer is really an international organization, with potential royalty income from all over the world," an early example of Peer's global business strategy reaping specific, tangible dividends.

The largest musical conundrum that had been facing Peer, and for that matter, other publishers of Latin music, was *not* how to further the familiar rumba, as the new competitor firm's name implied it might, but how to deal with the rise of the highly syncopated, often dissonant, disruptive new sounds of the mambo. Conservative Havana nightclub proprietors had initially fought those, the very sounds that would spell "Cuban music" to the world a decade later, as an intrusion of foreign (as in "American") bebop jazz influence into the city's local dance scene. That pushback had sent mambo popularizer Pérez Prado and his orchestra packing for Mexico City in 1947.

Some associated Fernando Castro with that sort of conservative, nativist reaction to the mambo and saw him as an opponent of the music. There was an element of truth in it, if a limited one. Potent transportable *songs* had not been developing out of the jazzy early mambo wave, and the string of marketable hits from the island had come to a virtual halt, which was why Castro was no early mambo enthusiast. As *Billboard* would note, Ralph Peer and other publishers had been "bombarding the Cuban writers with pleas to return to songs with singable melodies," songs that could be sold and promoted.

Now things were changing; Prado was proving to be the latest successful importer of novel Afro-Caribbean music into Mexico, and Peer, adjusting to musical circumstances, as he tended to do, began to publish the pop brew that Prado was creating from music that had so recently been a limited product of a local scene. One Prado piece became a smash international hit of 1949, "Mambo No. 5," which enjoyed the benefit of the great Cuban vocalist Beny Moré singing lead. Vocals, as they had at least as far back as the Bristol sessions, helped the novel music break through. That specific Prado record, of that song, is generally credited with launching the global mambo craze. The song would be played often, by many musicians, in many places. Returning to work for Peer and company just then was fortuitous timing for Castro; Peer quickly promoted him to the professional manager level, responsible for a program indicative of a new level of Peer-Southern commitment to Latin as general pop, plugging Latin tunes on the same general basis as any pop song. Castro would retain this role into the mid-1950s.

That clash in Cuba over newfangled rhythms, sounds, and blends versus familiar, undiluted, homegrown regional music was just one of many "authenticity" preservation arguments traditionalists were raising amid the stress of fast-changing social and musical times. In the States, there was both a notable wave of nostalgia for the prewar, premodernized era and a related reflective, rigorous wave of self-consciousness about popular music history and preservation of roots music. Ralph Peer was well positioned to make the most of both.

Alan Lomax's wartime efforts at the Library of Congress to call attention to the lasting importance of 1920s and early '30s recordings, Peer-recorded acts such as Fiddlin' John Carson and the Carter Family included, had been effective enough to be reflected in popular culture. The early stages of a commercial folk revival were seen in phenomena such as Merle Travis's 1947 *Folk Songs of the Hills* collection, which was actually made up of such evocative new songs he'd written as "Sixteen Tons" and "Dark as a Dungeon," perfect models of Peer's "new songs built along the same lines" imperative—though not, in that case, published by Peer-Southern. A country musician, songwriter, and song plugger from out of Pennsylvania whom Peer hired for the New York office, Vaughn Horton, was beginning to succeed placing songs much like those with Burl Ives, the appealing star of the *Sing Out, Sweet Land* Broadway show.

The throwback Dixieland revival in jazz was at hand, too, including publication of Eddie Condon's memoir, his stories of Ralph Peer and racially integrating bands included, and writers in the United Kingdom and the United States, in magazines such as *Downbeat* and *Esquire*, began to look back longingly at New Orleans and Chicago jazz days. There were notable nostalgic turns toward musical stories of both the Gay Nineties and the Roaring Twenties in Hollywood films and pop song revivals—a good situation for Peer-Southern's deep song catalog, which Peer added to with acquisitions.

For example, during the war, he'd acquired the old Charles K. Harris firm and copyrights from Harris's widow, which meant that when the likes of "After the Ball," the hit 1891 waltz, started showing up in movies such as the 1951 remake of *Showboat*, the royalties flowed in Peer's direction. He had also acquired the holdings of his friend L. Wolfe Gilbert, composer of "Ramona" and "Waiting for the Robert E. Lee" and known as "the Dean of Tin Pan Alley," by buying Gilbert's firm La Salle Music Publishers from him when he put it up for sale. As the veteran songwriter recalled in his memoir, Peer would call him in 1951 wondering if he'd gotten some singer to take up an obscure old song of his, "Down Yonder," which he had not. As it turned out, the ragtime-influenced Nashville piano player, Ms. Del Wood, had sold hundreds of thousands of copies of her instrumental version of it, not even knowing where it had come from.

It was in that context that the earliest stirrings of a Jimmie Rodgers music revival began, a revival that would change the standing and memory of Peer's most closely managed A&R client, while revealing the untapped new potential of both Southern Music's song catalog and of Peer's own "present at the creation" history. Jim Evans, a Texas printer, had slowly put together a full mint set of Jimmie Rodgers out-of-print 78s in the mid-1940s, set up a fan club, and won the encouragement of Carrie Rodgers and Rodgers acolytes Ernest Tubb and Hank Snow for his effort. In 1947 Evans began to press and sell bootleg dubs of the records, at such a rate that he attracted RCA Victor's attention—in the form of both lawyers' warnings to stop the record presses, and a tentative promise to begin to bring Rodgers's recordings back into circulation, in many cases, for the first time in twenty years.

At that point, Ralph Peer became personally involved, pressing RCA Victor's Steve Sholes, by then the manager of the label's country and western and rhythm and blues lines, to get on with the first in a series of Rodgers reissues. The collection emerged in the Spring of 1949, with country music albums still an extreme rarity, after continuing pressure from Peer, Tubb, Snow, and Mrs. Rodgers, as *Yodelingly Yours—Jimmie Rodgers, a Memorial Album to a Great Entertainer*. Sholes's personal and family connections to the label went back to the days Peer had worked there, which helped; it also came to be understood that experimenting to see how this six-side "Volume One" 78 collection might do was in the interest of all concerned.

Peer had his organization provide relevant scripts for the increasingly powerful radio disc jockeys, scripts that reminded listeners who Jimmie was and how he'd mattered, as material for broadcast specials about the memorial album and its sequels. Further Rodgers reissue albums would be released in the years ahead, eventually putting all of his recordings back in circulation, but for Peer, placing Rodgers's repertoire with stars of the day became a new, intriguing priority. Over the next three years, as albums' place in the recording firmament grew and long-playing records began to be released, there would be full albums of Rodgers songs by Lefty Frizzell, Ernest Tubb, Hank Snow, and about an album's worth of singles from Bill Monroe. Ralph Peer worked to become a more visible country music presence in that context, appearing at the new disc jockey conventions in Nashville, and sometimes on the air—for example, in the Washington, DC, area, along with Carrie Rodgers, Snow, and Tubb, on young disc jockey Don Owens's 1952 salute to Rodgers on the nineteenth anniversary of his death.

The renewed domestic activity and catalog shaking after Peer's return from the "world tour" had an immediate and pressing impetus. The basic cash-flow problem that was affecting Peer-Southern for the first time since the early 1930s had still not been entirely overcome, for all of the new hiring and global strategizing. Even longtime employees found Christmas bonuses skipped in 1950, with apologies. "We have gone a long time without a sufficient number of hits," Peer wrote to Provi Garcia, an assistant in the Latin department who would head it a few years later. He was putting his finger on what for a music publisher is generally the core problem, when there is one, that lack of large hits—and also expressed some informed optimism about the firm's prospects: "It seems to me that the situation is about to change for the better."

It did, in the form of a song that would do for Peer-Southern in 1951 what "Lazybones" had done a generation before. Song plugger Vaughn Horton and his younger brother Roy, back together in their Pinetoppers country band as a sideline, recorded a new song for Coral Records featuring a lyric Vaughn put to an obscure World War I era Scandinavian tune, one that had never been copyrighted and was virtually unknown in the United States. It was quietly released a few weeks before that coal-in-the-stocking 1950 Christmas, and was likely the cause of Peer's unexplained optimism. It was an upbeat, even cheery song called "Mockingbird Hill," about waking up in the morning to the sound of "a mockingbird's trill," in a place—possibly a country house, but just as easily a 1950s suburban home—where there's "peace and goodwill."

Just after the break of the new year, it was recorded by both Patti Page and the hot guitar-vocal duo Les Paul and Mary Ford, acts that were leading examplars of a new style of country music and pop fusion, with the greater emphasis clearly on pop; *both* versions proved to be top pop hits. Tellingly, the record Page's "Mockingbird Hill" replaced as number one on the *Cash Box* chart late in May 1951 was the Weavers' heavily orchestrated, Gordon Jenkins–produced pop folk version of "On Top of Old Smokey." Happy days indeed had returned for popular roots music in general, for Peer-Southern, and for the Peer household. Peer would report to friends by that summer that his son, nearly seven, was going around the house singing "Mockingbird Hill" in French.

Peer had rarely made appearances or given interviews in which he'd speak about his own experiences and interests, or wrote bylined articles about them before Monique's arrival and their time working in Latin America. Now, his radio appearance saluting Jimmie Rodgers was just one of many. With the increased interest in popular music history, calls for Ralph Peer to make broadcast and print appearances became more frequent.

On July 24 of that year he appeared on the popular *Luncheon at Sardi's* radio talk show, where he was asked about Latin pop hits, and about the size and scope of Peer-Southern. "We have the *only* global music publishing business," he answered. "The latest count is twenty-one countries," with two more on the way. It was the interview in which host Bill Slater asked what it took to be a music publisher of that scope, and Peer spoke of needing to be a businessman, a prophet, and a gambler, and then he added, "I think most music publishers are accidents."

He would spend much of the eight and a half years he had left seeing to it that what he had created—the global business, and the possibilities for popular roots music, too—would last and expand in a new, flush musical era, and even beyond his days. They would, and it was not simply an accident.

8

Locking a Legacy, 1952–1960

By 1952 Ralph Peer had been in the music business for over forty years, through most of the era in which mass-distributed and mass-reproduced popular music had existed—and, over the course of those years, markedly changed. It was a commonplace, heralded by some, decried by others in the United States and throughout the broadening list of places around the world where American sounds had become more influential, that by the early 1950s the most broadly popular music was less decorous, less "refined." Down-home music was having ever more impact on popular tastes, BMI and its affiliates having remade the American airwaves. Commonly experienced pop was earthier, hotter, sometimes blunter and less sentimental, occasionally more manifestly emotional, built on more varied rhythms and themes. Peer was working in a transformed musical world that, over the course of four decades, he'd played a large role in transforming.

As he marked his sixtieth birthday that May, the top pop records told the tale of growing roots music influence. They included Kay Starr's "Wheel of Fortune," Ella Mae Morse's clanging "Blacksmith Blues," and, instructively, Eddie Fisher's pop version of Eddy Arnold's hit country turn on "Any Time (You're Feeling Lonely)," a song Peer had first recorded with Emmett Miller in 1924. With the era of collecting rare records at hand, at least a few specialists were again aware of Miller's "Any Time" record, and of his version of the Broadway-originated tune "Lovesick

Blues," too, recorded by Peer at the same session, and much better known by this point as Hank Williams's theme song.

Ralph Peer and his organization now found increasing opportunities to revive pre–World War II jazz and blues and hillbilly music he'd identified and recorded for specialized audiences of an earlier era as more modern mainstream pop hits. Given the scope of his A&R work in the 1920s and '30s, it's not surprising that close to a third of the recordings deemed significant and era-defining by Harry Smith in his eventually famed 1952 *Anthology of American Folk Music* collection for Folkways had been recorded by Peer—records by G. B. Grayson, the Carter Family, Furry Lewis, the Carolina Tar Heels, Jim Jackson, Reverend Gates, Bascom Lamar Lunsford, Ernest Phipps, Rabbit Brown, Ernest Stoneman, the Memphis Jug Band, and Sleepy John Estes, among others.

Ralph Peer had not been going out of his way to remind people of his more youthful A&R work, Carter Family and Rodgers records aside; Smith did. ("The modern era of folk music recording began shortly after World War I," his widely influential liner notes read, "when Ralph Peer, of Okeh Records, went to Atlanta.") Increasingly, Peer's historic role and legacy were coming to his own attention. Through the rest of his life, he would work to leverage the new public and music industry understanding of what he'd contributed, and to lock down his legacy in music while overseeing a reviving business.

R. S. (Bob) Gilmore, who'd been there for close to twenty-five years, from Southern's first days, now had considerable operational and decision-making responsibility as executive vice president at Peer-Southern; Robert Iversen, Monique's brother, had increasing leeway in handling the timing of payments and of accounting matters, and as such was not always the most popular man in the room. Dorothy Morrison, Ralph Peer's secretary when Southern was formed, was still at work, the head of global copyrights servicing.

This crew's capabilities freed Peer to concentrate on the likes of national and international copyright and trade issues, the relationships of performing rights organizations between countries—the large global issues. It was in the forefront of his thoughts that the future value of his firm's copyrights and of its ability to publish new music around the world could be decided by those relatively lofty and technical questions. He was in a position to do things about them, as a storied veteran in the field. Both government and industry agencies actively sought out his ideas.

Peer's work with Carrie Rodgers, Ernest Tubb, Hank Snow, and RCA Victor's Steve Sholes on gaining new recognition for America's Blue Yodeler took another substantial step forward with the planning and execution of the first Jimmie Rodgers Memorial Day, in Meridian, on May 26, 1953. Tubb and Snow had come up with the idea of putting up a Jimmie Rodgers monument in his Mississippi hometown and generating maximum publicity for the event with a major show—in part to generate more interest, in part to generate more song royalty income for Carrie Rodgers, to whom they continued to feel beholden for her early support of their careers. To the degree that they were successful in that, it was going to be a boon for Peer-Southern, still publisher of all the Rodgers songs, and also for the Nashville country music industry, for whom establishing a strong historic legacy lent added credibility that country music radio coveted, as it sought prestigious, lucrative national advertising. That was a useful confluence of interests for the Jimmie Rodgers catalog.

Postwar country music needed to be perceived as modernizing, varied in musical backing and possibilities, a font of great new songs, star-powered and multimedia friendly, with a deep, rich, rooted past and a strong, inventive future—virtually a reiteration of the very qualities that Ralph Peer had been looking for and seen in Jimmie Rodgers when they found each other in 1927. In 1953 the country music industry came to recognize Rodgers as its own perfect personification, and it was these concerted efforts twenty years after his death, in which Peer actively took part, that effectively established Jimmie as "the Father of Country Music," a title not much considered or cared about before then.

Peer wrote and bylined an article for a pre–Rodgers Day issue of *Billboard*, "Discovery of the 1st Hillbilly Great," in which he offered one detailed version of meeting Jimmie at Bristol, with a few details off (confusing "Sleep, Baby, Sleep" with "Rock All Our Babies to Sleep," for example), suggesting that Rodgers's talent, energy, and optimism were very evident even if his song material wasn't ready then, and reiterating how after "Blue Yodel (T for Texas)" hit, Jimmie "was able to lead a new life because of his income from recordings and copyright royalties; . . . eventually Victor gave him a royalty contract on a basis similar to a grand opera star." Peer's mental analogy of Rodgers and Caruso had apparently never entirely faded, nor, of course, had his accent on lasting copyrightable songs. "Many of the compositions he wrote wholly or in part," Peer duly noted, "have become perennial standards."

He would be prominent among the musical and political dignitaries who convened in Meridian that day and took part in the ceremony, before a crowd estimated at thirty thousand and a regional radio audience across the South. His own ceremonial role was unveiling a flagpole with a bronze plaque at its base that read, "To the Everlasting Memory of Jimmie Rodgers, 1897–1933, America's Blue Yodeler—Dedicated by Ralph S. Peer."

Hank Snow referred to Rodgers in his speech as "the daddy of us all . . . the originator of hillbilly and folk music," and the designation stuck. Representatives of the quite varied wings of postwar country music who all felt the connection to Rodgers's music and image took part in the ceremony and performed, including such Peer-published artists as Bill Monroe, Lefty Frizzell, Jimmie Davis, and for the first and only time after their breakup at the outset of the war, the Original Carter Family, as Maybelle, Sara, and A.P. were now called, to distinguish them from Maybelle Carter and her daughters.

Just weeks before, Sara and A.P. had been in the same room long enough to be part of a small-time recording session for regional Acme Records, along with their son Joe and daughter Janette, in hopes that Acme might get their branch of the Carters back into the Sears mail-order catalog. Maybelle had long since gone off on her own, performing with her daughters and finding considerable success doing so; they were now stars of the Grand Ole Opry, and daughter June Carter and her husband, Peer publishing client Carl Smith, were currently the hot young "royal" couple of country music. Flatt & Scruggs recorded A. P. Carter's "Jimmy Brown the Newsboy" in 1951, and Mac Wiseman had a top five country hit with it in 1959, but it would be a few more years before the Carters saw the revival of interest in their music and esteem that Jimmie Rodgers was now undergoing. In the early 1960s, such advocates as Earl Scruggs,

Johnny Cash, and Mike Seeger would do for them what Tubb and Snow were doing for Jimmie now. Meanwhile, Ralph Peer was doing what he could.

That first Jimmie Rodgers Memorial Day proved to be a milestone not just for Rodgers's reputation, but also for country music's self-understanding, self-recognition, and promotion. Peer was much in evidence, as well, at that event's first important follow-up—the country disc jockey convention in Nashville that November, where *Billboard*'s Paul Ackerman handed awards to the "All-Time Greats of Country Singing"—a short list that included Jimmie Rodgers and Carl Smith, but not the Carters; Ralph Peer would present the award to Smith, and then, quite uncharacteristically up to this point, posted a signed letter as an ad in *Billboard* addressed to all of "his friends in the Country and Western music field," which read:

> I have just gone through a wonderful experience down in Nashville, and it certainly does my heart good to know that Country music is contributing so much to our American way of life. In working with the Country and Western music field since the days of old Fiddlin' John Carson—Jimmie Rodgers—The Carter family—I view with humble pride our contribution to the development of this great field of entertainment. I have enjoyed working with you all in the past and it will be my pleasure to work with all of you in the future.
> P.S.: Onie Wheeler's "Run 'Em Off" looks good.

The reminders both of his own role in "the start of it all" and that Peer-Southern was still very much in the game couldn't have been more explicit. (They'd recently signed Onie Wheeler as a songwriter and the song referenced was a hit in the making, as Troy Martin landed Wheeler a recording contract.)

At this time when music researchers and historians were more often looking into Peer's past, so was he. It was not strictly business that led him in that direction; personal factors undoubtedly played a role as well. As early as the summer of 1945, the Peers, and Monique in particular, had expressed concern about their new son's religious status—baptized Roman Catholic but son of an Episcopalian father and Catholic mother, a marriage not recognized by the Church at that time. As Ralph II grew, they were more concerned that he might suffer for it in either Episcopal or Catholic schools, both of which he attended at different periods in his childhood. As Peer later explained the situation, "We took it for granted that as I had been divorced, it would be impossible to marry in the Catholic Church . . . [but] I learned that even though I had been twice married before knowing Monique, it might be possible for me to become a Catholic, then remarry in the Church . . . because I had not been married previously in a church."

The process of trying to make that happen, which involved various priests, lawyers, interrogations, searches for old documents, signed and witnessed affidavits, and renewed, memory-tugging contact with previous wives Sadie Peer and Anita Peer, went on for more than a decade. Peer's related correspondence with his first young bride, Sadie, and hers with him, is consistently cooperative and concerned, tinged with a degree of nostalgic affection. In midsummer 1950 Peer returned to Kansas City, some thirty years after he'd permanently moved away, to pick up needed affidavits from Sadie, met with her and some of her family, and renewed some old acquaintances while he was in town. He wrote to his mother that "the surprising thing about Kansas City is that it changes so little."

Anita Peer hadn't changed a great deal either; still stinging from the outcome of their marriage, still caustic in response ("I don't give a damn if he wants to turn Hindu"), Ralph's dealings with her were all through attorney Arthur Fishbein as go-between and buffer. Anita, not particularly aware of the very active role Monique was taking in the family business, suggested in notes to Fishbein at several points during the process that she'd be more inclined to be cooperative (as she eventually was) if they could come up with a new car "or a few bonds or something. . . . Tell your client not to be impatient; if his wife had to work as hard as his ex-wife has to she wouldn't have time to think about religion!"

Sorting through which marriages counted with the Church under what circumstances and which might be considered officially dissolved eventually defeated all involved. Being the son of what was perceived in the 1950s to be "a mixed marriage" had no notable effect on the younger Ralph in any case. Peer continued his contact with Sadie after that visit, and later in the decade, when she became too ill to work anymore, volunteered to send additional money her way.

It was likely the digging into his family's religious past, as the son of a Catholic father and Protestant mother himself, that sparked Ralph Peer's intensifying interest in his own roots. In an era long before common use of Internet databases and easily shared information on genealogy, Ralph and Monique took some detours at the beginning of their 1948 world business tour to visit Crookhaven, Ireland, Peer's great-great grandfather's hometown in the late 1700s, where they looked into old church records and heard remote cousins' recollections of family history.

In the autumn of 1951, along with seven-year-old Ralph II, they revisited Crookhaven, as well as Dublin, Donegal, Belfast, and Skibbereen, in County Cork, and traveled on to Austria and Switzerland for more record checking and sightseeing. There had been some reasons to believe that Peers might have emigrated to the United Kingdom from Switzerland or Bohemia, but the continental connections first proved impossible to make, then dubious. The Peer name had been applied as a title to so many village heads in many places, as in "peerage," and sometimes become a surname in the process, that most Peers were not related to each other.

Meanwhile, Ralph Peer's growing role as a music industry elder statesman was pulling him further into new discussions, even battles concerning issues that had been lurking throughout his career—revisiting how royalties were meted out by the performance rights societies, what their roles and power would and wouldn't include, how copyright and performance rights would operate in an ever faster changing media world, and, once again, his long-standing disapproval of the US copyright law's compulsory license provision. Disruptive technological realities were putting all of these issues back into play once more, and it must have felt like déjà vu.

Both the Hollywood studio production system in which he'd placed so many songs in its heyday and radio as a prized live music broadcast medium were ending, fallout from the rapid rise of network and regional television. As other music-business-disrupting technologies—from records to radio to today's digital media—would be in turn, television had become a focus of both fear and hope. A second disrupter of the rules of the game was a 1948 US federal court consent decree that all at once brought into question ASCAP's involvement with song performance rights in films (the hoary "movie producers control ASCAP music" issue updated into an outright monopoly issue), and the relation of television to that question (was it like radio or like the movies when it came to song use?).

Few people around had been through more of the analogous earlier changes and could understand the implications faster than Ralph Peer could. He made global trade paper headlines in late August 1951 by taking on ASCAP's ancient grandfathered publisher seniority system, the procedure for divvying up ASCAP collected funds that had been a sore point for him from the first day of his publishing career. Arbitration of rankings assigned under that system had been made possible by the recent court decisions, and he was the very first music publisher ever to demand it.

Under the fossilizing procedures, Southern Music and small ASCAP houses that Peer had acquired along the way, such as Charles K. Harris, were still second-class citizens when performance royalties were handed out, and seemingly always would be. There was extra impetus to challenge that now, from Peer's standpoint, with the increasing interest in older songs in his catalog—whether ASCAP- or BMI-affiliated. "One of the sensitive points which arose," *Billboard* reported, "was whether or not the Southern catalogs were being discriminated against [by ASCAP] *because* of Peer's extensive Broadcast Music Inc. copyrights." The effort would prove an industry-shaker. In February 1952 the arbiters awarded Peer a substantial victory, a doubling of Southern's royalty allocation. It was a milestone move toward paying royalties on catalog songs based more on their actual, ongoing performance rather than on their publisher's historic "prestige" importance to ASCAP.

Washington, meanwhile, was coming to view *both* ASCAP and BMI, as they were functioning, as private monopolies. If resulting actions were mishandled, it could easily have decreased song performance royalties for songwriters and publishers alike. In the summer of 1952, Arthur Fisher, the register of copyrights of the US Library of Congress, began corresponding with Ralph Peer about the performing rights royalty "morass."

In this private correspondence, Peer called the laws as they stood "disgraceful" and antithetical to the encouragement of American arts and art makers. He soon took these thoughts on cultural integrity public, in a speech to the National Music Council of the United States, an organization set up to both represent the whole US music industry in cultural issues before the United Nations, and to further music education.

"We are left," he told that gathering, "with a most archaic law in a country which should provide artistic and intellectual leadership for the rest of the world," and called for a rewrite of the antimonopoly laws as applied to the performance rights organizations at the very least, so they could collect royalties due unhindered. While he was at it, he called for truly global copyright agreements, for the end of the 1909 compulsory license rule (no surprise there), for updating laws to account for jukeboxes and television, and, in a prescient suggestion that would resonate years later, a change in the copyright law's length to a simple one-time-only extension to thirty or perhaps fifty years after the death of the creator, *period*—no further extensions. It would actually take some twenty years before the laws he was questioning would be changed in systematic ways.

If Peer described his accomplishments to folklorist John Greenway at that time as essentially *business* accomplishments, he was also specific and outspoken in stressing that the popularized, commercial forms of roots music he'd spent a career fostering were important expressions of national culture. He never quite used the latter-day phrase "pop culture," but he was thinking about it, and thinking that it mattered, mattered not less than "folk culture" or "high culture" for being tied to commerce. Asked in 1957 by a US Senate committee to address the economic impact of that compulsory license clause he'd so long decried, he began with a direct statement about popular roots music's power source, and, yes, the importance of people getting properly paid for making it, if it were going to thrive: "It must always be remembered that the 'standard popular' repertoire in any country, and the current hits, are the product of what must be called a 'national urge.' It is the *population itself* which created this form of 'property;' the intangible values are extremely high and practically never capitalized. . . . Music has always brought joy and pleasure to the human race . . . [but] the number of persons engaged in *producing and distributing* commercial music is in direct relation to the total available compensation for this work. . . ."

As may have been inevitable, given his executive temperament, the break Peer was supposedly going to derive from the pleasurable distraction of identifying and cultivating camellias fell by the wayside by the mid-1950s. In that specialized field, too, he became an untiring organization head and advocate, not just a solitary shrub tender. Monique was nearly as involved with "camellia affairs" by this point as he was.

With the first import into the United States of those "Kunming Reticulates" species he'd identified in the Far East, his contributions to the field were quickly recognized. He rose from being a founder and president of the Los Angeles Camellia Society to vice president of the Southern California Camellia Society, state director of the national society, and in 1957, president of the American Camellia Society and a director of the American Horticultural Council. When Peer sent a new strain of camellia seeds to the United Kingdom's Royal Horticultural Society that he saw could stand up to the muggy British climate, he became honored there as well. He went on to found a camellia society in Japan, presenting a hundred species to be grown in that country for the first time, and was regularly quoted in general-interest magazines and newspapers on camellia shrubs' charms. At least one news report identified Ralph and Monique Peer *only* as "successful camellia detectives."

Their floral and global corporate music work became so intertwined that when they took their second world trip in the spring and summer of 1954, stopping in at Peer-Southern headquarters around the world again, they made global headlines for an attempt to locate a long-lost, naturally growing yellow camellia in what was still called Indochina. The place they attempted to reach proved unreachable—since it was in the French–Viet Minh war zone in Vietnam, squarely in the middle of the climactic battle of Dien Ben Phu. ("What I am afraid of now," Peer wrote to a fellow enthusiast back in California, "is that the battle in Tonkin may become so extensive that the species for which I am searching will be destroyed.")

The Peers spoke to students in Taiwan about their effort, and funded an attempted expedition by a Professor Takasi Tuyama of Japan, with the same negative result. That wasn't quite the end of it, though; Tuyama went on to find an actual example, located in China, in the 1970s, and hybridization of yellow variations began at that time. In camellia enthusiast circles, the Peers' efforts a generation before had by then become legendary. In 1958 an ongoing International Ralph Peer Sasanqua Award was established for new variations of camellias developed in that sasanqua variety.

Ralph and Monique's travel schedule was as frenetic as ever. In the late spring of 1956, on the heels of their second world trip, they traveled to capitals across Scandinavia all the way to Moscow. Peer was finally able to take up that long-standing Soviet invitation to discuss opening a Peer-Southern branch there, and hoping, while he was at it, to get the Soviets to sign onto the global Berne copyright conventions for the first time. Wedged between Khrushchev's Secret Speech on the calumnies of the late Joseph Stalin and the oncoming Hungarian uprising, it didn't prove a particularly fruitful time for discussions with the Soviets about music.

The relentless business travel and work on behalf of camellias were, between them, the sort of "relaxation" from which most any of us could use a break, to some retreat where the subjects of the music business, copyrights, and even flower specimens would rarely come up. That impulse led the Peers to purchase a getaway oasis at Lake Tahoe, where the family had spent a frozen-in Christmas break in 1953. The lakeside property, which they dubbed White Firs, became a regular family retreat through the following summers and Christmases, a place for some sailing and waterskiing, for very regular well-oiled cocktail parties and dinners out with neighbors, and, occasionally at least, checking in at Harrah's Lake Tahoe for dinner shows by the likes of Louis Prima, with Keely Smith and his band the Wildest.

It was still a relatively remote, pioneering place to go. Neighbors who became ongoing friends included a former president of Safeway supermarkets, physicians, and oilmen and their families—people with money and much to talk about, but not the music business. Peer remained adept, as always, at not saying things; some of these friends would not know exactly what it was that he did in music until years later. Getting to White Firs in the winter was an adventure in itself; Peer kept a sixteen-foot outboard motorboat in tow, a rarity at the lake at the time, in case they were snowed in during the winter breaks and he needed to communicate with the outside world fast. Being cut off there could happen, with hand-to-hand bucket brigades sometimes being the only way even to get water to houses when the pipes froze.

Sons and daughters of their Tahoe neighbors have vivid and parallel impressions of reserved Ralph and flamboyant, life-of-the-party Monique at that time. "Monique and Mr. Peer were so sophisticated," then twenty-year-old neighbor Betsy Bingham recalls, "yet, on the other hand, they loved meeting everybody at the lake; if you'd be over there, there would be highway patrolmen, too, just a whole variety of people. They had a lot of art from their travels—boomerangs from Australia. . . . Mr. Peer was always so quiet, but Mrs. Peer was bigger than life."

The Binghams would fashion a bobsled-style run in the snow behind their house at Christmastime for use with trashcan lid–sized sledding discs called Snowflakes, and as Betsy relates, "I'll never forget one time Mrs. Peer came over in a full-length sable fur coat and matching hat and went right down that run on a Snowflake. Everyone was petrified." She also recalls Monique, as Christmas 1958 arrived, calling Peer-Southern offices around the world, one by one, and offering them all Christmas and New Year's wishes in their own languages: "I sat there watching this, fascinated."

Neighbor David Marston, son of the owner of the Marston oil refinery near Bakersfield, and later a vineyard operator and classical music impresario, was a boy eight to ten when he first knew the Peers at Tahoe, and was likewise struck by Ralph Peer: "My parents were a bit in awe of the man, because it was clear that he was a great intellect and sometimes a great wit, too, but he was also a really guarded, private person. He'd listen to all ten conversations going on in a room simultaneously and nod to one, then another. He was one of the politest people I've ever encountered, but usually he'd hover near Monique, who kind of *ran* the small talk, let her do most of the talking and just gently correct her if she exaggerated or got something wrong, tossing in, 'No, Monique, that was in *Barcelona*.' . . . We didn't see Ralph II that much then, because he always seemed to be spending the summer in Italy or Germany or France, where he was to learn the language; he was obviously being groomed for the publishing company at eleven or twelve, when we were just running around on little outboards."

Victor Brochard, then fifteen, the son of a French émigré physician neighbor, recalls, "Ralph Peer was unassuming; you would never know that he was so successful in his field in everyday life; he wouldn't bring up music at all." He also recalls the Peers asking his father pointed medical questions, sometimes with new urgency.

For the first time in his life, in the summer of 1954, at the age of sixty-two, Peer was facing a serious and rather obscure medical challenge—polycythemia vera, a rare, chronic bone marrow disorder in which too many red blood cells are produced, the first effect of which is a floridly ruddy complexion, soon visible in photos of him, and recalled from that time by both David Marston and Victor Brochard. The latter would later be a physician, as his father had been before him, and is able to describe the situation Peer was facing—one encountered, it is estimated, by perhaps one person in a hundred thousand:

"He looked like Santa Claus. He was being bled; it's what was done in those days, though I've never seen a case myself in thirty years in medicine. If you have too many red cells, they could clot and cause a stroke at any time, and you're aware of that danger. It slows you down, but after you're bled, which may be needed frequently, you perk up, even have euphoria, and you carry on. Well, he was a doer—and he wasn't going to stop doing anything."

Which was true; Ralph S. Peer's activities after 1954 never let up, but from that time on he would sometimes be more energetic and sharper than at others and was from time to time quietly seeing hematologists for phlebotomies—bleedings—as necessary, wherever his travels took him. Those factors had to have increased his sense of urgency about firming up his company's positions for the long run, and about firming up his own legacy.

One issue still very much on his agenda in 1955 was revitalizing the Peer-Southern country music roster. The firm had dropped, dramatically, to no better than third in placing country songs on the charts, behind both Hill & Range and Acuff-Rose. In-house that year he would express "disgust" that they (and Nat Vincent, in particular) had lost a chance to lock in a new agreement with longtime Peer-Southern songwriter Ted Daffan, who would sign with Hill & Range to form Ted Daffan Words & Music in partnership with Hank Snow. "I have the feeling," Peer wrote to Gilmore, "that we will never get out of the present rut unless we can get a little more gumption into our business. It is no comfort to me that Daffan 'likes us' and hopes that we will still talk to him [again] next year."

He located that "gumption" he was searching for within the firm; if his old buddy Vincent seemed slow in responding to new challenges, and Troy Martin undependable, Roy Horton, the younger Horton brother, who'd been a song plugger and assistant to Bob Gilmore at the firm since 1948, had made personal connections in country music and was ready for the job. Peer had come to see the firm's strong hillbilly-era back catalog as underexploited but still potentially powerful, a linchpin for an "entirely fresh start" in the field, and Horton proved particularly good at making that so.

The annual Jimmie Rodgers memorials, known also as the National Country Music Festival by this point, provided access for Peer to lobby for recording of Rodgers songs with the cream of contemporary country music artists. Direct results of the new Rodgers catalog push were seen in the overdubbing by Hank Snow's band, the Rainbow Ranch Boys, of contemporary, steel guitar and drums–driven arrangements over selected Rodgers records for reissue, with some success. By the end of 1955, Webb Pierce's jumping update of the Jimmie Rodgers version of "In the Jailhouse Now" would top the country charts as the biggest single of honky-tonker Pierce's entire career, and be voted "record of the year" by the jukebox operators. Early in 1957, Jim Reeves's Number 3–hit take on Rodgers's "Waiting for a Train" followed.

These successes would have been considerably less exciting for Peer if he had not succeeded in standing up to a serious attempt to entice away Carrie Rodgers and the Rodgers estate in the summer of 1955, as renewal of the increasingly valuable Jimmie Rodgers songbook contract came up. He'd been somewhat bemused by Mrs. Rodgers's efforts to suggest, in her published memoir and elsewhere, that she'd been directly influential in her late husband's career, which didn't correlate with his experience, having actually been there, but he saw the usefulness of her being a rallying point for interest in Rodgers and his songs. (He remained, as he always had, openly appreciative of her sister Elsie McWilliams, who was also on hand at the Meridian events. She had, he knew, been game and important as a working songwriter who contributed much to the catalog; Elsie continued to collect royalties for her work throughout her life.)

That summer, Ernest Tubb approached Carrie with an offer from his Hill & Range–managed publishing company for the whole Rodgers repertoire, including a bonus for signing, with the somewhat disingenuous suggestion that only the Aberbachs would substantially beat the 1930s terms of Jimmie's old Southern contract. Peer was in London at the time, and Gilmore was bedridden with pneumonia, so there were some very detailed, explanatory Ralph-to-Carrie letters hurried back from England: "The contract which we are talking about will be the most favorable covering renewals ever given by any firm," he assured her. "It is only Jimmie Rodgers, the Carter family and Jimmie Davis whose compositions have continued in vogue through the years. Maybe this is because . . . we know our business."

Nat Vincent had to handle the closing of Peer's substantial counteroffer, and would recall "telling Tubb off" and unblushingly volunteering to Carrie that "Jimmie would come out of his grave and see that she was haunted" if she left Ralph. It's doubtful that that particular tactic swayed her, but Vincent also upped the royalty rate for Rodgers's songs to 1950s standards and added a $25,000 signing bonus, and that did it. Peer signed the new agreement with Mrs. Rodgers soon after, in Nashville, in the back of the Ernest Tubb Record Shop, no less, just in time, it turned out, for the terms to apply to those new hit versions of Rodgers's songs.

Peer also continued to write about Jimmie Rodgers's importance in national publications, speak to the subject in interviews, and he backed the introduction of an annual Ralph Peer Award just before the 1954 Meridian event, to be given to an outstanding promulgator of country music. The first award went to Mississippi congressman Arthur Winstead for his support of National Country Music Day; in 1955, Peer and Tennessee governor Frank Clement presented the second Peer Award to Tennessee Ernie Ford in Hollywood, since the singer and comedian was so busy with television work and recording that he was unable to take time off to travel to Meridian. (With his musical mixture of honky-tonk, boogie-woogie, folk balladry, gospel, and pop, his intelligence, comedy sense, and his broad media reach, Ford was a perfect exemplar of Peer's notion of what a popular roots music star could be.)

Former Grand Ole Opry manager–turned–Cedarwood Music Publishing executive Jim Denny would be the 1957 Ralph Peer Award recipient, presented at a banquet at Meridian's Lamar Hotel on May 22 of that year, an event attended by the Peers, Carrie Rodgers, Ernest Tubb, and Hank Snow, and the governors of both Mississippi and Tennessee. At the time, Denny was on the outs with his former Opry employers, and the selection was no doubt Peer's way of sending a message to them about the need for change in their relations with the Rodgers Festivals, an attitude he was expressing outright in private correspondence with the festival sponsors.

The festival was becoming a focus of politicking, contention, and distrust, precisely because it was seen as so central to country music. The Opry's management, which had eagerly encouraged its cast members to perform at the Jimmie Rodgers memorial festivals since 1953, had upset the festival organizers by staging a paid show of their own in Meridian, during the festivities, with no proceeds going to the festival itself. Meanwhile, competing barn dance–style live country broadcasts such as the *Louisiana Hayride* from Shreveport, the *WWVA Jamboree* from Wheeling, West Virginia, and the Cincinnati, Ohio–area *Renfro Valley Barn Dance* felt locked out of participation by the Opry people; a growing cadre of country disc jockeys felt slighted by them as well. Hard-nosed parties in the fast-growing Nashville music business, such as Acuff and Rose, quickly began working behind the scenes and in public to relocate major country music events to Nashville, despite their affection for Tubb and Snow personally.

From the pressures, protest meetings, and serious discussions these clashes generated emerged the idea that there needed to be something unheard of anywhere in the music industry, a genre-wide trade organization that would not favor any particular aspect of the business, any region or flavor of country music, and that could promote it broadly, particularly in its growing fight to maintain radio presence in the face of the rock 'n' roll explosion. These were the beginnings of what would emerge by the end of the decade as the Country Music Association, the CMA, and Ralph Peer was actively involved in its inception. All of the music publishers—Peer-Southern, Acuff-Rose, Hill & Range, Cedarwood—wanted to see the music flourish on multiple record labels, and in any broadcast or performance arena possible, so they were understandably among the first to advocate for a broad CMA organization. Mac Wiseman, a CMA founding board member who'd been a singer and guitar player in both Bill Monroe and Flatt & Scruggs's bluegrass bands, a country star in his own right who would eventually be inducted into the Country Music Hall of Fame, and also an A&R executive with Dot Records, emphasizes that credibility and a focused agenda were central needs of the fledgling organization, and that Ralph Peer proved to be a key contributor on both fronts: "He was an idea man, and also ethical and 'legit,' you see. So that was important for us."

Peer's mid-1950s campaign to revitalize Peer-Southern's song catalog was hardly limited to the "hillbilly" arena. With growing immigration of Latin populations, particularly Caribbean ones, into the United States and to New York in particular, the musical scenes and sounds from Havana, San Juan, Mexico City, and New York City were increasingly interrelated, with more than a few bands residing in combinations of those cities over the course of the year. In the autumn of 1955, the once "hard to sell" Pérez Prado, who'd had to move to Mexico from Cuba to be heard, was breaking a ten-year attendance mark previously held by Jimmy Dorsey at the Hollywood Palladium, drawing over six thousand dancers in a week. A popularized version of the mambo was by that time material for regularly scheduled dance lessons in the upstate New York Catskill resorts, far from the handful of Havana hipster clubs where it had started, and Prado proved to be a great popularizer of still-newer Latin dance rhythms that came along as well. He reached Number 1 on the US pop charts in 1955 with a cha-cha version of "Cherry Pink and Blossom White" (published by Chappell Music), ripe for *that* next dance craze; his catchy "Patricia" would be another Number 1 cha-cha soon after, and that new song was published by Peer.

Another Cuban, Southern Music–published cha-cha tune, Otilio Portal's "Me Lo Dijo Adela," was transformed into "Sweet and Gentle" with a new lyric by George Thorn, and reached the top of the pop charts as rendered by Prado with Eartha Kitt, and also by Georgia Gibbs, among others. And Tomás Méndez's Mexican ranchero "crying dove" song "Cucurrucucú Paloma," broadly introduced through movies, as so many Mexican Peer copyrights had been, and a signature ballad for Lola Beltrán in Mexico, was now transformed into a slower, almost stately commercial folk version hit by Harry Belafonte—who was about to prove prescient, as had the Andrews Sisters' "Rum & Coca-Cola" in

1945, Peer's predictions of the 1920s about periodic comebacks for calypso in pop music.

Peer was not yet through playing a key role in turning distinctive, localized Latin music into global pop. An energetic new genre, beat, and dance that emerged just then onto the international scene, with both Peer and his Latin division very much involved in promulgating it, was merengue, which had a history going back to guitar and rhythm instrument music in working-class, rural brothels in the Dominican Republic before the 1930s. It had evolved by adding more instruments, the accordion in particular, and then full orchestration with horns. The dance rhythms had been slowed somewhat during World War I so American soldiers who then occupied the country could manage to keep up with it, beginning internationalization of the music. By the mid-1950s, it was a product of the Caribbean–Mexico City–New York City axis.

In the middle of it all was Luis Kalaff, a gifted and trenchant, alternately mischievous and intense guitar-playing singer-songwriter who wrote of everyday life, often of his own love life, unfiltered. Upon relocating to New York City in 1956 for most of each year, while fronting his group Los Alegres Dominicanos (the Happy Dominicans), he began introducing a vast, versatile array of songs that would become global standards, such as the infectious "La Empaliza" ("The Stockade"). That one was still being recorded by Celia Cruz and Julio Iglesias decades later; Kalaff became a national legend in his home country in the process. Kalaff had signed with Peer while he was still obscure, back in Santo Domingo, and stayed with the publishing company for over sixty years.

In an interview at his Bronx apartment near Yankee Stadium, not long before his death at age ninety-four in 2010, Kalaff told this author, "When I came to New York, I changed the merengue known here to singing *faster*, and that was my success. In 1949, I'd met Mr. Ralph Peer, who was extremely tall; we had lunch at Mario's in Santo Domingo. Though many other companies approached me, I never wanted to change. You see, I hadn't known that recorded songs generated publishing money, and I became more inspired after I received the first checks! We would send the lyrics and music to New York, so my music came to New York before I did, which accounts for my loyalty."

As much as Ernest Stoneman and family saw their lives transformed by Peer's interest in their music and the money that followed in 1925, so, as he emphasized himself, did Luis Kalaff and family thirty years later. "I've heard composers complain that they have many songs with Peer and received no money. I ask them who recorded their songs, and it's nobody, so how can they expect any money?" volunteered the man whose songs have been recorded by so many.

When the role became open again at that time, Peer elevated Provi Garcia to international manager of the Latin division; she'd been with the firm even longer than Roy Horton had been, having been hired while on vacation from Puerto Rico as a bilingual stenographer in 1937; it was still quite unusual for a woman to rise to such a position in the music business, but it was a second-nature decision for Ralph Peer, who'd promoted Dorothy Morrison in copyrights, worked with Monique as a virtual partner, and never shown any signs of hesitating to empower the women in his business.

Peer wanted to revitalize the Melody Lane pop music business for the fast-changing era, and for that he relied heavily on Murray Deutch, one of another pair of brothers who worked for him, as the Hortons did. Murray's identical twin, Irving Deutch, spearheaded the New York office's pop music song-placement efforts for two years, with Murray as his assistant, before he left in March 1955 to work for Les Paul and Mary Ford; Murray then moved up to the top job. The Bronx-raised twins had been performers on *Major Bowes' Amateur Hour* on network radio as boys, gone on to appear in Irving Berlin's wartime musical film *This Is the Army*, and sung with Woody Herman's swing band before moving to the business side.

It was well known in the music business that the brothers were far from identical in character; when Frank Sinatra heard that Pamela Wolkowitz, who'd been leading his global bobby-soxer fan clubs, had married a Deutch, he asked her pointedly, "Who did you marry, the good one or the bad one?" (It was Murray, "the good one.")

Irving, while known as a charmer, would have a succession of short-term wives and short-term music industry jobs for years to come, and by multiple accounts also enjoyed socializing with street toughs, mobsters, and gamblers. Those associations led to one of the more colorful episodes in the history of Peer's Brill Building home office, when well after Irving had left the firm, leg-breaker types to whom he owed a gambling debt showed up there, insisted that Murray was his identical twin, Irving, despite all protests, and dangled him out the window over Broadway. Irving's connections paid off musically, though, when Danny DiMinno, an ex-hood he'd befriended who'd worked on his songwriting while serving twenty-five years in prison for killing a policeman, proved musically talented. After his release, Murray, introduced to him by Irving, would bring DiMinno into the Southern Music fold, and his song "Return to Me (Ritorna-Me)" became a huge hit for Dean Martin in 1958, and a lasting pop standard.

If the "good" Deutch became one of Peer's most relied-upon executives, a key reason was that he proved quite adept at doing what Peer always liked to see and tasked him with doing—matching the right artists with the right songs from the Peer-Southern catalog. Murray Deutch, for instance, revived the old 1905 waltz "Fascination," which Peer had published with English lyrics in 1932, got it into Billy Wilder's Gary Cooper–Audrey Hepburn film *Love in the Afternoon*, and as recorded by pop singer Jane Morgan, helped it become one of the defining songs and hit singles of that era. The same ear would hear something in the patter song "Sugartime," by Charlie Phillips and Odis Echols, and foster it into becoming a hit first for the McGuire Sisters as pop, then for Johnny Cash as country.

It would become Deutch's special role, sometimes abetted by in-house song plugger Lucky Carle (the brother of pianist and bandleader Frankie Carle), to put the organization firmly back into the rhythm and blues field that Peer had lost touch with while focusing on Latin music, and into the new rock 'n' roll arena, which was then sometimes barely distinguishable from R&B but was showing global pop potential.

Peer quickly understood the implications of the rise of Elvis Presley, and it would have been difficult for him to miss them. After all, Presley's very first 1954 Sun Records single, obscure but well reviewed in the trade magazines, had had that energetic new pop adaptation of Bill Monroe's Peer copyright "Blue Moon of Kentucky" on one side and a turn on Arthur Crudup's "That's All Right," from the RCA Victor blues line Peer had founded, on the other. An early Deutch success for Peer-Southern in the rock 'n' roll arena was establishing a relationship with songwriter-producer Buck Ram, whose songs "Only You" and "The Great Pretender" would be global hits for the Platters vocal group—significantly, not exclusively as R&B, as Mercury Records had first viewed the music, but as global pop—and both were Peer copyrights.

Ralph Peer's meticulously expanded and tended global publishing network would prove the key to his rock 'n' roll involvement; just as he'd once taken Latin American songs first published by tiny local outfits out to the world, now Peer-Southern would sign up small US regional publishers, some of those tied to small regional record labels, for global marketing of the songs. Outside of the United States, Little Richard songs, the likes of "Long Tall Sally," "Tutti Frutti," and "Good Golly Miss Molly," songs at the very heart of rock 'n' roll, would be published and serviced by Peer-Southern, by means of an arrangement with Art Rupe of Specialty Records. Similarly, the songs of the Big Bopper, J. P. Richardson, including "Chantilly Lace," "White Lightning," and "Running Bear," would be taken global by Peer by a similar arrangement with his small publisher.

Peer had Deutch and Carle looking in particular for singing, song-writing rock 'n' rollers, song-creating, song-promoting potential stars working at the latest intersection of roots and pop music, who could be new incarnations of his long-standing model—effectively, as heirs to Jimmie Rodgers, a connection he made explicit in a letter regarding the state of country music to C. H. Phillips of the *Meridian Star*, the publicist for the Jimmie Rodgers Festivals:

> There are drastic changes taking place in the Hillbilly, or shall we call it Country Music business. Hillbillies as such are passing out of the picture because in recent years they have been educated or brought into the towns and . . . the result is that recordings of pure Hillbilly music sell in only limited amounts. The biggest sellers in the record business, however, are the offshoots of Jimmie Rodgers—what is usually called Rock Billy music. This is sometimes difficult to differentiate from old-fashioned jazz, and, of course, the roots are the same. I would say that the original Jimmie Rodgers Blue Yodel is the ancestor to the whole lot, if we confine ourselves to the white artists.

Deutch and Carle found Peer his first rockabilly singer-songwriter in Jack Scott, in the Detroit, Michigan–Windsor, Ontario area. He'd recorded a few obscure singles when Carle heard him, and, along with Deutch, bought out his existing contract, with Murray signing him to Peer International and Lucky working as his de facto manager. Scott proved successful as a singer and writer with both ballads such as "My True Love" and "What in the World's Come Over You," and seminal "cool cat" rockers such as "The Way I Walk."

The organization's working relations with small regional producing outfits also brought a legend-to-be into the Peer-Southern fold. Deutch was working with Clovis, New Mexico, producer and pop performer Norman Petty, which resulted in a 1957 roller rink organ–centered instrumental hit "Almost Paradise," for his Norman Petty Trio. They then signed a working agreement under which Peer's Melody Lane became the "sole selling agent" for songs from Petty's Nor-Va-Jak Music, both nationally and internationally, publishing and promoting the songs, as Petty's small outfit could not. Petty sent some demos to Deutch of an impressive but stymied young band from Texas that he'd started to record, an outfit that could write, perform, and sound good on records— Buddy Holly and the Crickets. Deutch liked what he heard in a more hard-hitting new version of their previously, unsuccessfully recorded rocker "That'll Be the Day" and got the band not one but two recording contracts with his friend Bob Thiele—for the group, as such, on Coral Records and for Holly, for whom they saw solo potential, with the same concern's Brunswick affiliate, though there would be no clear pattern as to what song appeared under which name.

Ralph Peer met Buddy Holly directly on at least two occasions, once at the Brill Building offices in New York, which Crickets drummer, sometime songwriter, and close Holly friend Jerry "J. I." Allison recalls as "a good place to hang out," as they often did, and another at his Park Hill home, when Buddy and the band (minus Allison, who was busy getting married to his soon famous bride Peggy Sue) had a television appearance in Los Angeles.

Peer had to have spotted in this ambitious young singing songwriter a particularly striking realization of his model of the "live wire" starting out from local roots music, very rapidly expanding his musical frontiers toward broadly appealing pop, and with the demonstrated ability to handle more, including even record producing. Peer-Southern began placing Holly's songs with others from the start of the relationship; the doo-wop vocal group the Diamonds would have a version of "Words of Love" on the charts before the Crickets. As any follower of pop music history will be aware, Holly's star-crossed career at the top would turn out to be even shorter than Jimmie Rodgers's, when he died in the February 1959 plane crash that also took the life of the Big Bopper and Richie Valens.

It was only a few weeks after meeting Ralph Peer in Los Angeles that Holly had had his first date with his bride-to-be, the receptionist at the Peer-Southern New York office, Provi Garcia's bilingual, Puerto Rico–born niece, María Elena Santiago.

"It was an entire floor of the Brill Building," María Elena recalls, "and when they opened the elevator doors, my desk was right there, so they all saw me first, and I would call Murray Deutch, who was a very good friend of my aunt, or Roy Horton, or whoever they were looking for. I received the people and was mailing out records to the deejays; at first, when I would mail out Buddy's records, I didn't even know who he was. Everybody was working all the time, working till late, even the secretaries, until they finished setting appointments or whatever they had to finish. There were no hours! And most everybody was very cordial with everybody."

The story of the Buddy and María Elena Holly romance has been oft told and dramatized; less so were her occasional trips accompanying her aunt Provi to Latin American capitals, where she met Agustín Lara, for one, and saw her aunt treated with great affection by Latin songwriters—partly because she was a bilingual music executive, but also because she was empowered by Peer to offer additional advances when it seemed appropriate. There was, María Elena observed, little of the cultural resistance that might have been expected in Latin music circles at that time about Provi Garcia being a woman.

The global network and efforts by Peer-Southern executives, especially in England, played a substantial role in spreading the rock 'n' roll of Buddy Holly and Little Richard overseas, where it would resonate for years to come. It must also be noted that, things operating as they did at the small regional outfits with which the artists had signed, it was often difficult for them to receive the full royalties to which they were entitled. The Peer organization's contracts were with the smaller publishers in those cases, not directly with the artists. Even as Peer had looked the other way regarding his client Jimmie Davis's claims to have written (and not just owned) "You Are My Sunshine," he followed the letter of the contract with Nor-Va-Jak, and didn't intercede to pressure middleman Norman Petty, for example, to pay the songwriters, or to question how valid Petty's own songwriting claims were.

Of collecting his writer's shares, Jerry "J. I." Allison recalls, "In some cases, it was impossible. Buddy Holly and I wrote 'Not Fade Away,' for instance, but when it came out it didn't have my name on it. [It was credited to Holly and Petty.] And 'That'll Be the Day,' Norman hadn't even *heard* it when we first recorded it [but Petty's name joins Holly and Allison's on that one]. Norman was always the middleman in charge of getting paid on the copyrights and he had our power of attorney. But, I've never had a bad word to say about the Peer-Southern folks themselves."

Relatively unusually for managers of the firm's units and their families, Murray and Pamela Deutch were occasionally the Peers' guests at Lake Tahoe and Park Hill. Ralph Peer, later in life, was generally keeping his out-of-industry social contacts and his business associates compartmentalized, presenting somewhat different faces to each. The founder and chief executive of Peer-Southern, after some thirty years in that role, did not let key business underlings forget easily who was in charge, so his reticence and sometime silences off the job are interpreted differently by Mrs. Deutch, a demonstrative, talkative product of swing era New York, than they are by the Peers' Lake Tahoe friends. The Ralph Peer she remembers best was not the one who'd have policemen and local boat mechanics over to the house along with the doctors and oilmen: "Ralph Peer was very, very fond of Murray," she'd recall, "but he wasn't the type of a man who'd just *say* that. And he could be brusque; I always thought of him as Winston Churchill—he looked like him, and his attitude could be, well . . . 'higher than thou.' Yet, still, he was a wonderful host!"

She was taken aback once, in the late 1950s, to find that Marlon Brando was living in the Peers' extra guest house at Park Hill, on the hill above the property proper, a bungalow that had a bottom floor decked out as a tiki bar, and where she heard the star actor and proto-hipster "practicing playing the conga drum all day." Brando was indeed a tenant there whenever not on location filming from 1954 through 1957, and noted in a letter to the Peers that he considered "Tower House," as it was called, his home, which "has afforded me a great measure of comfort in many ways."

In the later 1950s, another in the succession of peaks for the commercial folk music revival offered renewed evidence of the pop potential of down-home, regional songs—and of the legal entanglements that the "roots to pop" journey could create. It concerned "Tom Dooley," folk's commercial high-water mark, selling six million copies in 1958 as recorded by the Kingston Trio. The "eternal triangle" hit recalled an actual case, the murder of one Laura Foster by Wilkes County, North Carolina, Civil War veteran Tom Dula, and how, in 1868, the doomed killer was tracked down by Major James Grayson and executed for the crime. Multiple ballads about those much-publicized events surfaced not long after, but the story had become relatively obscure by the late 1930s.

Ralph Peer sometimes found the public 1958 tussle amusing, sometimes less so, and with good reason. He'd recorded "Tom Dooley" with his old friend Henry Whitter and his fiddling partner G. B. Grayson for Victor all the way back in 1929, in a spirited, hoedown version, and the Grayson & Whitter record had sold thousands of copies. It was little wonder that the duo knew the song; the quite real Major Grayson in the ballad was blind fiddler Grayson's great-uncle, and the song had been in the family for years, a nice "folk" touch.

The song history had since become tangled. Folk song collectors Frank and Anne Warner recorded a version of the Dula ballad they'd heard sung by North Carolina performer Frank Proffitt in 1940; it had the famous "Hang down your head, Tom Dooley" chorus, and the "hanging on a white oak tree" fate of the later Kingston Trio hit. Frank Warner taught a slimmed-down version to his friend Alan Lomax who included it, modified slightly, in his 1947 book *Folk Song USA* and copyrighted that version, in his own and Warner's names, with revenues also assigned to Proffitt. Then Warner recorded his version in 1952 without registering it, which technically rendered it public domain under US law, and it had apparently been *that* version, recorded by Erik Darling's

Folksay Trio the following year, that the Kingston Trio learned. A tremendous legal tangle came down to the question of whether the hit Kingston Trio song was derived from the copyrighted Lomax version or the accidentally public domain Frank Warner record—while totally ignoring some relevant history.

The song had also been in Southern Music's catalog ever since Grayson and Whitter recorded it, without interruption, in a version virtually identical in key verses to the one Frank Proffitt knew.

"In this case," Peer would laugh, "I have a contract signed by Whitter and Grayson jointly . . . and the 'Tom Dooley' which was finally recorded on Capitol and became a number one song . . . just happens to have the same words that these fellas have. . . . It also has the same melody, so the inference is that this contract is good." He would have his attorneys look into the matter, and they came to the conclusion that nothing could be done about it. "There's a little hitch legally," Peer would note at the time. "It would be very difficult to start a lawsuit about it."

The hitches included the way Frank Warner had handled copyright on his version, and Peer didn't enter the complicated case, as tempting as it was to point out the obvious. The fairly well-known Grayson & Whitter record, to music historians' regular surprise, was never mentioned by the lawsuit litigants at all, since none of them would have benefitted from doing so. For those interested in how credits are dished out legally, the case was instructive: Alan Lomax and Frank Warner's names remained attached as authors to the folk revival hit version of "Tom Dooley," the one most performers encounter to this day. But singers can, of course, still choose to turn to the alternative Grayson and Whitter version that Ralph Peer recorded long before, copyrighted in their names but, in keeping with his lifetime practice, not in his.

Late in 1958, Peer suddenly heard from an author seemingly unlikely to be asking him questions about such subjects, the automobile and auto racing authority Griffith Borgeson, who was particularly interested in knowing what it would take to get Sara Carter a new recording deal. A decade earlier, Griff and his freelance writer wife, Lil, had been thrilled to discover that the couple who lived in a trailer right next to theirs in Altaville, California, were Sara and husband Coy Bayes; as roots music enthusiasts who "worshipped" the Carter Family, they were proud to strike up a friendship. In the years since, Griff, Lil, their sometime writing collaborator Jack Speirs, and his wife, Hazel, had organized themselves into a hobbyist folk group. In April 1958 they had all stopped in to see Sara and Coy again, at Angel's Camp, California, where they taped Sara doing a few numbers, and they thought they might help her get back into professional music making.

Jack Speirs, coincidentally, when not coauthoring books on outdoor topics such as recreational vehicles and scuba diving with Lil, or doing a little side singing, was an old Hollywood hand and a once and future mainstay at the Walt Disney organization—the screenwriter of the talks Walt would give to his TV audience every week, of narrations for Disney nature films, and writer of lyrics for Disney film songs. Speirs was not the composer of "It's a Small World, After All," but it would have been fitting; he had also worked off and on with Carrie Rodgers on one of the seemingly endless, never-realized writing efforts to bring the life of Jimmie Rodgers to the movie screen. So while no one had ever succeeded in getting Ralph Sylvester Peer to sit down and discuss his memories and accomplishments in detail, this set of writer friends, with their Carter, Rodgers, and Disney connections, did.

On December 6, 1958, Jack Speirs and Griff Borgeson, as the latter would report, "spent many hours with Mr. Peer today, listening to him recall the crucial old days. It was quite an unforgettable experience." That initial conversation was not recorded, but the whole discussion was preliminary to two epic interviews that would be, at Peer's office at Park Hill with Lil Borgeson asking the questions, the first a few weeks later in January with a follow-up session in May 1959. It was an interesting, complex moment to be interviewing Ralph Peer. Though Peer never refers to either event, Fidel Castro had taken power in Havana on New Year's Eve, just before the January interview, which posed questions about the fate of musical copyrights in Cuba (battles lay ahead); and by the time of the second May interview with Lil, Buddy Holly and the Big Bopper were dead.

The Lil Borgeson interviews, often mistakenly described as having taken place a year earlier, were intended as research notes for a potential "Ralph Peer story" movie or book ("something that will be of permanent value to all who honor these traditions," Griff called the unspecified project), and they have been both a boon and a bane to understanding Ralph Sylvester Peer ever since. They include nearly eight taped hours of Peer discussing his life, work, and thoughts on the music industry, in a style Mrs. Borgeson refers to accurately as "casual chatter." Precisely because the occasion was unique, the comments have frequently been taken as the definitive word on Peer's experiences, his views, and even his character, though he was often attempting to recollect events that took place twenty to forty years earlier, offhandedly, without notes, and at a point in life in which his health and sometimes his memory were not perfect. (The degree to which things he recollects *do* prove to be accurate is impressively high, under the circumstances.) If Lil Borgeson was interested in a topic, such as the Jimmie Rodgers and Carter Family stories, they discuss it a great deal; if she was less interested, not so much. And her knowledge of the matters at hand varies considerably, by her own admission. But interviewer and interviewee do take up the overarching theme of his key role in making roots music broadly and commercially popular.

There on the record is Ralph Peer on growing up in Kansas City, his entry into the music business, his thinking and the industry's in developing the race and hillbilly records, on the Bristol sessions and location recording, the birth of his music publishing business, the Latin American adventures, and the growth of the global publishing network. He is often acerbic, frequently witty, occasionally weary sounding, and since none of it was meant for publication or quotation, but as background, less careful about language and characterizations of others than he might usually have been. Mrs. Borgeson raises the point, late in the conversation, that he'd have to go over it all, and have his lawyer Arthur Fishbein go over it all, so he could authorize use of any of the testimony for a book or film. That never happened, so what's come down to us is, for better and for worse, unedited, unchecked, and uncorrected.

Peer alternately takes credit for his early A&R work in down-home music and makes light of it, evidently viewing the Hollywood, pop, and classical music publishing work as more prestigious, which is a core reason the erroneous notion that he never liked country music and blues at all has been with us since. He expresses doubt that his life story would appeal to the public, especially the moviegoing public, and wonders aloud what the sales pitch would be on that sort of story line: "I haven't seen the punch line, if you've got a story of a music publisher, that will *get* you any place. . . . You might even go to the *other* extreme [though] and say it was the beginning of a new era in popular music. There are better words than that—but even then, nobody gives a damn!"

Lil Borgeson supplies a potential answer, though, elsewhere in their talks: "I do think," she suggests, "this music [country, blues, popular roots music in general], whether you will admit it or not, and your part in it, are a lot more important than you will credit. I think that a hundred years from now this will be something that will have a lot of meaning to a lot of people."

And Ralph Peer reluctantly agrees, conceding, "Somebody had to discover it. And I did . . . and I figured out these things in my own mind. But if I hadn't, somebody else would have." He goes on to offer a reasonably objective compact dissertation on the economic and social situation in the United States post–World War I, adding, "They would come to me, people who could play a guitar very well, and sing very well—and I'd test them. . . . *'Do you have any music of your own?'* That was the test."

He appeared at the May 1959 edition of Jimmie Rodgers Day in Meridian a few weeks after the second Borgeson interview, sponsoring a luncheon for Mrs. Rodgers there, and on the Fourth of July, agreed to a phone interview, almost a monologue, with Don Owens on Washington, DC, radio again, to discuss the Fiddlin' John Carson session back at the birth of country music: "This, of course, has lasted to this day; some call them 'hillbilly records,' and to others they are 'country music,' but mixed in with all of this we have rock and roll, Western music and, finally, we are at the state when it is hard to tell the dividing line for *popular* music."

There had to have been considerable satisfaction lurking behind that remark. What's shocking about the interview, though, conducted just six weeks or so after the second Lil Borgeson interview, is how Ralph Peer sounds—congested, rasping, suddenly older, and speaking exactingly to be sure to be understood; he doesn't sound like himself and he wasn't feeling quite right, either. He submitted to a series of hospital physicals in the weeks following, and doctors reported in October that "your recent studies . . . were the best that they have been . . . [indicating] that the polycythemia is under good control." He paused briefly to look into such matters as updating his will and life insurance policies, then proceeded right on with his typical activities.

As a boy he had been a tinkerer, amateur experimenter, and would-be scientist, and he was still sending letters off to his old friends at RCA Victor offering detailed suggestions on how to improve their new color TVs, and to the manufacturer of his latest dictation machine on its pluses and minuses. He also sent instructions to schoolmasters where young Ralph, by this point a tall teenager, was staying and studying, seeing to it that his son had some good new, well-fitting pants. He wrote his brief autobiographical sketch for use by camellia organizations that summer, noting at the end that "Mrs. Peer and I are now planning our third trip around the world, to start March 1, 1960 in a westward direction," and he ordered tickets for the 1960 Winter Olympics, set for Squaw Valley, California, in February.

The whole family descended on White Firs at Lake Tahoe that Christmas, and sent out Christmas Day letters in addition to Monique's usual round of multilingual phone calls. In a note to Hoagy Carmichael, Ralph Peer reported: "We are having a fine White Christmas with a beautiful sunny day, temperature 20 degrees. Our trip to the Midnight Mass through a blinding snowstorm was good fun, although the rather violent weather reduced attendance. . . . We stay here until January 6, when young Ralph flies back to school at Concord, New Hampshire."

The Peers, son Ralph, and a visiting British friend of his, Kenneth Carlisle, spent New Year's Eve 1960 at a Spike Jones show in Reno. Jones's wacky "Happy New Year" resolution song was no doubt part of the festivities; there's no record as to whether Jones revived the Peer-published "(Right in) Der Fuhrer's Face" for the occasion. At the local airport, on January 4, while returning Kenneth to Los Angeles, Peer ran into his old friend Walt Disney, who mentioned having been put in charge of the upcoming pageant at the Olympics.

Ralph Peer's plans to be there as well would not pan out, nor would he be on hand to implement his musical ideas for the years just ahead. On the evening of January 19, 1960, he was suddenly stricken with pneumonia and was rushed to Good Samaritan Hospital in Los Angeles, where he rapidly succumbed to it. He was, for all of the contributions and adventures he had fit into his event-filled life, just 67. Monique had her brother Bob Iversen rush a cable to Peer-Southern executives and to her husband's many friends around the world: "With deepest regret I wish to inform you of the passing of my darling husband Ralph 7:30 PM January 19."

Many would miss him personally; that his contributions would reverberate well beyond his time was understood at his passing. Reflecting the way popular music history and Ralph S. Peer's role in it were beginning to be taken more seriously, and appreciated enough to be referenced in some detail for the general public, the *New York Times* obituary report would remind readers of his role in recording Mamie Smith, the Carter Family, Jimmie Rodgers, Rabbit Brown, and Furry Lewis, and his role in publishing "You Are My Sunshine," "Bésame Mucho," and "Up the Lazy River."

Variety, in its inimitable style, was more encompassing: "Ralph Peer, music publisher and onetime recording exec . . . was a pioneer in several areas of the music biz. On the artistic front, he was among the first to see the potential in hillbilly, rhythm & blues and Latin American music; on the business end, he took the lead in thinking of the music biz in worldwide terms. . . . A shrewd businessman, Peer was highly regarded by songwriters for his scrupulous honesty. He was a man noted for his long silences while in conversation with others. Close associates ascribed his taciturnity to shyness. . . . He is survived by his wife, Monique Iversen Peer, a son, Ralph Iversen Peer, and his mother."

Ralph Peer was interred at Forest Lawn in Los Angeles, after a funeral service there on January 22 attended by family, friends, and many from the camellia community. On the same day, a memorial service was conducted at the Frank Campbell funeral home in New York attended by the gathered leading lights of the American music industry. Sydney Kaye, the founder of BMI, provided the eulogy:

Ralph . . . was a pioneer in the fostering of our native folk music. He was responsible for the universal recognition of the music of Latin America. . . . He created a worldwide organization for the interchange of music of every nation of the globe. . . . By the contributions he made in the fields which enlisted his boundless enthusiasm, and by his outstanding gifts of mind and spirit and character, has made certain that he will not be forgotten.

Ralph Peer heard regional roots music and detected potential pop that might speak to people broadly, far beyond the music's starting point, speak to them in the moment, and, sometimes, when a song's potential power was recognized and realized well enough, again and again. He envisioned markets and genres that hadn't been there at all, tested them and experimented with them. He matched music and artists that worked together in the areas he identified, and he kept finding fresh ways to repeat the outcome, expanding the musical possibilities for them all. He made many people a decent livelihood in the process, and he changed what we can hear.

These were not small things. For many, they were everything.

9

The Roots and Pop Aftermath

WHAT RALPH PEER WORKED A LIFETIME to build, he had designed to grow, evolve, and last. Starting soon after his death, dramatic effects that he did not live to see were plainly evident. By the mid-1960s, the songs of Little Richard and Buddy Holly would go global all over again in the hands of the British Invasion pop bands, not least of which, of course, the Beatles and Rolling Stones, the latter themselves initially published by Peer-Southern out of London.

Ray Charles's version of Hoagy Carmichael's "Georgia on My Mind," the soul-flavored version best known around the world ever since, was released in the autumn of 1960, a meeting of rooted pop styles old and new. In a reminder that neither corporate musical divisions nor genre definitions are constrained by solid walls, in 1963, some of the most fiery of Peer-Southern's Latin songs were successfully recorded as rock 'n' roll instrumentals by the Ventures—a band with global appeal.

During the mid-1960s the commercial folk music revival, and the New Lost City Ramblers, Johnny Cash, and Earl Scruggs in particular, advocated anew for the original Carter Family; A. P. Carter songs soon took on a new, robust, and profitable life—though A.P. died just ten months after Ralph Peer, later in 1960. Bill Monroe's catalog songs also found widening adaptation, as his role as the Father of Bluegrass became firmly established in the same years. Gus Cannon lived to see his 1928 jug band song "Walk Right In" top the pop charts in the Rooftop Singers' 1962 folk revival version, to get paid for it, and to record a new LP along with Will Shade, for Memphis's Stax Records.

The Country Music Association that Peer helped to organize in 1958, when only 150 country radio stations were left in the United States in the face of the rock 'n' roll assault, was a key impetus for resurgence of the field; some two thousand country stations were in operation by the early twenty-first century. In 1961 the CMA spun off the Country Music Foundation and simultaneously founded Nashville's Country Music Hall of Fame, where such Peer-recorded and -published artists as Jimmie Rodgers, the Carter Family, Ernest Stoneman, Jimmy Davis, Bob Wills, Bill Monroe, Floyd Tillman, Carl Smith, and Flatt & Scruggs would be inducted as honored members. Ralph S. Peer himself and long-time Peer-Southern country music executive Roy Horton were inducted in the early 1980s. Horton proved a strong continuing advocate for the Peer-Southern country catalog; with his aid and influence, artists from Doc Watson to Merle Haggard took up Jimmie Rodgers songs in more modern settings in the 1960s and '70s. Later, Haggard would record *The Peer Sessions*, released in 2002, an album of songs he loved, all culled from Peer's catalog.

The reputation of the Bristol sessions grew along with the renewed fame of Jimmie Rodgers and the Carters. Monuments marking the events were erected at their original site in 1971, and a huge mural depicting Ralph Peer and those he recorded at Bristol became part of the border-straddling town's landscape, as did streets named for Rodgers, the Carters, the Stonemans, and for Ralph Peer himself. The Birthplace of Country Music Museum opened its doors there in the summer of 2014.

For decades, Peer's organization would remain virtually the only US-based publisher with such a strong emphasis on Latin American music, and they added an office in Miami to address the ever-increasing integration of music of all of the Americas. When establishment of the Latin Songwriters Hall of Fame was announced at a 2013 gala in Miami, Ralph Peer was given its first Publisher of the Year Award, an award that will be named after him from now on.

The Peer-Southern organization, known today as Peermusic, remains a large but independent family-owned business in the twenty-first century, with units across the globe, as Ralph S. Peer had envisioned it. It has managed to remain so right through the era in which virtually every music publishing operation has changed hands or been merged into a larger corporation. The founding Peer's business strategy of focusing where others didn't is still in evidence there.

On Ralph Peer's death, his wife and partner, Monique I. Peer, succeeded him as president and CEO, and she held that position for twenty years, shaping the global firm as popular music moved into an era of mass communications and massive sales unforeseen before the 1970s. When Peer-Southern's fortieth anniversary was celebrated in a special section of *Billboard* in June 1968, such long-standing Ralph Peer associates as Dorothy Morrison, Provi Garcia, Roy Horton, Thomas Ward, Wladimir Lakond, and Lucky Carle were among those depicted, still at work, as many of them would be for years more after that. That same 1968 Peer-Southern anniversary publication announced the arrival of Ralph I. Peer, twenty-four, referred to from that point on for everyone's clarity and convenience as Ralph Peer II, as the firm's new vice president.

The very public face and level of authority of women in the organization, a personal legacy of Ralph Peer's temperament, continued, as would be expected, through Monique's presidency; she maintained close personal ties with artists Peer had recorded, with the songwriters and composers the firm published, overseeing the signing of many more, and did so, of course, in a panoply of languages. Kathy Spanberger, one of the young women who joined Monique's staff (in 1979, as a secretary to Ralph Peer II), would rise to the office of president and chief operating officer of the firm in 1995.

Monique would remarry briefly, twice; she passed away in 1987. Ralph and Monique's only child, Ralph Peer II, became Peermusic's CEO in 1980, and remains so nearly thirty-five years later, leading the firm into the digital music age. Ralph II married (Mary) Elizabeth "Liz" Wilson in 1970; Liz Peer would eventually become the firm's vice president and a director of the corporation. Ralph II and Liz have three children—Mary Megan, Elizabeth Ann, and Ralph Peer III; at the time of this writing, Mary Megan is a rising international executive within the firm.

The questions that Ralph Peer wrestled with at the dawn of the age of mass music production, distribution, and promotion have consumed people interested in popular music's direction and fate, and of roots music's direction and fate, ever since—whether they be in the music business themselves, music makers, fans, or commentators. Indeed, here at the tail end of the age of mass-marketed media, another time of enormous change, we find ourselves, inevitably, revisiting questions Ralph Peer addressed at its outset.

We still ask, as he did:

How far from its earliest definitions can music go and still be of the genre—and how much does that matter? How far can you stretch its limits to appeal to wider audiences and still have something usefully distinctive? And how far toward novelty can you go and still suit the core audience that a flavor of music was first shaped for? How can the music respond to changes in the lives, economic standing, and tastes of that original audience, and not so incidentally, how do you even figure out what they want?

Once you have some idea, or think you do, how long do you try to give them, again and again, what they've already wanted—and when do you try to lead tastes somewhere beyond that? How do you deal with an era of media globalization? How do you respond to an ever more rapidly changing technology and media environment, where what's paid for one day seems "free" and abundant the next? How does the music business best find and maintain arrangements that work and that fairly pay all concerned?

Ralph Peer's temperament, personal history, and business ambitions predisposed him to take small-audience music to a wider world, to broaden its popular potential. Far from diluting traditional regional music into "lowest common denominator corporate pop" for a mass consumer marketplace, even in the 1920s and '30s he was experimenting at the intersection of roots and pop, developing a complex of varied interest areas, clusters of musical gravity—music with flavors that could potentially all find favor. Eighty years later, that idea—that one size *does not* fit all, cannot meet all interests, that offering a cluster of variations on your themes (or "brands") all at once can appeal to more people, more effectively—is considered cutting-edge in business circles.

At a global forum conducted by the International Policy Network in London in 2008, Mark Schultz and Alec van Gelder presented a paper ("Nashville in Africa: Culture, Institutions, Entrepreneurship and Development") that outlined how Ralph Peer's fostering of royalty payments for writer/performers from the underdeveloped and widely poverty-stricken American South was crucial for development of Nashville, Tennessee, as an unexpected music production center, and how that story could work as a model across Africa today. A good song remains a form of intellectual capital available to all who can come up with one—as Ralph S. Peer kept telling us.

We can now readily stream, download, and play back pop that reflects where we've come from, where we've been, how we see ourselves, and what we aspire to. We also find ourselves riveted by engaging songs and sounds that reflect where somebody *else* has been and how they express that. These things are, in considerable measure, legacies of Ralph Peer.

Appendix

Key Recordings and Published Songs of Ralph Peer, 1920–1960

Okeh A&R Recordings

Mamie Smith: "Crazy Blues" (first blues recorded by an African American) 1920

James P. Johnson: "Carolina Shout" (first jazz piano recording) 1921

Norfolk Jazz Quartet: "Going Home Blues" "Preacher Man Blues" 1921

Vincent Lopez: "Nola" 1922

Sara Martin & Sylvester Weaver: "Longing for Daddy Blues" (first blues with guitar) 1923

Sylvester Weaver: "Guitar Rag" 1923

Fiddlin' John Carson: "The Little Old Log Cabin in the Lane" (country/on location) 1923

King Oliver & His Creole Jazz Band: "Sobbin' Blues" (with Louis Armstrong) 1923

Bennie Moten's Kansas City Orchestra: "Vine Street Blues" 1923

Charles Anderson: "Sleep, Baby, Sleep" 1923

Jelly Roll Morton: "London Blues" 1923

Henry Whitter: "The Wreck of the Southern Old 97" 1924

Butterbeans & Susie: "Get Yourself a Monkey Man" 1924

Bascom Lamar Lunsford: "I Wish I Was a Mole in the Ground" 1924

Johnny De Droit: "New Orleans Blues" (first jazz session in New Orleans) 1924

Roba Stanley: "Single Life" (first female country solo record) 1925

The Hill Billies: "Old Joe Clark" 1925

Ernest V. Stoneman: "The Titanic" 1925

Lonnie Johnson: "Mr. Johnson's Blues" 1925

Emmett Miller: "Lovesick Blues" 1925

Clarence Williams' Blue Five: "Cake Walking Babies from Home" 1925

Louis Armstrong and His Hot Five: "Gut Bucket Blues" "Heebie Jeebies" 1925

Clifford's Louisville Jug Band: "Get It Fixed Blues" 1925

Victor/RCA Victor A&R Recordings and Southern Publishing

Johnson Brothers: "Careless Love" 1927

Richard "Rabbit" Brown: "James Alley Blues" 1927

Fats Waller (on organ) & Alberta Hunter: "Beale Street Blues" 1927

Ernest Phipps & His Holiness Quartet: "Do, Lord, Remember Me" (southern gospel) 1927

Bobby Leecan's Need-More Band: "Shortnin' Bread" 1927

Uncle Eck Dunford: "Skip to Ma Lou, My Darling" (first recording of song) 1927

Carter Family: "The Storms Are on the Ocean" 1927, "Wildwood Flower" 1928

Furry Lewis: "I Will Turn Your Money Green" "Kassie Jones" 1928

Jimmie Rodgers: "Blue Yodel" 1927, "Waiting for a Train" 1928, "My Rough & Rowdy Ways" 1929

Sam Manning: "Touch Me All About, but Don't Touch Me Dey" (calypso) 1927

Memphis Jug Band: "Stealin', Stealin'" 1928, "K.C. Moan" 1929

Ernest V. Stoneman & His Dixie Mountaineers: "All I've Got's Gone" 1928

Jim Jackson: "I Heard the Voice of a Pork Chop" 1928

Blind Willie McTell: "Statesboro Blues" 1928

Cannon's Jug Stompers: "Walk Right In" "Minglewood Blues" 1928

Tommy Johnson: "Cool Drink of Water Blues" "Big Road Blues" 1928

Frank Stokes: "'Taint Nobody's Business" 1928

Leo Soileau & Maius Lafleur: "Mama Where You At?" (Cajun) 1928

Don Redman: "Cherry" 1928

Jimmie Rodgers: "My Little Lady" (E. McWilliams-Rodgers) 1928 {Roy Rodgers (as "Hadie Brown") 1940}

Blind Alfred Reed: "How Can a Poor Man Stand Such Times and Live?" 1929

Grayson & Whitter: "Tom Dooley" 1929

Carter Family: "I'm Thinking Tonight of My Blue Eyes" 1929

Eddie's Hot Shots: "I'm Gonna Stomp Mr. Henry Lee" (integrated band) 1929

Fats Waller & His Buddies: "Minor Rag" (with Eddie Condon, etc.) 1929

McKinney's Cotton Pickers: "Cherry" 1929

Allen Brothers: "A New Salty Dog" 1930

Bukka Washington White: "The New Frisco Train" 1930

Cannon's Jug Stompers: "Bring It with You When You Come" 1930

Jimmie Rodgers: "Blue Yodel No. 8" ("Muleskinner Blues") 1930 {Bill Monroe 1940, the Fendermen 1960}

Jimmie Rodgers: "Blue Yodel No. 9" (with Louis Armstrong) 1930

King Oliver: "Everybody Does It in Hawaii" 1930

Hoagy Carmichael: "Rockin' Chair" "Georgia on My Mind" 1930 {Ray Charles 1960}

Carter Family: "Worried Man Blues" 1930

Memphis Minnie: "Meningitis Blues" 1930

Jimmie Rodgers: "Travellin' Blues" "Jimmie Rodgers Visits the Carter Family" 1931

Blind Willie McTell: "Southern Can Is Mine" 1931

Jimmie Davis: "Red Nightgown Blues" 1932

Benny Moten's Kansas City Orchestra: "Toby" (with Count Basie, Hot Lips Page etc.) 1932

Agustín Lara: "Granada" 1932 {Carlos Ramirez in MGM movie 1944, Frankie Laine 1954}

Hoagy Carmichael: "Lazybones" (Carmichael & Mercer) 1933 {Bing Crosby & Louis Armstrong}

Agustín Lara: "Solamente Una Vez" 1933 {also see "You Belong to My Heart" 1945}

Carter Family: "Will the Circle Be Unbroken?" 1933

Publishing

"Guadalajara, Guadalajara" (Pepe Guizar 1936) Tito Guizar 1936, Desi Arnaz 1946, Elvis Presley 1963

"Lamento Borincano" (Rafael Hernández 1937)

"Baia (Bahia)" (Ary Barroso 1938) *The Three Caballeros* film soundtrack 1944, Bing Crosby 1945

"Truck Driver's Blues" (Ted Daffan) Cliff Bruner with Moon Mullican 1939

"Aquarela do Brasil" (Ary Barroso 1939) Xavier Cugat 1943, Geoff Muldaur 1969, *Brazil* film soundtrack 1985

"Perfidia" (Alberto Domínguez) Xavier Cugat 1940, the Ventures 1960

"You Are My Sunshine" (Jimmie Davis et al. 1939) Jimmie Davis 1940, Gene Autry 1941, etc.

"Frenesi" (Alberto Domínguez) Artie Shaw 1940

"Bésame Mucho" (Consuelo Velázquez 1940) Lucho Gatica 1953, Jimmy Dorsey 1944, Beatles 1962

"El Cumbanchero" (Rafael Hernández 1940) Rafael Hernandez 1940, Desi Arnaz 1943, Xavier Cugat MGM 1948, the Ventures 1963

"Maria Elena" (Lorenzo Barcelata 1933) Gene Autry 1941, Los Indios Tabajaras 1962

"Green Eyes" (Adolfo Utrera–Nilo Menendez 1932) Helen O'Connell 1941

"Amor, Amor, Amor" (Gabriel Ruiz–R. L. Mendez–Sunny Skylar 1941) Bing Crosby 1944, Julio Iglesias

"Deep in the Heart of Texas" (June Hershey–Don Swander 1941) Perry Como with Ted Weems 1942, Jimmy Wakely 1942, Bing Crosby, 1942

"When My Blue Moon Turns to Gold Again" (Wiley Walker–Gene Sullivan 1941) Cindy Walker 1944, Elvis Presley 1956

"Take Me Back to Tulsa" (Bob Wills–Tommy Duncan) Bob Wills 1941

"Do I Worry?" (Bobby Worth–Stanley Cowan 1940) Ink Spots 1941, Frank Sinatra with Tommy Dorsey 1941

"Cimarron" (Johnny Bond) Johnny Bond 1942

"Tico-Tico no Fubá" (Zequinha de Abreu 1917) *Saludos Amigos* film soundtrack 1942, Ethel Smith 1944, Carmen Miranda 1947

"That's What I Like About the South" (Andy Razlaff 1933) Bob Wills 1942, Phil Harris 1947

"Til Reveille" (Bobby Worth–Stanley Cowan 1942) Bing Crosby 1942, Kay Kyser 1942

"Der Fuehrer's Face" (Oliver Wallace 1942) Spike Jones 1942, Johnny Bond 1942, Disney cartoon 1943

"Night Train to Memphis" (Beasley Smith–Marvin Hughes–Owen Bradley 1942) Roy Acuff 1943, Dean Martin 1951

"Born to Lose" (Ted Daffan as "Frankie Brown" 1942) Ted Daffan 1942, Ray Charles 1962

"No Letter Today" (Ted Daffan as "Frankie Brown" 1942) Ted Daffan 1942, Bill Haley 1960

"You're Nobody Till Somebody Loves You" (Russ Morgan 1944) Mill Brothers 1946, Dean Martin 1965

"Champagne Polka" (Lawrence Welk 1945) Lawrence Welk 1945

"You Belong to My Heart" (Agustín Lara–Ray Gilbert) Bing Crosby & Xavier Cugat 1945

"Babalú" (Margarita Lecuona 1939) Desi Arnaz 1946

"Kentucky Waltz" (Bill Monroe 1946) Bill Monroe 1946

"Blue Moon of Kentucky" (Bill Monroe 1946) Bill Monroe 1946, Elvis Presley 1954

"Rocky Road Blues" (Bill Monroe 1946) Bill Monroe 1946

"La Bamba" (Serrano version) *Fiesta* film soundtrack 1947

"Stay a Little Longer" (Bob Wills–Tommy Duncan) Bob Wills 1947

"I Want to Live and Love Always" (Wiley Walker–Gene Sullivan 1947) Maddox Bros. & Rose 1948

"Mambo No. 5" (Pérez Prado 1948) Pérez Prado 1948

"I Love You So Much (It Hurts Me)" (Floyd Tillman 1948) Floyd Tillman 1948, Jimmy Wakely 1948, Mills Brothers 1949, Patsy Cline 1961

"Cuanto La Gusta" (Gabriel Ruiz–Ray Gilbert) Carmen Miranda & Xavier Cugat MGM 1948

"Slippin' Around" (Floyd Tillman 1949) Floyd Tillman 1949, Jimmy Wakely 1949

"I Overlooked an Orchid" (Carl Smith–Carl Story–Shirly Lyn 1950) Carl Smith 1950, Mickey Gilley 1974

"I've Got Five Dollars and It's Saturday Night" (Ted Daffan 1950) Ted Daffan 1950, Faron Young 1956

"If You've Got the Money, I've Got the Time" (Lefty Frizzell 1950) Lefty Frizzell 1950, Willie Nelson 1976

"Down Yonder" (Wolfe Gilbert 1921) Del Wood 1950

"I Love You a Thousand Ways" (Lefty Frizzell 1951) Lefty Frizzell 1951

"Mockingbird Hill" (Vaughn Horton 1949) Patti Page 1951, Les Paul & Mary Ford 1951

"If Teardrops Were Pennies" (Carl Butler 1951) Carl Smith 1951, Porter Wagoner & Dolly Parton 1973

"Lonesome Whistle" (Jimmie Davis & Hank Williams 1951) Hanks Williams 1951

"Goober Peas" (Burl Ives 1952) Burl Ives 1952

"I Know an Old Lady" (Burl Ives 1952) Burl Ives 1952

"It Wasn't God Who Made Honky Tonk Angels" (J. D. Miller 1952) Kitty Wells 1952

"Big Mamou" (Link Davis 1953) Link Davis 1953, Smiley Lewis 1953

"Run 'Em Off" (Onie Wheeler–Tony Lee 1953) Onie Wheeler 1953, Lefty Frizzell 1953

"Cucurrucucú Paloma" (Tomás Méndez 1954) Harry Belafonte 1959, Lola Beltrán 1965

"La Empaliza" (Luis Kalaff 1954) Luis Kalaff 1954, Julio Iglesias (as "La Empalizada") 2000

"A Satisfied Mind" (Joe Hayes–Jack Rhodes 1954) Jean Shepard 1955, Porter Wagoner 1955, Ella Fitzgerald 1955

"Sweet and Gentle/Me Lo Dijo Adela" (George Thorn–Otilio Portal 1953) Georgia Gibbs 1955, Alan Dale 1955

"Only You" (Buck Ram 1954) the Platters 1955, Ringo Starr 1975

"The Great Pretender" (Buck Ram 1954) the Platters 1955, Freddie Mercury 1987

"Alright, Okay, You Win" (Sid Wyche–Mayme Watts 1955) Joe Williams 1955, Ella
   Johnson 1955, Peggy Lee 1959

"Ooby Dooby" (Wade Moore–Dick Penner 1956) Roy Orbison 1956

"Fascination" (Fermo Dante Marchetti 1932) Jane Morgan 1957

"Almost Paradise" (Norman Petty) Norman Petty 1957

"Everyday" (Norman Petty–Buddy Holly) Buddy Holly 1957

"That'll Be the Day" (Buddy Holly–Norman Petty–Jerry Allison 1956–57) the Crickets
   1957, Linda Ronstadt 1976

"White Silver Sands" (Red Matthews 1957) Don Rondo 1957, Sonny James 1972

"Sugartime" (Charlie Philips–Odis Echols 1958) McGuire Sisters 1958, Johnny Cash 1961

"Return to Me/Ritorna a Me" (Danny DiMinno–Carmen Lombardo 1957) Dean Martin
   1958

"My True Love" (Jack Scott 1958) Jack Scott 1958

"Chantilly Lace" (J. R. Richardson 1958) the Big Bopper 1958, Jerry Lee Lewis 1972

"Patricia" (Pérez Prado–Bob Marcus 1958) Pérez Prado 1958

"The Way I Walk" (Jack Scott 1959) Jack Scott 1959

"Running Bear" (J. R. Richardson 1959) Johnny Preston 1959 (on charts Jan. 1960 at
   Peer's death)

Acknowledgments

COMPILING, GRASPING, AND RELATING THE STORY of Ralph Sylvester Peer called for investigation of over one hundred years of popular music and the music business of multiple countries, an array of musical genres and styles, the careers of innumerable performing artists and songwriters, and a hoard of archival documents—some more accessible, some less so. My answer to the inevitable question "How did you handle all of that?" is very simple: not single-handedly. This would not be the book it is without the aid, advice, and encouragement of many people well versed in these subjects, and I want to acknowledge and thank them here.

This project could not have begun in the first place, or been possible to see through, without the care, insights, and extraordinary support of the Peer family. Their involvement began, in effect, back when Monique Peer (whom I never had the opportunity to meet) assembled and maintained the personal and professional papers of her late husband, Ralph, of his mother, Ann, her own papers and diaries, and photographs and other media relating to them all. That cache, filling enough cartons and files to take up a good-sized room, was carefully preserved over the decades by Ralph Peer II and tended to and organized by his wife, Liz, a trained historian. Liz Peer's unceasing efforts to make the material accessible to me, to find answers in long-buried documents, and to help contextualize the personal family material when necessary were absolutely indispensible.

As my research got under way, Ralph and Liz proved to be exceptional information resources and connection facilitators, insightful commenters, and, from time to time as I worked in the family archive, charming, accommodating hosts. Their shared aspiration for this project was always quite clearly the same as mine—that this biography should be an unblinking, fair, and unbiased look at Ralph S. Peer's life and work and how they mattered. They'd waited a long time to see someone write one, and I will always be tremendously grateful and appreciative for the trust and confidence they placed in me in making so much unseen documentation available for my research.

In writing about a man whose life ended a half century before work began on this story, it was a happy privilege to be able to speak directly with people who knew Ralph Peer and his important associates personally, and I want to express my personal thanks to those vital interviewees: Patsy Stoneman, Georgia Warren, Flo Wolfe (granddaughter of A.P. and Sara Carter), Hoagy Bix Carmichael, Elisabeth Waldo, James Monroe, Betsy and Bob Bingham, David Marston, Victor Brochard, Mac Wiseman and Jo Walker-Meador, Pamela Deutch and Howard Deutch, Maria Elena Holly, Jerry "J. I." Allison, and the late Hoyt "Slim" Boyd, Luis Kallaff, and Diane Disney Miller.

I am indebted also to the immensely knowledgeable and helpful professionals at some of the leading American music history archives and libraries; I encourage anyone reading these words to find ways to support the efforts of those institutions. Thanks to: Stephen Weiss and Aaron Smithers of the University of North Carolina's Southern Folklife Collection; John Rumble, Michael Gray, Alan Stoker, and Tim Davis of the Country Music Hall of Fame and Museum; Tad Hershorn and Ed Berger of the Institute of Jazz Studies at Rutgers (Newark); Lynn Abbott and Bruce Boyd Raeburn of the Hogan Jazz Archive at Tulane University; Bill Osment of the Kansas City Public Library; Karen Paar of the Southern Appalachian Archives at Mars Hill College; Silas House of the Loyal Jones Appalachian Center at Berea College; Brenda Colladay of the Grand Ole Opry Museum; Georgia Greer and Ted Olson of the Archives of Appalachia at East Tennessee State University; Lucinda Cockrell, John Fabke, Stacey Wolfe, and Martin Fisher of The Center for Popular Music at Middle Tennessee State University; Megan Halsband, Judith Gray, and

David Sager of the US Library of Congress; Candy Novak of the Midwest Genealogy Center (Independence, Missouri); David Jackson of the Jackson County (Missouri) Historical Society Archives; J. B. Kaufman of the Walt Disney Family Museum; Greg Hatcher and Betty Lou Jones of the Jimmie Rodgers Foundation; and Jeanne Powers of the Bristol Public Library.

One of the pleasures and opportunities of working as an author, researcher, and journalist focusing on popular roots music, as I do, are the ongoing opportunities to share ideas, potential directions, research materials, and possible sources with knowledgeable colleagues, so many of whom are friends as well. For various shared research, observations, and pointers, I certainly want to acknowledge the contributions to this effort and suggestions made by writers Patrick Huber, Nolan Porterfield, Paul Garon, Karl Hagstrom Miller, Tony Russell, Allan Sutton, Eddie Stubbs, Colin Escott, Martin Hawkins, Daniel Cooper, Loyal Jones, Peter Guralnick, Christopher King, John Beecher, Elijah Wald, Fred Hoeptner, Michael Gray (of the United Kingdom), Tony Thomas, Neil Rosenberg, Dick Spottswood, Alex Beattie, and Wayne Daniels, and for help with translation from Spanish, spoken and written, from Anthony Collado, Luis Soto, and Catalina Schindler. A special thank-you is due to my good friend, author David Cantwell, for his astute comments and suggestions on an early reading of the entire manuscript. I also want to recognize the late Richard Sudhalter, an excellent biographer, particularly of jazz figures; he'd begun research on the life and work of Ralph Peer for a biography of his own but was waylaid by an illness that ultimately took his life before he could get far with that announced effort.

While working on this book I had ample need and gratifying opportunities to seek research help from many who hold key positions with today's Peermusic. I'm particularly indebted to Gudrun Shea, assistant to Ralph Peer II at his Northern California office, whose help was vital throughout the project in incalculable ways; to Kevin Lamb, vice president of Peermusic Nashville, who'd been a great help while I was working on my previous book, *Meeting Jimmie Rodgers*, and brought that effort to the Peers' attention, and to Peermusic chief operating officer Kathy Spanberger in Burbank, California, who has been enthusiastically supportive of this project from its beginnings. Elias Andrade and Yvonne Drazan of that office were also of considerable help at important times.

Sincere and special thanks for the book you've been reading, as it has emerged, go to my editor at Chicago Review Press, Yuval Taylor, whose support for my work—and his welcome willingness to prod me to take it further and make it sharper—are gratifying and have been much appreciated, as has the dedicated work of the full production staff there. While I have written articles and reviews and conducted interviews about music since the early 1970s, I would not be writing books, including this one, without the encouragement, guidance, and successful efforts on my behalf of my literary agent, Paul Bresnick. And, finally, I have a satisfying life, not just deadlines and bylines, and a home in which I can work, because of the care, affection, companionship, advice, and considerable patience of my wife, Nina Melechen.

Notes and Sources

TWO INVALUABLE RECURRING SOURCES used in research for this book are the papers and memorabilia that reside in the Peer Family Archives, referenced in these notes as "PFA," and the extensive Ralph Peer interview by Lillian Borgeson, which resides on tape at the Southern Folklife Collection, Wilson Library, University of North Carolina at Chapel Hill. (Tapes FT-2772-2775 in the John Edwards Memorial Foundation Records collection there.) The Borgeson tapes, used with permission, are referenced as "BT." Ralph Peer is referenced as "RSP." Books noted here are referenced selectively.

Introduction: "Something New—Built Along the Same Lines"

"As a pioneer": RSP, letter to John Greenway, March 28, 1955, PFA.

Music industry focus pre-Peer: Russell Sanjek, *American Popular Music and Its Business: The First Four Hundred Years*, vol. 2, *1790–1909*, and vol. 3, *1900–1984* (New York: Oxford University Press, 1988); Allan Sutton, *A Phonograph in Every Home: The Evolution of the American Recording Industry, 1900–1919* (Denver: Mainspring Press, 2010).

"I do think that if I hadn't": RSP, BT.

"He was not a person to *display*": Ralph Peer II, interview by the author.

"This music publishing business": RSP, radio interview by Bill Slater, July 24, 1951, transcript in PFA.

1. Starting Out: Independence, 1892–1919

Abram and Ann Peer family backgrounds: US Census and city directory records, 1892–1920, Ancestry.com; affadavit of Peer cousin Mercie Peer DeSeyn and family Bible records on their marriage; RSP, letter to Arthur Fishbein, April 29, 1949, PFA.

Peer childhood gardening prize: RSP, "Biographical Highlights" memoir, August 17, 1959, PFA.

"I was going in and out of Kansas City": RSP, BT.

Independence during Peer's childhood: Jackson County *Examiner* articles, collected in Terry L. Anderson, ed., *Come and Spit on the Floor and Make Yourself at Home*, vols. 1–5 (Independence, MO: Waneek Enterprises, 1995); Pearl Wilcox, *Independence & 20th Century Pioneers* (Independence, MO: privately printed, 1979).

Peer in high school: *Centralian*, Kansas City Central High School, 1907, 1908, and 1909, Kansas City Public Library collections.

Electric light essay: RSP, *Centralian*, 1907.

Abram Peer takes gramophone to poor farm: "Concert at Poor Farm," Jackson County *Examiner*, April 26, 1907.

Peer Supply fair prize: Jackson County *Examiner*, September 27, 1907, in Terry L. Anderson, ed., *Come and Spit on the Floor and Make Yourself at Home*, vol. 4 (Independence, MO: Waneek Enterprises, 1995).

Race relations in Kansas City and Independence: Sherry Lamb Schirmer, *A City Divided: The Racial Landscape of Kansas City, 1900–1960* (Columbia: University of Missouri Press, 2002); Charles E. Coulter, *Take Up the Black Man's Burden: Kansas City's African American Communities 1865–1939* (Columbia: University of Missouri Press, 2006).

"drawing the color line": "The Color Line at Jenkins?" *Kansas City Sun*, December 15, 1917.

"The nut of it was": RSP, BT.

Recording industry in 1909 and mechanical copyrights: Russell Sanjek, *American Popular Music and Its Business: The First Four Hundred Years*, vol. 2, *1790–1909*, and vol. 3, *1900–1984* (New York: Oxford University Press, 1988); Siva Vaidhyanathan, *Copyrights and Copywrongs: The Rise of Intellectual Property and How It Threatens Creativity* (New York: New York University Press, 2001).

Sadie Hildebrand and family: US Census and city directories, Ancestry.com.

Peer at Columbia Phonograph: "Men Identified with Progress of Columbia Co.," *Music Trade Review*, December 1912; Brian A. L. Rust and Tim Brooks, *The Columbia Master Book Discography* (Westwood, CT: Greenwood Publishing Group, 1999).

"I was promoted": RSP, BT.

Peer local business campaign: "At Home Day," Jackson County *Examiner*, March 29, 1912.

"I wasn't old enough," "Chicago, of course," "W.C. Handy and his band," "In 1918, I enlisted": RSP, BT.

Peer in World War I: "Easier to Run a Ship than a Car" (United Press RSP interview), *Chillicothe Constitution-Tribune*, August 23, 1919.

2. Getting the Music: Okeh, Records, and Roots, 1919–1926

Return from war: RSP's army demobilization correspondence, 1919, PFA.

Divorce from Sadie H. Peer: Divorce proceeding legal correspondence, 1920–27, PFA; RSP and Sadie Peer, correspondence, 1950–58, PFA.

Sadie Peer's arts career, businesses, and later life: "New Art Institute Classes," *Kansas City Star*, September 23, 1922; Kansas City directories, Ancestry.com; RSP and Sadie Peer, correspondence.

Sadie Peer's tennis career: Sports reports, *Kansas City Star*, June 15 and 22, 1919, July 18–19, 1921, and July 31, 1922; "Tennis: Western Championship," in *The Chicago Daily News Almanac and Year-Book for 1920*, ed. James Langland (Chicago Daily News Company, 1919).

Otto Heineman and Okeh Records background: Ross Laird and Brian A. L. Rust, *Discography of Okeh Records 1918–1934* (Stanhope, NJ: W. C. Allen, 1970); Allan Sutton, *A Phonograph in Every Home: The Evolution of the American Recording Industry, 1900–1919* (Denver: Mainspring Press, 2010); Tim Gracyk with Frank Hoffman, *Popular American Recording Pioneers 1895–1925* (Binghamton, NY: The Haworth Press, 2000); Allan Sutton, "Odeon in America," Mainspring Press official website, 2004, www.mainspringpress.com/odeon.html.

"They were way down": RSP, BT.

"Today, there is a machine": Otto Heineman, interview, *Talking Machine World*, May 15, 1919.

Mamie Smith's "Crazy Blues" session: Kyle Chichton, "Thar's GOLD in Them Hillbillies," *Collier's* April 30, 1938; Perry Bradford, *Born With the Blues* (New York: Oak Publications, 1965); Willie the Lion Smith with George Hoefer, *Music on My Mind: The Memoirs of an American Pianist* (Garden City, NY: Doubleday, 1964); Ed Kirkeby with Duncan P. Schiedt and Sinclair Traill, *Ain't Misbehavin': The Story of Fats Waller* (New York: Da Capo Press, 1975).

"I discovered and developed": RSP, BT.

Okeh race records development: William Barlow, *Looking Up at Down: The Emergence of Blues Culture* (Philadelphia: Temple University Press, 1989); Robert M. W. Dixon and John Godrich, *Recording the Blues* (New York: Stein & Day, 1970); advertisements, *Talking Machine World*, November 15, 1920, and July 15 and August 15, 1921, and reports on live shows.

Guitar blues beginnings: RSP, letter to Sara Martin, 1924, courtesy of Paul Garon; Paul Garon, "On the Trail of Sylvester Weaver," *Living Blues* 52 (Spring 1982); Keith Briggs, liner notes for *Sylvester Weaver: Complete Recorded Works*, vol. 1, Document Records, 1992.

"I recorded all of them": RSP, BT.

First location recording trip background: "Warner's Seven Aces Accept Offer to Make Okeh Records," *Atlanta Constitution*, April 22, 1923; "Warner Seven Aces Play for WGM Fans This Week," *Atlanta Constitution*, April 29, 1923; "Warner's Seven Aces Will Make Okeh Phonograph Records Soon," *Atlanta Constitution*, May 6, 1923; "Dixie's Noted Orchestra at 'Old Reliable,'" *Atlanta Constitution*, June 12, 1923; research by Patrick Huber; Sutton, *A Phonograph in Every Home*.

"The machines themselves": RSP, BT.

Fiddlin' John Carson session: RSP, interview by Don Owens, July 4, 1959, from the audio collection of Eddie Stubbs; Gene Wiggins, *Fiddlin' Georgia Crazy: Fiddlin' John Carson, His Real World, and the World of His Songs* (Champaign: University of Illinois Press, 1987); Archie Green, "Hillbilly Music: Source and Symbol," *Journal of American Folklore*, 1965; Polk Brockman, interview by Archie Green and Ed Kahn August 11, 1961, Southern Folklife Collection, UNC; Bill C. Malone and Jocelyn R. Neal, *Country Music, U.S.A.*, 3rd rev. ed. (Austin: University of Texas Press, 2010); Richard A. Peterson, *Creating Country Music: Fabricating Authenticity* (Chicago: University of Chicago Press, 1997).

"The problem was": RSP, BT.

"When the wax recordings got back to New York," "I took the precaution": RSP, interview by Owens.

"We just had to learn": RSP, BT.

Henry Whitter: *Familiar Folk Songs as Sung by Henry Whitter*, songbook in Southern Folklife Collection, UNC; *Asheville Citizen* reports, August 26 and 30 and September 2, 1925; RSP, BT.

"Old Familiar Tunes" hillbilly line development: Okeh advertisements, *Talking Machine World* June 15, 1924, and December 15, 1924; Laird and Rust, *Discography of Okeh Records*.

Ernest Stoneman: Ernest V. Stoneman, interview by Ed Kahn and Mike Seeger, and Ernest V. Stoneman, interview by Ed Kahn, April 1961, Ed Kahn Collection, Southern Folklife Collection, UNC, with permission of Margaret J. Moore Kahn; Ivan M. Tribe, *The Stonemans: An Appalachian Family and the Music That Shaped Their Time* (Champaign: University of Illinois Press, 1993).

"A recording artist worked for everybody": RSP, BT.

Asheville 1925 sessions: "Okeh Company May Make Records Here," *Asheville Citizen*, August 26, 1925; "Mountain Songs Recorded by B.L. Lunsford of Asheville," *Asheville Citizen*, August 30, 1925; "Orchestra Will Record in City," *Asheville Citizen*, September 2, 1925; Kent Priestly, "Okeh Record's Historic Session in Asheville," Native Ground, http://nativeground.com/okeh-records-historic-session-in-asheville-by-kent-priestly/; Nick Tosches, *Where Dead Voices Gather* (New York: Little, Brown and Company, 2001).

Butterbeans & Susie: RSP, BT.

Detroit and Chicago jazz line events: "Recording by Okeh Expedition in Detroit Is Viewed by Thousands of Spectators," *Talking Machine World*, February 15, 1925; "Carnival of Colored Entertainers and Record Artists in Chicago a Big Success," *Talking Machine World*, March 15, 1926.

Jazz line development in Kansas City: Ross Russell, *Jazz Style in Kansas City and the Southwest* (Berkeley: University of California Press, 1973).

RSP in New Orleans: Johnny De Droit, interview by Dick Allen, December 2, 1969, Abbey Foster, interview by Bill Russell and Ken Mills, June 29, 1960, and Nick Larocca, interview by Dick Allen, May 26, 1958, Hogan Jazz Archive, Tulane University; Richard Sudhalter, "Setting Peer Apart—New Orleans, etc.," unpublished notes and comments, PFA.

RSP and Louis Armstrong: Brian Harker, *Louis Armstrong's Hot Five and Hot Seven Recordings* (New York: Oxford University Press, 2011); Gene H. Anderson, *The Original Hot Five Recordings of Louis Armstrong* (New York: Pendragon Press, 2007); Laurence Bergreen, *Louis Armstrong: An Extravagant Life* (New York: Broadway Books, 1997); Terry Teachout, *Pops: A Life of Louis Armstrong* (New York: Mariner Books, 2009).

"I *invented* Louis Armstrong": RSP, BT.

Johnson conversation with Peer, 1925: Guy Benton Johnson, "Memorandum: Notes on 'the Blues' Negro Songs," Guy Benton Johnson Papers, collection no. 03826, Southern Historical Collection, Wilson Library, University of North Carolina at Chapel Hill.

"It was the custom": RSP, BT.

3. To Victor, On to Bristol, and the Making of Giants, 1926–1927

Peer departing Okeh: "General Phono. Corp. Uses New Recording Principle" and "James K. Polk, Inc. Holds Its Annual Staff Dinner," *Talking Machine World*, January 15, 1926; "Allen W. Fritzsche Appointed General Sales Manager of General Phono. Corp.," *Talking Machine World*, February 15, 1926; RSP, BT; Allan Sutton, *A Phonograph in Every Home: The Evolution of the American Recording Industry, 1900–1919* (Denver: Mainspring Press, 2010).

Anita Jeffers Glander and Peer: Ship's passenger log, Ancestry.com.

"I had what they wanted," "I went back to New York one night": RSP, BT.

Peer's new arrangement with Victor: RSP, interview by Duncan Schiedt, December 15, 1950, Ed Kirkeby Collection, Institute of Jazz Studies, Rutgers University.

Victor and Caruso personality marketing; RCA Victor radio and sound films: Suisman, *Selling Sounds*; Russell Sanjek, *American Popular Music and Its Business: The First Four Hundred Years*, vol. 3, *1900–1984* (New York: Oxford University Press, 1988).

"I got a letter": RSP, BT.

Nat Shilkret: Nathaniel Shilkret, with Niel Shell and Barbara Shilkret, eds., *Nathaniel Shilkret: Sixty Years in the Music Business* (Lanham, MD: Scarecrow Press, 2005); Tim Gracyk with Frank Hoffman, *Popular American Recording Pioneers 1895–1925* (Binghamton, NY: The Haworth Press, 2000).

"I couldn't bother Victor": RSP, BT.

Peer's exclusive management contracts: Contract examples in PFA; Ralph Peer II, interview by the author.

"I always insisted": RSP, BT.

Mechanical rights retention implications: David Suisman, *Selling Sounds: The Commercial Revolution in American Music* (Cambridge, MA: Harvard University Press, 2009); Sutton, *A Phonograph in Every Home*.

"I never, never bought a copyright": RSP, BT.

Jimmie Rodgers's mechanical royalties: His quarterly statements from Southern Music and related correspondence, PFA.

RSP on song copyright disputes, "The Ballad of Charles Guiteau," and Alan Lomax: RSP, BT.

Earliest RSP recording sessions for Victor: Ernest V. Stoneman, recorded interview by Eugene Earle, 1964, courtesy of Patsy Stoneman; Shilkret, *Sixty Years in the Music Business*; "Columbia Co. Buys Okeh-Odeon," *Talking Machine World*, October 15, 1926; Robert M. W. Dixon and John Godrich, *Recording the Blues* (New York: Stein & Day, 1970).

"At that early age," "They asked me for recommendations": RSP, BT.

Lead-up to Bristol session: Johnson Brothers: *Bristol Herald Courier*, July 29, 1927; Victor Artists Database, University of California; Charles K. Wolfe and Ted Olson, eds., *The Bristol Sessions: Writings About the Big Bang of Country Music* (Jefferson, NC: McFarland & Co., 2005).

"That was the first recording trip for Victor": RSP, BT.

Toward electrical recording at Bristol: Allan Sutton, *Recording the 'Twenties: The Evolution of the American Recording Industry, 1920–1929* (Denver: Mainspring Press, 2008); RSP, BT; author discussion with Christopher King (Frank Walker effort); Tony Russell, *Country Music Records: A Discography, 1921–1942* (New York: Oxford University Press, 2004).

"I made it a rule": RSP, letter to John Greenway, March 28, 1955, PFA.

"I can't tell you why": RSP, BT.

Bristol preparation work with Ernest V. Stoneman: Patsy Stoneman, interview by the author, December 21, 2009; Ernest V. Stoneman, interview by Ed Kahn, April 1961, Ed Kahn Collection, Southern Folklife Collection, UNC, with permission of Margaret J. Moore Kahn; Ivan M. Tribe, *The Stonemans: An Appalachian Family and the Music That Shaped Their Time* (Champaign: University of Illinois Press, 1993).

"The preliminary trip": RSP, BT.

Cecil McLister: Cecil McLister, unpublished recorded interview by Elizabeth Justus, November 1973, MTSU Center for Popular Music; Ed Kahn, notes on interview with Cecil McLister, August 16, 1966, Ed Kahn Collection, Southern Folklife Collection, UNC, with permission of Margaret J. Moore Kahn.

Peer at Bristol: "Ralph S. Peer in Bristol to Arrange for Recording Here," *Bristol Herald-Courier*, July 13, 1927; "Record Engineers Locate in Bristol," *Bristol Herald-Courier*, July 24, 1927; "Johnson Brothers Heard by Kiwanians," *Bristol Herald-Courier*, July 29, 1927; "Victor Recording Crew Here Soon," *Bristol Herald-Courier*, October 12, 1928; "Mountain Songs Recorded Here by Victor Co.," *Bristol News Bulletin*, July 27, 1927; Wolfe and Olson, eds., *The Bristol Sessions*.

Daily session details: book accompanying *The Bristol Sessions*, Bear Family Records, 2011, box set.

"This fellow seemed to me," "After you read this": RSP, BT.

Carter Family at Bristol: Sara Carter, interview by Henry Young, May 29, 1971, and Ed Kahn, notes on interview with A. P. Carter, August 31, 1960, and interview with Virgie Hobbs, August 1, 1963, Southern Folklife Collection, UNC; Maybelle Carter, audio interview by Mike Seeger, April 24, 1963, and notes by Charles K. Wolfe, in *The Carter Family: In the Shadow of Clinch Mountain*, Bear Family Records, 2000, box set; Mark Zwonitzer with Charles Hirshberg, *Will You Miss Me When I'm Gone?: The Carter Family & Their Legacy in American Music* (New York: Simon & Schuster, 2002).

"They wander in": RSP, BT.

"True Lover's Farewell": Olive Dame Campbell and Cecil James Sharp, English Folk Songs from the Southern Appalachians (New York: G. P. Putnam's Sons, 1917), available at https://archive.org/details/englishfolk00camp.

Jimmie Rodgers at Bristol: Ralph S. Peer, "Discovery of the First Hillbilly Great," *Billboard*, May 16, 1953; Claude Grant, taped interview, Richard Blaustein Collection, Archives of Appalachia, East Tennessee State University; Georgia Warren, interview by the author; Nolan Porterfield, *Jimmie Rodgers: The Life and Times of America's Blue Yodeler* (Champaign: University of Illinois Press, 1992); Barry Mazor, *Meeting Jimmie Rodgers: How America's Original Roots Music Hero Changed the Pop Sounds of a Century* (New York: Oxford University Press, 2009).

"He could record *anything*," "I liked him": RSP, BT.

4. Reaching Out from the Roots: Southern Music, 1927–1933

John and Alan Lomax copyright and Library of Congress involvements: Nolan Porterfield, *Last Cavalier: The Life and Times of John A. Lomax* (Champaign: University of Illinois Press, 1996); John Szwed, *Alan Lomax: The Man Who Recorded the World* (New York:

Viking, 2010); Ronald D. Cohen, ed., *Alan Lomax, Assistant in Charge: The Library of Congress Letters, 1935–1945* (Jackson: University Press of Mississippi, 2011).

1927 "Wreck of the Old 97" dispute: Gregory D. Boos, JD, "The Wreck of the Old 97: A Study in Copyright Protection of Folksongs," *Seattle Folklore Society Journal* 9 (1977); Norm Cohen, "Robert W. Gordon and the Second Wreck of 'Old 97,'" *Journal of American Folklore*, January–March 1974; Larry G. Aaron, *The Wreck of the Old 97*, Charleston, SC: The History Press, 2010).

Robert W. Gordon's column: Old Songs That Men Have Sung, *Adventure*, reproduced in booklet form for tribute album *Folk-Songs of America* (Library of Congress, 1978).

Peer congratulating Lunsford: RSP, letter to Bascom Lamar Lunsford, January 4, 1926, Archive of Southern Appalachia, Mars Hill College.

Southern Music formation: Incorporation document, January 31, 1928, and new publishing agreement with Victor, April 4, 1928, PFA.

"I could split these royalty statements": RSP, BT.

RSP correspondence with Loren Watson and Eli Oberstein: PFA.

"I knew he was a live wire": RSP, BT.

"Victor is preparing a special Jimmie Rodgers album": RSP, letter to Jimmie Rodgers, August 18, 1931, PFA.

Recording sessions: Bengt Olsson, *Memphis Blues* (London: Studio Vista, 1970); Samuel B. Charters, *The Country Blues* (New York: Da Capo Press, 1975); Brian A. L. Rust, *The Victor Master Book*, vol. 2, *1925–1936* (Stanhope, NJ: W. C. Allen, 1970).

"I had to run the recording end," "I thought [Blue Steele] would fit": RSP, BT.

Cajun session, LaFleur and Soileau: Barry Mazor, *Meeting Jimmie Rodgers: How America's Original Roots Music Hero Changed the Pop Sounds of a Century* (New York: Oxford University Press, 2009).

Elsie McWilliams: Elsie McWilliams, interview by Douglas Green, May 23, 1974, Country Music Foundation Oral History Project; Elsie McWilliams, oral history taken by Mike Garvey, 1975, University of Southern Mississippi, Mississippi Oral History Program.

Sam Manning and calypso: John Cowley, "West Indies Blues," in *Nobody Knows Where the Blues Comes From*, ed. Robert Springer (Jackson: University Press of Mississippi, 2006).

Big Bethel Choir: RSP, BT.

Allen Brothers: Lee Allen, unpublished interview by Charles K. Wolfe, April 12, 1979, MTSU Center for Popular Music.

"My policy": RSP, BT.

Memphis, May 1930 sessions: RSP, correspondence with Loren Watson of RCA Victor, including notes on Memphis sessions sent June 6, 1930, PFA.

Booker T. Washington (Bukka) White comments: Fred J. Hay, *Goin' Back to Sweet Memphis: Conversations with the Blues* (Athens: University of Georgia Press, 2001).

Peer and Fats Waller: RSP, interview by Duncan Schiedt, December 15, 1950, Ed Kirkeby Collection, Institute of Jazz Studies, Rutgers University; Ed Kirkeby with Duncan P. Schiedt and Sinclair Traill, *Ain't Misbehavin': The Story of Fats Waller* (New York: Da Capo Press, 1975); Maurice Waller and Anthony Calabrese, *Fats Waller* (New York: Schirmer Books/Simon & Schuster, 1977).

Peer's racially integrated recording sessions; Jimmie Davis and Shreveport Home Wreckers: Tony Russell, booklet for *Governor Jimmie Davis: Nobody's Darlin' but Mine*, Bear

Family Records, 1998, box set; Eddie Condon with Thomas Sugrue, *We Called It Music: A Generation of Jazz* (New York: Da Capo Press, 1992; orig. publ. 1947).

Louis Armstrong and Jimmie Rodgers: Nolan Porterfield, *Jimmie Rodgers: The Life and Times of America's Blue Yodeler* (Champaign: University of Illinois Press, 1992); Terry Teachout, *Pops: A Life of Louis Armstrong* (New York: Mariner Books, 2009).

Rodgers and Carter Family: Eli Oberstein, letter to RSP, December 24, 1930, PFA.

Carter Family sessions and visits: RSP, BT; Gladys Carter Millard, "I Remember Daddy," in the Carter Family's *Sunnyside Sentinel* newsletter, Southern Folklife Collection, UNC, also reprinted in Charles K. Wolfe and Ted Olson, eds., *The Bristol Sessions: Writings About the Big Bang of Country Music* (Jefferson, NC: McFarland & Co., 2005); Ed Kahn, notes on Carter Family song origins, Southern Folklife Collection, UNC; Maybelle Carter, audio interview by Mike Seeger, April 24, 1963, in *The Carter Family: In the Shadow of Clinch Mountain*, Bear Family Records, 2000, box set.

Anita Peer's favorite Carter song: Griffith Borgeson, notes on interview with Sara Carter, July 7, 1961, Archie Green Collection, Southern Folklife Collection, UNC.

Managing Jimmie Rodgers: RSP and Jimmie Rodgers, correspondence, March 31, April 29, and November 4, 1930, October 2, 1931, and February 27 and March 8, 1932, PFA.

"Mr. Peer saw the possibility," "He had a man settin' at the piano": Hoyt "Slim" Bryant, interview by the author, February 14, 2007.

Peer on Rodgers accompaniment: RSP, BT.

Finhorn-Rodgers incident: RSP, correspondence, August 1930, PFA.

Depression effects at RCA Victor: Eli Oberstein, letters to RSP, December 24, 1930, and January 8 and February 6, 1931; RSP, letter to Clifford Hayes, February 24, 1931; Henry Whitter, letter to RSP, August 27, 1930; Willie McTell, letter to RSP, February 18, 1931; RSP, note to Loren Watson on Jim Jackson, June 6, 1930; all PFA.

"Mr. Sarnoff woke up to the fact": RSP, BT.

RCA Victor sell-back of Southern Music: Related documents, PFA.

Metronome profile: "Soulful Silhouettes: Ralph S. Peer," *Metronome*, February 1932, PFA.

5. Breaking Loose, Branching Out, Starting Over, 1933–1940

1933 "Home on the Range" dispute: "District Court of the US, Southern District of NY: Southern Music Publishing Co., Inc., William Goodwin and Mary Goodwin, Complainants, Against BiBO-LANG, et al.," PFA, and files of attorney Arthur Fishbein; John I. White, "Where the Deer and the Antelope Play," in *Git Along Little Dogies: Songs and Songmakers of the American West* (Urbana: University of Illinois Press, 1975); Karl Hagstrom Miller, *Segregating Sound: Inventing Folk and Pop Music in the Age of Jim Crow* (Durham, NC: Duke University Press, 2010).

"It amuses me—the people like Lomax": RSP, BT.

"I interviewed a great number of people": Samuel Moanfeldt, *The Story of Home on the Range* by Kirke Mechem (Topeka: Kansas State Historical Society, 1969; orig. publ. 1949).

"Home on the Range" dispute, continued: John Lomax's field notes on "Home on the Range," letters to George Jeffers of Southern Music, and correspondence of MPAA chairman John S. Paine to his publisher, Macmillan, The John A Lomax Family Papers, Center for American History, University of Texas, Austin.

RSP warning to Carter: RSP, note to A. P. Carter, April 25, 1933: Southern Folklife
    Collection, UNC.

"I never was able to really get what I wanted": RSP, BT.

RSP-Oberstein battle: Eli Oberstein, letter to R. S. (Bob) Gilmore, December 30, 1930,
    commented on by RSP; Oberstein, letter to RSP, January 19, 1931, on not using
    unfamiliar tunes; both in PFA.

"Theoretically, I continued," "Well, maybe Peer can help us about Mexico," "sitting on [his]
    shoulder," "We just operated like I did with the hillbilly": RSP, BT.

Emilio Azcárraga's broadcasting holdings: FCC commissioner Norman Goldstein,
    "Azcarraga Owns Huge Secret Empire," *Los Angeles Times*, June 2, 1989.

Agustín Lara: RSP, BT; Rita Pomade, "A Legend in His Time: Composer Agustin Lara,"
    Mexconnect, www.mexconnect.com/articles/1062-a-legend-in-his-time-composer
    -agustin-lara; Luis Carlos Buraya, *Agustín Lara* (Madrid: Datsin, S. L., 2003).

"Rooted in the past": Andrew G. Wood, "Nationalizing the Bohemian: The Mythogenesis
    of Agustín Lara," in *Masculinity and Sexuality in Modern Mexico*, ed. Victor M.
    Macias-Gonzalez and Anne Rubenstein (Albuquerque: University of New Mexico Press,
    2012).

"Peanut Vendor" incident: RSP, BT; E. B. Marks with A. J. Liebling, *They All Sang: From
    Tony Pastor to Rudy Vallee* (New York: Viking Press, 1934).

Oberstein on "stealing a march" in rumbas: Eli Oberstein, letter to RSP, February 6, 1931,
    PFA.

"I conceived the idea of an organized chain": RSP, "Biographical Highlights" memoir,
    August 17, 1959, PFA.

Leroy (Roy) Shield background: Leroy Shield website, www.leroyshield.com; Richard Lewis
    Ward, *A History of the Hal Roach Studios* (Carbondale: Southern Illinois University
    Press, 2005).

Jimmie Rodgers meets Laurel & Hardy: Carrie Rodgers, *My Husband, Jimmie Rodgers*
    (Nashville: Country Music Foundation Press, 1995; orig. publ. 1935).

Music in sound era movies: Donald Crafton, *The Talkies: American Cinema's Transition to
    Sound, 1926–1931* (Berkeley: University of California Press, 1999); Russell Sanjek,
    American Popular Music and Its Business: The First Four Hundred Years, vol. 3, *1900–
    1984* (New York: Oxford University Press, 1988).

Southern Music returns to Peer's control: Sale agreement document from RCA Victor to RSP,
    November 1, 1932, and RCA Photophone report to ERPI, October 21, 1932, PFA.

"I began to collect large royalties": RSP, BT.

Accounting of Southern movie music for ERPI: Related documentation, PFA.

RSP and Hoagy Carmichael: RSP, BT; Richard M. Sudhalter, *Stardust Melody: The Life and
    Music of Hoagy Carmichael* (New York: Oxford University Press, 2002); Hoagy
    Carmichael, *The Stardust Road & Sometimes I Wonder: The Autobiographies of Hoagy
    Carmichael* (New York: Da Capo Press, 1999; orig. publ. 1946 and 1965).

"Dad was a Bloomington guy": Hoagy Bix Carmichael, interview by the author.

"I was always trying to get away": RSP, BT.

"A decision was made": Ralph Peer II, interview by the author.

Death of Jimmie Rodgers: Nolan Porterfield, *Jimmie Rodgers: The Life and Times of
    America's Blue Yodeler* (Champaign: University of Illinois Press, 1992); Barry Mazor,

Meeting Jimmie Rodgers: How America's Original Roots Music Hero Changed the Pop Sounds of a Century (New York: Oxford University Press, 2009); Jimmie Rodgers's last notebook and letters to Mrs. Rodgers, Jimmie Rodgers Foundation.

RSP and Fats Waller: Waller payment documents, PFA; Maurice Waller and Anthony Calabrese, *Fats Waller* (New York: Schirmer Books/Simon & Schuster, 1977).

"He was patient, affable," Connie's Inn trip: RSP, interview by Duncan Schiedt, 1950.

"Lazybones was the first hit": RSP, BT.

"I wish those *were* Peer songs": Hoagy Bix Carmichael, interview by the author.

Managing the Carter Family: Anita Peer, letter to Sara Carter, May 3, 1933, Eli Oberstein, letter to A. P. Carter, May 26, 1935, and RSP, letter to Sara Carter, December 15, 1936, Southern Folklife Collection, UNC; Mark Zwonitzer with Charles Hirshberg, *Will You Miss Me When I'm Gone?: The Carter Family & Their Legacy in American Music* (New York: Simon & Schuster, 2002); notes by Charles K. Wolfe, in *The Carter Family: In the Shadow of Clinch Mountain*, Bear Family Records, 2000, box set; RSP, BT.

Relationship with Monique Iversen: Monique Iversen diaries, 1929–39; Monique Iversen, interview by Peter Wallenberg, June 1932; Monique Iversen profile, *New York Herold*, July 8, 1932; internal documents regarding Monique and her work, NBC Radio 1932–33; all PFA.

Jimmie Davis: Tony Russell, booklets accompanying Jimmie Davis box sets *Nobody's Darlin' but Mine* and *You Are My Sunshine*, Bear Family Records, 1998; Gus Weill, *You Are My Sunshine: The Jimmie Davis Story* (Waco, TX: Word, Inc., 1977).

Ted Daffan, Floyd Tillman, and Bob Wills: RSP, BT; correspondence in PFA.

RSP divorce from Anita Peer and settlement terms; Monique relocation to Mexico City, Monique and Ralph Peer marriage; Anita Peer's later life (in letters of the 1950s): Documentation in PFA.

Lomax's Library of Congress list: Alan Lomax, "List of American Folk Songs on Commercial Records," reprinted for the Library of Congress, first compiled for the Conference on Inter-American Relations in the Field of Music, September 3, 1940. US Library of Congress, Division of Music.

6. Crossing Borders: The War, Latin Music, and the Media, 1940–1945

"Unless you have the faculty": RSP, BT.

Ralph and Monique Peer as a team: Elisabeth Waldo and Diane Disney Miller, interviews by the author; Monique Peer diaries, 1940–45, PFA; and RSP, BT.

Hal Roach and politics: Monique Peer diaries, PFA; Leroy Shield website, www.leroyshield .com; Richard Lewis Ward, *A History of the Hal Roach Studios* (Carbondale: Southern Illinois University Press, 2005).

Background to birth of BMI: Russell Sanjek, *American Popular Music and Its Business: The First Four Hundred Years*, vol. 3, *1900–1984* (New York: Oxford University Press, 1988); and RSP, BT.

"ASCAP . . . would gradually bring more and more pressure": RSP, BT.

Los Angeles Times interview: "Popularity of Latin Music Held Due to ASCAP Fight," *Los Angeles Times*, December 27, 1940.

Rodgers songs 1938–48: Barry Mazor, *Meeting Jimmie Rodgers: How America's Original Roots Music Hero Changed the Pop Sounds of a Century* (New York: Oxford University Press, 2009).

Dorothy Morrison story, comment on APRS: Ralph Peer II, interview by the author.

Peer's comments in the *Chronicle*: "Publisher Finds ASCAP-BMI War a Blessing for Young Composers," *San Francisco Chronicle*, January 15, 1941.

New York Times report on the ASCAP-BMI battle: "Radio Music Dispute Raises Complex Issues," *New York Times*, February 9, 1941.

Peer acquisition of Melody Lane: Related documents, PFA.

Peers meet Lara and Cugat in New York: Monique Peer diary, 1941, PFA.

Cadillac purchase: RSP, correspondence in PFA.

Variety report: "Latin Music Subsids Multiply," *Variety*, June 18, 1941.

Rockefeller, Walt Disney, and RSP: Author interview with Diane Disney Miller; Monique Peer diaries, notebooks, and letters to Ann Peer on Mexican trips with Disneys, PFA; J. B. Kaufman, *South of the Border with Disney: Walt Disney and the Good Neighbor Program, 1941–1948* (New York: Walt Disney Family Foundation Press, 2009); *Walt & El Grupo*, Walt Disney Family Foundation Films, 2008, and related exhibits in the Walt Disney Family Museum, San Francisco; Neal Gabler, *Walt Disney: The Triumph of the American Imagination* (New York: Alfred A. Knopf, 2006).

Latin music involvement; Cugat: "Latin Music Subsids Multiply," *Variety*, June 18, 1941; Xavier Cugat, *Rumba Is My Life* (New York: Didier & Co., 1948); Monique Peer diaries, PFA.

Wartime Peer-Southern hits and music industry conditions: Reports in *Billboard* and *Variety*.

Orson Welles and RSP: Monique Peer wartime diaries, PFA; Catherine L. Benamou, *It's All True: Orson Welles's Pan-American Odyssey* (Berkeley: University of California Press, 2007).

"It was a *battle* to introduce the samba": RSP, interview in the *Sao Paulo Gazetta*, July 1945.

Peers' life in Mexico: RSP WW II draft registration papers; Monique Peer diaries; RSP, interview in *Estampa* magazine, January 26, 1943; all in PFA.

NBC Inter-American University of the Air programs: Series handbook in PFA.

"If I had another hundred years": Monique Peer diary, quotation from letter from Peer Music Mexico City executive Mario Alvarez, March 16, 1943, PFA.

"I have always proceeded": RSP, letter to Jose Luis Fernandez, April 29, 1952, PFA.

"Bésame Mucho" global success: RSP, BT; Consuelo Velázquez, letter to Ralph Peer II, May 7, 2003.

Nat Vincent and wartime country music: Nat Vincent, interview by Douglas Green, March 28 and 31, 1975, Frist Oral History Project, Country Music Hall of Fame and Museum.

MGM and Hollywood: Monique Peer diary, 1944, and RSP, letter to Fernando Castro, June 8, 1945, PFA; Will Friedwald, liner notes for *Maracas, Marimbas and Mambos*, Rhino Records, 1999, compact disc.

"Ralph and I have some exciting news": Monique Peer, letter to Enrique Losada, February 19, 1944, PFA.

Park Hill: Ralph Peer II, interview by the author; photos in PFA; John C. Brasfield report and photos in *Architectural Digest* 6, no. 1 (January 1926); Steve Vaught, "Then and Now—The John H. Blair and C. F. DeWitt Estates," *Paradise Leased* blog, http://paradiseleased.wordpress.com/2010/12/03/then-now-the-john-h-blair-and-c-f-dewitt-estates/.

Birth of Ralph I. Peer (Ralph Peer II): Monique Peer diaries and telegrams, PFA.

"'Amor, Amor' was very big in England": RSP, BT.

War's end reconnections: Ibid.; T. H. Ward, "Peer-Southern Organisation: The Eastern Hemisphere Story," report in PFA.

Sing Out, Sweet Land attendance: Monique Peer diary, 1945, PFA; liner notes for *Sing Out, Sweet Land!* cast recording, Decca, 1951, LP; Mazor, *Meeting Jimmie Rodgers*.

7. Going Global: Expansion, 1946–1951

Camellia interests: RSP, "Biographical Highlights" memoir, August 17, 1959, PFA.

Postwar business situation and trips: Monique Peer diaries, 1946 and 1947; "Incorporation Dates of the Companies Within the Peer-Southern Organization," January 14, 1960, document in PFA; Russell Sanjek, *American Popular Music and Its Business: The First Four Hundred Years*, vol. 3, *1900–1984* (New York: Oxford University Press, 1988).

"The Soviets seized all his music": Jimmie Fidler, In Hollywood (syndicated column), *Pottstown (PA) Mercury*, July 31, 1947.

"My personal participation necessarily becomes less": RSP, letter to staff, March 26, 1948, PFA.

Latin music in Japan: "Peer Opens Pubbery Branch," *Billboard*, September 22, 1951.

New Hill & Range and Acuff-Rose competition: RSP, letters to R. B. Gilmore, 1955, and to Nat Vincent, 1956; Monique Peer diary, 1946; all in PFA; Bar Biszick-Lockwood, *Restless Giant: The Life and Times of Jean Aberbach & Hill and Range Songs* (Champaign: University of Illinois Press, 2010); John W. Rumble, *Fred Rose and the Development of the Nashville Music Industry, 1942–1954*, PhD dissertation, Vanderbilt University, 1980; Colin Escott with George Merritt and William MacEwen, *Hank Williams: The Biography*, rev. ed. (Boston: Back Bay Books, 2004).

Bill Monroe: James Monroe, interview by the author; Neil V. Rosenberg and Charles K. Wolfe, *The Music of Bill Monroe* (Champaign: University of Illinois Press, 2007); Richard D. Smith, *Can't You Hear Me Callin': The Life of Bill Monroe, Father of Bluegrass* (New York: Da Capo Press, 2001).

RSP on Satherley: RSP, BT.

RSP on establishing relationships: Ibid.

Peers' first world trip: Monique Peer, "Flight of Ralph and Monique Peer Around the World, September 1948 to February 1949" (trip diary); Monique Peer's letter to friends, June 22, 1950; Ralph Peer's home movies; all in PFA.

Founding of Serious Music/Classical Department: RSP, BT; Ralph Peer II, interview by the author; Wladmir Lakond, memo on lineup of Southern's classical composers, February 1, 1961, PFA; "Southern Adds Longhair Dept," *Billboard*, August 14, 1948; "Southern Goes Longhair with Carnegie Bow," *Billboard*, March 24, 1951.

"There were so many talents": Elisabeth Waldo, interview by the author.

Aftermath of Ives publication: "Ives' Boom Boon to Peer-South'n," *Billboard*, April 23, 1967.

Troy Martin: Peermusic employment records; Daniel Cooper, unpublished notes on interview with J. D. Miller, August 27, 1993; Martin Hawkins, unpublished notes from interview with Arnold Rogers, November 2011; Martin Hawkins, liner notes for *Billy Brown*, Bear Family Records, compact disc; interviews with Don Law, Joe Allison,

Howard White, Joe Johnson, Curly Seckler, and Murray Nash, Frist Oral History Project, Country Music Hall of Fame and Museum; Rosenberg and Wolfe, *Music of Bill Monroe*; Rich Kienzle, liner notes for *Ray Price and the Cherokee Cowboys*, Bear Family Records, 1996.

"Rumbalero War" and Pérez Prado: "Fernando Castro Has Been Appointed," *Billboard*, February 5, 1949; "Peer-Rumbalero Tug-of-War," *Billboard*, February 19, 1949; "Peer's Castro Inks Flock of Cuban Writers," *Billboard*, April 23, 1949; "Peer to Plug Latin Tunes," *Billboard*, July 2, 1949; Joseph Levy, "Pérez Prado and Mambomania," Pérez Prado Pages, www.laventure.net/tourist/prez_bio.htm; Ed Morales, *The Latin Beat: The Rhythms and Roots of Latin Music, from Bossa Nova to Salsa and Beyond* (New York: Da Capo Press, 2003).

Wolfe Gilbert: RSP, BT; L. Wolfe Gilbert, *Without Rhyme or Reason* (New York: Vantage Press, 1956).

Rodgers country revival: Barry Mazor, *Meeting Jimmie Rodgers: How America's Original Roots Music Hero Changed the Pop Sounds of a Century* (New York: Oxford University Press, 2009); report on Peer radio appearance with Carrie Rodgers, Tubb, and Snow, *Billboard*, July 12, 1952.

"We have gone a long time without . . . hits": RSP, letter to employees such as Provi Garcia, December 1948, PFA.

"Mockingbird Hill" success: RSP company correspondence and Monique diary, PFA.

"We have the *only* global music publishing business": RSP, interview by Bill Slater, July 24, 1951, transcript in PFA.

8. Locking a Legacy, 1952–1960

Harry Smith comment: Smith's original liner notes reproduced in reissue of *The Anthology of American Folk Music*, Smithsonian Folkways, 1997.

RSP and Jimmie Rodgers Festivals: Barry Mazor, *Meeting Jimmie Rodgers: How America's Original Roots Music Hero Changed the Pop Sounds of a Century* (New York: Oxford University Press, 2009); Mike Paris and Chris Comber, *Jimmie the Kid: The Life of Jimmie Rodgers* (London: Da Capo Books, 1977); Ralph S. Peer, "Discovery of the First Hillbilly Great," *Billboard*, May 16, 1953.

RSP and Monique efforts to marry in Roman Catholic Church and Peers' genealogy research: Related letters and documents of 1948–58, including correspondence with Sadie Peer, Anita Peer, and Arthur Fishbein on marriage and religious histories; RSP, letters to relatives and possible relatives on his ancestry, 1949–52; RSP, letter to Ann Peer on Kansas City visit, 1950, and letter to her on European genealogy research trip, 1951; all in PFA.

RSP involvement in US federal examination of performance rights issues: RSP, correspondence with Arthur Fisher, July 1952, Register of Copyrights, Library of Congress.

Peer-Southern ASCAP classification arbitration effort: Russell Sanjek, *American Popular Music and Its Business: The First Four Hundred Years*, vol. 3, *1900–1984* (New York: Oxford University Press, 1988); "Southern Gripe vs. ASCAP Rating May Spark Look at Old Procedures," *Billboard*, August 25, 1951; "ASCAP Now Actively Sees New Pubber-Distribution Plan . . . as Result of Southern Music Case," *Billboard*, March 22, 1952; "Test Case Cues ASCAP Shakeup," *Variety*, February 27, 1952.

"We are left with a most archaic law": RSP, text of speech "Reforming Our Copyright Law," PFA.

"the product of what must be called a 'national urge'": RSP, "Comments and Views Submitted to the Copyright Office on the Economic Aspects of the Compulsory License in the Copyright Law," report, Senate Judiciary Committee, 86th Cong., October 16, 1957.

RSP Camellia positions and exploration: David L. Feathers, "Camellia Personality: Ralph Sylvester Peer," in *1959 American Camellia Yearbook*, ed. Milton H. Brown (Ft. Valley, GA: American Camelia Society, 1959); "The Yellow Camellia," in *1985 American Camellia Yearbook* (Ft. Valley, GA: American Camelia Society, 1985); "Again, It's Camellia Time," *Oakland Tribune*, February 17, 1952; United Press, "Collectors Search for Rare Yellow Camellia," *Palm Beach Post*, July 24 1954; "He Likes Camellias," *Better Gardens Institute*, 1956; RSP, letter to Julius Nuccio, April 19, 1954; RSP, "Biographical Highlights" memoir, August 17, 1959, PFA.

White Firs Lake Tahoe retreat: Bob and Betsy Bingham, Dr. Victor Brochard, David Marston, and Ralph Peer II, interviews with the author.

RSP polycythemia diagnosis: Dr. Victor Brochard and Ralph Peer II, interviews with the author; medical papers in PFA.

Revitalizing Peer-Southern country music division and country genre: RSP, BT; Peer advertisement letter, *Billboard*, December 5, 1953; report on "All-Time Country Greats" awards, *Hoedown*, January 1954; John W. Rumble, *Fred Rose and the Development of the Nashville Music Industry, 1942–1954*, PhD dissertation, Vanderbilt University, 1980.

"We will never get out of the present rut": RSP, letter to R. Gilmore, October 19, 1955, PFA.

Carrie Rodgers and song renewal: RSP, letter to Mrs. Rodgers, October 1955, PFA; RSP, BT; Nat Vincent, interview by Douglas Green, March 28 and 31, 1975, Frist Oral History Project, Country Music Hall of Fame and Museum.

Ralph Peer Award: Trade magazine and *Meridian Star* news reports; Jimmie Rodgers Foundation archives; Frist photo archive, Country Music Hall of Fame and Museum.

RSP and Country Music Association founding: Mac Wiseman and Jo Walker-Meador, interviews by the author.

"I'd met Mr. Ralph Peer": Luis Kalaff, interview by the author.

Murray Deutch, Irving Deutch, and pop and rock music, 1950s: Howard Deutch and Pamela Deutch, interviews by author; "PI May Revive Melody Lane with Deutch at Helm," *Billboard*, August 7, 1954; "Irving Deutch Quits Peer," *Billboard*, March 19, 1955; RSP, letters to Robert Iversen on Murray Deutch contract, July 7 and August 8, 1958, PFA.

RSP on Jimmie Rodgers and rockabilly: RSP, letter to C. H. Phillips, April 14, 1958, PFA.

Jack Scott: Rob Finnis, liner notes for *Jack Scott: The Way I Walk*, Roller Coaster Records, 1990, and Deke Dickerson, liner notes for *Jack Rocks*, Bear Family Records, 2006; Pamela Deutch, interview by author.

Buddy Holly: Maria Elena Holly and Jerry "J. I." Allison, interviews by author; John Goldrosen and John Beecher, *Remembering Buddy: The Definitive Biography of Buddy Holly*, rev. ed. (New York: Penguin Books, 1986); Elizabeth Peer and Ralph Peer II,

Buddy Holly: A Biography in Words, Photographs and Music (New York: Peer International, 1972).

Marlon Brando as tenant: Marlon Brando, letter to RSP and Monique Peer, January 17, 1955, PFA; Pamela Deutch, interview by the author.

"Tom Dooley" dispute: Oscar Brand, *The Ballad Mongers: Rise of the Modern Folk Song* (New York: Funk & Wagnalls/Minerva Press, 1962); Peter J. Curry, "'Tom Dooley': The Ballad That Started the Folk Boom," Kingston Trio Place, www.kingstontrioplace.com /tdooleydoc.htm; Robert Cantwell, *When We Were Good: The Folk Revival* (Cambridge, MA: Harvard University Press, 1996); O. Wayne Coon, *Some Problems with Musical Public-Domain Materials Under U.S. Copyright Law as Illustrated Mainly by the Recent Folk-Song Revival*, John Edwards Memorial Foundation, 1971.

"I have a contract signed by Whitter and Grayson": RSP, BT.

Lillian Borgeson RSP interview: RSP and Lillian Borgeson, BT; Griffin Borgeson, letters to Ed Romanink, April and December 1958 and March 1959, and "Sara Carter, Angel's Camp, April 1, 1958," audiotape FT-12517LC, Ed Kahn Collection, Southern Folklife Collection, UNC, with permission of Margaret J. Moore Kahn.

"We are at the state where it is hard to tell the dividing line for *popular* music": RSP, interview by Don Owens, July 4, 1959, from the audio collection of Eddie Stubbs.

RSP notes on health, insurance, RCA Victor TVs, and dictation equipment: RSP correspondence, 1959, PFA.

Christmas letters: RSP, letter to Hoagy Carmichael, Hoagy Carmichael official website, www.hoagy.com.

New Year's Eve 1960: RSP, letter to Mr. and Mrs. Peter Carlisle, January 4, 1960.

Monique Peer cable on RSP's death: Copy in PFA.

RSP obituaries: *Los Angeles Times*, January 20, 1960; *New York Times*, January 21, 1960; *Variety*, January 27, 1960.

Kaye's eulogy: Sydney Kaye, letter to Monique Peer with text of speech, January 22, 1960, PFA.

9. The Roots and Pop Aftermath

Peermusic directions since 1960: Ralph Peer II, interview by the author.

Peer-Southern anniversary in *Billboard*: "The Peer-Southern Organization 40th Anniversary Salute," *Billboard*, June 1, 1968.

Global forum paper: Mark Schultz and Alec van Gelder, "Nashville in Africa: Culture, Institutions, Entrepreneurship and Development," paper/presentation to International Policy Network, London, November 2008.

Index

R 12/14